The varieties of British political thought, 1500–1800

There is at present no overall history of English and British political thought and literature in the early modern period, although new approaches to the writing of its history have taken shape in the past forty to fifty years; and during that time British political history has itself been subjected to intensive revision.

This volume, written by directors of seminars at the Folger Institute Center for the History of British Political Thought in Washington DC, attempts to review the period from the English Reformation to the French Revolution, to suggest new ways of studying the articulation of political consciousness and the conduct of political argument, and to point out the extraordinary intellectual and linguistic richness of the ongoing English and British political debate.

The varieties of British political thought, 1500–1800

Edited by
J. G. A. Pocock

with the assistance of
Gordon J. Schochet and Lois G. Schwoerer

Published in association with the
Folger Institute, Washington, DC

CAMBRIDGE
UNIVERSITY PRESS

Published by the Press Syndicate of the University of Cambridge
The Pitt Building, Trumpington Street, Cambridge CB2 1RP
40 West 20th Street, New York, NY 10011-4211, USA
10 Stamford Road, Oakleigh, Melbourne 3166, Australia

First published 1993
First paperback edition published 1996

Printed in Great Britain at the University Press, Cambridge

A catalogue record for this book is available from the British Library

Library of Congress cataloguing in publication data
The varieties of British political thought, 1500–1800 / edited by
J. G. A. Pocock, with the assistance of Gordon J. Schochet and
Lois G. Schwoerer.
    p. cm.
Papers presented during a series of seminars, held between 1984
and 1987 at the Folger Shakespeare Library in Washington, D.C.
Includes bibliographical references.
ISBN 0 521 44377 6 (hardback)
1. Political science – Great Britain – History – Congresses.
I. Pocock, J. G. A. (John Greville Agard), 1924– .
II. Schochet, Gordon J. III. Schwoerer, Lois G.
JA84.G7V37   1993
320'.0941 – dc20   92-37772   CIP

ISBN 0 521 44377 6 hardback
ISBN 0 521 57498 6 paperback

Contents

Acknowledgements

The editors take great pleasure in expressing thanks to their benefactors, without whose support neither the Center for the History of British Political Thought nor this volume would have been possible. Above all we are grateful to the National Endowment for the Humanities for its continuing generous support, which initially enabled us to establish the Center, organize its seminars and carry on its diverse activities. Essential help came also from Barclays Bank of New York, the British Council, the Exxon Education Foundation, The George Washington University, the John Ben Snow Memorial Trust, the North American Conference on British Studies, and from the Honourable and Mrs Ronald S. Lauder and Dr Barbara Taft. We also thank the past and present officers of The Folger Institute, within whose structure the Center for the History of British Political Thought functions: Chairpersons John Andrews and Barbara Mowat; Associate Chairperson Susan Zimmerman; and Executive Director Lena Cowen Orlin. When Lena Cowen Orlin was on leave in 1989–90, Patricia E. Tatspaugh served as Acting Executive Director, and we warmly acknowledge her support during that time.[1]

We also express our deep gratitude to the directors of The Folger Shakespeare Library (under whose aegis the Folger Institute operates), who have sustained the Center and its work: the late O. B. Hardison, Jr, and his successor Werner Gundersheimer. We thank them for their confidence, support, and occasional forbearance. The Folger Library has been the locus of much of the work of this volume, and we and all others associated with the Center are deeply indebted to it. Its holdings include not only unrivalled printed materials for Elizabethan and Jacobean drama and literature, but also extensive sources for the study of political discourse in the sixteenth and seventeenth centuries and much of the eighteenth.

The financial assistance that the Center has enjoyed made it possible

---

[1] The members of the staff of The Folger Institute also won our admiration and appreciation. They include Pierrette Ashcroft, Gregory Barz, Carol Brobeck, Amy Brooks, Ivy Gilbert, and Patricia Kelly.

for it to sponsor seminars, conferences and lectures from 1984 to the present.[2] It enabled the Steering Committee to appoint Directors of the seminars and permitted the Directors of the initial series of six seminars, conducted over the three years 1984–7, to invite a number of distinguished scholars in the field to take part in their respective seminars. We thank those Directors and with them express our gratitude to their visiting scholars; the presentations of visiting scholars, together with those of participating members of the several seminars, form the basis of the six volumes of proceedings which Gordon J. Schochet has edited for distribution by The Folger Institute.[3] The publication of

[2] A full list of these to date runs as follows: *Seminars:* 'From Bosworth to Yorktown: The Development of British Political Thought from Henry VII through the American Revolution', directed by Gordon J. Schochet, Spring 1984; 'Political Thought in the Henrician Age, 1500–1550', directed by John Guy, Fall 1984; 'Political Thought in the Elizabethan Age, 1558–1603', directed by Donald R. Kelley, Spring 1985; 'Political Thought in Early Modern England, 1600–1660', directed by William Lamont, Fall 1985; 'Political Thought in the Later Stuart Age, 1649–1702', directed by Howard Nenner, Spring 1986; 'Politics and Politeness: British Political Thought in the Age of Walpole', directed by Nicholas Phillipson, Fall 1986; 'Political Thought in the English-Speaking Atlantic, 1760–1800', directed by J. G. A. Pocock, Spring 1987; 'Property, Power, and Politics', directed by Arthur J. Slavin (University of Louisville), Fall 1987; 'Kings, Courtiers, and Judges: Political Discourse in Early Stuart England', directed by Linda Levy Peck, Spring 1988; 'The Glorious Revolution', directed by Lois G. Schwoerer (George Washington University), Spring 1989; 'Political Thought in the English-Speaking World, 1485–1793', directed by Gordon J. Schochet, Lois G. Schwoerer, and J. G. A. Pocock, Part I, Fall 1989; Part II, Spring 1990; 'Preachers, Petitioners, and Prophets in the Age of Charles I', directed by Esther S. Cope (University of Nebraska), Spring 1990; 'Scots and Britons: Scottish Political Thought and the Union of 1603', directed by Roger A. Mason (University of St Andrews), Fall 1990; 'Union, State, and Empire: The Political Identities of Britain, 1688–1750', directed by John C. Robertson (St Hugh's College, Oxford), Spring 1991; 'Partisan Culture in an Age of Revolution: England, 1649–89', directed by Derek Hirst and Steven Zwicker (Washington University), Fall 1991; 'Empire Confederation, and Republic: From Atlantic Dominion to American Union', directed by J. G. A. Pocock, Spring 1992; 'The Politics of the Ancient Constitution: British Political Thought in the Early Seventeenth Century', directed by Glenn Burgess (University of Canterbury, New Zealand), Fall 1992. *Conferences and symposia:* 'The Treaty of Paris in a Changing States System', 26–7 January 1984; 'Political Thought in the Henrician Age, 1500–1550', 15–17 November 1984; 'Political Thought and the Elizabethan Drama', 21 February 1985; 'The Ancient Constitution and Elizabethan Political Thought', 4 April 1985; 'The New Model Army and the Levellers', 11 October 1985; 'Political Thought and Imaginative Literature in Seventeenth-Century England', 13–14 March 1986; 'The Images of Monarchy in Late Seventeenth-Century England', 11 April 1986; 'Civil Religion, 1690–1750', 25–6 September 1986; 'British Responses to the French Revolution', 26–7 March 1987; 'Conceptual Change and the Constitution of the United States', 16–18 April 1987; 'The Mental World of the Jacobean Court', 17–19 March 1988; 'The Political Thought of Thomas Hobbes: A 400th-Anniversary Commemoration', 2–3 December 1988; 'The Glorious Revolution, 1688–90: Changing Perspectives', 13–15 April 1989; 'England's Wars of Religion, 1625–1649', 23–4 March 1990; English Parliamentary Culture to 1689', 1–13 June 1992.

[3] *The Proceedings of the Center for the History of British Political Thought*, General Editor: Gordon J. Schochet (Washington, D.C.: Folger Shakespeare Library,

these volumes was supported in part by a generous grant from the Andrew W. Mellon Publishing Endowment of the Folger Shakespeare Library.

Publications have followed from some of the seminars and conferences associated with the work of the Center for the History of British Political Thought. To date they are: Terence Ball and J. G. A. Pocock (eds.), *Conceptual Change and the Constitution* (University Press of Kansas, 1988), Linda Levy Peck (ed.), *The Mental World of the Jacobean Court* (Cambridge University Press, 1991), and Lois G. Schwoerer (ed.), *The Revolution of 1688–1689 Changing Perspectives* (Cambridge University Press, 1992).

The present volume grew out of the conviction that the Directors of the initial six seminars, with other scholars who have directed seminars from time to time, should seek to organize and articulate the fruits of their own studies and those of participants in their seminars in the form of a volume of essays surveying the history of British political thought as it has been examined by the Center. The resulting volume has taken time to assemble. The editors are grateful to their colleagues and fellow contributors for their patience and hard work in the course of bringing it together. They also thank the staff at the Cambridge University Press for smoothing the road to publication.

There are three other groups of people, their membership changing over the years, who were indispensable to all that has been done and attempted: the bibliographical experts and Reading Room staff of The Folger Shakespeare Library; the faculty, graduate students, and independent scholars who have taken part in the Center's seminars and conferences; and the individual scholars in many fields who, whether or not they took part in the Center's activities, have made the Library and the Institute a uniquely stimulating and welcoming community of research and conversation.

Lastly, the three members of the Steering Committee of the Center for the History of British Political Thought who have acted as editors of

1990–93). Volume 1: *Reformation, Humanism, and 'Revolution'*, from the seminar: 'Political Thought in the Henrician Age, 1500–1550', directed by John Guy, Fall 1984; Volume 2: *Law, Literature, and the Settlement of Regimes*, from the seminar: 'Political Thought in the Elizabethan Age, 1558–1603', directed by Donald R. Kelley, Spring 1985; Volume 3: *Religion, Resistance, and Civil War*, from the seminar: 'Political Thought in Early Modern England, 1600–1660', directed by William Lamont, Fall 1985; Volume 4: *Restoration, Ideology, and Revolution*, from the seminar: 'Political Thought in the Later Stuart Age, 1649–1702', directed by Howard Nenner, Spring 1986; Volume 5: *Politics, Politeness, and Patriotism*, from the seminar: 'Politics and Politeness: British Political Thought in the Age of Walpole', directed by Nicholas Phillipson, Fall 1986; Volume 6: *Empire and Revolutions*, from the seminar: 'Political Thought in the English-Speaking Atlantic, 1760–1800', directed by J. G. A. Pocock, Spring 1987.

this volume, desire to thank a fourth: their colleague and friend, Lena Cowen Orlin, Executive Director of The Folger Institute. Words are inadequate to describe how much she has done for the efficient and happy conduct of their collaborative enterprise.

Editorial introduction

The essays presented in this volume offer compelling evidence of the remarkable varieties of British political thought in the early modern era, 1500–1800. Written by the Directors of seminars that were organized to cover that era in approximately fifty-year segments at a time and were held from 1984 through 1987 under the aegis of the Center for the History of British Political Thought at The Folger Shakespeare Library in Washington, DC, these chapters are the result – to that date – of the Center's ongoing project: to explore in depth the changing patterns of British political discourse over approximately three centuries, from the English Reformation and the advent of print culture to the impact of the American and French Revolutions upon Great Britain. Sponsored by the Center (whose affairs are conducted by a Steering Committee of the three editors of this volume and Dr Lena Cowen Orlin, Executive Director of The Folger Institute), this volume hopes to contribute to the creation of a comprehensive history of British political discourse in this era, and a reconceptualization of that discourse.

These essays are informed by certain assumptions and principles and shaped by a special circumstance. First, the history of political thought that the chapters present takes the form of a history of political 'discourse'; that is, they focus on the principal vocabularies or 'languages' which were available and exploitable for the conduct, discussion, vindication and criticism of political action and the principles on which it was seen to be founded. They also examine the major enterprises which were carried out or endeavoured in these 'languages'. As a history of published discourse this volume is in consequence also a history of 'theory' or 'philosophy' – even of 'literature' – as these terms denote special levels of analysis and reflection or modes of writing and debate *within* the changing modes of political discussion. For this reason, the term 'discourse' is not used here – as it may be and sometimes is – with the single purpose of 'deconstructing' history and reducing it to the modes of seeking and exercising power encoded within language systems, but rather is used with the aim of *including* that

1

dimension in a history 'reconstructed' as the activity of language-using political creatures, deeply involved in what they were doing and seldom unaware of its ambivalences.

A second principle is that major works which have attained special prestige and authority are studied as they occur in the overall narrative. Such works are usually situated in more than one historical context and can be studied from more than one viewpoint. The 'classics of British political thought' receive the attention they deserve, but in terms not only of their canonical character but also of the process of their canonization.

Third, the authors of these essays assume that history takes place within a political system, or group of systems, consisting of the institutions which have constituted such systems, the events which have been perceived as affecting them, and the languages available for conducting them and articulating the political and human experience seen as entailed by and implicit in them. The history dealt with in these essays is one of theology, jurisprudence, princely culture, poetic literature, history writing, and political economy, these components varying in importance over the era. Another element of central significance to the early modern era and to the understanding of its political discourse is print culture, especially that based in London, with subsidiary centres in Oxford, Cambridge and a few other places, and generated by the English political system of which it was the most important articulation. The London-based print industry is the circumstance that has imposed certain patterns of selection on these authors' presentation of history. For it is the product of that industry, preserved in great collections – of which George Thomason's was the first – that has been the most important to us. What the essays present, then, is a history of English-speaking politics and political discourse as interpreted and transmitted by the print culture.[1] It need hardly be said that no full history of that print culture has been attempted, but some crucial moments are implicit: the advent of a humanist discourse and a print medium capable of conveying it; the explosion of unlicensed printing at the outset of the mid-seventeenth-century internal wars; the growth of journalism and another explosion of printed matter in the troubled late seventeenth century; the appearance of the novel and essay in the early eighteenth century; and the further expansion of the reading market throughout that century.

Fourth, as a consequence of the nature of early modern print culture,

---

[1] We have benefited from the advice regarding print culture of Elizabeth L. Eisenstein and Peter Blayney.

our history is dominated by the genres of political literature produced by that culture: the broadsheet, the pamphlet, the newsletter, the journal, and the essay, treatise or learned folio seen as interacting with all these. The era was one in which the clerisies were on the streets and in the market; great works of jurisprudence, divinity, philosophy and history can and should be read in the context of an occasional, polemical and public literature with which they in fact interacted.

Fifth, it might have been expected that a group of scholars working in the setting of the Folger Shakespeare Library would have devoted themselves to studying the interactions between the printed discourse of politics and the major printed genres – poetry, drama, the novel – for which the term 'literature' is conventionally reserved. Probably all contributors share the wish that we could have done even more[2] in this direction than we have. William Shakespeare was perhaps the last great English poet unaffected by the constant production of political controversy in print; all his canonical successors – Milton, Marvell, Dryden, Defoe, Swift, Pope, Johnson, Blake, Wordsworth, Coleridge, Byron, Scott – not only wrote their poems and other literary works surrounded by this component of a print culture, but contributed to it, very often in the prose genres peculiar to it. The history of the theatre and the rise of the novel can be studied as part of this history of print culture, and of course have been. But at present there is a division of labour between those who study genres which make them 'historians of political thought' and those whose studies make them 'historians of literature', and to some extent the two groups produce, for both good and ill, non-identical understandings of what 'politics' and even 'history' are.[3] More needs to be done towards bridging the gaps between these understandings, and perhaps some day will be.

Sixth, since the archive on which this history of discourse is based is predominantly that laid down by the London printing industry, the history that emerges is decidedly Anglocentric. This can be defended. England was the dominant partner among the Anglophone cultures; its printed discourse was largely a dialogue with and about itself, and enough entered into it from the continental *républiques des lettres* to

---

[2] The seminar conducted in 1991 by Derek Hirst and Steven Zwicker was specifically concerned with the location of literary texts in the context of political polemic. See also Kevin Sharpe and Steven N. Zwicker (eds.), *The Politics of Discourse: The Literature and History of Seventeenth-Century England* (Berkeley and Los Angeles, 1987).

[3] Historians and 'new historicists' constitute distinct though not competing groups. Their possible interactions are fruitfully developed in two recent works: David Harris Sacks, *The Widening Gate: Bristol and the Atlantic Economy, 1450–700* (Berkeley and Los Angeles, 1991) and Richard Helgerson, *Forms of Nationhood: The Elizabethan Writing of England* (Chicago, 1992).

ensure that it was one of the discourses of Europe. Grotius entered the vocabulary of English political thought as Hobbes did that of the Netherlands. Yet there is a necessary enterprise of enlarging English into British history, to which this volume pays only limited attention. The political works of James I (as McIlwain called them)[4] are shown to have been those of James VI, but after Linda Peck's essay the British dimension appears only when Nicholas Phillipson and J. G. A. Pocock examine the eighteenth century.[5]

But, since the completion of the series of seminars which give rise to this volume, two further seminars, conducted by Roger A. Mason and J. C. Robertson, have sought, in the first place, to establish a canon and a historical scheme for Scottish political thought,[6] and in the second, by focusing on the Unions of 1603 and 1707, to establish the character of 'British' political thought as that concerned with creating and maintaining the Kingdom of Great Britain and its derivative settler societies beyond seas. Both seminars have been the origin of published volumes,[7] and the book now presented may profitably be read in conjunction with these. A third seminar examined the imperial crisis and American secession of 1763–1776 in the light of the decision of 1707 that the union of England and Scotland should be an incorporation and not a confederation,[8] and has left its imprint on the penultimate chapter of the present volume. It is beginning to seem likely that the picture may have to be completed by a study of Irish, Anglo-Irish and Scottish-Irish political thought down to the fateful Union of 1801. The history of British political thought includes the history of those who cease to be British, as well as those who become or remain so; the beginnings of American political thought are also the beginnings of Canadian.

Seventh, these essays deal with history on two levels. First, there is history as presented and interpreted by persons immediately involved in it, together with the history of their modes of responding to it – modes

---

[4] C. H. McIlwain (ed.), *The Political Works of James I* (Cambridge, MA, 1918).

[5] Indeed, it is the necessity of treating such large subjects as the Scottish Enlightenment and the American Revolution which explains the allocation of two chapters to the first thirty years of George III's reign; only the reiterated permission of his colleagues has justified one of the editors of this volume in what would otherwise have been an unforgivable encroachment.

[6] They were preceded in this by Arthur Williamson, *Scottish National Consciousness in the Age of James VI* (Edinburgh, 1979).

[7] R. A. Mason (ed.), *Scots and Britons: Scottish Political Thought and the Union of 1603* (Cambridge University Press, forthcoming); J. C. Robertson (ed.), *A Union for Empire: The Union of 1707 in the Context of British Political Thought* (Cambridge University Press, forthcoming).

[8] 'Empire, Confederation and Republic: From Atlantic Dominion to American Union', see p. x, n. 2, above.

which, over the early modern era, seem to have become increasingly historiographical and even, within limits, historicist.[9] And second, there is early modern English and British history as presented and interpreted by the contributors to this volume, who are at the same time historians of discourse reading history in the light of the materials in which they are specialists, and historians working in the closing years of the twentieth century. As the latter, they are involved in and well aware of all the remarkable changes that have happened in the last twenty or so years, and are still happening, in Anglo-American historiography. In these linked capacities our authors would probably agree in hoping that they have indicated the contours of a post-revisionist history of the Anglo-British political system. It bears observing that the history of published discourse in a highly centralized print and political culture like the Anglo-British encourages its own perception of the debate over consensus and conflict,[10] for one is studying the history of shared languages (and therefore of consensus) within which are found the histories of many bitter and profound disagreements (and therefore of conflict). Thus, conflict is found within consensus, sometimes breaking it down and sometimes transforming or restoring it. Revisionist historiography, as post-revisionists see it, emphasizes both the fragility and the durability of British political practices, and that on the whole seems to be the image conveyed by these essays.

Finally, the obvious point must be made: this volume is a collection of essays by different authors, who have discussed their contributions with each other and whose offerings have been co-ordinated by the editors to the limits within which such a thing is possible. The essays differ in the extent to which their authors have attempted to cover the field surveyed in the seminars they originally directed. Some authors – Guy, Kelley, Pocock – have sought to portray in breadth the changing diversity of languages of discourse in the periods their chapters cover; but even this cannot be done without selection and arrangement. Nicholas Phillipson has selected a limited number of themes and pursued them as far – and it is quite a distance – as they will carry him; while William Lamont, for reasons that will appear, has chosen to survey a crucial moment in the light of its historiography rather than its history. Other essays, those by Peck and by Pocock and Schochet in collaboration, were not based on any of the original seminar series, but were written especially for this

---

[9] The applicability of this term before the late eighteenth century is of course debatable. See Zachary Sayre Schiffman, 'Renaissance Historicism Reconsidered', *History and Theory*, 24 (1985), 170–82.

[10] See the observations of Kelley and Peck below, pp. 48, 63–4, 78–9, 82–3, 102–6, and the references that are given.

volume, to give it greater comprehension. This volume, then, is not the work of a single mind. There is to date no unifying book-length study of the field of early modern British political discourse by a single author, but an essay published at the outset of the Center's project suggests a major outline with which it is interesting to compare the essays in this book.[11]

This book is divided into three sections. The first, with its emphasis on the sixteenth century but covering the years from 1530 to 1642, depicts the ideology of counsel surrounding a post-medieval monarchy and its court, engaged in bringing about that profound series of transformations in the relations between *sacerdotium* and *magisterium* which we subsume under the name of Reformation. A discourse of humanism plays an effective part in this, and is reinforced by the advent of typography, but the author sending his book to be printed is primarily a counsellor to his prince or a client to his patron. There is an avid and often heterodox lay public waiting to consume books, but the predominant discourse is still that of court and counsel; it is the gentleman and doctor of laws John Hayward who is in trouble for publicizing the deposition of Richard II 200 years after that event, not the obscure mountebank William Shakespeare. Nevertheless, it is this closed and courtly world of monarchy which wreaks the revolution that lies at the foundation of all early modern English history, proclaiming in 1533 that England is an 'empire', sovereign over itself in matters civil as well as ecclesiastical, and leaving it to be decided whether this sovereignty is to be exercised centrally (over a church both apostolic and 'as by law established') by a crown imperial or a crown in parliament, but not less sovereign or imperial for being there located. After the deep changes of the 1530s, where there is a church there is also a congregation, and where there is a court there is also a country. These pairs profoundly desire unity, but may not always find it easy to achieve. As David Hume perceived in the middle of the eighteenth century,[12] after about 1603 the minds of men began to change, and what had seemed consensus began to display incoherence.

John Guy and Donald Kelley explore the world in which court and counsel co-existed with a discourse of law that taught every proprietor of land his place in the national community, and a Christian humanism

---

[11] J. G. A. Pocock, 'The History of British Political Thought: The Creation of a Center', *Journal of British Studies*, 24, 3 (1985), 283–310. See further the same author's 'Transformations in British Political Thought', in Mark Francis (guest ed.), 'Theory in History: English Political Thought, 1640–1832', *Political Science*, 40, 1 (1988), 160–78.

[12] David Hume, *The History of England* (1754; edn of 1778, reprinted Indianapolis, 1983), V, p. 18.

sought to co-exist with a potentially subversive priesthood, either in obedience to the heirs of the apostles or consisting of all believers. Linda Peck pursues the discourse of court and national church under the sometimes indiscreet shrewdness of James VI and I and the disastrous insensitivity of his son. The calamitous years between 1637 and 1642 are not here covered in narrative detail; but with Charles I's departure from Whitehall in 1642 – to return only for his execution in 1649 – we enter upon the central trauma of English history and the great efflorescence of print culture and ideas in conflict that marks the years of civil war, dissolution of government and interregnum. These may be considered years either of profound constitutional and ecclesiastical conflict, or of a catastrophic breakdown that imprinted on the English mind forever the lessons that king and parliament must never again be separated and that dissensions among the clerisy and the godly were the most likely causes of this disaster. In either reading, the decades in which Milton and Winstanley, Hobbes and Harrington, and later Sidney and Locke wrote and were read by publics as deeply perplexed as they were, are the epic years of the English political intellect, which still debates how far they were interpreting change or struggling to explain away anarchy. It is because this debate goes on and shows no sign of ceasing that William Lamont's essay is a study in contemporary historiography; but it is because the notion of an 'English revolution' has been losing ground to that of the Interregnum as 'the quest for a settlement', that Pocock and Schochet have juxtaposed their study of Hobbes and Harrington with Lamont's study of Conrad Russell, Christopher Hill and J. C. Davis. We have to move through Interregnum to Restoration if we are to break down the watertight compartments, divided and sealed at 1640 and 1660, into which English history has been organized, and understand that the English exposed themselves to a revolutionary experience, but rejected it with abhorrence before they could understand what it was. The rejection of priestcraft and enthusiasm, the attempt against all the odds to ensure that king and parliament would never again become separated, are keys to the history of the 'long eighteenth century' from 1660 to 1830, itself as much 'the quest for a settlement' as 'the growth of political stability'.[13]

The history of that 'long century' is not co-terminous with a history of political stability. Howard Nenner's perception of the Restoration period is resolutely constitutionalist; firmly, if unfashionably, he holds with Blackstone that amid all those 'wicked, sanguinary and

---

[13] The first phrase is that of Gerald Aylmer (ed.), *The Interregnum: The Quest for a Settlement, 1646–60* (London, 1972); the second, that of J. H. Plumb, *The Growth of Political Stability in England, 1675–1725* (London, 1967).

turbulent'[14] politics serious issues of law and liberty were known to be involved, and that English politics were about themselves and not merely a marginal explosion of the last European wars of religion.[15] The parliamentary classes, willing to go to the edge of absolutism and beyond in their need to maintain unity with the crown, were unable to rely on the monarchy's resolution to preserve the foundations laid down in the Act in Restraint of Appeals. The Restoration kings' flirtation with political Catholicism underlined the ineradicable presence of nonconformity, and the Anglican 'confessional church-state' had to be maintained until 1830 precisely because it had been challenged at its roots between 1642 and 1662, and because there was continuing organized dissent from it. It was in large measure because the monarchy shifted between laxity and rigour in its relations with the church that it had to be challenged by both Tories and anti-clericals in parliament; the ambiguities in the position of John Locke, expounded for the most part elsewhere than in this volume,[16] were the ambiguities of his age, though the extremism to which he had been reduced when he wrote the *Second Treatise* receives the emphasis which it has deserved since the researches of Peter Laslett. The unity of crown, church and parliament was restored by the Revolution of 1688–89 at the high price of legalized dynastic revolution and a partial toleration of nonconformists. Whether it is to be described in the classic constitutionalist language of an abandonment of prerogative for parliamentary monarchy, or of a return to the mixed and balanced monarchy momentously invented in the *Answer to the Nineteen Propositions* nearly half a century before, continues – to all appearances, endlessly – to be debated.

The debate is complicated by the shift in historical perspective that made it a commonplace of eighteenth-century readings of the Glorious Revolution that the crown's prerogatives had been curbed but at the same time its influence enormously expanded. As the reader of this volume turns from part II to part III and the chapters written by Phillipson and Pocock, a profound change comes over the subject-matter and the historiography of British political thought. The classic themes of church and state, authority and liberty, dissolution and foundation of government, in no case disappear and are not lost to sight in an age of Augustan stability – neither Macaulay nor Trevelyan nor

---

[14] For Blackstone's employment of these well-chosen adjectives, see Robert Willman, 'Blackstone and the "Theoretical Perfection" of English Law in the Reign of Charles II', *The Historical Journal*, 26, 1 (1983), 39–70, esp. p. 40.

[15] The thesis of Jonathan Scott, *Algernon Sidney and the Restoration Crisis, 1677–1683* (Cambridge, 1991).

[16] See, in particular, John W. Marshall, *Resistance, Responsibility and Religion: The Thought of John Locke* (Cambridge, forthcoming).

Plumb ever said that they were – but the discourse of *jus*, of authority and right, property and sovereignty, in which they were classically discussed, is joined, modified and within limits displaced by an entirely new discourse of commerce and culture, virtue and corruption, and perception of historical change. So strongly has the older discourse supplied the paradigms of 'political thought' that historians of this subject still have difficulty in coming to terms with the eighteenth century, though it is nearly thirty-five years since Caroline Robbins began enabling and obliging them to do so.[17]

Between the fall of James II studied by Nenner and the later years of Anne examined by Phillipson, there intervenes the extraordinary decade of 1688–98, during which a series of innovations convinced English and Scottish thinkers, for the first time, that they were living in a new and unprecedented stage of civil history. The needs of King William's wars converted England from an unstable rural polity where the sword was in the hands of the subject and the danger of civil war endemic, to a powerful military state which must think about its parliamentary structure in a new financial and imperial age; cults of republican militia and Roman virtue were a critical, not merely a nostalgic, response. By 1707, the new state was enlarged into Great Britain by the Union with Scotland and faced itself in the character of an 'extensive' or 'enormous empire' of the Atlantic archipelago; while at the same time it was brought to be a major player in a European states-system, first, by involvement in William III's grand alliance, and later, by the reactions and counter-reactions of the Treaty of Utrecht and the Hanoverian succession. The sovereignty of a Hanoverian crown in a Whig parliament was enforced, by such harsh measures as the Septennial Act, to ensure a regime capable both of shouldering these new responsibilities and of maintaining the unity necessary to guard against a danger of civil war which dynastic and ecclesiastical instability rendered by no means obsolete. As a further response to these uncertainties, we are at least learning to trace the character of an English and British Enlightenment; it appears clerical, conservative and verging toward Socinianism in the case of the English latitudinarians and later the Scottish Moderates, but anti-clerical, republican and frequently Spinozist in that of the English and Anglo-Irish deists and freethinkers.

Nicholas Phillipson explains how a cult of manners and politeness arose in answer to all of these disturbing challenges. It was 'modern' in the philosophical sense, celebrating the replacement of an 'ancient'

---

[17] Caroline Robbins, *The Eighteenth-Century Commonwealthman: Studies in the Transmission, Development and Circumstance of English Liberal Thought from the Restoration of Charles II until the War with the Thirteen Colonies* (Cambridge, MA, 1959).

philosophy that sought to perceive substances by a Lockean and Humean limitation of the intellect to studying its own workings, but still 'ancient' in the ethical sense that it preferred Ciceronian and Epicurean manners and morals to those of Christian devotion. The British Enlightenments were debates between 'ancients' and 'moderns', reflecting the shaping of 'modernity' in a society and culture still aristocratic and patronal enough to be called 'early modern' and an *ancien régime*. Pocock's concluding chapters examine the defeat of David Hume's never very strong hopes for a moderate political culture, and the advent of the 'present discontents' and the 'imperial crisis'. These bring the foundations of authority and liberty back to the forefront of political discourse; the United States depart to found a new federalism and republicanism, and by the time of the French Revolution the United Kingdom can be seen shedding much of its neo-classicism and laying the foundations of a new liberal positivism and utilitarianism. Pocock states – he hopes with sufficient caution – the case for holding that while the structure of the British *ancien régime* predominated until 1829–32, the language of discourse and some of its social assumptions were ceasing to be 'early modern' in the decade of the 1790s. The character of The Folger Shakespeare Library and its Institute have made it expedient to halt the Center's programme here; there is a case against, as well as a case for, going on to yet another half-century (say 1780–1830).

The study of political thought belongs both to the discipline of history and to that of political theory and philosophy. In his epilogue, Gordon Schochet examines the history which he has helped present, adopting the standpoint of a political theorist concerned with the contemporary state and its uncertain future. He reviews the early-modern history of discourse the better to ask in what ways the paradigms and values of the modern liberal state emerged from it; his concern here is not with teleology but with continuity. Turning to a present and future which we must term post-modern, he calls attention to the increasing contingency and marginalization of the 'state' which was once considered the focus of all civil existence, and asks what may be the consequences for both politics and civility. This leads him to consider the role of a shared discourse in maintaining the fabric of political life, and to enquire in conclusion whether the discourse of a stable society can persist without some sort of a past and a capacity to relate past and present to one another. His essay in political theory brings our historical enterprise into contact with a present and future in which, considered merely as historiography, it can be expected to continue.

Part I

Church, court and counsel

1 The Henrician age

John Guy

The humanist debate of 'counsel'

Renaissance political thought, insofar as it existed as a sub-discipline, was the branch of moral philosophy which taught men how to govern.[1] Moral philosophy was adjunct to law and theology, and was closely related to logical philosophy, itself divided into dialectic and rhetoric. The Ciceronian debate on 'office and duty' was central, but so was the link between politics and rhetoric. Sir Thomas Elyot claimed that young noblemen, by the use of rhetoric, might rival Cicero and Quintilian through their ability to speak wisely whenever and wherever required, whether acting as courtiers, counsellors or adminis-

[1] J. W. Allen, *A History of Political Thought in the Sixteenth Century* (London, 1928; repr. 1964); W. G. Zeeveld, *Foundations of Tudor Policy* (Cambridge, MA, 1948); A. B. Ferguson, *The Articulate Citizen and the English Renaissance* (Durham, NC, 1965); his *Clio Unbound: Perception of the Social and Cultural Past in Renaissance England* (Durham, NC, 1979); J. K. McConica, *English Humanists and Reformation Politics under Henry VIII and Edward VI* (Oxford, 1965; repr. 1968); F. Caspari, *Humanism and the Social Order in Tudor England* (Chicago, 1954; repr. New York, 1968); Q. Skinner, *The Foundations of Modern Political Thought*, 2 vols. (Cambridge, 1978); A. G. Fox and J. A. Guy, *Reassessing the Henrician Age: Humanism, Politics, and Reform* (Oxford, 1986); G. R. Elton, *Studies in Tudor and Stuart Politics and Government*, 3 vols. (Cambridge, 1974–83); his *The Tudor Revolution in Government* (Cambridge, 1953); his *Reform and Reformation: England, 1509–1558* (London, 1977); J. A. Guy, *Tudor England* (Oxford, 1988) and works cited in bibliography at pp. 514–37. For various methodological approaches to the history of Renaissance political discourse, see Skinner, *Foundations of Modern Political Thought*; A. Pagden (ed.), *The Languages of Political Theory in Early Modern Europe* (Cambridge, 1987); T. Ball, J. Farr and R. L. Hanson (eds.), *Political Innovation and Conceptual Change* (Cambridge, 1989); J. G. A. Pocock, *Virtue, Commerce, and History* (Cambridge, 1985); H. White, *Tropics of Discourse: Essays in Cultural Criticism* (Baltimore, MD, 1978); his *The Content of the Form: Narrative Discourse and Historical Representation* (Baltimore, MD, 1987); D. LaCapra, *History and Criticism* (Ithaca, NY, 1985). In this chapter I adhere to the decision taken at an editorial conference at the Folger Shakespeare Library in May 1988 that the earlier contributions to this volume be confined to English political thought. A valuable introduction to the preoccupations of Scottish writers in this period is provided by Roger A. Mason, 'Kingship, Nobility and Anglo-Scottish Union: John Mair's *History of Greater Britain* (1521)', *The Innes Review*, 41 (1990), 182–222. For critical comments on an earlier draft of this chapter I am especially indebted to Alistair Fox and Linda Levy Peck.

trators.[2] George Cavendish, Wolsey's gentleman-usher and earliest biographer, said of his master, 'He had a special gift of natural eloquence with a filed tongue to pronounce the same, that he was able with the same to persuade and allure all men to his purpose'.[3]

Dialectic was the technique of rigorous argument, rhetoric the art of speaking well. If the former was a clenched fist, the latter was an open hand. By means of rhetoric, kings, courtiers and patrons might be influenced and loyalty and obedience induced in clients and subordinates. Politics and discourse were therefore closely related. As Count Ludovico advised in Castiglione's *Il libro del cortegiano*, the courtier unable to mould language 'like wax after his own mind' would fail. The 'greatness and gorgeousness of an Oration' was that 'at the first shew' of the words, their dignity and brightness would appear like 'tables of painting placed in their good and natural light'.[4]

'The end of all doctrine and study is good counsel. . . wherein virtue may be found'.[5] So Elyot began the final chapters of *The Book Named the Governor* (1531). From the time of Sir John Fortescue, writing in the 1460s and early 1470s, to that of Francis Bacon over a century later, the duties of courtiers and magistrates were discussed in a humanist-classical vocabulary. Basic concepts were virtue, civility, self-rule, corruption, and the *res publica*. Standard theses for debate were (1) that the 'best state' was attained where active citizens inhabited a self-governing commonwealth; (2) that princes and rulers should choose 'good counsellors' and disregard flatterers and time-servers; (3) that 'true nobility' sprang from virtue and learning; (4) that action not based on knowledge was worthless and knowledge wasted without resulting action. As in Italian civic republicanism the authoritative source-book was Cicero's *De officiis*, bolstered by Aristotle's *Politics* and *Ethics*, and with Plato's *Republic* some distance behind. The difference for the English humanists was that they were obliged to mould their material to suit the models of service, benefits and the *cursus honorum* prevailing at the royal court. Their objective became to define the role of the active citizen as a 'counsellor' of the ruler.

Archetypal was the defence of the *vita activa* rendered in answer to Hythlodaeus by the fictional 'Thomas Morus' in Book I of *Utopia*

---

[2] *The Book Named the Governor*, ed. S. E. Lehmberg (London, 1962; repr. 1975), pp. 34–59; F. W. Conrad, 'A Preservative against Tyranny: The Public Career and Political Theology of Sir Thomas Elyot', unpublished PhD thesis, Johns Hopkins University, 1988.

[3] *Two Early Tudor Lives*, ed. R. S. Sylvester and D. P. Harding (New Haven, CN, 1962), p. 14.

[4] *The Book of the Courtier*, ed. W. H. D. Rouse (London, 1928; repr. 1966), p. 56.

[5] *Book Named the Governor*, p. 238.

(1516).[6] It was a line of argument modelled to a remarkable extent on *De officiis*, and was so powerful and effective that when Thomas Starkey began his *Dialogue between Pole and Lupset* thirteen years later, debate was virtually pre-empted by Lupset's robust assertion that if anyone 'by his own quietness and pleasure moved, leaveth the care of the common weal and policy, he doth manifest wrong to his country and friends, and is plain unjust and full of iniquity, as he that regardeth not his office and duty'.[7] Some genuine discussion ensued in Starkey's *Dialogue*, but it was not long before 'Pole' was persuaded to reject Plato's ideal commonwealth on account of its impracticality.[8] Sir Thomas Smith's *Discourse of the Commonweal of this Realm of England*, written in 1549, but not printed until 1581, likewise incorporated the gist of Cicero's defence of the active life.[9] Furthermore, these were the values of Tudor politicians generally. It was said of Sir William Cecil, secretary of state and a privy councillor under Edward VI, and Elizabeth I's chief counsellor, that 'he would always carry Tully's *Offices* about him, either in his bosom or his pocket'.[10]

Emphases and slants inevitably varied. Erasmus was the leading European humanist whose *Praise of Folly* (1511) and *Education of a Christian Prince* (1516) propounded a Christian-humanist synthesis rooted in Platonism, neo-Stoicism and the transcendental. He treated with scepticism the ideal of the active citizen, an outlook shared by John Colet that was echoed, in turn, by Elyot and Sir Thomas Wyatt. Its finest exposition was given by Hythlodaeus in reply to 'Morus' in Book I of *Utopia*, where he reiterated Plato's view that intellectuals did not belong in the service of princes. Unless kings themselves turned to philosophy 'they would never approve of the advice of real philosophers because they have been from their youth saturated and infected with wrong ideas'.[11] In the *Book Named the Governor*, Elyot signalled his preference for Plato in several passages, choices which mirrored his

---

[6] Skinner, 'Sir Thomas More's *Utopia* and the Language of Renaissance Humanism', in Pagden (ed.), *Languages of Political Theory*, pp. 123–57; his *Foundations of Modern Political Thought*, I, pp. 115–16, 217–19.

[7] *A Dialogue between Reginald Pole and Thomas Lupset*, ed. K. M. Burton (London, 1948), pp. 21–6, 36–40. The date of composition of the *Dialogue* is discussed by T. F. Mayer, *Thomas Starkey and the Commonweal* (Cambridge, 1989), pp. 89–102. I differ slightly in thinking Starkey to have been revising the work as late as 1535–6.

[8] *Dialogue between Pole and Lupset*, pp. 150–1.

[9] *A Discourse of the Commonweal of this Realm of England*, ed. M. Dewar (Charlottesville, VA, 1969), pp. 16–17.

[10] R. B. Wernham, *Before the Armada: The Emergence of the English Nation, 1485–1588* (New York, 1966; repr. 1972), pp. 236–7.

[11] E. Surtz and J. H. Hexter (eds.), *The Complete Works of St Thomas More* [hereafter cited as *CW*], IV: *Utopia* (New Haven, CT, 1965; rev. edn, repr. 1979), pp. 87, 101–3.

personal struggle to reconcile himself to political obscurity.[12] His opposition to Henry VIII's first divorce was his undoing, and he tried to square the circle by urging politicians 'called' to counsel to retreat to 'a secret oratory' in order to contemplate virtue.[13]

Yet the overriding preoccupation of the English humanists was the debate upon 'good counsel'. Classical studies shaped this outlook. As Francis Bacon later remarked, antiquity 'set forth in figure both the incorporation and inseparable conjunction of counsel with kings ... whereby they intend that Sovereignty is married to Counsel'.[14] In this mode, *imperium* was represented as male and *consilium* as female: their relationship was conjugal. (A married woman shared in the administration of her husband's household and mitigated his *imperium* just as equity tempered the rigour of the common law.) By curbing human passions and mitigating misjudgements, 'good counsel' stood between order and chaos. By instructing rulers who would otherwise become tyrants or near-tyrants in the ways of virtue and honesty, it was the touchstone of government.

'Counsel' was not, however, a neutral concept nor even one intrinsically suited to the conduct of politics. On the contrary, it subsumed competing moral and political values which were the subject of continuous discussion and negotiation. The politics of 'counsel' were in a fundamental sense the unceasing politics of discourse. This applied whether 'counsel' was tendered directly within established institutions or the law courts, or whether it was presented indirectly in the form of advice books, histories, commentaries, dramas, or even sometimes verse. It was through 'counsel' offered by whatever means that the process of conversion of politicians from evil to good might begin. Hythlodaeus complained that rulers invariably disregarded the advice of worthy counsellors. Yet *Utopia* was itself an advice book which sought to influence events on the Platonic grounds that root-and-branch reform required the 'miraculous effort' of dialogue.[15]

Elyot spoke the common language when he explained: 'every counsel is to be approved by three things principally, that it be rightwise, that it be good, and that it be with honesty'. What is 'rightwise' is approved by 'reason'; goodness springs from 'virtue'; and 'honesty' from virtue and reason'. The counsellor should be 'void of all hate, friendship, dis-

[12] Fox and Guy, *Reassessing the Henrician Age*, pp. 52–73.
[13] *Book Named the Governor*, pp. 95–9.
[14] *Bacon's Essays* (Chandos edn, London, n.d.), p. 37.
[15] A. J. Slavin, 'Platonism and the Problem of Counsel in *Utopia*', in Gordon J. Schochet (ed.), *Reformation, Humanism and 'Revolution': Proceedings of the Folger Institute Center for the History of British Political Thought* (Washington, DC, The Folger Shakespeare Library, 1990), I, pp. 207–34.

pleasure, or pity'. His duty is to consider the 'state of things present' and thereafter to advise 'what is to be followed and exploited, but also by what means and ways it shall be pursued, and how the affair may be honourable; also what is expedient and of necessity, and how much is needful, and what space and length of time, and finally how the enterprise being achieved and brought to effect may be kept and retained'. The object of the consultative process is good 'governance', either of a single individual (which is 'moral' governance) or of a multitude or public weal (which is 'politic' governance). In particular, 'the general and universal estate of the public weal' should always be preferred 'before any particular commodity' or concern of private persons.[16]

Such abstract ideas might be applied to political affairs by means of *exempla*. Historical parallels were constantly invoked: almost every humanist advocated the study of history equally for pleasure and profit. Typical arguments were that there was 'no study or science . . . of equal commodity and pleasure'; that the annals of past ages were 'statues and images' of human acts and minds; and that history was 'the nurse of practical wisdom' (the metaphor of Juan Luis Vives, whom Wolsey nominated to his endowed lectureship in classical literature at Oxford in 1523).[17]

Fortescue idealized the Augustan Principate on account of its commitment to 'counsel', a position invaluable to theorists anxious to set republican virtue firmly into the context of monarchical rule.[18] His thesis was that Augustus succeeded because he consulted the senate, 'which lordship and monarchy the emperor[s] kept all the while they were ruled by the counsel of the Senate.' But when they 'left the counsel of the senate', and Nero and Domitian slew 'great party of the Senators' and were ruled by their 'private' counsellors, 'the estate of the emperor fell in decay, and their lordship wax alway since then less and less'. From this Fortescue drew the simplest explanation of the Wars of the Roses:

We also Englishmen, whose kings some time were counselled by sad and well chosen councillors, beat the mightiest kings of the world. But since our kings have been ruled by private councillors, such as have offered their service and counsel and were not chosen thereto, we have not been able to keep our own

---

[16] *Book Named the Governor*, pp. 236–41.
[17] *Book Named the Governor*, pp. 37, 39; Thomas Starkey, *An Exhortation to the People Instructing them to Unity and Obedience* (1536), fo. 32ᵛ; *STC²* no. 23236; Skinner, *Foundations of Modern Political Thought*, I, pp. 220–1; J. K. McConica (ed.), *The History of the University of Oxford*, III, *The Collegiate University* (Oxford, 1986), pp. 26–7, 338.
[18] *The Governance of England*, ed. C. Plummer (2nd edn; Oxford, 1926), pp. 149–50, 347–8.

livelihood . . . And our Realm is fallen thereby in decay and poverty, as was the Empire when the emperor left the counsel of the Senate.[19]

Elyot, too, wrote in terms of a failure of 'counsel' when he deplored the fall of his patron, Cardinal Wolsey.[20] He feared the rise at court of an exclusive cabinet council which spoke only for the anti-clerical, anti-papal caucus planning Henry VIII's first divorce.[21] He was the earliest commentator to observe the shift towards a select privy council in the 1530s, and he sought to mitigate this development by annexing its intellectual context. He argued that privy councillors advised Henry VIII at Court in the same manner as the Roman emperors were advised by their *amici principis*. So he formulated an educational programme designed to create model Tudor equivalents of the *amici* whom he could deploy rhetorically against Henry VIII's 'private counsellors'.[22] He knew that the Roman *amici* had been drawn from those provincial governors, military commanders and special commissioners who had represented the emperor in the localities. He also believed – with Thomas Starkey and (later) Sir Philip Sidney – that a monarchy limited by a strong nobility would insure the state against tyranny. Hence, Elyot conceptualized the *amici* almost exclusively in terms of the hereditary nobility and landed gentry who served the crown in the localities. His humanism and (even more so) Starkey's had a keen aristocratic edge.[23] While this contrasted sharply with the ideas of Richard Moryson whose emphasis on 'true nobility' was tantamount to a defence of meritocracy, Elyot's reading is immediately explicable. For his overriding motive was to recreate the mechanism of 'good counsel' whereby the exclusivity of the break with Rome might be ameliorated and traditional links restored between the crown and its provincial affinities. What ultimately underpinned the *Book Named the Governor* was the axiom that rulers should promote the 'best' and most 'experienced' counsellors and that no 'good'

---

[19] *Ibid.*, pp. 347–8.
[20] For the evidence of Wolsey's patronage, see J. A. Guy, *The Court of Star Chamber and its Records to the Reign of Elizabeth I* (London, 1985), pp. 11–12; Fox and Guy, *Reassessing the Henrician Age*, pp. 54–6.
[21] Fox and Guy, *Reassessing the Henrician Age*, pp. 138–40; Guy, *Tudor England*, pp. 116–64.
[22] *Book Named the Governor*, pp. 15–94, 238–40; Fox and Guy, *Reassessing the Henrician Age*, pp. 138–40; J. A. Crook, *Consilium Principis: Imperial Councils and Counsellors from Augustus to Diocletian* (Cambridge, 1955), pp. 21–30. A comprehensive study of Elyot's political thought by Dr F. W. Conrad is in preparation. See his article, 'The Problem of Counsel Reconsidered: The Case of Sir Thomas Elyot', in T. Mayer and P. Fideler (eds.), *Political Thought and the Tudor Commonwealth* (London, 1992).
[23] For Elyot's preference for birth and lineage, see *Book Named the Governor*, pp. 2, 13–14.

(in this sense 'noble') counsellor should 'be omitted or passed over'.[24] For Elyot as for other English humanists apart from More, the problem of government itself was reducible to one of 'good counsel', because it was 'counselling' and conciliar institutions which effectively guided the ruler and bridled his inclinations to cruelty and vice.[25]

In *A Dialogue between Pole and Lupset*, begun about 1529 and completed between 1532 and *c.*1535, Starkey sang the same song but to a different tune. He had studied at Oxford and Padua, and served as Reginald Pole's secretary in the 1520s. He had seen at first hand Florentine refugees and Venetian patricians fusing their traditions of civic humanism into a 'myth of Venice', and was attracted to their outlook because it retained the princely office of *doge* but relied on the *Consiglio maggiore* as the guarantor of liberty and equality and of aristocratic government by the *ottimati*.[26] In consequence, Starkey stressed the limits of monarchy more strongly than his contemporaries. More than any other writer between the time of Fortescue and the Nineteen Propositions in 1642, he blended the idioms of civic humanism with those of feudal-baronial rhetoric in order to construct a thesis of limited monarchy.[27] His point of departure was public authority as enshrined in parliament, something almost obligatory given the prevailing conditions of Henrician political practice. Since, however, parliament was an intermittent institution, Starkey endowed a Venetian-style Council of Fourteen with the 'authority of the whole parliament' (the latter understood in a baronial sense) when parliament was not in session. The function of this Council was to 'represent the whole body of the people . . . to see unto the liberty of the whole body of the rea[l]m, and to resist all tyranny which by any manner may grow upon the whole commonalty'.[28] Its membership was to comprise four of the 'greatest and ancient lords of the temporalty', two bishops, four judges, and 'four of the most wise citizens of London', and it would ensure that the king and his own (privy) council did 'nothing again[st] the ordinance of his laws and good policy'. It should have power 'to call the great parliament whensoever to them it should seem necessary for the reformation of the

[24] *Book Named the Governor*, pp. 236–41, esp. 238.

[25] For some discussion of counselling as a 'bridle' upon royal power in Valois France, see J. A. Guy, 'The French King's Council, 1483–1526', in R. A. Griffiths and J. Sherborne (eds.), *Kings and Nobles in the Later Middle Ages* (Gloucester, 1986), pp. 274–94.

[26] Mayer, *Thomas Starkey and the Commonweal*, pp. 44–5, 132–3.

[27] For resonant echoes of feudal-baronial idioms during the Pilgrimage of Grace in 1536, see Fox and Guy, *Reassessing the Henrician Age*, pp. 121–47; J. A. Guy, 'The Rhetoric of Counsel in Early Modern England', in D. Hoak (ed.), *Tudor Political Culture* (Cambridge, forthcoming).

[28] *Dialogue between Pole and Lupset*, pp. 155–6, 164–7.

whole state of the commonalty' and should also 'pass all acts of leagues, confederation, peace and war'. The Fourteen were even to 'elect and choose' the privy council, since 'this may in no case be committed to the arbitrament of the prince – to choose his own counsel – for that were all one and to commit all to his affects, liberty and rule.'[29] By imposing such severe restraints of 'counsel' on the king's exercise of *imperium* in the *Dialogue*, Starkey therefore remodelled the English constitution rhetorically in the image of that of Venice.[30]

The humanists also played with ideas of transformation and conversion. The kernel was reached in the 'medical' metaphor in which 'counsellors' diagnosed sickness and disease in rulers or their subjects and appealed for 'physic'. Within this idiom, which ultimately derived from Aristotle, 'counsel' is medicine, and vice, corruption and absolutism are the diseases. Elyot ended his *Book Named the Governor* by comparing unworthy counsellors to 'evil physicians seeking for medicines ere they perfectly know the sicknesses'.[31] In *Pasquil the Playne*, a Lucianic dialogue first printed in 1533, he developed an extended triple analogy between the good physician who cures his patient's sickness, the good confessor who discharges a penitent's soul of 'vicious affections', and the good counsellor who purges his master's political passion. He stressed that counsellors should eschew flattery, which implants 'false opinions and vicious affects' into the hearts of rulers and 'is the poison that we so much spake of'. Should the counsellor resort to flattery: 'though ye after repent you, and perceive the danger, yet shall it perchance be impossible with speech to remove those opinions, and cure those affects, except ye loved so well your master, that for his health ye would confess your own errors'.[32] Again, Starkey urged that 'like as to physicians little it availeth to know the body, complexion thereof, and most perfect state, except they also can discern and judge all kind of sickness and diseases which commonly destroy the same', so the art of statecraft required that counsellors 'truly search out all common faults and general misorders, which, as sickness and diseases, be manifest impediments and utterly repugn[ant] to the maintenance of the same'.[33]

Yet theory and practice conflicted, and it is striking that the author who best understood the character of Henry VIII criticized the ideal of 'good counsel' with one voice at the same time that he endorsed it with

---

[29] *Ibid.*   [30] Mayer, *Thomas Starkey and the Commonweal*, p. 132.
[31] *Book Named the Governor*, p. 241.
[32] *Pasquil the Playne* (London, 1533), sig. D2ʳ–ᵛ; *STC²* 7672.
[33] *Dialogue between Pole and Lupset*, pp. 73, 79, 81–5, 97–8; Mayer, *Thomas Starkey and the Commonweal*, pp. 111, 128–9.

another.[34] Whereas More so crafted the civil philosophy of 'Morus' at the climax of Book I of *Utopia* that we may suppose his personal decision to enter the king's council was already taken, his overall attitude is highly ambivalent.[35] More's genius was his ability to debate both sides of a question, and in *Utopia* he subverted from within the view that 'good counsel' is the 'end of all doctrine and study'. In a mode clearly modelled upon Plato, Hythlodaeus insists, 'If I proposed beneficial measures to some king and tried to uproot from his soul the seeds of evil and corruption, do you not suppose that I should be forthwith banished or treated with ridicule?'[36] He cites examples to show that 'good counsel' is ignored by rulers while flattery and evil counsel are rewarded. He retorts that by playing the active citizen, 'I should accomplish nothing else than to share the madness of others as I tried to cure their lunacy'. It is true that More controlled this debate in such a way as to leave intact the Ciceronian 'civil philosophy' of 'Morus'. But Hythlodaeus scores palpable hits. He plants genuine misgivings in the minds of his audience that the humanist infatuation with the ideal of 'good counsel' is misplaced.[37]

Still more striking, the Utopian institutions which Hythlodaeus meticulously describes in Book II allot only the most superficial role to 'good counsel'. True, the Utopian senate is given legislative and judicial functions reminiscent of the senate of Rome. Again, provision is made for consultation between the people and their elected officials, and for a public assembly (*comitia*) of the people.[38] Yet it is less the 'counsel' of senators which guarantees the welfare of the Utopians than their rule of life which limits their opportunity for choice and thereby reduces the risks of evil and corruption. Utopian social institutions so innately embody justice and simplicity that few laws and no lawyers are in practice required.[39] Civic virtue is built into the system of government. The values and institutions of Utopia *by themselves* define the path to virtue, and it is by this route that the Utopians attain as much happiness as it was possible for a Christian humanist to accord to pagans. As More's vision of Utopia unfolds, so the functions of 'counselling' diminish and his pessimistic view of human nature is revealed. Why he

---

[34] Skinner, 'Sir Thomas More's *Utopia* and the Language of Renaissance Humanism', pp. 123–57; Fox and Guy, *Reassessing the Henrician Age*, pp. 131–3; A. G. Fox, *Early Tudor Literature: Politics and the Literary Imagination* (Oxford, 1989), ch. 6.

[35] J. A. Guy, *The Public Career of Sir Thomas More* (Brighton and New Haven, CT, 1980), pp. 6–11.

[36] Surtz and Hexter (eds.), *CW*, IV: *Utopia*, p. 87.   [37] *Ibid.*, pp. 101–3.

[38] *Ibid.*, pp. 112–13, 123–5. The exact constitutional role of the *comitia* is left unexplained by More.

[39] *Ibid.*, pp. 193–5.

did not share the optimism of his fellow humanists is a question beyond the scope of this inquiry, but that he was personally attracted to the system of government he put into the mouth of Hythlodaeus is suggested by the concluding speech of 'Morus', and by a letter More wrote to Erasmus in which he confessed to dreaming of himself as a Utopian king.[40]

Debate concerning law and jurisprudence

Henrician political thought was crammed with statements rooted in law and jurisprudence. Henry VIII insisted that his marriage to Catherine of Aragon infringed divine and natural law, and that therefore the papal dispensation was invalid. The Acts of Appeals and Supremacy defined the king's *imperium* in church and state and asserted the autonomy of the Church of England in relation to Rome.[41] Magna Carta and its confirmations linked issues of politics and property directly to the common law: 'no man shall be taken nor imprisoned, nor disinherited, nor put to death ... save *per legem terrae*'.[42] The Reformation was therefore declared by parliamentary statutes and enforced by common law procedures. Parliamentary statute became omnicompetent in the sense that the 'king-in-parliament' could legislate for church and state alike. Treason, not heresy, became the penalty for denying the royal supremacy and, in Elizabeth's reign, for Catholic priests or laymen who withdrew subjects from their allegiance to the queen or the Church of England. Common law triumphed over canon and papal law; the privileges and immunities enjoyed by clergy and sanctuarymen were stifled by parliament. Canon law was retained in the church courts on a selective basis, but was emasculated as a subject for study at the universities.[43]

The crux of Henry VIII's strategy was his contention that his marriage to Catherine of Aragon infringed divine and natural law. In the *libellus* he delivered in person to Wolsey's legatine court in 1529, he laid down the principles that his scholars defended in print. The earliest tracts were revisions of the *libellus* intended to bolster the favourable

---

[40] Skinner, 'Sir Thomas More's *Utopia* and the Language of Renaissance Humanism', p. 156; *St Thomas More: Selected Letters*, ed. E. F. Rogers (New Haven, 1961; reissued 1967), p. 85.

[41] See below, pp. 35–46.

[42] J. C. Holt, *Magna Carta* (Cambridge, 1965; repr. 1969), pp. 9, 326. The wording changed significantly between 1215 and 1354. My quotation conveys the meaning reached by the middle of the reign of Edward III.

[43] D. M. Owen, *The Medieval Canon Law: Teaching, Transmission and Literature* (Cambridge, 1990), pp. 43–65.

opinions which Henry secured from some French and Italian universities.[44] *Gravissimae atque exactissimae illustrissimarum totius Italiae et Galliae Academiarum censurae* (published in the spring of 1531), and Cranmer's translation *The Determinations of the Most Famous and Most Excellent Universities of Italy and France* (published the following November), maintained that the Levitical prohibitions against sexual intercourse between a man and his brother's wife were divine law, and that marriage to a brother's wife was incestuous and unnatural. In reply, Catherine of Aragon's supporters claimed that these prohibitions applied only during the brother's lifetime, that the levirate (i.e. marriage to a brother's widow) was validated by God in the Book of Deuteronomy, and that it was unproven that Henry's marriage was against the law of nature. Their arguments were rejected by the king's scholars, who denied that the levirate was commanded by God and that its observance brought honour to the deceased brother. They countered that the levirate was simply a Jewish custom not binding on Christians.[45]

Hence, Julius II, according to Henry VIII, had contravened divine and natural law by granting the dispensation that originally authorized his marriage to the widow of his elder brother, Prince Arthur. It followed that, if Clement VII declined to correct the matter, the pope was no better than another human legislator who had exceeded his authority. Rome had to respond, because Henry held that 'conscience' must always be obeyed when a particular course of action was prohibited. If the pope declined to act, Christians might lawfully resist him: the distinction between human law and natural (or moral) law, according to Henry, justified such resistance. Natural (or moral) law was inscribed on men's hearts 'instinctu spiritus sancti'.[46] It was known by means of 'conscience' and took precedence over human law. Anyone who sought an annulment, as Henry did, on grounds of 'conscience' was neither rebellious nor disobedient to the church.[47] His argument was publicized in tracts which included Edward Foxe's *De vera differentia* (1534), where bishops and holy men were shown to have rightfully resisted papal encroachments when guided by 'conscience' written in their hearts by the Holy Spirit. The 'spirit of God' was a superior 'law', and persons

---

[44] See the introduction to *The Divorce Tracts of Henry VIII*, ed. E. Surtz and V. Murphy (Angers, 1988).

[45] For the arguments of the king's opponents, see John Fisher's 'Apologia' in BL, Arundel MS. 151, fos. 202–339v; Thomas Abel, *Invicta veritas* (Lüneberg [?Antwerp], May 1532); *STC*² 61; *Tumultuaria apologia* (Lüneberg [?Antwerp], September 1532).

[46] On this point Henry VIII followed the classic exposition of the Middle Ages; St Thomas Aquinas, *Selected Political Writings*, ed. A. P. D'Entreves (Oxford, 1965), pp. 128–9.

[47] *Divorce Tracts of Henry VIII*, ed. Surtz and Murphy, pp. xxxiii–xxxiv, 167–85, 266–77.

guided by the Holy Spirit were ordered after the 'law of God'.[48] *Mutatis mutandis* Henry's contention that human law was subordinate to moral law provided philosophical support for Thomas More's opposition to the Act of Supremacy, but this point was overlooked.

Henry VIII did not, of course, argue his case against the pope in a vacuum. Since 1485, a vocal lobby at the inns of court had demanded the subordination of canon and papal law to the common law. The 'conflict of laws' underpinned this rhetoric.[49] The Statutes of Provisors and *Praemunire* were the chief legislation of the Middle Ages regulating papal jurisdiction in derogation of royal prerogative or the laws and customs of the realm. Whereas the Yorkists did not much invoke these acts, *praemunire* actions were encouraged under Henry VII, when belief in the supremacy of common law and parliamentary statute over canon law and ecclesiastical custom gained ground.[50] Chief Justice Hussey asserted in 1485 that the king of England was answerable directly to God and was therefore superior to the pope within his realm. Thomas Kebell, an Inner Temple barrister, said in the same year that 'if all the prelates should make a provincial constitution, it would be void, because they cannot change the law of the land' (i.e. canon law was invalid if it contradicted common law). Again, John Hales, in a Gray's Inn reading of 1514, expounded his objections to the problems of dual authority caused by parallel jurisdictions in church and state. He thought it 'inconvenient' that similar questions should be decided differently by different courts – this argument became a hallmark of the royal cause in the 1530s.[51]

In 1512, parliament restricted benefit of clergy to persons ordained in the three higher orders of clergy.[52] The statute was denounced by Richard Kidderminster (February 1515), who claimed that it infringed divine law and the liberties of the church; that it was void and sinful to put it into effect; and that those who had made it were liable to censure if they remained obdurate.[53] His attack caused a furore; Henry VIII personally ended the debate when he declared: 'By the ordinance and sufferance of God we are king of England, and the kings of England in

---

[48] E. Foxe, *Opus eximium. De vera differentia regiae potestatis et ecclesiasticae, et quae sit ipsa veritas ac virtus utriusque.* (London, 1534); *STC²* 11218–20.

[49] *The Reports of Sir John Spelman*, ed. J. H. Baker, 2 vols. Selden Society (London, 1977–8); his 'English Law and the Renaissance', *Cambridge Law Journal*, 44 (1985), 46–61; Fox and Guy, *Reassessing the Henrician Age*, pp. 95–120.

[50] Guy, *Tudor England*, pp. 72–3.

[51] *Reports of Sir John Spelman*, ed. Baker, II, intro., p. 65.

[52] 4 Henry VIII, c.2.

[53] J. D. M. Derrett, 'The Affairs of Richard Hunne and Friar Standish', in J. B. Trapp (ed.), *CW*, IX: *The Apology* (New Haven, CT, 1979), p. 226.

time past have never had any superior but God alone. Wherefore know you well that we shall maintain the right of our crown and of our temporal jurisdiction as well in this point as in all others'.[54] Henry knew that a king who does not recognize a superior is free from outside jurisdiction, and he spoke following a judicial opinion that the writ of *praemunire facias* ran against all members of Convocation who appealed to Roman canon law not expressly based on divine law or approved in advance by the king. Almost twenty years before the Act of Supremacy, Henry VIII defined his regality in terms of his right to monitor the reception of canon law, in which case his 'superiority' included denial of the pope's right to infringe his territorial sovereignty on the basis of the Petrine commission.

The common lawyers' position was cemented when Christopher St German wrote the two dialogues known as *Doctor and Student*, printed in 1528 and 1530 respectively.[55] By publishing in Latin and English rather than Law French, St German revealed his intention to address an audience beyond the inns of court. His first dialogue was translated from Latin into English, and the second was in English from the start. As he explained: 'It is right necessary to all men in this realm both spiritual and temporal for the good ordering of their conscience to know many things of the law of England . . . Therefore for the profit of the multitude it is put into the English tongue rather than into the Latin or French tongue'.[56] What St German taught the multitude, however, was anti-clericalism. His *Treatise Concerning the Division between the Spiritualty and Temporalty* (1532) exasperated Thomas More, who rebuked him for publicizing clerical abuses 'in the vulgar tongue'. Whereas Gerson, his intellectual mentor, had written in Latin out of respect for the clergy, St German printed the faults of the clergy in the vernacular, as More believed, 'because he would have the lay people both men and women look on them'.[57]

St German's jurisprudence was reiterated in *A Little Treatise Concerning Writs of Subpoena* (1532), where he defined the litigable limits of

[54] Henry E. Huntington Library, San Marino, CA, Ellesmere MS. 6109 (in vol. 34/C/49); J. A. Guy, 'Henry VIII and the *Praemunire* Manoeuvres of 1530–1531', *English Historical Review*, 97 (1982), 497 n2.
[55] *St German's Doctor and Student*, ed. T. F. T. Plucknett and J. L. Barton, Selden Society (London, 1974). The alleged '1523' edition of the first dialogue seems to be a ghost; no surviving copy has been identified. For a fuller discussion of St German's legal theory, see J. A. Guy, *Christopher St German on Chancery and Statute*, Selden Society, Supplementary Series, vol. 6 (London, 1985); Fox and Guy, *Reassessing the Henrician Age*, pp. 95–120, 179–98.
[56] *Doctor and Student*, ed. Plucknett and Barton, pp. 176–7. The first dialogue was translated into English in 1531 (*ibid.*, pp. lxx–lxxiii).
[57] Trapp (ed.), *CW*, IX: *The Apology*, p. 60.

'conscience'. He reviewed a series of cases where equitable jurisdiction was admissible, and then discussed others where it was not despite *prima facie* grounds in canon or natural law. His thesis was that a suitor whose case conflicted with the 'maxims' of the common law was no more eligible for relief at equity than at law.[58] He formulated the issue thus: 'there lieth no *subpoena* directly against a statute, nor directly against the maxims of the law, for [if] it should lie, then the law should be judged to be void, and that may not be done by no court, but by the parliament'.[59] The effect of this theorem depended upon the question of agency. Who precisely was empowered to define the 'maxims' of the common law and interpret the scope and force of statutes? Since St German assigned these functions exclusively to the common lawyers, the effect was to deny a plea of 'conscience' to litigants whose grounds of action were derived from principles which the common lawyers rejected. The result was to sever equity from its medieval roots and annex it as a branch of the common law. While this process was neither begun nor completed in the reign of Henry VIII, St German's theory both reflected and informed the politics of the 1530s whereby philosophic denials of the Reformation statutes were inadmissible at law.[60]

If, however, Henry VIII and the common lawyers shared anti-clerical objectives, they disagreed upon the extent to which the Acts of Appeals and Supremacy validated 'imperial' kingship. From the autumn of 1530 onwards, Henry VIII maintained that his *imperium* was divinely ordained. He quoted the Old Testament and early chapters of Justinian's Code to establish the sovereignty of rulers who 'gave' laws *de episcopis et clericis*.[61] Bishops Foxe and Gardiner used these and other sources to claim that 'imperial' authority embraced matters of faith as well as discipline.[62] Gardiner had lectured in canon and civil law at Cambridge in the early 1520s.[63] Later he denied insinuating to Henry VIII that the king would magnify his power if English law were assimilated to the *lex regia* in Roman civil law, which enshrined the principle 'What pleases the prince has the force of law'. He put the blame for this suggestion on his rival, Thomas Cromwell, claiming that he himself had advised the king to make the laws his will: '"And by this

---

[58] Guy, *Christopher St German on Chancery and Statute*, p. 117.
[59] *Ibid.*, p. 116.
[60] The legal background to this issue is treated by N. Doe, *Fundamental Authority in Late Medieval English Law* (Cambridge, 1990).
[61] D. Wilkins (ed.), *Concilia Magnae Britanniae et Hiberniae*, 4 vols. (London, 1737), III, pp. 762–5; Fox and Guy, *Reassessing the Henrician Age*, pp. 151–78.
[62] *De vera differentia*, fo. 47ᵛ; P. Janelle (ed.), *Obedience in Church and State* (Cambridge, 1930), pp. 116–18.
[63] J. A. Muller, *Stephen Gardiner and the Tudor Reaction* (New York, 1926), p. 9.

form of government ye be established", quoth I, "and it is agreeable with the nature of your people." [64]

It is likely that Cromwell himself tempted Gardiner to make the insinuation in order to refute it publicly.[65] In 1532 Cromwell had orchestrated the Submission of the Clergy to Henry VIII.[66] Initially, he sought to subordinate Convocation to parliament, a prospect even less tolerable to the prelates than surrender to the supreme head alone. Cromwell drafted a bill to this effect, but the king recognized its significance and intervened to protect his command of 'his' church's institutional structure.[67] Henry modelled his *imperium* upon that of Solomon in Israel and Constantine in Rome.[68] The crown assumed full responsibility for the government of church and state. Hence, the royal supremacy was potentially a Trojan horse. Whereas Bracton's *On the Laws and Customs of England* stated that the king of England is 'under God and the law, because the law makes the king',[69] Henry VIII's propagandists recast the passage to read: the king is 'under God but not the law, because the king makes the law'.[70] They annexed the vocabulary of Roman civil law to assure to the 'imperial' crown the sovereignty that the law and its institutions embodied. The Leviathan they created in the minds of the common lawyers was the thesis of 'imperial' kingship.

Yet the lawyers already had a counter-thesis. They replied that the prerogatives of the crown were the common law rights of the king, which were themselves granted by English law.[71] The king might issue letters patent exempting named individuals from the provisions of statute within limits to be determined by the judges, but he could not 'give' the law, tax his subjects, nor enact or repeal statute by himself.[72]

---

[64] *The Acts and Monuments of John Foxe*, ed. G. Townsend, 8 vols. (London, 1843–9), VI, pp. 45–6.

[65] Elton, *Studies in Tudor and Stuart Politics and Government*, II, pp. 219–20.

[66] Guy, *Public Career of Sir Thomas More*, pp. 175–201.

[67] Two versions of the draft bill are PRO, SP 2/L, fos. 78–80; SP 2/P, fos. 17–19.

[68] G. D. Nicholson, 'The Act of Appeals and the English Reformation', in C. Cross, D. Loades, and J. J. Scarisbrick (eds.), *Law and Government under the Tudors* (Cambridge, 1988), pp. 22–3; W. Ullmann, '"This Realm of England is an Empire"', *Journal of Ecclesiastical History*, 30 (1979), 175–203; Janelle (ed.), *Obedience in Church and State*, pp. 106–8, 128–30.

[69] Bracton, *De Legibus*, Bk. I, c.8.   [70] BL, Cotton MS. Cleopatra E. vi, fo. 28ᵛ.

[71] William Stanford, *An Exposition of the King's Prerogative* (London, 1567); *STC²* 23213–18. S. B. Chrimes, *English Constitutional Ideas in the Fifteenth Century* (Cambridge, 1936), pp. 55–8, 279–80.

[72] Only in 1491, 1522–3, 1525, 1543–6, and the 1590s were attempts made to levy forced loans or non-parliamentary taxation on any significant scale during the Tudor period. Furthermore, the benevolence of 1491 was granted by a Great Council, and on every subsequent occasion except that of the Amicable Grant of 1525, the loan or benevolence was legitimized as a tax by Parliament *ex post facto* or substantially repaid by the Crown. The principal exception was the Amicable Grant, which provoked a revolt in East Anglia and had to be abandoned.

His *imperium* was limited by the 'assent of the kingdom' in parliament. Or, in Fortescue's idiom, his *dominium* was *politicum et regale*. Kings 'do not make laws nor impose subsidies on their subjects without the consent of the three estates of their kingdom'. The king 'cannot at his pleasure change the laws of his kingdom'. Statutes are established 'by the assent of the whole kingdom', and the civil law maxim 'What pleases the prince has the force of law' is unknown to English law.[73]

St German took this formulation further. In *A Little Treatise Called the New Additions* (1531) he annexed the sovereignty of the law to the 'king-in-parliament', which was 'the high sovereign over the people, which hath not only charge on the bodies, but also on the souls of his subjects'.[74] He muffled the effect by citing precedent from the reign of Richard II, but his argument for parliament's power in *New Additions* went beyond anything contemplated before. In *A Treatise Concerning the Power of the Clergy and the Laws of the Realm* (1535?) he even doubted that statute could infringe divine law.[75] The pith, however, was his contention that the assent of the 'kingdom' (defined as 'the king and the estates of the realm') was the touchstone of *both* ecclesiastical and secular legislation. In *An Answer to a Letter* (1535) he invoked 'populist' language to ask 'Why should not the Parliament then which representeth the whole catholic church of England expound scripture?' All human positive law, secular or ecclesiastical, was properly made in parliament, 'for the Parliament so gathered together representeth the estate of all the people within this realm, that is to say of the whole catholic church thereof'.[76] St German was emphatic about the 'ascending' basis of political power and his viewpoint was echoed by William Marshall, Cromwell's client, when he translated Marsiglio's *Defensor Pacis* for publication.[77] The legitimacy of government rested upon the consent of the governed. Henry VIII was to exercise his 'imperial' authority in parliament.[78]

---

[73] See Fortescue's *De natura legis naturae*, in *The Works of Sir John Fortescue, Knight, Chief Justice of England and Lord Chancellor to King Henry the Sixth*, ed. T. Fortescue (Lord Clermont), 2 vols. (London, 1869), Bk. I, ch. 16; *De laudibus legum Anglie*, ed. S. B. Chrimes (Cambridge, 1949), chs. 9, 18, 34, 36; Chrimes, *English Constitutional Ideas in the Fifteenth Century*, pp. 58–61, 300–32.

[74] *Doctor and Student*, ed. Plucknett and Barton, p. 327.

[75] *STC²* no. 21588, esp. ch. 6.

[76] *An Answer to a Letter*, sigs. G3–G6ᵛ; *STC²* 21558.5.

[77] *The Defence of Peace: Lately Translated out of Latin into English* (London, 1535); *STC²* 17817. Marshall glossed Marsiglio's citizen legislative body as meaning parliament on fos. 27ᵛ, 28ᵛ, 35, 91ᵛ, 138.

[78] Nor was this viewpoint seriously contested in practice. Although proclamations were a valid weapon of the prerogative, Henry VIII made no attempt to augment their scope or

Central to the common lawyers' position was the axiom that anyone who invoked the king's *imperium* in a manner derogatory to common law or statute was liable to the charge of *praemunire*. When Gardiner questioned in parliament the legality of a *praemunire* action against the bishop of Exeter on the grounds that every bishop was 'authorized' directly by the king, Lord Chancellor Audley told him to consult the Act of Supremacy, where he would 'find' that the royal supremacy was restricted to purely spiritual matters. Audley also claimed that the Act for the Submission of the Clergy (1534) proved that spiritual law could not override common law or statute. '"And [if] this were not", quoth he, "you bishops would enter in with the king, and, by means of his supremacy, order the laity as ye listed. But we will provide . . . that the *praemunire* shall ever hang over your heads; and so we laymen shall be sure to enjoy our inheritance by the common laws, and acts of Parliament."'[79] Audley's argument was tendentious, but the definitions of *praemunire* and prohibition were subsequently extended by the common law judges to enable them to regulate not only ecclesiastical jurisdiction under the crown, but even litigation in the temporal courts of equity and admiralty.

The common lawyers' achievement was therefore to ensure that the word 'law' in Tudor political practice meant 'the laws and customs of England'. Hence, the property of the ex-religious houses and chantries was remitted to royal coffers by the authority of parliament. Again, the theology of the Church of England was declared and enforced by the Act of Six Articles (1539) and the Act for the Advancement of True Religion (1543) in Henry VIII's reign, and by the Acts of Uniformity of 1549 and 1552 under Edward VI. When the Catholic Mary ascended the throne, she had little choice but to repeal the Reformation statutes in order to deny them. When in 1559 the Elizabethan Acts of Supremacy and Uniformity passed into law despite Convocation's formal protest, it seemed that the only law of immediate practical significance was common law and statute, even if martial law might be proclaimed in such emergencies as the Northern Rising of 1569 and if in time of war or

---

force. On the contrary, the Act of Proclamations (1539) firmly reinforced the existing exceptions which barred proclamations from infringing common law and statute, or from touching subjects' lives, lands, goods or liberties. True, the new act's purpose was to enable proclamations to be enforced in star chamber as if they had the force of statutes. But this supposed 'innovation' was no more than the common law judges already allowed. See 31 Henry VIII, c.8; G. R. Elton, *The Tudor Constitution* (2nd edn; Cambridge, 1982), pp. 21–3, 27–30.

[79] *Acts and Monuments of John Foxe*, ed. Townsend, VI, 43.

revolt the queen acting alone might in theory tax or impress her subjects 'for the safety of the kingdom'.[80]

Religious debate on the eve of the Reformation

The agenda raised by Henry VIII's quarrel with the pope was far less novel than it appeared because it focused chiefly upon issues of regality and jurisdiction inherited from the Middle Ages. Since the late eleventh century, the papacy had emphasized the church's institutional, universal and temporal qualities at the expense of its charismatic, provincial and eschatological ones. Gregory VII and Innocent III blazed the trail whereby the pope's authority as 'vicar of Christ' was augmented. Canon law proclaimed the 'liberty' of the church from secular interference and the pope's right to intervene in secular affairs 'by reason of sin'. The inference was that the pope's authority was equivalent to that of Christ. All ecclesiastical power derived from the pope as St Peter's successor; the 'descending' thesis of authority and hierarchy in the church was asserted.[81]

By the late thirteenth century, canon law affirmed the pope's role as the church's superior legislator, the primacy of the priesthood, and the unitary spiritual goals of church and state to the point where temporal rulers were claimed as papal subjects. The justification was Innocent III's doctrine of the 'plenitude of power', which held that the pope's authority was so extensive that nothing could be determined in the church without it. Gradually the scope of this authority was extended in order to annex regal as well as ecclesiastical power for the pope. The culmination was Boniface VIII's bull *Unam sanctam* (1302), which codified this monarchic theory and concluded: 'We declare, we affirm, we define and pronounce that for every human creature it is absolutely necessary for salvation to be subject to the Roman pontiff'.[82]

---

[80] See Fortescue's *De natura legis naturae*, in *Works of Sir John Fortescue*, Bk. I, chs. 16, 24, 25. Occasions when martial law was imposed by the Tudors included 1487, 1495, 1513, 1536–7, 1549, 1569–70, and spasmodically for purposes of military discipline during the Elizabethan war with Spain. In general, the Tudors preferred the ordinary machinery of common law and statute to the extraordinary procedures of the law of arms when dealing with Englishmen. (Irishmen received different treatment.) There was a tangible incentive, since martial law did not secure forfeiture of the victim's lands to the Crown. Aliens could not be indicted at common law unless they had been naturalized as 'denizens'.

[81] W. Ullmann, *A History of Political Thought: The Middle Ages* (London, 1965); his *Principles of Government and Politics in the Middle Ages* (2nd edn; London, 1966).

[82] E. Lewis, *Medieval Political Ideas*, 2 vols. (New York, 1954; repr. 1974), II, pp. 626–7; Ullmann, *History of Political Thought*, pp. 114–15.

The counter-thesis came from the French civil lawyers who held that the king was 'emperor' in his realm (*rex in regno suo est imperator*), that he recognized no superior save God in 'temporal' matters, that the clergy's jurisdiction was confined to 'spiritual' affairs, and that the king might tax his clergy. In particular, the pope had no authority to legislate for the kingdom in temporal affairs, because the prerequisite for legislation was dominion, and the pope had no dominion over the king's subjects.[83] Such claims reflected the civil lawyers' view, echoed in St German's *Doctor and Student* and *New Additions*, that the clergy's jurisdiction should be restricted to their spiritual duties, and that all issues involving property were subject to the jurisdiction of the temporal ruler who was empowered to regulate both the clergy's possessions and social relationships. Increasingly, lawyers on both sides of the English Channel defined regality in terms of the provincial autonomy and territorial independence of the kingdom.

The papal 'plenitude of power' was also attacked by conciliarists who held that the church was a community of believers entitled to secure their own good government. The politics of the Great Schism (1378–1415) underpinned their claims: (1) that papal law was subordinate to divine law; (2) that the clergy possessed the *potestas ordinis* but not the *potestas jurisdictionis*; (3) that the general council of the church was superior to the pope; (4) that sacerdotal jurisdiction was partly based on spurious documents, partly on mistaken interpretation of scripture, and partly on usurpation by the papacy; (5) that the pope was an officer of the church charged with specific duties and responsible to the whole Christian people (including the laity) through their representative general council; (6) that the pope was as prone to error as any Christian; (7) that the pope could be deposed by the general council.[84] These arguments formed the basis of a 'populist' or 'ascending' thesis of government in the church.

Disputes over papal provisions aside, the English church escaped significant conflict before 1500. Scandals involving simony or sexual misconduct were relatively infrequent, even if tithes disputes, probate and mortuary fees, and inquisitorial procedure in cases of suspected heresy could become flashpoints. Dissent was confined to London and the south-east, parts of East Anglia, and towns such as Bristol, Coventry

---

[83] Lewis, *Medieval Political Ideas*, II, pp. 451–3, 468–70, 528–31, 567–74; W. Ullmann, '"This Realm of England is an Empire"', pp. 188–90, 202–3; his *History of Political Thought*, pp. 155–8.

[84] Ullmann, *History of Political Thought*, pp. 200–28; B. Gogan, *The Common Corps of Christendom* (Leiden, 1982), pp. 33–63; Lewis, *Medieval Political Ideas*, II, pp. 453–615.

and Colchester.[85] The most numerous dissenters were the Lollards, who challenged clerical power and the doctrine of transubstantiation; they also anticipated the reformers' solifidian platform. But they were largely drawn from the mercantile or artisan community and spoke *sotto voce*. More audible were a group of itinerant preachers based in Cambridge. By the 1520s they had laid the foundations of an evangelical movement which taught that salvation was God's free gift to believers and that scripture was antecedent to the church. They verged on Luther's doctrine of 'justification by faith alone', and questioned the theology of the mass. But they failed to agree upon a valid Protestant alternative.[86]

The humanists also nourished anti-clericalism. In a powerful sermon to Convocation in 1512, John Colet attacked clerical abuses and demanded reform of the church from within. He compared negligent priests to heretics: his language was so pungent that he narrowly escaped a charge of heresy himself! But the humanists spoke from a position of strength. Their scholarship drove a wedge between 'faith' and 'reason' forcing literate men and women to choose whether they were prepared to believe as 'necessary to salvation' Catholic traditions not documented by scripture. Erasmus was acclaimed for his critical editions of the primary Christian texts, notably the Greek New Testament (1516). His achievement served to authenticate his Biblical 'philosophy of Christ' which he propagated in a manner subversive of clerical authority. He embellished his *oeuvre* with witty satires on priests and monks, ritual and superstition, and even the papacy. The upshot was that scholasticism was discredited and scripture re-established as the authentic witness to the church's original constitution.

The foremost English Lutheran was William Tyndale. When he failed to win Bishop Tunstall's approval for a vernacular edition of the Bible, he migrated to Germany and the Low Countries to print his English *New Testament* (1525). Reprints in 1526, 1534, and 1535 reflected his conviction that scripture came first and determined the doctrines, institutions and ceremonies of the church. His outlook was summarized in his *Preface unto the Epistle of Paul to the Romans* (1526), where an ideal of Christian 'liberty' served as a foil to the institutional

---

[85] Guy, *Tudor England*, pp. 25–7, 118–53, 178–88; C. Haigh (ed.), *The English Reformation Revised* (Cambridge, 1987).

[86] J. F. Davis, *Heresy and Reformation in the South-East of England, 1520–1559* (London, 1983); D. D. Wallace, *Puritans and Predestination: Grace in English Protestant Theology, 1525–1695* (Chapel Hill, NC, 1982); H. Davies, *Worship and Theology in England from Cranmer to Hooker, 1534–1603* (Princeton, NJ, 1970); W. A. Clebsch, *England's Earliest Protestants, 1520–1535* (New Haven, CT, 1964).

imperium of Rome and the papacy.[87] Imitating Luther's own deployment of humanist rhetoric, Tyndale wielded *libertas* against *imperium*, Pauline against Petrine authority, in order to proclaim the 'liberty' of the Christian faith as instilled by the Holy Spirit into the hearts of believers born again in Christ.

Tyndale's most political work was his *Obedience of a Christian Man* (1528). He identified the pope with Antichrist and argued that the Catholic church was so powerful and tenacious that only the 'godly king' could rescue England from its thraldom. He adopted the position of Henry IV of Germany during the Investiture Contest: kings were anointed by God, therefore they were godly servants for the reform of the church. He even came close enough to an 'imperial' theory of kingship to catch Henry VIII's ear. He wrote of kings: 'God hath made the king in every realm judge over all, and over him is there no judge. He that judgeth the king judgeth God; and he that layeth hands on the king layeth hand on God; and he that resisteth the king resisteth God, and damneth God's law and ordinance'.[88] But Tyndale declined to champion Henry VIII's divorce; his *Practice of Prelates* (1530) positively condemned it. He therefore remained in exile, but helped to mould opinion for the king. Indeed, his ideas 'Truth as revealed in scripture' and 'We must rather obey God than men', when fused with the claim that scripture was divine law, provided slogans for Henry VIII. For the strength of the king's case against the pope was precisely that it defined the powers of kings and church government in terms that were Biblical.

Tunstall commissioned his friend Thomas More to refute the reformers. In 1523 More had attacked Luther at Henry VIII's request. He immediately realized that the vital terrain was not the papal supremacy but Catholic tradition and ecclesiology. His *Dialogue Concerning Heresies* (1529) and *Confutation of Tyndale's Answer* (1532–3) defined the Catholic church as the visible or 'common known church' comprising 'the common known catholic people, clergy, lay folk, and all'.[89] He repudiated the Lutheran claim that the church was 'a spiritual thing and no exterior thing but invisible from carnal eyes'.[90] No 'invisible' or 'church unknown' comprising only the 'elect' could be

---

[87] *STC²* 24438.

[88] *Doctrinal Treatises and Introductions to Different Portions of the Holy Scriptures by William Tyndale*, ed. H. Walter, Parker Society (Cambridge, 1848), p. 177; *STC²* 24446.

[89] L. A. Schuster, R. C. Marius, J. P. Lusardi, and R. J. Schoeck (eds.), *CW*, VIII: *The Confutation of Tyndale's Answer*, 3 vols. (New Haven, CT, 1973), pp. 379–82, 477–9, 480–1, 1004–13, 1029–34.

[90] *Ibid.*, appendix A, p. 1042.

believed 'since it cannot be heard'.[91] The 'Catholic church' had prevailed since the time of the apostles and – above all else – was antecedent to scripture; not the other way round, as Tyndale and his adherents supposed. The Catholic church had canonized the texts that together comprised the holy scriptures; its role was decisive. The Holy Spirit inspired consent, which had permitted the canonization of scripture by the church.[92] Hence, the church was not to be judged by the opinions of individuals, even if their scholarship was rooted in what they believed was scripture itself. Only the church as an institution could provide authentic interpretations of scripture. Furthermore, Catholic tradition not expressly warranted by scripture was as valid as if it *were* documented in scripture, because such tradition had been substantiated by the councils of the church, when the Holy Spirit had inspired consent as much as in the time of the apostles themselves.

Henry VIII left More's ecclesiology unchallenged at this point. The king was not a Lutheran, but his suit for divorce threw down the gauntlet to papal authority. By the autumn of 1530 his campaign raised fundamental questions about the original constitution of the Catholic church, the 'true difference' between royal and ecclesiastical power, and the pope's role as 'vicar of Christ'. One of the earliest decisions of his propagandists was to publish Latin and English editions of the *Disputation between a Clerk and a Knight*, originally written by the French civil lawyers to repudiate papal jurisdiction during the clash between Boniface VIII and Philip the Fair.[93] The tract denied the papal plenitude of power on the grounds that 'no man hath power to ordain statutes of things over which he hath no lordship'. It then maintained that clerical privileges existed only 'by the goodness and liberal benignity of kings and princes'. For the king was the superior legislator in his kingdom; his regal power was above the 'laws, customs, privileges and liberties' of the clergy. He could curtail the clergy's privileges whenever these were 'hurtful and grievous to the common weal' or 'for the necessary business of the realm'. His power was chronologically antecedent to that of the pope – this argument reflected the search at the

---

[91] *Ibid.*, pp. 379–82, 476–9; J. M. Headley (ed.), *CW*, V: *Responsio ad Lutherum*, 2 vols. (New Haven, CT, 1969), pp. 180–5.

[92] Headley (ed.), *CW*, V: *Responsio ad Lutherum*, pp. 242–4; T. M. C. Lawler, G. Marc'hadour, and R. C. Marius (eds.), *CW*, VI: *A Dialogue Concerning Heresies*, 2 vols. (New Haven, 1981), pp. 116–21, 180–2, 253–5; Schuster, Marius, Lusardi, and Schoeck (eds.), *CW*, VIII: *Confutation of Tyndale's Answer*, pp. 377–83, 476–81, 996–1006.

[93] *Disputatio inter clericum et militem super potestate prelatis ecclesiae atque principibus terrarum commissa sub forma dialogi* (London, ?1531); *A Dialogue between a Knight and a Clerk, Concerning the Power Spiritual and Temporal*; *STC*² 12510–12511a; Ullmann, *History of Political Thought*, pp. 156–7. The work was originally written in 1296 or 1297.

University of Paris for the 'ancient' or 'original' constitution of the
Gallican church. Indeed, the original authors of the *Disputation* had
expressly derived their thesis of 'imperial' kingship from the 'acts of
great Charlemagne' and the 'ancient approved histories' of France.[94]

Other propaganda included *A Glass of the Truth* (printed in 1532, but
written the previous year) and *Articles devised by the Whole Consent of
the King's Most Honourable Council* (1533). The *Glass of Truth* first
linked the arguments of *Gravissimae atque exactissimae ... censurae*
explicitly to Henry's suit for divorce. It then argued that the Church of
England was an autonomous province of the universal church, and that
by the authority of church councils legal cases must properly be heard in
the province wherein they arose. This set the stage for the following
spring, when the Act of Appeals cut the Gordian knot and, at Henry
VIII's insistence, Convocation resolved as a general principle that
marriage to a brother's widow contravened divine law. Thereafter, the
Articles ... of the King's Most Honourable Council justified the Act of
Appeals and Cranmer's sentence of divorce at Dunstable. The tract also
claimed that the pope had no more jurisdiction outside his own diocese
than any other bishop; that the pope was subordinate to the general
council; that no one could legitimately be excommunicated 'except it be
for deadly sin prohibite[d] by God's law and scripture'; and that
Clement VII was a heretic.[95] Cromwell evidently feared that More
would refute this publication, since he interviewed William Rastell,
More's printer, shortly after copies were nailed up in London to
discover what More had in the press. But More did not answer the tract.
As he informed Cromwell, on some points he knew not the law, on
others the facts. In any case, his 'duty' to the king and council forbade
him to reply to works openly published in the council's name.[96]

The 'imperial' crown and the Church of England

The classic conspectus of Henrician political thought was the preamble
to the Act of Appeals:

Where by divers sundry old authentic histories and chronicles it is manifestly
declared and expressed that this realm of England is an empire, and so hath been
accepted in the world, governed by one supreme head and king having the
dignity and royal estate of the imperial crown of the same, unto whom a body
politic, compact of all sorts and degrees of people divided in terms and by names
of spiritualty and temporalty, be bounden and owe to bear next to God a natural

[94] *Dialogue between a Knight and a Clerk*, fos. 2ᵛ–3ᵛ, 22ᵛ–3, 24, 24ᵛ–5.
[95] *STC²* 11918–19 (*Glass*); 9177–8 (*Articles*); quotation from *STC²* 9177, 'The VII Article'.
[96] Fox and Guy, *Reassessing the Henrician Age*, pp. 116–18.

and humble obedience; he [the king] being also institute and furnished by the goodness and sufferance of Almighty God with plenary, whole and entire power, preeminence, authority, prerogative and jurisdiction to render and yield justice and final determination to all manner of folk resiants or subjects within this realm, in all causes, matters, debates and contentions happening to occur, insurge or begin within the limits thereof, without restraint or provocation to any foreign princes or potentates of the world . . .⁹⁷

This was the language of 'imperial' kingship and its immediate context has been identified. During and after 1530, Henry VIII's scholars compiled a fresh collection of sources inspired by, but distinct from, the original collection linked to the king's *libellus* of 1529 and *Gravissimae atque exactissimae . . . censurae*. New sources were harvested and old ones revisited: the result was the 'Collectanea satis copiosa', first shown to the king in the autumn of 1530.⁹⁸ Whereas the original collection had been designed to prove that the Levitical prohibitions against marriage between a man and his brother's wife were divine law which no pope could dispense, and that sexual relations with a brother's wife were incestuous and unnatural, the purpose of the 'Collectanea' was different. It was to define the *imperium* of the king of England, to document the original constitution of the Church of England, and thereby to establish the 'true difference' between royal and ecclesiastical power. The theses which the 'Collectanea' advocated were (1) that Henry VIII possessed secular *imperium* and spiritual supremacy within his realm; (2) that these powers were tantamount to a right of 'empire'; (3) that the Church of England under the crown was an autonomous province of the Catholic church. These were the assumptions which underpinned the Acts of Appeals and Supremacy.

Many authorities cited in the 'Collectanea' were the same as those in *Gravissimae atque exactissimae . . . censurae* and its translation *The Determinations of the . . . Universities of Italy and France*.⁹⁹ But they

---

⁹⁷ Elton, *Tudor Constitution*, p. 353.
⁹⁸ BL, Cotton MS Cleopatra E. VI, fos. 16–135; Nicholson, 'Act of Appeals and the English Reformation', pp. 19–30; *Divorce Tracts of Henry VIII*, ed. Surtz and Murphy, pp. xxii–xxxvi; Fox and Guy, *Reassessing the Henrician Age*, pp. 151–78.
⁹⁹ The closing pages of the *Determinations of the . . . Universities of Italy and France* contain some new material not contained in the Latin original. In one instance this new material derives from the 'Collectanea'. This suggests that by November 1531, when the sheets of the *Determinations* were in the press, it was the 'Collectanea' and not the original source collection which was making the running. Again, where the two research projects intersected in the composition of the *Glass of Truth*, most of the material was derived from the first source collection, but fresh arguments at the end proleptic of the Act of Appeals came from the 'Collectanea'. The original source collection was compiled by Henry VIII's scholars in *c*.1527–30. It is unfortunately lost, but its contents may be reconstructed from the king's *libellus* of 1529 and from the 'elenchus' printed in *Gravissimae atque exactissimae . . . censurae*. See *Divorce Tracts of Henry VIII*, ed. Surtz and Murphy, pp. xxxii–xxxvi, 4.

were slanted differently. This shift of focus also explains the basis of selection of the new materials, which came chiefly from the Old Testament, the records of church councils, Roman civil law, the laws of Anglo-Saxon theocrats, and English histories and chronicles. No longer did Henry VIII's scholars limit themselves to a study of the *privilegium Angliae* and right of the English bishops to pronounce the king's divorce in England; they proceeded to construct a novel and coherent theory of English regal power, demonstrating how kings in general, and the kings of England in particular, exercised their power in handling the clergy. They argued that the king's *imperium* was ordained by God and embraced 'temporal' and 'spiritual' jurisdiction equally. They invoked historical precedents to prove that the power of the king was magisterial. Henry VIII was invested with an 'imperial' sovereignty, part of which had been 'lent' to the priesthood by previous English monarchs. Royal *imperium* was chronologically antecedent to the jurisdiction of the clergy. Moreover, it was an inalienable right of the 'imperial' crown. Despite its partial 'loan' to the clergy by earlier rulers, it could be resumed at will by Henry VIII.

The simplest justification of the king's *imperium* was derived from the *leges Anglorum*, a thirteenth-century interpolation of the so-called *leges Edwardi Confessoris*. A passage concerned the mythical King Lucius I, allegedly the first Christian ruler of Britain, who endowed the British church with all its liberties and possessions and thereupon wrote to Pope Eleutherius asking him to transmit the Roman laws. In reply, the pope confirmed that Lucius did not need any Roman law, because he already had the Old and New Testaments from which he might take a law (i.e. the *lex Britanniae*) for his kingdom. The king was 'vicar of God' (*vicarius dei*) in his kingdom; he was the superior legislator who governed church and state equally. The papal letter was quoted twice in the 'Collectanea', the second time immediately beneath the heading 'Institutio officium et potestas Regum Anglie'.[100]

More radical was the thesis first publicized in the *Glass of Truth* that the English church was autonomous. Citations from Jacques Merlin's *Conciliorum quatuor generalium tomus* were inserted in the 'Collectanea' to argue that the Church of England was privileged to determine its affairs unilaterally in national synods and without reference to Rome and the papacy. Again, references were culled from scripture, legal texts, and

---

[100] BL, Cotton MS Cleopatra E. VI, fos. 27, 35. Cf. Ullmann, *Principles of Government and Politics*, pp. 161–2.

histories and chronicles to illustrate the *imperium* of kings who had exercised a *potestas jurisdictionis* in the church.[101]

The most accomplished defence of the royal supremacy was Bishop Gardiner's *De vera obedientia* (1535). This described the *imperium* of rulers from Solomon onwards who appointed lay and clerical judges, disciplined their clergy, and determined the spiritual and temporal affairs of their kingdoms. Gardiner also constructed a theory of obligation consistent with the Acts of Appeals and Supremacy. Unlike other Henrician propagandists, he did not merely recite Biblical or historical precedents. He invoked abstract theory by formulating a concept of 'true obedience' which he defined as obedience to God and his law and therefore to rulers whom God had appointed as his representatives on earth. Such obedience was enjoyed by scripture, which was 'the most certain voice of God' (*certissima dei vox*). It also accorded with reason. Inferiors must obey their superiors, just as masters, servants and even kings are bound to obey God. The royal supremacy was authorized by scripture and therefore securely grounded in law. When in 1534 the people of England consented to it by their free votes in parliament, they did not innovate, but simply recognized God's law more expressly than they had before.[102]

Superficially this theory of obligation resembled Tyndale's. But it differed in three fundamental respects. First, it attributed magisterial as well as jurisdictional authority to Henry VIII. Second, it defended Henry VIII's divorce and marriage to Anne Boleyn. Thirdly, Gardiner's soteriology was that of an orthodox Catholic, even if he differed from More and Bishop Fisher, the leaders of the Catholic resistance to Henry VIII, by reason of his willingness to defend the king's proceedings on the lines envisaged by the 'Collectanea satis copiosa'.[103] Whether he was motivated by principle, ambition, or a personal conviction that only royal authority could close the door against Protestantism remains unclear. Whatever his objective may have been, it was the ecclesiology of *De vera obedientia* which established his reputation.[104]

Gardiner defined the church as the body (*corpus*) of people united in

---

[101] Nicholson, 'Act of Appeals and the English Reformation', p. 28. Editions of Merlin's collection appeared in 1524 and 1530. The link between the 'Collectanea' and Act of Appeals is even clearer if drafts of the act are examined. See Fox and Guy, *Reassessing the Henrician Age*, pp. 162–3.

[102] Janelle (ed.), *Obedience in Church and State*, pp. 68–92.

[103] See Glyn Redworth, *In Defence of the Church Catholic: The Life of Stephen Gardiner* (Oxford, 1990).

[104] Gardiner was known to the participants in the Elizabethan Admonition Controversy and was cited by Anglican apologists in the post-Restoration period, especially Gilbert Burnet; see Burnet, *History of the Reformation of the Church of England*, 3 vols. (London, 1679–1715).

the profession of Christ, but qualified his definition by reference to provincial boundaries. The Church of England was 'English' because it comprised the gathering (*congregatio*) of Christian people resident in England. A native of England was subject to the headship of the king as a subject and also as a member of the church. Church and state were co-extensive: this was the nub of the argument. At a 'universal' level, the church was the communion of Christians dispersed throughout the world, while at a 'particular' level the Church of England was the gathering of Christians who were the king of England's subjects. The Gallican and Spanish churches existed in France and Spain in the same manner, as did the Roman church in Rome.[105]

A distinction between the church 'universal' and the 'particular' churches became the Church of England's trademark. It was adopted by Henry VIII's official formularies of faith, the *Institution of a Christian Man* (1537) and *Necessary Doctrine and Erudition for any Christian Man* (1543), where the 'Holy Catholic Church' was said to be the 'visible' church 'spread universally throughout all the whole world', of which the 'very parts, portions or members' were the 'particular' churches found in specific regions.[106] Again, when John Jewel wrote *An Apology of the Church of England* (1562) in defence of the Elizabethan settlement, this ecclesiology was reasserted.[107] The dissonance with John Foxe's *Acts and Monuments* (1563 and innumerable later editions) which defined the 'true' church in terms of the 'invisible' elect or 'secret multitude of true professors' of the Gospel proved subversive. The establishment view was nevertheless maintained, because it enabled clergy as diverse as Whitgift under Elizabeth, Bancroft under James I, Laud under Charles I, and Gilbert Burnet under Charles II to defend the 'imperial' interpretation of the royal supremacy and the provincial autonomy of the English Church whilst continuing to deny that the Church of England was schismatic.

To Gardiner's dismay, the royal supremacy became an instrument of Protestantism in the reign of Edward VI. Influenced by exiles who flocked to England after Charles V's victory at the battle of Mühlberg, Cranmer underwent a 'conversion' to a Swiss memorialist view of the Eucharist. Between 1550 and 1552, he revised the theology of the church and drafted the Second Book of Common Prayer. Yet he continued to claim that scripture validated the structure of the Church of England.

[105] Janelle (ed.), *Obedience in Church and State*, pp. 92–6, 114–16.
[106] *Miscellaneous Writings and Letters of Thomas Cranmer*, ed. J. E. Cox, Parker Society (Cambridge, 1846), pp. 91–2.
[107] John Jewel, *An Apology of the Church of England*, ed. J. E. Booty (Charlottesville, VA, 1963; repr. 1974).

The pattern was therefore unchanged whereby the mission of the 'imperial' crown was to 'renovate' or 'restore' throughout the ruler's dominions that 'church of the apostles and of the old Catholic bishops and fathers' which had first borne witness to scripture.[108] Even when the Marian exiles and first generation of Elizabethan bishops injected Calvinist soteriology into the English Reformation, the institutions of the church were not reconstructed. This disjuncture could plausibly be overlooked in the decades before 1585, when a Calvinist consensus prevailed in the upper echelons of the Elizabethan church. But later, when a powerful lobby of conformists sought to neutralize Calvinism's hold over the church on the grounds of order, decency and hierarchy, a struggle began for the identity of the Church of England.[109]

All Tudor exponents of ecclesiastical *renovatio* accorded the decisive authority to scripture as the authentic witness to the practice of the apostolic church. Disputes became inevitable over sanction to interpret the Bible.[110] Papal jurisdiction had been rejected by Henry VIII.[111] Neither was the authority of the general council much invoked after the Acts of Appeals and Supremacy.[112] Cranmer made valiant but unsuccessful attempts in Edward's reign to convene a general council of the

---

[108] See Jewel, *Apology*, ed. Booty, esp. pp. 100–1, 120–1. The problem lay in the different readings of 'renovate on scriptural lines' taken by successive rulers and their advisers. In the reign of Henry VIII this objective dominated the agenda both before and after the fall of Thomas Cromwell. G. Redworth, 'Whatever happened to the English Reformation?', *History Today* (Oct. 1987), pp. 29–36; see also his *In Defence of the Church Catholic.*

[109] P. Lake, *Anglicans and Puritans? Presbyterian and English Conformist Thought from Whitgift to Hooker* (London, 1988). A wide-ranging and provocative discussion of these issues is provided by D. MacCulloch, 'The Myth of the English Reformation', *Journal of British Studies*, 30 (1991), 1–19. See also C. Hill, 'Archbishop Laud and the English Revolution', in *Religion, Resistance and Civil War*, ed. G. J. Schochet (Washington DC, 1990), pp. 127–49.

[110] The author most exercised by this question in Henry VIII's reign was St German. He agreed with Gardiner that church and state were co-extensive, but differed by applying Fortescue's concept of *dominium politicum et regale* equally to church and state. He saw the need to withhold from Henry VIII and the clergy the power to interpret scripture and therefore to expound divine law. He believed that Parliament should itself perform this vital role since 'the whole catholic church' came together in Parliament. However, he later argued in manuscript that Biblical interpretation was the function of the general council See *An Answer to a Letter*, sigs. G3–G6ᵛ; *STC²* 21558.5; Fox and Guy, *Reassessing the Henrician Age*, pp. 199–220; J. A. Guy, R. Keen, C. H. Miller, and R. McGugan (eds.), *CW*, X: *The Debellation of Salem and Bizance* (New Haven, CT, 1987), pp. 395–417.

[111] Gardiner's *De vera obedientia* allowed the pope a moral role as a teacher and pastor. However, all residual components of papal authority in England were extinguished by statute in 1536. Janelle (ed.), *Obedience in Church and State*, p. 148; 28 Henry VIII, c.10.

[112] Henry VIII acknowledged the authority of general councils in theory, but his demands that they be summoned only with the consent of secular rulers, meet in an 'indifferent' place, and comprise laity as well as clergy meant that he would ignore them in practice.

reformed churches in order to settle church doctrine.[113] This was consistent with his previously expressed opinion that the council's power extended to points of faith.[114] But when decrees enacted at Trent threatened the doctrine of the Elizabethan church as much as imminent papal excommunication threatened its supreme governor, the council was treated with circumspection despite a nod by Jewel in its direction.[115] Even the Catholic Mary had been intimidated when the issue of competing claims to ex-religious property arose to frustrate the policy of a ruler inclined to throw the 'imperial' crown at the feet of the pope.[116] Like her father before her, she refused to allow the reception into England of decrees which infringed the *privilegium Angliae*.

It followed that problems of scriptural interpretation had to be settled within the realm. How were points necessary to salvation to be decided? Also, how were conflicts over rites, ceremonies or matters of church government to be resolved where scripture was silent or ambiguous? Debate focused especially upon the rites and ceremonies variously described as *adiaphora*, 'indifferent things' or 'unwritten verities' (i.e. opinions upheld by tradition which were not documented in scripture).[117] Cranmer and Gardiner concurred that the Christian ruler had the final authority over rites and ceremonies.[118] Where the articles of faith were at stake, opinions differed. Henry VIII affirmed *his* right to define them. He even briefly claimed the 'cure of souls' until rebuffed by an outraged episcopate.[119] Whether the 'imperial' king was Moses or Aaron was a vitally important question, though one more dangerous to answer than to ask. It was circumvented under Henry VIII, eclipsed by

---

[113] D. MacCulloch, *The Later Reformation in England, 1547–1603* (London, 1990), pp. 13–18.

[114] *Miscellaneous Writings and Letters of Thomas Cranmer*, ed. Cox, pp. 77, 463–4.

[115] The exception was James I's evidently genuine, but unsuccessful call for a general council to resolve differences between the Catholic and reformed churches. See W. Brown Patterson, 'King James I's Call for an Ecumenical Council', in *Councils and Assemblies*, ed. G. J. Cuming, *Studies in Church History*, 7 (1971), 267–75.

[116] Guy, *Tudor England*, pp. 226–47.

[117] The usage of the terms *adiaphora*, 'indifferent things' and 'unwritten verities' was imprecise. Sometimes the meanings overlapped or were interchangeable. Essential writings are: T. F. Mayer, 'Starkey and Melanchthon on Adiaphora: A Critique of W. Gordon Zeeveld', *Sixteenth Century Journal*, 11 (1980), 39–49; his *Thomas Starkey and the Commonweal*, pp. 220–23, 238–40; Fox and Guy, *Reassessing the Henrician Age*, pp. 201–3, 217–19; R. Marius, 'Thomas More and the Heretics', unpublished PhD dissertation, Yale University, 1962, pp. 258–64; Guy, Keen, Miller, and McGugan (eds.), *CW*, X: *The Debellation of Salem and Bizance*, pp. 409–17; *Miscellaneous Writings and Letters of Thomas Cranmer*, ed. Cox, pp. 1–67.

[118] *Memorials of Thomas Cranmer*, ed. J. Strype, 2 vols. (Oxford, 1840), I, p. 43; Janelle (ed.), *Obedience in Church and State*, pp. lxi–lxii, 116–18, 130–2.

[119] J. J. Scarisbrick, 'The Pardon of the Clergy, 1531', *Cambridge Historical Journal*, 12 (1956), 22–39. Cf. Guy, 'Henry VIII and the *Praemunire* Manoeuvres', p. 495.

the political nation's preoccupation with the ex-monastic estates and the scramble to purchase them.

'Indifferent things', according to Starkey in his *Exhortation to the People Instructing them to Unity and Obedience* (1536), were properly 'left to worldly policy, whereof they take their full authority'.[120] They included 'all such things which by God's word are neither prohibited nor commanded'. They were in themselves 'neither good nor ill', but once they were 'set out with authority', then 'the people are to them bound, yea by virtue of God's own word, who commandeth expressly his disciples to be obedient to common policy'. Later he explained that 'the decree of princes in things indifferent bindeth us under pain of damnation'.[121] This was a highly conservative line. It is unlikely that Cranmer went so far. On the other hand, Cranmer's opinion was more conservative than is usually thought. When he explained that 'in matters indifferent men ought to be left to their freedom', the context of the discussion was the power of the general council and he was probably arguing that the 'particular' churches were at 'liberty' to resolve 'indifferent things' by the power of rulers whose decision would be final.[122]

When Elizabeth expounded her royal supremacy in *A Declaration of the Queen's Proceedings*, prepared during the Northern Rising, she said her power came from 'the laws of God and this realm always annexed to the Crown of this realm and due to our progenitors'. She was 'bound in duty to God to provide that all estates, being subject to us, should live in the faith and the obedience and observance of Christian religion'. Whereas Christian princes had 'care' of their subjects' souls, pagan rulers 'take only a worldly care of their subjects' bodies'.[123] This was not far short of Henry VIII's opinion. Yet Elizabeth denied herself power 'to define, decide or determine any article or point of the Christian faith and religion'. That function she thought belonged to Convocation. As a matter of principle as much as to sidestep the Presbyterian lobby in pulpit and parliament, she upheld the separation of church and state in practice, ruling both but through different channels of administration.[124]

---

[120] *STC²* 23236, fos. 6ᵛ, 24ᵛ, 42ᵛ; Mayer, 'Starkey and Melanchthon', p. 47; his *Thomas Starkey and the Commonweal*, p. 221. When Cromwell considered the issue of *adiaphora* at the vicegerential synod which he convoked at the House of Lords in 1537, he argued (possibly ingenuously) that Henry VIII would no longer tolerate 'any articles or doctrine not contained in the scripture, but approved only by continuance of time and old custom, and by unwritten verities'. See A. Alesius, *Of the Authority of the Word of God against the Bishop of London* (Strassburg, ?1544), sigs. A6–A6ᵛ; *STC²* 292.

[121] *Exhortation*, fos. 6ᵛ–8, 43, 70; Mayer, 'Starkey and Melanchthon', pp. 47–8; his *Thomas Starkey and the Commonweal*, pp. 221–2.

[122] *Miscellaneous Writings and Letters of Thomas Cranmer*, ed. Cox, p. 77.

[123] PRO, SP 12/66/54 (quotations from fo. 150ᴿ⁻ᵛ).

[124] G. R. Elton, *The Parliament of England, 1559–1581* (Cambridge, 1986), pp. 199–216.

Elizabeth enforced strict conformity to the settlement of 1559 and declined to allow objections to 'indifferent things' on grounds of conscience. All she would concede was that petitions approved by her in advance might be referred to the bishops, whereupon it was the business of Convocation to enact appropriate canons. Whenever points affecting church government and worship were tested by critics of the settlement, strict conformity was required. After puritan attacks on *adiaphora* and vestments in the Convocation of 1563, Archbishop Parker issued his *Advertisements* (1566) which demanded compliance with the rubrics of the Prayer Book and required the clergy to dress in accordance with royal instructions. Later, assent to the Thirty-Nine Articles was demanded despite puritan howls of anguish. Finally, Whitgift required clergy to subscribe to the royal supremacy, Prayer Book and Thirty-Nine Articles or else be deprived.

The puritan experience bred a gradual realization that the 'indifferent things' were not 'indifferent' in a confessional state. When the Presbyterian campaign approached its climax with the publication of Cartwright's *Second Admonition to the Parliament* (1572), the lines were drawn for a twenty-year battle over *adiaphora* and external church government out of scripture, a battle in which episcopacy as much as the 'imperial' supremacy became a legitimate target.[125] Moreover, the puritans were encouraged by the fact that Burghley, Leicester, Walsingham and other leading members of the privy council were themselves far from uncritical adherents of royal supremacy and episcopacy, especially before the trial and execution of Mary, Queen of Scots in 1586–7. Only when the Catholic heir to the 'imperial' crown had been excluded from the succession did the privy council reinforce Whitgift's subscription campaign with the panoply of the Court of Star Chamber.

The Admonition Controversy and its sequels were corrosive, because they turned the debate over *adiaphora* and scriptural interpretation into a fundamental clash of principle upon the role of the civil magistrate in the church, the relationship between church and state, and the ecclesiology of the reformed churches. The far-reaching discovery was made that to argue *for* one form of church government was to deny the legitimacy of a related form of civil administration. When Cartwright propounded the Polybian 'mixed' polity as the ideal form of government in both church and state, he touched a nerve which the political establishment could not ignore. Although the Elizabethan state *was* in many practical respects a 'mixed' polity, it was divisive to declare this fact in print or assert that there were things the queen could not do

---

[125] Lake, *Anglicans and Puritans?*, pp. 13–66.

without parliament. Cartwright's concept of 'edification' was particularly subversive, since it implied the existence of a community of active citizens empowered to attain their full potential in church and state by the true interpretation of God's Word.[126]

When, therefore, conformists after 1589 accused both their puritan and Catholic opponents of 'popularity' and countered with defences of *jure divino* monarchy and episcopacy, a gulf began to open between 'absolutist' and 'populist' accounts of regality which reached its extremity during the Civil War and remained a source of conflict in the 1680s.[127] Hitherto, 'descending' and 'ascending' interpretations of the 'imperial' supremacy had co-existed. The complementary roles of Gardiner and St German under Henry VIII epitomized this compromise, which subsisted in the pages of the (unpublished) eighth book of Richard Hooker's *Of the Laws of Ecclesiastical Polity* (1593–1600). James I sought peace and unity in the Church of England, and cannot be held personally responsible for the failure of the Hampton Court Conference.[128] Yet the appointment of Bancroft to the see of Canterbury in 1604 signalled an intensified drive for order, hierarchy and conformity in the church. For the first time since Mary's reign the argument began to be voiced that the church formed a *societas* separate from the civil state. While this reflected the increasing emphasis which leading conformists placed upon worship and the sacraments and was proleptic of the Laudian attack on sacrilege, it was easily mistaken for sacerdotalism. When accompanied by the conversions to Rome and *jure divino* culture which pervaded the Caroline court in the 1630s, it was constructively taken for popery.

Especially damaging to Charles I's regime were the canons enacted by Convocation in 1640. These declared that the 'most high and sacred Order of Kings is of Divine Right, being the ordinance of God himself, founded in the prime laws of nature, and clearly established by express texts both of the Old and New Testaments'. They also claimed that 'tribute', taxation, 'and all manner of necessary support and supply' were 'due to kings from their subjects by the Law of God, Nature and

[126] *Ibid.*
[127] See J. P. Sommerville, *Politics and Ideology in England, 1603–1640* (London, 1986); J. A. I. Champion, 'The Ancient Constitution of the Christian Church: The Church of England and its Enemies, 1660–1730', unpublished PhD thesis, University of Cambridge, 1989, now *The Pillars of Priestcraft Shaken: The Church of England and its Enemies, 1660–1730* (Cambridge, 1992); John Spurr, *The Restoration Church of England, 1646–1689* (New Haven, 1991).
[128] K. Fincham and P. Lake, 'The Ecclesiastical Policy of James I', *Journal of British Studies*, 24 (1985), 169–207; P. Collinson, 'The Jacobean Religious Settlement: The Hampton Court Conference', in *Before the English Civil War*, ed. H. Tomlinson (London, 1983), pp. 27–51.

Nations'.[129] While this thesis was not new – some Laudians had proclaimed it from the pulpit as early as 1627 – the difference was that in 1640 it was enacted as part of canon law under the sanction of the 'imperial' crown.[130] Furthermore, the canons were promulgated in a way which was believed to impugn the terms of the Henrician Submission of the Clergy and the subordination of canon law to common law and parliamentary statute.[131] It was this latter belief that precipitated Laud's impeachment and provoked members of the Long Parliament in 1641 to accuse the bishops of infringing *praemunire*. Not even the compilers of Henry VIII's 'Collectanea satis copiosa' had affirmed the king's right to tax the laity without parliamentary assent. Nor had they embodied the principle of *jure divino* kingship in ecclesiastical law, since this was seen from the beginning as a threat to individual liberty and property rights.

With the canons of 1640 ringing in their ears, the opponents of Charles I glimpsed Leviathan in clerical clothes. This is not the place to consider the events of 1640–2, which contemporaries interpreted as a failure of 'counsel' as much as a 'popish' plot.[132] The immediate cause of civil war sprang from parliament's insistence in 1642 that it should have control over the militia and any expeditionary force raised to crush the Irish Rebellion of 1641. Yet it is a false choice to debate the *casus belli* in terms of 'constitutional' *versus* 'religious' issues.[133] Under attack from his adversaries in England and Scotland, Charles I abandoned the political and religious protocol which had sweetened the pill of Henry VIII's break with Rome and thereafter underpinned a process of Protestant acculturalization. He sought to bolster his authority by advancing his *imperium* beyond the limits recognized either by the common lawyers or by previous instruments imposing religious uniformity within the Church of England. The apparatus of royal supremacy began to be dismantled in 1641 when Parliament abolished the High Commission and *ex officio* oath. Thereafter, the Grand Remonstrance declared that the king was 'entrusted with the ecclesiastical law as well as with the temporal, to regulate all the members of the Church

---

[129] J. P. Kenyon, *The Stuart Constitution* (2nd edn; Cambridge, 1986), pp. 149–53.

[130] For important background, see R. Cust, *The Forced Loan and English Politics, 1626–1628* (Oxford, 1987); N. Tyacke, *Anti-Calvinists: The Rise of English Arminianism, c. 1590–1640* (Oxford, 1987).

[131] M. Judson, *The Crisis of the Constitution* (New York, repr, 1976), pp. 361–2. See also J. Davies, *The Yoke of Bondage: The Caroline Captivity of the Church, 1625–1641* (Oxford, 1993).

[132] For the Popish Plot interpretation, see Caroline Hibbard, *Charles I and the Popish Plot* (Chapel Hill, 1983). For a discussion of the events of 1640–2 as a failure of 'counsel', see Guy, 'The Rhetoric of Counsel' (forthcoming).

[133] For the best recent discussion, see C. Russell, *The Causes of the English Civil War* (Oxford, 1990).

of England, by such rules of order and discipline as are established by Parliament, which is his great council, in all affairs both in Church and State'.[134] This statement radically redefined the thesis of 'imperial' kingship. 'Descending' and 'ascending' interpretations disengaged: this was the *damnosa hereditas* of Henry VIII.[135] In these circumstances it was hardly surprising that a politics of consensus ceased to be attainable and a politics of ideology ensued.

[134] *The Constitutional Documents of the Puritan Revolution, 1625–1660*, ed. S. R. Gardiner (3rd edn; Oxford, 1906), pp. 228–9.
[135] The phrase is Russell's; *Causes of the English Civil War*, p. 61.

2 Elizabethan political thought

Donald R. Kelley

Ius: Law: right: authoritie: libertie: power.
Thomas Cooper, *Thesaurus linguae Romanae et Britannicae* (1565)

The languages of political thought

Public discourse in the second half of the sixteenth century was carried on through an extraordinary confusion of tongues, and the history of political thought can be reconstructed only through a serious effort of discrimination, translation, and decipherment. The interpretation of political texts often requires highly problematical judgements. Is a particular work an illocutionary 'act' (whether a legal enactment or a 'speech act' more generally)? A pedagogical treatise or an entertainment? A serious statement or a satire, a parody, or even a hoax? A piece of conventional rhetoric or a real cry of pain? A conscious expression or a discourse in which the author is overwhelmed by the inertial force of literary tradition? A personal statement or a 'contribution' to a canon? A 'classic' or just a historical document? Does it address 'our' questions or merely reflect bygone contexts and predicaments? Or is it a mixture of all of the above?

Context is hardly less problematical than text, involving as it does questions of time as well as space. Political texts, in other words, may be considered in a long intellectual continuum going back to Aristotle or Cicero or in what Conal Condren calls a 'political theory community' extending down to our own day, but it may also be placed in a particular cultural environment remote from our experience; and here it is essential to be aware of the values, assumptions, linguistic and conceptual resources, and social and political predicaments of the actors and speakers of a bygone age.[1]

[1] Conal Condren, *The Status and Appraisal of Classic Texts: An Essay on Political Theory, Its Inheritance, and the History of Ideas* (Princeton, 1985), 81. Other recent discussions of these questions include David Boucher, *Texts in Context: Revisionist Methods for Studying the History of Ideas* (Dordrecht, 1985), and James Tully (ed.), *Meaning and Context: Quentin Skinner and his Critics* (Princeton, 1988).

The range of political languages and idioms in post-Reformation Europe was both an illustration of the rich ideological heritage of classical and Judaeo-Christian thought and feudal experience, and a measure of the misunderstandings and conflicts which disrupted European society in the age of religious and civil war from the second quarter of the sixteenth century to the second quarter of the seventeenth.[2] In general my purpose is not so much to identify the arguments and propositions – political theory in a modern sense – as to examine the historical grounds, linguistic environment, and social, institutional, and religious sources of political thought in a period before political science was conceived of in a formal and canonical way. I do so by focusing on such themes as Law, Resistance, the Ancient Constitution, Political Authority and Individual Liberty.

In many respects the clash of religious and political parties was a struggle over language and the values attached to particular sacred words; and the semantic polarization resulting from this logomachy was extraordinary. For Protestants, 'law' could refer either to the righteousness of God (*justitia Dei*), which promised salvation or to 'Judaic' or 'Romanist' tyranny; 'authority' to fundamentalist scriptural or to the corrupt human variety; and liberty either to the spiritual condition produced by faith or to the sinful pride associated with 'free will'. Every term and value had a good and a bad, a spiritual and a carnal, face; and there was no way except personal conviction or submission to authority – inner light or outer direction – to tell them apart.

Consider more closely the term 'liberty', its connotations and reverberations. In his famous speech in the Commons in 1576 Peter Wentworth, so he declared to the speaker, found 'written in a little volume these words in effect: sweet indeed is the name of liberty, but the thing itself is a value beyond all estimable treasure'.[3] Whether he knew it or not, he was reciting one of the ancient Roman maxims preserved in the Digest, that authoritative anthology of Romano-Byzantine jurisprudence. The scholarly judge William Lambarde was drawing on the oldest of national conventions when, in his charge to a jury fifteen years later, he invoked 'the native liberty and ancient preeminence of the

---

[2] See *The Languages of Political Theory in Early-Modern Europe*, ed. Anthony Pagden (Cambridge, 1987), especially J. G. A. Pocock, 'The Concept of a Language and the *métier d'historien*: Some Considerations on Practice', pp. 19–40, Nicolai Rubinstein, 'The History of the Word *Politicus* in Early-Modern Europe', pp. 41–56, and D. R. Kelley, 'Civil Science in the Renaissance: The Problem of Interpretation', pp. 57–78.

[3] Wentworth's speech of 1576 in T. E. Hartley (ed.), *Proceedings in the Parliament of Elizabeth I* (Wilmington, Del., 1981), 425, G. R. Elton (ed.), *The Tudor Constitution* (Cambridge, 1982), p. 271; and in Leonard J. Trintrud (ed.), *Elizabeth Puritanism* (New York, 1971), p. 171 – none noting the source (*Digest*, 50, 17, 122).

English policy'.[4] By this time, however, confessional emotions had injected a more threatening note, with 'Christian liberty' taking human form – as indeed Luther himself had learned – not only from the 'murdering hordes of peasants' which he condemned but also from the 'protestant' Princes whose defiance of imperial power he supported. In England the 'godly' and the 'ungodly' alike displayed radical inclinations, and there was careless talk of 'liberty' across all orders of society. As Randall Hurlestone complained at mid-century, 'There be certaine rude feloes which when thei heare mention of libertie in sermones, straightwayes with out iudgement despise all maners, lawes & honestie'.[5]

The nickname 'Puritan', accompanied by its own terminology and counter-terminology, originated in a pejorative judgement made by orthodox critics, but it became finally a badge proudly worn by its designees.[6] Puritans found and freely distributed even more pejorative labels for the abuses and abusers it protested, drawing especially on the vocabulary of contamination and turning words such as 'mass', 'image', and 'priest' into abominations. Under the influence of the 'Pauline Renaissance' the terms of Puritan worship were spiritualized – purified and made edifying – and associated with religious faith rather than ecclesiastical order.[7] Thus, the church was no longer the hierarchy but the Lord's home, where His children gathered for supper and song, not led by a 'massing-priest' but accompanied by a 'godly minister'. Puritan vocabulary was replete with soul- and self-words and neologisms, many of them (self-affection, self-eater, self-lust, self-lying, self-sermon, self-sophistry, etc.) unknown to the new OED. Behind this process of logogenesis lay a whole world of psychological, religious, social, and potentially political upheaval.

In pursuing the question of Elizabethan political thought it is essential to attend critically to questions of the resources, limitations, impulses, and strategies of language and the means of communicating and moving people through this medium. It is important, too, to distinguish and analyze the various political and social languages of sixteenth-century public experience and expression. W. H. Greenleaf has distinguished two varieties of political argument in English political thought in this period – that based on conceptions of cosmic 'order' and that based on a

---

4 *William Lambarde and Local Government*, ed. C. Read (Ithaca, 1962), p. 108.
5 *Newes from Rome concerning the Blasphemous Sacrifice of the Papisticall Masse* (Canterbury, [c.1550]), sig. Gi\ᵛ.
6 M. van Beek, *An Enquiry into Puritan Vocabulary* (Groningen, 1969).
7 John S. Coolidge, *The Pauline Renaissance in England* (Oxford, 1990).

more pragmatic 'empirical' approach[8] – but this view is hard to maintain except on the highest level of theory and in any case under-values the uses of history and of modern 'natural law'. Political and social criticism in the Elizabethan age drew upon vocabularies that were feudal as well as civic, evangelical as well as corporatist, and employed the legitimizing resources of canon and civil as well as English common law. What is more, 'political thought' involves not only the ruling elite or its protesting rivals but also marginal groups alienated from power; and it should be explored not only in canonical texts but in the social, religious, and linguistic contexts of sixteenth-century thought, exper-ience, and action. Attention to such questions of language, law, and social thought may make possible a more discriminating and historically accurate map of 'political' thinking in the age of collapsing hierarchy and emergent naturalism – which was also an age of collapsing universalism and emergent nationalism.

Medieval background

In many respects the sixteenth century was an extension of the Middle Ages, most conspicuously in terms of the revival of Scholastic thought (the so-called 'second scholasticism'), legal as well as philosophical, of canon law and conciliarism, of revitalized feudal ideas, of deep-rooted heretical movements, and of the chronic disputes between church and state. These are themes which (though often overlooked) have informed the classic works of J. N. Figgis, C. H. McIlwain, and A. P. d'Entreves as well as, more recently, those of Francis Oakley and Brian Tierney.[9] The languages of Elizabethan public discourse richly illustrate the

---

[8] W. H. Greenleaf, *Order, Empiricism and Politics: Two Traditions of English Political Thought, 1500–1700* (Oxford, 1964), and cf. the criticisms of Robert Eccleshall, *Order and Reason in Politics: Theories of Absolute and Limited Monarchy in Early Modern England* (Oxford, 1978).

[9] Brian Tierney, 'Medieval Foundations of Elizabethan Political Thought', in Gordon Schochet (ed.), *Law, Literature, and the Settlement of Regimes* (Proceedings of the Folger Institute for the History of British Political Thought, II) (1990), pp. 1–3. See also Tierney, *Religion, Law, and the Growth of Constitutional Government* (Cambridge, 1982); Francis Oakley, *Omnipotence, Covenant, and Order* (Ithaca, 1984), and (in the old McIlwainian mode) Arthur P. Monihan, *Consent, Coercion, and Limit: The Medieval Origins of Parliamentary Democracy* (Kingston, 1987). Despite large-scale interpre-tations and small-scale studies of particular authors and texts, there is no satisfactory historical account of political theory in Tudor England, although some aspects are usefully treated by Quentin Skinner, *The Foundations of Modern Political Thought* (Cambridge, 1978), II; J. P. Sommerville, *Politics and Ideology in England, 1603–1640* (London, 1986); and *The Cambridge History of Political Thought, 1450–1700*, ed. J. H. Burns with the assistance of Mark Goldie (Cambridge, 1991), henceforth cited as *CHPT*.

variety, complexity, and ambiguity of the medieval intellectual heritage, including continental traditions as well as continuities associated with parliament and common law. Echoes of medieval contention can be heard in various invocations of history, legal precedent, national mythology, and oral tradition (even if one would not wish to push such continuities as far as Alan MacFarlane has done).[10] Politically at least, the 'Elizabethan world picture' was still in many ways idealized and backward-looking.

One connecting theme has been 'medieval constitutionalism', a view old-fashioned in provenance and Whiggish in implications but indelibly part of the tradition of interpretation of English 'mixed government' since the seventeenth century. The idea of the mixed constitution, retrieved from ancient, especially Aristotelian and Polybian, political theory, was reinforced by the assumptions, terminology, and metaphors of what Ernst Kantorowicz called 'political' (and Walter Ullmann 'juristic') theology.[11] These arguments, emphasizing the corporate and proto-representative character of government, secular as well as ecclesiastical, presented a popular model for modern political speculators, especially in the wake of the conciliar movement and its impact on England. Concepts of the body politic and the body ecclesiastic, with their organic strengths, disorders, patterns, and processes, also continued to inhabit the political imagination of the Elizabethans, while the second of the 'king's two bodies' continued to haunt as well as to inspire the realm of public representation and debate. Lambarde reinforced the organic analogy and the 'natural' condition of the English nation with a conventional musical simile: '*Naturall* in that it hath an imitation of the naturall "bodie" of man, truly called a *little World* . . .; and Harmonicall, because from, as so well-turned a Base, Meane, and Treble, there proceedeth a most exquisite *consent*, and delicious melodie'.[12]

Another less naturalistic constitutional model, also developed in canon law, was that of the family. Conjugal organization, especially as contrasted with patriarchy, was a voluntary relationship implying that the ruler was a steward (or 'tutor') rather than a lord, and that the state was in the legal condition of a dowry. Like classical and conciliar precedents, this conjugal paradigm was elaborated in the effort to promote limited, responsible, and in a sense 'representative' govern-

---

[10] Alan Macfarlane, *The Origins of English Individualism* (London, 1978); cf. E. M. W. Tillyard, *The Elizabethan World Picture* (New York, 1929).

[11] E. H. Kantorowicz, *The King's Two Bodies: A Study in Political Theology* (Princeton, 1957), and Walter Ullmann, *Principles of Government and Politics in the Middle Ages* (London, 1961), p. 94, etc.

[12] *Archeion, or a Discourse upon the High Courts of Justice in England*, ed. C. H. McIlwain and P. C. Ward (Cambridge, MA, 1959), p. 126.

ment, which in England was illustrated by the crown in its relations with the royal council, the parliament, and the common law courts. Elizabeth in particular was wedded to these notions and tended indeed to give them amatory and sexual overtones. Nor were her overtures normally rebuffed; and in reaction to the old historiographical habit of seeking 'causes' of the Puritan revolution in this period, revisionist scholars have emphasized the cordial and productive relationship which usually prevailed between crown and parliament, at least for everyday business.[13]

Carrying over from medieval times, too, was the tradition of religious protest against the established church, its secular appendages and pretensions; and this was – quite apart from the Henrician break with Rome – much intensified by the Lutheran 'scandal', whose repercussions could be heard in England even before Luther's own famous break with Rome in 1520.[14] In social terms the 'slow Reformation' thesis is persuasive, but on the more visible level of public opinion and political consciousness Protestant attitudes and ideas were a conspicuous feature of printed literature. Moreover, as A. G. Dickens continues to argue, organized Protestantism had a solid foundation in Henrician England, in the countryside as well as among urban folk and intellectuals, notably in the 'Protestant heartland' of Kent and Essex (especially as shown by residual Lollardy, anti-clericalism, iconoclasm, and the evidence of wills).[15] Despite the recent efforts of scholars to minimize the pre-Elizabethan Reformation, there was numerical as well as moral growth, with attendant political implications.

Still, in terms of political thought, the Reformation under Henry VIII, despite various kinds of 'proto-Protestantism' and pockets of surviving Lollardy, was muted and peripheral, often in or on the edge of exile, and generally opposed by royal policy. The programme of evangelical reform flourished briefly under Edward VI, when continental contacts were secured and extended; and it came to a head under Mary, though largely through the commotion generated by the exiles in Geneva, Strasbourg, Frankfurt, and other Protestant refuges. Calvin was often looked to for counsel from persons wondering 'how they should behave them selves among ye papistes where it is not lawful for

[13] Geoffrey Elton, *The Parliament of England* (Cambridge, 1986).
[14] Basil Hall, 'The Early Rise and Gradual Decline of Lutheranism in England (1520–1600)', in Derek Baker (ed.), *Reform and Reformation* (Oxford, 1979), pp. 103–31.
[15] W. G. Dickens, *The English Reformation* (rev. edn, London, 1991), and paper on 'English Protestant Society 1520–58' (20 April 1987) given at the Folger Library. 'Revisionist' criticism includes Christopher Haigh (ed.), *The English Reformation Revised* (Cambridge, 1987), pp. 3, 19, etc, and most recently 'The English Reformation: A Premature Birth, a Difficult Labor and a Sickly Child', *Historical Journal*, 33 (1990), 449–60, and J. J. Scarisbrick, *The Reformation and the English People* (Oxford, 1984).

them to worshyppe God purely: but every man is constrained to use many ceremonies which have been invented against ye word of God, an be full of superstition'.[16] His advice was either 'that he should get hym hence from thence if he can', for the only alternative was to follow the way of the martyrs. In a broad perspective, English notions of religious and, by inference, political resistance were derivative (especially compared to Lutheran, sacramentarian, and Calvinist doctrine) and richly supplemented by translations of the works of magisterial Reformers (such as the previous passage from a pamphlet of 1548 on 'the mind of the godly and excellent learned man John Calvin'); but in human terms the Marian ideologists seem pioneers and innovators in subversive political thinking, if only because of their extraordinary predicament.

The grounds of resistance

For Milton, the Marian exiles were 'true Protestant divines of England, fathers in the faith we hold'.[17] Yet, with regard to sixteenth-century ideas of resistance, the conventional questions of priority and degree of radicalness may well be (to transpose the judgement of Lucien Febvre about mistaken notions of 'pre-reform' in France) 'badly posed'.[18] In a certain general sense, Christopher Hill's notion of a radical tradition 'from the Lollards to the Levellers' seems plausible, and indeed histories

[16] *The Mynde of the Godly and excellent lerned man M Jhon Calvin*, tr. R. G. ('Ippswyche', 1548; *STC* 4435), Aviii.

[17] *The Tenure of Kings and Magistrates*, ed. W. T. Allison (New York, 1911), 50. This section is based on my 'Ideas of Resistance before Elizabeth', in *The Historical Renaissance*, ed. R. Strier and H. Dubrow (Chicago, 1988), pp. 48–76, with further references (also in Schochet, II, pp. 5–28). See John N. King, *English Reformation Literature* (Princeton, 1982), seeking to rehabilitate the literature of the period between Henry VIII and Elizabeth; and Edward J. Baskerville, *A Chronological Bibliography of Propaganda and Polemic Published in England Between* 1553 and 1558 from the Death of Edward VI to the Death of Mary I (Memoirs of the American Philosophical Society, Philadelphia, 1979); Michael R. Watts, *The Dissenters, From the Reformation to the French Revolution* (Oxford, 1978), vol. I; and G. Bowles, 'Marian Protestants and the Violent Resistance to Tyranny', in *Protestantism and the National Church in England*, ed. P. Lake and M. Dowling (London, 1987), pp. 124–43, N. M. Sutherland, 'The Marian Exiles and the Establishment of the Elizabethan Regime', *Archiv für Reformationsgeschichte*, 78 (1987), 253–84; Catharine Davies, 'Poor Persecuted Little Flock of Commonwealth Christians: Edwardian Protestant Concepts of the Church', in *Protestantism and the National Church*, pp. 78–102, and especially Jane Dawson, 'Revolutionary Conclusions: The Case of the Marian Exiles', *History of Political Thought*, 11 (1990), 257–72, from her unpublished thesis on Goodman (Durham University, 1978); and, in general, Ludwig Cardauns, *Die Lehre vom Widerstandsrecht des Volks gegen die gegenmässige Obrigkeit in Luthertum und in Calvinismus des 16. Jahrhunderts* (Darmstadt, 1973).

[18] 'The Origins of the French Reformation: A Badly-Put Question?' *A New Kind of History*, tr. K. Folca (London, 1973), pp. 44–107.

of dissent and nonconformity have taken just this tack. So have studies of puritanism such as that of Michael Walzer, following a method not all that different from the martyrological approach of John Foxe and Flacius Illyricus's *Catalogue of the Witnesses of the Truth* (1559), relied on by Foxe himself.[19] Yet a historical inquiry into political thought must attend to questions of context as well as a retrospectively constructed canon.

In European society there was a common heritage of resistance thought and action; and the form of expression had more to do with social context and political predicament than with logical progression of thought – whence the various contradictions and turn-abouts of argument with regard to obedience, not only of particular authors but also of particular parties. Moreover, there were various competing, yet overlapping, traditions with distinct vocabularies, conceits, and styles of argument as well as intended audiences. Among the most conspicuous of these traditions are the classical (invoking Roman formulas of self-defence and popular sovereignty), the feudal (asserting contractual restraints and remedies), the commercial (or civic in a modern sense, associated with urban 'liberties'), the ecclesiastical (extending the old *libertas ecclesiae* of Gregorian reform), the conciliar (rejecting papal supremacy), and the fundamentalist (joining in the Pauline celebration of Christian 'liberty' over Judaic, and by analogy Romanist, 'bondage').[20] Of these the latter, especially in quantitative terms, was the most significant; for the Bible was surely the most influential and – in the construction of hot gospellers – the most incendiary of all texts.

The social environment of post-Reformation England encouraged and exacerbated dissent in various ways, especially through its potential for spontaneous and organized violence. On the secular side official concern for the secular threat of unauthorized and crypto- or para-political assemblies is illustrated by the laws, directed against the enclosure revolts continuing in this era, making it treasonable for forty or more persons to gather for over two hours and a felony to remain together an hour after being dispersed by the magistrate.[21] Technically, a meeting of at least three persons marked the dividing line between a merely private gathering and a public one subject to the jurisdiction of Star Chamber. The religious counterpart was the 'conventicle', which (as Laud later defined it) meant ten or more meeting to pray, read,

---

[19] *The Revolution of the Saints* (Cambridge, MA, 1956).
[20] Further discussion in D. R. Kelley, *The Beginning of Ideology* (Cambridge, 1981), ch. 8.
[21] Roger B. Manning, *Village Revolts: Social and Popular Disturbances in England, 1509–1640* (Oxford, 1988) 55ff; Barnett Beer, *Rebellion and Riot: Popular Revolt in England during the Reign of Edward VI* (Kent, Ohio, 1982).

preach, or expound scripture.[22] Since Wycliffe's time such conventicles were associated with 'faction, sedition, and insurrection'; and they inspired the conventicle acts of 1593 and 1664. Protestants characteristically took a more 'spiritual' view of what they regarded as 'godly conferences', but more legal-minded scholars like William Lambarde saw them as conspiracy; and indeed, according to Patrick Collinson, they had significant links with the 'gathered church' of the puritans. Another form of group violence was represented by iconoclasm, but this popular sport, though commonly associated with religious extremism, was to some extent accommodated by Elizabethan government as a necessary companion of religious reform and the rejection of popery.[23]

What constituted legitimate protest? English resistance, expression in part of a more general 'mid-Tudor crisis', was caught on the horns of a devilish dilemma: the opposition between the hated (popish as well as Judaic) 'law', or bondage, and the spiritual 'liberty of the Christian man' (in Luther's phrase), but which could also be construed as an opposition between social order and the worst sort of 'sedition' or 'rebellion' – charges ranking only slightly below that of 'heresy' in legal terms. The challenge to public order was only intensified by the Protestant aversion to 'Nicodemitism' – the offense of hypocrites who (wrote John Bale) 'will visit Christ only in ye dark and by night'.[24] The only way to avoid such soul-threatening 'temporizing', sharply condemned by Calvin and other evangelical leaders, was to 'publish' one's faith openly and take the consequences, whether exile from 'Egyptian' persecution or martyrdom. In combination the exile mentality and the martyr-complex significantly increased the emotional forces underlying resistance thought.

This premise is what made Protestantism a public threat and so a target of public action – most especially when the drive to bear witness to one's faith was joined to the new engine of publicity, which was the printing press. 'God hath opened the Presse to preach', declared John

---

[22] Patrick Collinson, 'The English Conventicle', in *Voluntary Religion*, ed. W. J. Shiels and D. Wood (London, 1986), pp. 223–59; also Robert Whiting, *The Blind Devotion of the People: Popular Religion and the English Reformation* (Cambridge, 1989); D. M. Palliser, 'Popular Reactions to the Reformation during the Years of Uncertainty, 1530–70', in *English Church and Society: Henry VIII to James I*, ed. F. Heal and R. O'Day (London, 1977), pp. 35–56; and J. W. Martin, *Religious Radicalism in Tudor England* (London, 1989).

[23] John Phillips, *The Reformation of Images: Destruction of Art in England, 1535–1660* (Berkeley, CA, 1973), and Margaret Aston, *England's Iconoclasts*, vol. I, *Laws against Images* (Oxford, 1988).

[24] *The Pageant of Popes* (London, 1574 [1538]), and Leslie P. Fairfield, *John Bale: Mythmaker of the English Reformation* (West Lafayette, IN, 1976). Cf. Wolfgang Musculus, *The Temporisour* (n. p., 1555; *STC* 18313), and Matteo Gribaldi, *A notable and marvalous epistle . . . concerning the terrible Judgement of God, 'upon him that for feare of man, denyeth Christ* (n. p. 1556; *STC* 12365).

Foxe, himself a Marian exile in contact with continental propagandists such as Jean Crespin and Flacius Illyricus.[25] In order to celebrate Protestant martyrs – 'seed of the church', in Tertullian's famous phrase – and to publicize their 'cause' to all nations, Foxe exploited this device to the fullest. Of course, oral transmission of doctrine, especially through sermons and public disputations, remained a primary vehicle of propaganda and proselytism, as illustrated by the spread and effectiveness of the 'Puritan lectureships' and the growing numbers of seditious preachers whom Hobbes, in the next century, thought should all have been killed.[26]

But more important, at least in the longer run, was what Foxe celebrated as the 'miracle' of print, which disseminated vernacular scriptures and martyrologies, and other genres of religious discourse with political overtones and resonances.[27] In less than a half-dozen years the Marian exiles – the first of the 'alienated intellectuals' of the Tudor age – produced over eighty pamphlets illustrating their passage across the whole spectrum of protest from religion to politics and from passive to active resistance, as the Calvinists would also do (likewise with the aid of the printed book) over a generation and more and as the Lutherans had already done, although in a rather more 'constitutional' fashion.

Although often neglected by English historians, the links with continental Protestantism were of major significance throughout the sixteenth century, beginning with the pilgrimage of William Tyndale and others to Wittenberg and continuing especially through the Marian exiles and the foundation of the 'stranger churches' (French and Dutch) in 1550.[28] From the 1520s heretical literature had come into England

[25] D. R. Kelley, 'Martyrs, Myths, and the Massacre: The Background of St Bartholomew', *American Historical Review*, 77 (1972), 1323–42 (repr. *The Massacre of St Bartholomew*, ed. A. Soman [The Hague, 1974]); also W. R. D. Jones, *The Mid-Tudor Crisis, 1539–1563* (New York, 1973); R. Tattler and J. Loach (eds.), *The Mid-Tudor Polity, c. 1540–1560* (Totowa, NJ, 1980), Winthrop Hudson, *The Cambridge Connection and the Elizabethan Settlement of 1559* (Durham, NC, 1980); and K. R. Firth, *The Apocalyptic Tradition in Reformation Britain 1530–1645* (Oxford, 1979).

[26] Paul S. Seaver, *The Puritan Lectureships* (Stanford, 1970).

[27] William Haller, *Foxe's Book of Martyrs and the Elect Nation* (London, 1963), and Jane Facey, 'John Foxe and the Defense of the English Church', in *Protestantism and the National Church*, pp. 163–92. Despite massive specialized literature the fundamental question of the impact of printing on political thought has not progressed far beyond the suggestions of Elizabeth Eisenstein, *The Printing Press as an Agent of Change* (Cambridge, 1978).

[28] Andrew Pettegree, *Foreign Protestant Communities in Sixteenth-Century London* (Oxford, 1986); Elton, 'England and the Continent in the Sixteenth Century', *Reform and Reformation*, (Oxford, 1979); Patrick Collinson, 'Calvinism with an Anglican Face: The Stranger Churches in Early Elizabethan England and their Superintendent', *ibid.*,

through the communities of 'Alians' (aliens) in London; and from the reign of Edward VI the activities of printers and translators forged new links between English evangelicals and the churches of Zurich and Geneva. These ties were continued during the Elizabethan period, when the stranger churches again served as refuges (during the religious wars and particularly after the massacres of St Bartholomew) and points of contact between English and continental Protestants. The intellectual exchanges are difficult to determine precisely, but the extraordinary volume of translated literature (including French ordinances as well as historical and theological works and resistance pamphlets) is some measure of the community of discourse preserved in the international Protestant network, a special province in the Republic of Letters celebrated by Erasmus.

Another essential ingredient in political polemic, though difficult to describe precisely, was the development of the theory and practice of rhetoric, and its extension into the vernacular, most famously in the form of Ramism, which attracted many of the younger generation in Elizabethan universities, especially Cambridge.[29] Ramism had many aims, including the reform of learning and teaching, but its goal was what amounted to a theory of indoctrination and propaganda, whether through sermons, disputations, or pamphlets. Protestant theories and practice of oratory, combined with their preaching and amplified by printing, constituted a major political force, and threat – as indeed did the new 'merchant adventurers of the mind', as Elizabethan writers like Kit Marlowe have been called.[30] Not only knowledge (to adapt the Baconian adage) but also persuasive and well disseminated opinion was 'power'.

The most striking illustration of this dimension of public discourse is perhaps the *Arte of Rhetorik* published in 1553 by the Protestant (and future statesman) Thomas Wilson – freshly back from Italy and full of enthusiasm for the humanist programme. Wilson praised the power of eloquence as superior to either 'force of arms or Policys' and emphasized its proselytizing potential: 'For if the writings of eloquence may move us, what worthier thing can there be, then with a word to winne cities

---

pp. 71–102; Claire Cross, 'Continental Students and the Protestant Reformation in England in the Sixteenth Century', *ibid.*, pp. 35–57.

[29] Kelley, *The Beginning of Ideology*, ch. 4. Despite Walter Ong's classic *Ramus, Method and the Decay of Dialogue* (Cambridge, Mass., 1957), and much of recent literature on Renaissance rhetoric, Ramism, especially in its relations to Aristotelianism, needs further exploration. Most recently, see Donald K. McKim, *Ramism in William Perkin's Theology* (New York, 1987).

[30] M. T. Jones-Davies, *Victimes et rebelles: l'écrivain dans la société elizabethaine* (Paris, 1980).

and whole countries?'[31] Eloquence, first given by God, then lost by man, and now recovered, was essential in matters both religious and political; and in both cases the aim was 'always to have the victorie'. On this rule, if on few others, the champions of all doctrines could agree.

Expressions of resistance

The weapons of controversy were at hand and the lines of division drawn; it remained only to set the fires of ideological war. Perhaps the most seminal stage in the development of resistance ideas was the colourfully vituperative portraits of the enemies of the 'godly', beginning with the Romish 'wolf' or 'fox' (John Bale's terms) which preyed on the Christian flock. There is a definite Joachimite coloration to the polemic of Bale and John Ponet, aimed at the 'buggery' of monasticism and similar 'blasphemies', including idolatry, pagan costume and ceremony, and the cannibalistic ritual of the mass, requiring (as Ponet lamented) 'that we must eat and chaw with our corporeal teeth ... Christes blessed fleshe and bones'.[32] This often scatological denunciation was all too easily turned from the popish Antichrist to the 'Jezebel' Mary and her unspeakable consort Philip II of Spain, and later to Mary Queen of Scots. Similar personalized assaults on tyranny had been made by French Protestants, who concocted 'black legends' of Catherine de Médicis and the Cardinal of Lorraine.[33] Identifying the human aspect of the confessional enemy was an essential step in the politicization of religious protest and its transmutation into resistance theory.

The culmination of this process of personalizing the ideological came with the construction of the new myth of Italianate skulduggery, 'Machiavellianism', which came to stand for tyranny and assassination as well as popery and 'atheism'.[34] *Machiavelisme*, a fabrication of French Huguenots in the wake of the massacres of St Bartholomew, was taken up by Elizabethan English authors. Although Machiavelli's political 'virtues' were not entirely overlooked, the counter-myth associated with his 'republican' face was quite overshadowed by the more lurid image of 'old Nick' depicted by Shakespeare and Marlowe, as well as

---

[31] *Arte of Rhetorique*, ed. G. H. Main (Oxford, 1909), p. 5.

[32] *A notable sermon concerninge the right of the lordes supper* (Westminster, 14 March 1550; STC 20177), sig. Ciii.

[33] [Henri Estienne], *A mervaylous discourse upon the life, deedes, and behaviours of Katherine de Medicis* ('Heidelberg', 1575).

[34] These two 'faces of Machiavelli' are reflected in D. R. Kelley, 'Murd'rous Machiavel in France', *Political Science Quarterly*, 85 (1970), 24–51, and J. G. A. Pocock, *The Machiavellian Moment* (Princeton, 1975); see also Felix Raab, *The English Face of Machiavelli* (London, 1964).

political writers. Though the world might think Machiavel dead, as Marlowe said, he was alive and well in this age of fascination with power, not only on the Elizabethan stage but in the counsels of princes and prelates, who looked with increasing favour on extreme and 'political' solutions for complex problems.

In England, the assembling of resistance theory came to a head with the work of Ponet, Christopher Goodman, John Knox, and other exiled members of the English Protestant community, which perhaps only a minority of English historians are willing to associate with the puritan movement that emerged under Elizabeth. The exiles lamented, petitioned, and objected, but finally came to the conclusion expressed perhaps most succinctly in Goodman's *How Superior Powers Oght to be obeyed*, that 'it is both lawful and necessarie some tymes to disobeye and also to resist Vngodly magistrates'.[35] Yet, added Goodman (following Calvinist convention), 'This is no doctrine of Rebellion, but only doctrine of Peace'. Goodman's ambiguity about what was lawful, and peaceful, was further highlighted by his defence of the 'cause' and the 'enterprise', but what others would call 'rebellion' – 'the only refuge of heretics', wrote John Proctor in 1554 – of Thomas Wyatt and his anti-Marian fellows, including Ponet.[36]

The most comprehensive statement of Marian resistance ideas was John Ponet's *Short Treatise of Politike Power*, published in Strasbourg in 1555. For Ponet, thundering against modern tyranny like an Old Testament prophet and celebrating the great tradition of Christian martyrs from the time of Nero, 'politike power' was the product not merely of reason and natural law but of the Almighty himself, who, after the fall, authorized it for the good of 'the people'.[37] 'Before magistrates were, Goddes lawes were', Ponet argued; rulers were always subject to the 'positive lawes of their countreyes', as shown by the famous Roman formula, *Digna Vox*, which made the *princeps* subject to the *populus* and which underlay the authority of the diets and parliaments of the European states. The final cause of 'civile power' Ponet assigned to 'the libertie of the people', which he then conflated with the evangelical idea

[35] Photorepr. of this work (Geneva, 1558), with a note by C. H. McIlwain (New York, 1931), p. 41.
[36] *The historie of Wyates rebellion* (London, 1554), ded. to Queen Mary, sig. Aiᵛ. Cf. William B. Robinson, 'The National and Local Significance of Wyatt's Rebellion in Surrey', *Historical Journal*, 30 (1987), 769–9; also Anthony Fletcher, *Tudor Rebellions* (London, 1973).
[37] Photorepr. (Strasbourg, 1556) in Winthrop S. Hudson, *John Ponet (1516–1556)* (Chicago, 1942), p. 43; also E. J. Baskerville, 'John Ponet in Exile: A Ponet Letter to John Bale', *Journal of Ecclesiastical History*, 37 (1986), 442–7, and David H. Wollman, 'The Biblical Justification for Resistance to Authority in Ponet's and Goodman's Polemics', *Sixteenth Century Journal*, 13 (1982), 29–41.

of Christian liberty. Identifying 'the people' of English political tradition with the Christian flock in an Augustinian sense (*congregatio
fidelium*, if not *communitas sanctorum*) also promoted the politicization of
religious protest.

A rival for the revolutionary sweepstakes (at least in the judgement of
Quentin Skinner) is the Protestant, Gallicized Scottish scholar – and
'monarchomach' – George Buchanan, who defended the rights of the
Scottish nobles in their revolt against Queen Mary.[38] In his defamatory
biography of Mary, his *Right of the Kingdom of the Scots* (1579), and his
history of Scotland Buchanan formulated a secular theory of popular
sovereignty based especially on the contractual 'regal law' (*lex regia*) by
which the Roman people had bestowed their sovereignty (*majestas*) on
the emperor. On these grounds Buchanan declared an inalienable right
of resistance and even of tyrannicide on the part not just of a political
elite but of the 'people' (modern analogue of the Roman *Populus
Romanus*) as a whole.

In certain ways the trajectory of Protestant thought, from passive to
active resistance, was recapitulated by Catholics in the next generation,
especially in the publication of the 'Allen-Persons' party under Elizabeth (especially in 1584–96). Catholic resistance ideas were affected by –
if not actually drawn from – the arguments of the Marian exiles, but with
significant differences, most notably in dependence upon papal power
('corner-stone of Catholic resistance theory', as it has been called) and in
a more elaborate casuistry. But like the Protestants, Catholics blamed
the troubles of Tudor England on their confessional adversaries; they
developed a horror of – and a 'recusant' remedy for – conformity with
Protestant religious practice; and they sought political legitimacy in
history and martyrology, or 'counter-martyrology', to replace Foxe's
'stinking dung-hill' of a book.[39] In search of their own brand of
'Christian liberty', they became the new generation of political exiles;
and from this position they elaborated their own political views,
especially radical ideas of popular sovereignty derived from scholastic
tradition and the same Biblical line of argument previously developed

---

[38] Buchanan, *De jure regni apud Scotos* (Edinburgh, 1579). See Skinner, *Foundations of
Modern Political Thought*, II, p. 343, and Robert M. Kingdon in *CHPT*, pp. 214–18;
also Roger A. Mason (ed.), *Scots and Britons: Scottish Political Thought and the Union of
1603* (Cambridge, forthcoming).

[39] William Allen, *A True, Sincere and Modest Defense of English Catholics*, ed. R. M.
Kingdon (Ithaca, 1965), p. 134, referring to Protestant defences of resistance; in general,
see Peter Holmes, *Resistance and Compromise: The Political Thought of the Elizabethan
Catholics* (Cambridge, 1982), T. Clancy, *Papist Pamphleteers* (Chicago, 1964), and
J. H. M. Salmon in *CHPT*, pp. 241–4.

and secularized by Protestants: God must in every case be obeyed before man.[40]

Religious settlement

The Elizabethan settlement of 1559 rendered the Marian protest obsolete, but it could not in the long run resolve the religious differences which had come to maturity in the times of exile and contact with continental Protestantism.[41] The assault on vestments was continued as a programme for the 'purifying' of ceremonial abuse; both were symbols of and surrogates for more straightforward attacks on episcopal authority. Elizabeth's task, inherited from her father, was to build a national church, and she could only do this through the Anglican hierarchy centred on the bishops and the ecclesiastical prerogative embodied in the Court of High Commission. In the Elizabethan period, this 'Erastian' premise was tempered by a 'constitutional' corollary emphasizing what Richard Hooker called 'general consent', surely meaning to the role of Parliament as well as the episcopate in ecclesiastical organization.

The Settlement has been an endless source of controversy among historians as well as among squabbling Elizabethan denominations. If recent revisionist scholarship has seen it mainly as a difficult political manoeuvre, the major problems in a long perspective were doctrinal and ideological. Based in part on adiaphorist premises deemphasizing external forms of worship, the Settlement tied royal supremacy to monarchical episcopacy, as Collinson put it – such was the theme of Bishop John Jewel's 'challenge sermon' of 1559 – and soon the disputes over vestments and ceremonies were superseded by debates over church 'polity', which included English government and society more generally. So the Anglican establishment formed its own idea of legitimacy. Rejecting the extremes of popish convention and puritan idealism, Anglican political theory urged the conservative and traditional character of Elizabethan ecclesiastical order – 'no new thing', said Jewel[42] – and its justification in terms of historical precedent, as Hooker did more elaborately a generation later.

[40] The last paragraph of Calvin's *Institutes of the Christian Religion*, 1536 and all later editions.

[41] Norman L. Jones, *Faith by Statute: Parliament and the Settlement of Religion, 1559* (London, 1982), p. 189; and cf. Claire Cross, *The Royal Supremacy and the Elizabethan Settlement* (London, 1969); W. M. Southgate, *John Jewel and the Problem of Doctrinal Authority* (Cambridge, MA, 1962), and Bernard J. Verkamp, *The Indifferent Mean: Adiaphorism in the English Reformation to 1554* (Athens, OH, 1977).

[42] John Jewel, *An Apology of the Church of England*, ed. J. E. Booty (Ithaca, NY, 1963), p. 134.

By contrast, 'puritan' social attitudes were based on the assumption that the church should live by a 'new law', essentially Calvin's new ecclesiastical order. This was the message of the first Admonition to Parliament of 1572, 'first manifesto of Puritanism', as it has been called, which established the line of argument pursued, explicitly or implicitly, by Cartwright, Perkins, and other opponents of a church but 'half-reformed'.[43] Bucer's and Calvin's ideas of church organization, based on supervision of pastors and elders, was clearly a political as well as an ecclesiastical threat. To challenge clerical habit and ceremonial practice was to subvert the hierarchy, but to question church government was, because of its Erastian base, to challenge the monarchy itself; and ecclesiological controversy under Elizabeth – carried on by sermons, disputations, and prophesies as well as printed pamphlets – always had these dangerously political overtones. As John Penry wrote, 'The puritans say truly, that all the Lord Bishops are petty antichrists, and therefore that the magistrates ought to thrust you out of the common-wealth'.[44]

Penry's declaration came at the high point of the ecclesiological debate, the Marprelate controversy of 1587–8, centring on a series of satirical denunciations of the 'swinish rabble' of bishops, the 'pettie Antichrist, pettie popes', who (behind the skirts of the Queen) stood in the way of full reformation. The author, writing anonymously or under the pseudonym 'Martin Marprelate', was probably Job Throkmorton, who was also a parliamentary critic of James VI of Scotland.[45] Like the Anglican establishment, the Protestant opposition sought legitimation in a particular reading of history, as exemplified in the notion of the 'true church' offered in William Harrison's 'Great English Chronology', which followed Lutheran and Calvinist precedents in retracing a tradition of 'pure doctrine' back to the primitive church and its 'lively' descendant.[46]

The 'puritan' movement was complex, and the ideological coherence and continuity with the Civil War, argued by Michael Walzer and others, has been dissolved by discriminating research into divergent

[43] W. H. Frere and C. E. Douglas, *Puritan Manifestos* (London, 1954), and Donald Joseph McGinn, *The Admonition Controversy* (New Brunswick, 1949). See also J. Knott, *The Sword of the Spirit: Puritan Responses to the Bible* (Chicago, 1980).

[44] [John Penry], *A Man of Worship*, in *Images of English Puritanism*, ed. Lawrence A. Sosek (Baton Rouge, 1989).

[45] Leland H. Carlson, *Martin Marprelate, Gentleman: Master Job Throkmorton Laid Open in his Colors* (San Marino, 1981), p. 9; and see Paul Christianson, *Reformers and Babylon: English Apocalyptic visions from the Reformation to the Eve of the Civil War* (Toronto, 1978), pp. 65ff.

[46] G. J. R. Parry, *A Protestant Vision: William Harrison and the Reformation of Elizabethan England* (Cambridge, 1987).

trends of Protestant opposition.[47] Most prominent was the division between 'separatists' like Robert Browne, who, invoking the radical tradition of the martyrly 'elect', rejected compromise with notions of episcopacy and uniformity, and certain 'moderate Puritans' (as Peter Lake calls them), who professed a covenant theology based on acceptance of social conventions and who would be satisfied pursuing 'presbytery within episcopacy'. The situation was complicated, too, by an 'anti-Calvinist' move against egalitarianism and back to hierarchy associated with the rise of English Arminianism in the later sixteenth century.

Yet the public image and subsequent myth was much simpler. Richard Hooker took little notice of these complications in his defence of Anglican tradition and the connections between the 'civil' and the 'ecclesiastical polity'. For Hooker, the central concept in both contexts was that of 'law', and for him this was precisely what Calvinists of all persuasions, following Luther, had recklessly put in question. Like Erasmus and other critics of fundamentalist Protestantism, Hooker pointed to the learned fascination with disputation, a tendency which had fragmented continental movements of 'reform'; and he turned back to neo-scholastic traditions of natural law – that is, the 'secondary natural law' of man's fallen condition as contrasted with the primary natural law celebrated by Stoics – to provide legitimacy for the Church of England as it had grown out of statutory law and the policy of the queen.[48] In other words Hooker attempted to restore political controversy to the sphere of 'Civill society' and its various laws – to human convention rather than transcendent or radical ideas, which threatened

---

[47] Efforts to link 'Puritanism' to large political and social patterns (capitalism, democracy, revolution), exemplified by Michael Walzer's *The Revolution of the Saints* (Cambridge, MA, 1965), and David Little's neo-Weberian *Religion, Order, Law* (Chicago, 1969, 1984) have been criticized and overshadowed by more socially analytical and differentiating studies, beginning especially with Patrick Collinson, *The Elizabethan Puritan Movement*, followed by his *Godly People* (London, 1983) and *The Religion of Protestants: The Church in English Society, 1559–1625* (Oxford, 1982). See also Peter Lake, *Moderate Puritans and the Elizabethan Church* (Cambridge, 1982), and 'Calvinism and the English Church, 1570–1635', *Past & Present*, 114 (1987), 32–76, with Margo Todd, 'The Godly and the Church: New Views of Protestantism in Early Modern Britain', *Journal of British History*, 28 (1989), 418–26; Nicolas Tyacke, *Anti-Calvinists: The Rise of English Arminianism, c. 1590–1645* (Oxford, 1987); Peter White, 'The Rise of Arminianism Reconsidered', *Past & Present*, 101 (1983), 34–54; B. R. White, *The English Separatist Tradition from the Marian Martyrs to the Pilgrim Fathers* (Oxford, 1971); William Hunt, *The Puritan Movement: The Coming of Revolution in an English County* (Cambridge, MA, 1983), and Elliott Rose, *Cases of Conscience: Alternatives to Recusants and Puritans under Elizabeth I and James I* (Cambridge, 1975). Of broader intellectual studies see, most recently, David Zaret, *The Heavenly Contract: Ideology and Organization in Pre-Revolutionary Puritanism* (Chicago, 1985), and Margo Todd, *Christian Humanism and the Puritan Social Order* (Oxford, 1987).

[48] *Of the Laws of Ecclesiastical Polity*, ed. W. Speed Hill (Folger Library edition; Cambridge, MA, 1977), preface, Bk. I.

liberty as well as order. In the works of Hooker, English political thought, marking an intersection between national ecclesiology and constitutionalism, became in large part an eclectic and apologetic commentary on the Settlement.

Conflict of Laws

But the larger, more theoretical questions would not go away, and Hooker's synthesis was carried out within a larger constitutional framework. In general, European political thought in the sixteenth century drew upon two major resources – Aristotelian philosophy, 'practical' as well as 'theoretical', and Roman jurisprudence, which included canon and some parts of feudal as well as civil law. In England, Roman law played a limited role, especially after Henry VIII's break with the church; and of course common lawyers (like the feudists on the continent) rejected its 'authority'. In certain practical and theoretical ways, however, the civilian tradition, as Hooker insisted, continued to be significant. In Scotland, moreover, civil law prevailed – its being (as Henry Spelman judged) 'liken to Fraunce'[49] – and this intensified controversies over the Union in the early years of James I. For most Englishmen Roman law signified absolutism and popery; and in Hooker's time the dark images of Romanist and Italianate influence flourished on the stage, in public opinion, and in political thought, contributing to the ideological divisions later separating Stuart policy from common law and parliamentary opposition, which drew on its own non-Roman (and anti-Norman) mythology.

On the whole, except in subordinate jurisdictions like the admiralty and ecclesiastical courts and in the little civilian guild known as 'Doctor's Commons' – 'seed-bed of popery', as Puritans viewed it – Roman law failed to take root in England.[50] There never was a serious threat of a 'reception' of Roman law, and its political associations

---

[49] 'Of the Union', in Bruce R. Galloway and Brian Levack (eds.), *The Jacobean Union* (Edinburgh, 1985), p. 180; and see also Levack, *The Formation of the English State: England, Scotland and the Union, 1603–1707* (Oxford, 1987).

[50] Richard Helmholz, *Roman Canon Law in Reformation England* (Cambridge, 1990), p. 154. See also C. D. Squibb, *Doctors Commons* (Oxford, 1977). I have not basically altered the views expressed in my 'History, English Law and the Renaissance', *Past & Present*, 65 (1974), 24–51, repr. *History, Law and the Human Sciences* (despite the later exchange with Kevin Sharpe and Christopher Brooke, *ibid.*, 72 (1978), 133–46), although much further research has been done; e.g., Daniel R. Coquillette, 'Legal Ideology and Incorporation: English Civilian Writers, 1523–1607', and Louis Knafla, 'The Influence of Continental Humanism on English Common Law in the Renaissance', both in *Actus Conventus Neo-Latini Bononiensis*, ed. R. J. Schoeck (Binghamton, 1985); and especially the work of Helmholz cited. See also D. R. Kelley, *The Human Measure: Social Thought in the Western Legal Tradition* (Cambridge, MA, 1990), ch. 10.

ensured that common lawyers would continue to resist its influence. Yet this influence had a positive as well as negative side; for Roman law offered a model of rational and systematic jurisprudence from which civilians like John Cowell, William Fulbeke, John Doderidge, and Francis Bacon hoped that the common law might be reformed and made more 'equitable', in the classical rather than English sense of the term developed in Chancery. Politically, moreover, Roman law contained concepts and devices of constitutional as well as absolutist rule – including the idea (from the law *Digna vox*) that the prince should rule under the law and that 'what touches all should be approved by all' (the formula *Quod omnes tangit*, which passed into English law via the canonists).[51] Finally, the Romanist distinction between the private sphere of individual liberty and the public sphere of legislative activity helped to simplify questions of obedience and the abuse of power.

The major significance of civil law in Elizabethan England was felt in a more indirect way; and according to Brian Levack this was in providing 'a set of questions, a vocabulary, and in some cases a set of political principles, with which [Elizabethan and early Stuart writers] approached some very difficult constitutional questions around the turn of the sixteenth century'.[52] This influence can be seen in the work of such disparate authors as Thomas Smith, Alberico Gentili, John Davies, and continental authors like Jean Bodin, whose translated work played a vital part in English political controversy. The upshot was to shift the terms of the debate from limited government to the sovereign power (*maiestas* and *praerogativa*) of the king, its legal limits, and the means of redress for its abuse. This shift may have been reinforced, too, by growing interest in continental political debates reflected in the numerous translations from official as well as oppositional declarations of political principles – French royal ordinances, for example, as well as pamphlets produced by the Huguenot opposition.[53]

It may be that English equity as developed in the court of chancery ('twin sister of Star Chamber', as Maitland remarked) owed something to civil law; but formally it depended on the 'conscience' of the lord

---

[51] Gaines Post, *Studies in Medieval Legal and Political Thought* (Princeton, 1964), pp. 163–240.

[52] See Brian Levack, 'The Civil Law, Theories of Absolutism, and Political Conflict in Late Sixteenth- and Early Seventeenth-Century England', in *The Historical Renaissance*, cited above, n. 12 (also in Schochet, II, pp. 29–48); *The Civil Lawyers in England, 1603–1641* (Oxford, 1977), and 'The English Civilians, 1500–1700', in *Lawyers in Early Modern Europe and America*, ed. Wilfrid Prest (New York, 1981), pp. 108–28.

[53] This is an important question which has not been pursued since the path-breaking book of J. H. M. Salmon, *The French Religious Wars in English Political Thought* (Oxford, 1959).

chancellor and applied, only after petition, to 'singular' rather than to 'common' cases. The purpose of 'equitable interference' was to remedy defects in the law, and its theory accepted two maxims: equity follows the law, and it acts *in personam* (rather than *in rem*).[54] The jurisprudence of equity accumulated since the fourteenth century did soften the rigours of common law, most notably in the protection of women and their property rights. In general this rival jurisdiction and the literature it produced strengthened connections between the Aristotelian conception of *epieikeia* (applied a century earlier by conciliarist reformers to heal the Great Schism which had afflicted the church for over a generation) and political thinking in the sixteenth century.

Continental influences were substantial, even when not wholly visible: and in the work of a Protestant (and Ramist) jurist like Henry Finch even religious conceptions of 'law' were drawn on for the improvement of English legal traditions.[55] Yet the common law, by choice as well as habit, continued for the most part in the insular channels it had cut since the time of Bracton and Glanvil, or so at least professional convention and English historiography would have it. For English law, the sixteenth century was a time of judicial expansion, not only in the activities of the courts but also in the practice and elaboration of judicial 'interpretation' of statutes, with the result that judges as well as the parliament enjoyed a larger role in the 'making' of law. This was an age, too, of increasing litigation, especially over questions of property and debt – between 1560 and 1606 cases 'in advanced stages' before King's Bench increased over sevenfold, and the proportion of attorneys in the general population increased fivefold (from 20,000:1 to 4,000:1). This order of increase is apparent too in the large quantities of published works on legal issues, and it is time that historians of political theory, all too often tied to the classical and formal philosophical canons, take these factors into account for the generations between the Reformation and the Puritan Revolution. The problem is that the sixteenth century continues to represent, in terms of historical exploration 'the dark age of English legal history' – and so, to a degree, of political thought.[56]

[54] D. E. C. Yale (ed.), *Lord Nottingham's 'Manual of Chancery Practice' and 'Prolegomena of Chancery and Equity'* (Cambridge, 1965); also F. W. Maitland, *Equity* (Cambridge, 1909), and John Guy, 'Law, Equity and Conscience in Henrician Juristic Thought', in John Guy and Alistair Fox (eds.), *Reassessing the Henrician Age* (Oxford, 1986), pp. 179–98.

[55] See also Wilfred R. Prest, 'The Art of Law and the Law of God: Sir Henry Finch (1558–1625)', in *Puritans and Revolutionaries* (Oxford, 1978), 94–117.

[56] J. H. Baker, 'The Dark Age of English Legal History (1500–1700)', *Legal History Studies* 1972, ed. D. Jenkins (Cardiff, 1972), pp. 1–27, and C. W. Brooks, 'Litigants and Attorneys in the King's Bench and Common Pleas, 1560–1640', *Legal Records and the Historian*, ed. J. F. Baker (London, 1978).

The ancient constitution

Central to these considerations is what J. G. A. Pocock has called the 'common law mind', referring to the expression of a set of professional attitudes, assumptions, prejudices, methods, and 'authorities', together with a very special language, beginning with Law-French and ending in the seventeenth century with a kind of legal jargon which only graduates of the Inns of Court could be trusted to employ. The common law mind was tied also to a particular national pedigree which had attained the level of a myth by the time of Elizabeth. This applied not only to the 'high court of parliament' and the statutory canon but also to the unique features of English private law. 'The law or policy of this realm of England', as William Lambarde instructed one of his juries, 'as it is a peculiar government, not borrowed of the imperial or Roman law (as be the laws of the most part of other Christian nations) but standing upon the highest reason, selected even for itself; so doth it in one special thing above any other most apparently vary from the usage of other countries: I mean in the manner of proceeding that we have by jurors, which our law callest the judgement by peers or equals . . .'[57]

Crucial to the common law mind was the appeal to tradition – a peculiar combination of history, myth, common sense, and legal divination suggested by the clichés 'immemorial custom' and 'time out of mind'. This was a mentality which contrasted in many respects with continental conceptions of the European legal tradition. Yet in a longer perspective this conception was an insular development of the old civilian theory of custom (*consuetudo*), and it might apply to local usages as well as the 'high' conventions of King's Bench and Common Pleas. This has been well illustrated by the studies made by Louis Knafla of the court of Romney Marsh and its own pre-Bractonian 'ancient customs'.[58] Looking at English customs 'from the bottom up', as Knafla suggests, might give us a larger and more critical view than psycho-historically analyzing the 'common law mind' – or trying to read the devious one of Edward Coke.

In recent times, the historiographical locus of these topics has been the question of the 'ancient constitution', which Pocock's book has

---

[57] *William Lambarde and Local Government*, p. 100. And see Norman Doe, *Fundamental Authority in Late Medieval English Law* (Cambridge, 1990).

[58] 'Common Law and Custom in Tudor England: or, "The Best State of a Common-wealth"' (Schochet, II, pp. 171–86), and 'Common Law and the Problem of Authority' (presentation at the Folger Library, April 1985); also Glenn Burgess, 'Common Law and Political Theory in Early Stuart England', *Political Science*, 40 (1988), 4–17, and *The Politics of the Ancient Constitution* (London, 1992, and University Park, PA, 1993).

provoked and illuminated.[59] The idea of an original organizational ideal, which was shared by ecclesiastical as well as secular authorities throughout Europe, required above all locating the source and inspiration of political values and standards in a remote past, and the corollary that improvement – 'reform' – entailed a return to this original state. This dream of a political golden age resembled the classical – Stoic but also Machiavellian – idealization of the ancient virtue of the Roman fathers (*mos maiorum*); but it included a more literal attempt to imitate particular ancient, and perhaps obsolete, laws and institutions, whether the arrangements of the 'primitive church' (an ecclesiological ideal itself going back at least to the time of Gregorian reform) or that of a political structure based on counsel and consent (a pattern perhaps going back, with the help of modern readings of Tacitus, to the ancient Germanic tribes and their alleged social and moral virtues).[60] In both cases there was an assumption of a kind of populist purity which had been lost in the course of generations of corruption and usurpation – which in England was usually blamed on the Norman yoke and papal tyranny.

Retrospective utopianism, 'constitutional antiquarianism', or the never-never-land of political virtue – however it should be characterized – is the most ancient of illusions and myths. Cicero had spoken of the *status antiquus* of Rome, when *boni mores* were more potent than *leges*, and Tacitus had sharpened the point by invidious contrast between imperial Romans and barbarian Germans. Elizabethan authors cited these precedents, too ('Without manners, what are laws?' William Lambarde asked).[61] Modern imitators, however, were at least two removes from this sort of political nostalgia; and in speaking of the Ancient Constitution, it is essential to recall that we are dealing not only with a political construct, or reconstruction, but also with an almost prehistorical trope. Nor would it be surprising to find that sixteenth- and seventeenth-century constitutional antiquarians were at least as aware as we are of this phenomenon of literary *longue durée*, products as they were of political disillusionment as well as of humanist learning, and inclined as they were, on a variety of levels, to historical reflection as well as imitation.

At the foundations of the Ancient Constitution too, however, lay

[59] *The Ancient Constitution and the Feudal Law* (Cambridge, 1957; rev. edn 1987); also J. H. M. Salmon, 'The Ancient Constitution in European Perspective', *Renaissance and Revolt* (Cambridge, 1987), pp. 155–88; and Corinne C. Weston in *CHPT*, pp. 374–411.

[60] D. R. Kelley, 'Tacitus Noster: The *Germania* in the Renaissance and Reformation', in *Tacitus and the Tacitean Tradition*, ed. T. J. Luce and A. J. Woodman (Princeton, 1993), pp. 152–67.

[61] *William Lambarde and Local Government*, p. 69.

something less self-conscious than literary mimesis; and this again was the very old idea, or social instinct, of custom. *Consuetudo* represents not only an essential legal category but also one of the most fundamental forms of cultural memory – just as its obverse *desuetudo* defined a form of social forgetting.[62] 'Custom', in the famous formula of Ulpian, 'is the tacit consent of people confirmed by long-established practice', and as such it was associated with the legal notion of 'prescription', or 'long prescription' (*praescriptio longa*, or *longissima consuetudo*), which also joined social action to social value, fact to law, and in effect might to right. English law itself, in the often-quoted opening lines of Bracton, developed uninterruptedly under the rubric of *consuetudo* (though later confirmed by statute). As 'unwritten law and usage' emerging in preliterate culture, custom represented the putative 'original' of English law, but it is important to notice that it survived into early modern times in the form of oral tradition and judicial procedure. As John Cowell wrote, 'It is enough for the proofe of a custom by witness in the common law (as I have credibly heard), if two or more can agree, that they have heard their fathers say, that it was a custom all their time and that their fathers heard their fathers also say, that it was likewise a custome in their time'.[63] To judge from the writing of Coke, we might add, it was sometimes enough for the proof of a custom for a common lawyer to search his own memory and learning; certainly it was enough for speculations about the Ancient Constitution and even about the royal prerogative.

In various ways English common law resembled continental *droit coutumier* and *Gewohnheitsrecht* and had ties with feudal concepts, which had been incorporated into the civil law. The famous chapter (39) of Magna Carta guaranteeing due process to all 'freemen', for example, was itself taken from the Lombard *Libri Feudorum*.[64] Like continental feudists, English lawyers avoided Romanist conventions, preferring native tradition to 'written' law, *ius commune* to the *ius civile*; and so, again like the feudists, their framework of judgement was not Roman law but the 'law of nations' (*ius gentium*) by which every 'people' enjoyed its own law (*ius proprium*). The law of nations was the field in which ideas like 'the people', legal 'action', 'tyranny', and other social and political categories received definition and legitimation (*populi*, *actiones*,

---

[62] Further discussion, with full references in D. R. Kelley, '"Second Nature": The Idea of Custom in European Law, Society, and Culture', *The Transmission of Culture in Early Modern Europe*, ed. A. Grafton and A. Blair (Philadelphia, 1990), pp. 131–72.

[63] *The Interpreter* (Cambridge, 1607).

[64] *Consuetudines Feudorum*, V, c. 1.

tyrannia . . . sunt de iure gentium are the civilian formulas).[65] This is the true source of that theory of political independence declared by Bartolus and others (*civitas sibi princeps*), an idea which was elaborated not only in a 'civic' context but also, and more extensively, in connection with the national monarchies. Like his French and Spanish brothers, the English king was – as Cromwell had usefully recalled during the Reformation parliament – 'emperor in his kingdom' (*imperator in regno suo*) and enjoyed the same rights of self-government, law-making, and law-interpreting (which was also, notoriously, a kind of law-making).[66] The identification of *rex* and *lex*, implying 'legislative sovereignty', suggested also that common law was the king's law.

Yet in national contexts the interpretation of custom, with attendant assumptions about the nature of history and politics, became the monopoly of professional jurists. For ultimately it was the judges who determined, defined, and applied customs; and often they did so with remarkable political licence. On the continent they might, in given circumstances, have recourse to various neighboring customs, civil or canon law, natural law, equity, or, explicitly or implicitly, their own conscience. These were some of the devices, too, which informed the theory and practice of English jurists like John Fortescue, Christopher St German, Lambarde, Coke, and Matthew Hale – though the English were more likely to be content with judgements about the rational or natural character of English law. In the course of time such judgements, invoked and taught in the Inns of Court, came to form not only a legal tradition and a jurisprudence but also an idea of history very different from the reconstructions made by antiquarians – the original 'Whig fallacy', as it were, and politically even more functional, aiming at nothing less than 'cognizance' over the whole legacy of English legal history.[67]

In a sense Coke's achievement was, through his 'theory of custom', to raise legal convention and myth to a political art. What common lawyers created, in effect, was a juridical ideology which reinforced their professional monopoly, authority, and, frequently, political potential –

---

[65] Baldus, comm. on *Digest* 1.1.1; see my 'Civil Science in the Renaissance: Jurisprudence Italian Style', *Historical Journal*, 22 (1979), 777–94, repr. in *History, Law and the Human Sciences* (London, 1984), and now especially Joseph Canning, *The Political Thought of Baldus de Ubaldis* (Cambridge, 1987).

[66] Act of Appeals, 1533 (24 Henry VIII), in Elton (ed.), *The Tudor Constitution* (Cambridge, 1982), p. 53.

[67] Herbert Butterfield later documented his own famous view of *The Whig Interpretation of History* (Cambridge, 1931) in *The Englishman and his History* (Cambridge, 1944). See John W. McKenna, 'How God Became an Englishman', in *Tudor Rule and Revolution*, ed. De Lloyd, J. Guth and J. McKenna (Cambridge, 1982), pp. 25–44.

especially as applied to competing jurisdictions and mentalities and, occasionally, to the sovereign. In civil as well as common law, the rivalry between the makers and the interpreters of law was evident from the beginning; and it established a fundamental, though not always publicly displayed, dialectic of history: *lex* v. *rex*. It was a competition of rival myths: divine right v. immemorial custom, Romanoid kingship v. a Germanic or 'Gothic' Ancient Constitution. As always this rivalry involved a struggle for terminology and over the meaning of such ambiguous terms as 'prerogative', 'liberty', and 'law' itself, and an appropriation of the language of legitimacy. This logomachy, echoing the power struggles of Elizabethan and Stuart England, also defines the primary target of historians of political thought.

The notion of custom was applied by Richard Hooker to the English ecclesiastical tradition in order to establish a national *via media* between the extremes (as he saw them) of popery and Calvinism.[68] Hooker had few ties either with late Elizabethan antiquarian scholarship or with the common law, and his defence of human law rested instead on Biblical and philosophical foundations. In the *Laws of Ecclesiastical Polity*, Hooker's aim was to demonstrate the 'natural character' of Anglican organization, and in this connection he introduced the ancient (Aristotelian) principle that custom constituted a 'second nature' (*usus altera fit natura*), as Fortescue had expressed this conceit and applied it to English institutions.[69] For Hooker, the 'laws made concerning religion, do originally take their essence from the power of the whole realm and church of England'. Like English government more generally, the Anglican church had accumulated its own usages and institutional arrangements in accordance with nature – but in the sense not of universal reason (as in civil law or natural philosophy) but of common sense and the development of English national character within a Christian framework.

Interpreting the past through custom and constitutional antiquarianism is hardly to be distinguished from historical scholarship in Elizabethan England, although the influence of humanist philology is evident in the work of such authors as Lambarde, William Harrison, and

[68] Charles Gray, 'Category Confusion as a Confused Category' (Schochet, II, 221–36), remarking on the very eclectic and sometimes confused character of Hooker's view of the varieties of law, human, natural, and divine. See also J. H. M. Salmon, 'Gallicanism and Anglicanism in the Age of the Counter-Reformation', *Renaissance and Revolt*, pp. 155–88.

[69] Fortescue, *De Laudibus legum Anglie*, ed. S. Chrimes (Cambridge, 1949), p. 16; Hooker, *Of the Laws of Ecclesiastical Polity*, V, p. 6 etc; and see Lawrence Manley, *Convention 1500–1750* (Cambridge, MA, 1980), pp. 90ff. According to Thomas Wilson's *Arte of Rhetorique*, English law was 'grounded wholly upon natural reason'.

Camden. But legal and ecclesiastical controversy remained the primary motive even of great scholars like John Selden, Henry Spelman, and perhaps Harrison and Roger Owen; and erudition remained in the service of ideology.[70] Arguments from reason and 'laws of nature' were available (and frequently used by civilians). Before the seventeenth century, however, polyhistorical learning and legal, Biblical, and classical tradition, tended to prevail in political debate; and demonstrations of antiquity or particular precedents were the basis of disputation, a mode of argumentation reinforced by the increased availability of printed records and sources and the growing practice of co-operative scholarship. Before the age of Hobbes and the fashionable natural-law style of argumentation ('antique-modern' Gierke called it) political theory, following the patterns of theological controversy, depended heavily on quantitative and eclectic erudition and especially on historical interpretation to demonstrate legitimacy.

Political authority

Conceptions of state, or society, and subject, or citizen, were likewise eclectic; and observers of all persuasions and parties shared notions about general political structures and goals. In England, absolutist and imperial ideas of the 'state' were unpopular even with rulers, except in certain circumstances, such as conflicts with the papacy. Though opposed in religion, John Ponet and John Aylmer agreed on the desirability of 'mixed' government, as did Thomas Smith in his *De Republica Anglorum* (1565); and indeed continental scholars often associated this ancient ideal with English government. During the religious wars, some French jurists hoped to revive the estates general, that sadly debilitated counterpart of the English parliament – although in France the idea of 'mixed monarchy' was tainted by association with Huguenot resistance and stigmatized as *'lese majesté'*.[71] Indeed, it was in part to counter this political heresy that Jean Bodin composed his *Republic*, which (whether or not Bodin had contact with Smith) was very influen-

---

[70] See Paul Christianson, 'John Selden, the Five Knights Case, and the Genesis of the Petition of Right', *Criminal Justice History*, 6 (1985), 65–87; the late David Berkowitz's unfinished *Young John Selden* (Cambridge, MA, 1988); also Edith Bershadsky, 'Controlling the Terms of Debate: John Selden and the Tithes Controversy' (Schochet, II, pp. 187–220); William Klein's 'Ruling Thoughts: The World of Sir Roger Owen of Condorer', unpublished PhD dissertation, Johns Hopkins University, 1987; Parry on William Harrison (above, n. 28).

[71] See Michael Mendle, *Dangerous Positions: Mixed Government in the Estates of the Realm and the Making of the Answer to the XIX propositions* (University, ALA, 1985).

tial in England, giving systematic form not only to the king's prerogative but also to the general idea of 'absolute' and 'perpetual' sovereignty.[72]

Celebrations of absolute and divinely instituted monarchy, though often muted, preceded the advent of the Stuarts, as historians are beginning to note; and indeed, as Geoffrey Elton has remarked, 'Figgis studied the divine right of kings ... on its deathbed'.[73] John Jewel and others defended the 'majesty', that is, as Bodin had written, the 'Sovereignty', of the queen against the pretensions of the 'bishop of Rome'; and royalists like Thomas Bilson pressed such arguments for 'supreme power' further. God himself, wrote Bilson, speaks through the laws of the prince, who should be obeyed, he added, 'though they be very wicked'.[74] As George Whetstone wrote in 1586, 'The dignitie Royall, is so great and holy, as kings that are protectors and defenders of human society, imitates the providence of God, whose office & action is to govern al things ... And he himselfe calleth them gods ... [since they] should imitate God, whose lieutenants they are: in their religion, Justice and government'.[75] (The same formula – religion, justice and police – had been used some seventy years before in Claude de Seyssel's celebration of the *Grand Monarchy of France*, which likewise regarded this trinity as a mark of the power and honor as well as the limits of kingship.)

These ideas were reinforced by various ceremonies and symbols employed in the cult centring specifically on that second Virgin, Elizabeth, who had inherited from her father Henry VIII that imperial authority invoked on his behalf and against the Roman church by Cromwell. To illustrate this more personalized worship of 'majesty', Frances Yates points out that in Foxe's *Book of Martyrs*, which is dedicated to Elizabeth, she is represented as enthroned first (in the 1563 edition) within the 'C' of the name of Constantine (the emperor who established imperial primacy over the church) and then (in the 1570

---

[72] Several volumes of Bodiniana have been published since the important collection of Horst Denzer (ed.), *Jean Bodin: Verhandlungen der internationalen Bodin Tagung* (Munich, 1973), with full bibliography.

[73] 'The Divine Right of Kings', *Studies in Tudor and Stuart Politics and Government* (Cambridge, 1974), II, pp. 193–214, commenting on J. N. Figgis, *The Divine Right of Kings* (Cambridge, 1896); also J. P. Sommerville, 'Richard Hooker, Hadrian Saravia, and the Advent of the Divine Right of Kings', *History of Political Theory* (1983), 229–45.

[74] Thomas Bilson, *The True Differences between Christian svbiection and vnchristian rebellion* (Oxford, 1585); *The perpetuall government of Christs Church* [1585] (London, 1610). Cf. *The Works of John Jewel* (Cambridge, 1848), III, p. 75.

[75] *The English Mirror* (London, 1586), p. 201. Cf. Seyssel, *The Monarchy of France*, tr. J. H. Hexter and ed. D. R. Kelley (New Haven, 1981), and also Geoffrey Fenton, *A Form of Christian policy Gathered out of French* [1574] (New York, 1972) [photorepr.]).

edition) in the 'C' of 'Christ'.[76] Elizabeth was also identified with Pandora, Gloriana, Cynthia, Belphoebe, and especially Astrea, who was, among other things, empress of the world, guardian of religion, patroness of peace, and restorer of virtue; and her destiny (it was said) was to bring forth that 'golden age' foretold by Virgil. As John Davies wrote in his eighth hymn to Astrea, all European rulers would be well advised to make a pilgrimage – 'in politique devotion' – to this model ruler to see her 'true beames of maiestie'.

But these images portrayed England from the heights of political power; what of the society governed thereunder? In English political discourse (aside from the technicalities of legal traditions) there were at least three vocabularies, which by the sixteenth century had become intermingled in the extraordinarily hybrid language that English was becoming. One came from the Greek *polis*, another from the Latin *civitas* and *respublica*, and the third from the communality of medieval England; and each of these institutional complexes had its own connotations, associations, and possibilities. 'Politics' invoked the philosophy of Plato, Aristotle, and their commentators; 'civility' the civic tradition of the Roman jurists; and the 'commonwealth' the vernacular discourse of native English society, institutions, and ideals.[77]

Again the contrast with Roman law was striking. Civil lawyers – 'civilians' – interpreted their *ius civile*, as they said, *civiliter* and with *civilitas*; but with common lawyers it was different. For them the words to conjure with – and to impress people with – were not 'civil' or 'civic' but common, and not 'empire' or 'republic' but 'common wealth'.[78] This tendency was reinforced by the vernacularist fashions of the day which preferred English to French or Latinate roots (as in the attempt to substitute 'witcraft', for example, for 'logic'). As John Rastell wrote in his *Expositiones terminorum legum anglorum* (1527), 'a good resonable commyn lawe maketh a gode commyn pease and a comyn welth among a grete commynalte of people'.[79] Whether or not one can distinguish a 'commonwealth party' in Edwardian times, the economic, social, and religious concerns of English statesmen and parliaments gave pride of

[76] Yates, *Astrea: The Imperial Theme in the Sixteenth Century* (London, 1975), pp. 42–3; Roy Strong, *The Cult of Elizabeth: Elizabethan Portraiture and Pageantry* (Wallop, Hampshire, 1977); and David Loades, *The Tudor Court* (Totowa, NJ, 1987).

[77] See Thomas Cooper, *Thesaurus linguae Romanae et Britannicae* (1565).

[78] See G. R. Elton, 'Reform and the "Commonwealth-men" of Edward VI's Reign', *The English Commonwealth 1547–1640*, ed. P. Clark *et al.* (Leicester, 1979), pp. 23–38, and David Starkey, 'Which Age of Reform?' in Christopher Coleman and Starkey (eds.), *Revolution Reassessed* (Oxford, 1986), pp. 13–28; also Donald W. Hanson, *From Kingdom to Commonwealth: The Development of Civil Consciousness in English Political Thought* (Cambridge, MA, 1970).

[79] Rastell, *Expositiones terminorum legum* (London, 1527), 'prohemium'.

place not to 'interest of state' but to the 'common wealth' (not unlike the Huguenots in France, who justified their actions in terms not of policy but of public welfare). Elizabethan notions of royal 'prerogative', too, were associated with such communal language; and in her golden speech, Queen Elizabeth emphasized not just royal authority but also royal duty, social order, and – with a variety of medical metaphors – the common 'health' as well as the common wealth.

On the level of civil society Elizabethan political thought reflected not only class and religious differences but also gender questions, explicitly as well as implicitly. About women in general, published opinions were divided, and stereotypical 'praises' as well as 'dispraises' of women were common after 1540.[80] Prejudice against the public role of women (which for Protestants reached a high point in the polemics directed against Catherine de Médicis and Mary Tudor) were muted in the England of Elizabeth in the wake of the reaction to the ill-timed 'blast' issued by John Knox against the 'monstrous regiment of women'. Nevertheless, the old cliché persisted, that woman, descended from Eve, was the source and locus of vice, while man embodied 'virtue' – a patriarchal and public quality which Thomas Cooper defined as 'strength: puissance: valiantnesse: manliness: power: help, Merite or desart'. To this cliché, however, there was at least marginal dissent, beginning with *The Schoolhouse of Women* published in 1541 and again in 1560, as a reply to Knox. Another work, situated by a modern historian in the canon of feminist thinking, was *Jane Anger, her Protection for Women* (1589), a work of significant political as well as social implications. This defence of feminine qualities cried 'fie on the falsehood of men', with their 'slanderous tongues' and the deceptive rhetoric, which hid their 'unspeakable' desires and ambitions.

But aside from Elizabeth, it was the other half of humanity that dominated the political stage. The political if not the moral centre of the English commonwealth was of course the 'High Court of Parliament', which was the generator of numerous myths, the largest of them the 'Whig view of history' itself. According to Thomas Smith's *De Republica Anglorum*, the Parliament constituted 'the most high and absolute power of the realme of England'; and unlike the estates of France, the

---

[80] Katherine Henderson and Barbara F. Macmanus (eds.), *Half Humankind: Contexts and Texts about Women in England, 1540–1640* (Urbana, 1985); and see also Retha M. Warnicke, *Women of the English Renaissance and Reformation* (Westport, CT, 1983); Constance Jordan, 'Women's Rule in Sixteenth-Century British Political Thought', *Renaissance Quarterly*, 40 (1987), 421–51; Maria L. Cioni, 'The Elizabethan Chancery and Women's Rights', *Tudor Rule and Revolution*, ed. D. Guth and J. McKenna (Cambridge, 1982); and Ralph Houlbrooke, *Church Courts and the People in the English Reformation* (Oxford, 1979).

cortes of Spain, and the diets of the Empire, the English parliament indeed had since the fifteenth century attained a share of sovereignty and 'majesty' – the law-making power in Bodin's definition – in the sense that bills were initiated in Commons or Lords and that statutes were passed, according to formulas established by the fifteenth century, both by the advice and 'by the authority of Parliament'.[81] 'The Parliament abrogateth olde lawes, maketh newe, giveth orders for things past, and for things hereafter to be followed', wrote Smith, adding further privileges which corresponded more or less to the 'marks of sovereignty' later assembled by Bodin for the French monarchy in particular and for his 'Republic' – rendered into English, in Richard Knolles's translation, naturally, as 'Commonwealth' – in general.[82]

Ultimately, of course, the basis of this power was popular consent; and Smith went on to declare that, like the old Roman assemblies, the parliament 'representeth and hath the power of the whole realme both the head and the bodie'. Similarly, John Hooker, in his *Order and Usage* (1572), argued that the 'commons' (in the sense of responsible English-men as a whole) were 'represented' in the assemblies of 'Kings, Commons, and Burgesses', and the English legal tradition itself flowed from this corporate talking ground ('parlement').[83] The privileges and 'liberties' of the parliament, entangled also in the myth of Magna Carta, became identified with those of the people – that is, propertied English-men – in general. In particular, 'freedom of speech' (in a technical sense) became a major Elizabethan issue and contributed to the mythical, and mystical, conception of parliament which revisionist scholars have ignored.[84] It contributed, too, to an even more hotly contested topic, which is the emergence of the modern idea of liberty.

Individual liberty

What of the subject of this political authority – the subject who, at least in the law, had a will no less to be reckoned with that of the sovereign? This history of liberty, unfashionable as it has become in the wake of

---

[81] *De Republica Anglorum*, ed. Mary Dewar (Cambridge, 1982), p. 78; and cf. S. B. Chrimes, *English Constitutional Ideas in the Fifteenth Century* (Cambridge, 1936), pp. 134ff.

[82] As important as, and published prior to Bodin, *The Six Books of a Commonweale* (London, 1606), was Louis Le Roy, *Aristotles Politiques or Discourses of Government*, tr. I. D. (London, 1598).

[83] Vernon Snow, *Parliament in Elizabethan England: John Hooker's Order and Usage* (New Haven, 1977), p. 182.

[84] For the 'revisionist' view, see especially Elton, *The Elizabethan Parliament*, and cf. Michael A. R. Graves, *The Tudor Parliaments* (London, 1985).

revisionist scholarship, has been central to the history of political thought; and (despite revisionist criticism) it has always been associated, however indirectly and inferentially, with parliamentary privilege.[85] From the late sixteenth century, moreover, natural law theory operated to give clarity, sharpness, and (arguably) generality to these ideas. Before Hobbes, however, it was probably in the economic arena that the modern concept of liberty received most precise definition, and in particular in the debate over the monopolies created by royal grant. To many late-sixteenth-century Englishmen, these monopolies represented a tyranny of private interest and a restraint on free trade, and they had violated 'the General Liberties of the Subjects'. In this sense, liberty shifted from a heterogeneous 'positive' to a general 'negative' signification, suggesting liberation from what some called the 'bondage' of monopolies, and opened up an early stage of the career of modern liberalism.

'The dispute [over monopolies] draws two great things in question', declared Robert Cecil. 'First, the prince's power. Secondly, the freedom of Englishmen.'[86] As monopolies, while embodying the 'liberties' of a few, threatened the 'liberties' of many, so they tested and also confused the royal meanings of duty and authority. Under Elizabeth, assertions of royal prerogative were muted, or seldom heard over the talk of duty and the public interest, and for that reason there were few to question its limits. Precisely on the question of monopolies the dialectic of liberty and prerogative was expressed in 1601 in this way by Bacon: 'The Queen, as she is our sovereign, hath both an enlarging and a restraining power. For by her prerogative she may first set at liberty things restrained by statute law or otherwise; and secondly by her prerogative she may restrain things that be at liberty ... I say and say again that we ought not to deal, to judge, or to meddle, with her majesty's prerogative.'[87] But the potential conflict would soon be made manifest by the attitudes and actions of a ruler with a very different

---

[85] A comprehensive study of the question has been launched by J. H. Hexter in a series entitled 'The Making of Modern Freedom', which begins with J. H. Hexter (ed.), *Parliament and Liberty: From the Reign of Elizabeth to the English Civil War* (Stanford, 1992). See also Hexter's 'Power Struggle, Parliament, and Liberty in Early Modern England', *Journal of Modern History*, 50 (1978), 1–50, and 'The Early Stuarts and Parliament: Old Hat and *Nouvelle Vague*', *Parliamentary History*, 1 (1983), 181–215.

[86] David Harris Sacks, 'Private Profit and Public Good: The Problem of the State in Elizabethan Theory and Practice' (Schochet, II, pp. 121–42). On the general background, see also Margaret Judson, *The Crisis of the Constitution* (New Brunswick, 1949), and Corinne Comstock Weston, *English Constitutional Theory and the House of Lords, 1556–1832* (New York, 1965).

[87] D'Ewes reporting on Bacon, 20 Nov. 1601, in Elton, *The Tudor Constitution*, p. 25.

political upbringing, style, and destiny – and a very different impact on political thought.

The most eclectic and ecumenical view was that expressed by Richard Hooker, who was moved to give every part of the 'body politic' its due, especially for the sake of harmony and stability. 'Without order there is no living in public society', Hooker wrote, 'because the want thereof is the mother of confusion, whereupon division of necessity followeth; and out of division destruction.'[88] Thus, he defended the 'sweet form of kingly government' against the claims both of pope and of national clergy. For Hooker, the king was under but not subject to the law; he enjoyed his prerogative, but his law-making power was assumed only in parliament. In defending English tradition, Hooker drew also on the precedents and values of Roman laws – including not only ideas of divine right but also the quasi-legendary *lex regia* asserting the popular origin of imperial authority – which had given ancient emperors such as Constantine control over their church. But it was not Hooker's nature to push arguments to an extreme, and the fanaticism of fundamentalists was abhorrent to him. 'Howbeit, too rigorous it were', as he concluded in his *Laws of Ecclesiastical Polity*, 'that the breach of every human law should be a deadly sin: a mean there is between these extremities, if so be we can find it.' In the perspective of the next century such complacent wisdom seems far from prophetic.

Conclusion

By the end of Elizabeth's reign political discourse was carried on in a Babel of tongues, in an ideological pandemonium, which historians are still trying to sort out and link somehow to the course of events. The semantic confusion noted earlier had increased with the urgency and sharpening of issues, economic and social as well as religious and political, with the accession of James Stuart; and the meanings in question were 'real' as well as verbal. Liberty implied the free employment of 'will', and the debates over this ancient ideal turned indeed on the poles of royal prerogative and individual rights; and property, rendered by the Latin term *dominium*, was torn between royal 'dominion' and individual proprietorship. So it was, too, in the literary arena, where human creations were (in Stephen Greenblatt's words) the

[88] *Lawes of Ecclesiastical Polity*, III, 331 (7.2); IV, 401 (8–2). See especially W. Speed Hill, *Studies in Richard Hooker* (Cleveland, 1972); Olivier Loyer, *L'Anglicanisme de Richard Hooker* (Lille, 1979); Robert K. Faulkner, *Richard Hooker and the Polity of a Christian England* (Berkeley, 1981); and Peter Munz, *The Place of Hooker in the History of Thought* (London, 1952).

product of 'collective negotiation' and 'exchange' as well as conflict – and which likewise reflected the feeling of 'all coherence gone'.[89] Above all, the tensions were expressed as different and divergent perspectives on English, and European, history, which – in the works of Selden, Spelman, and their like – remained the principal mode of the legitimation and communication of English ideals.[90]

Although the hard lines of party politics were not drawn until the Stuart period, most of the fundamental questions of the religious, social, and political predicaments of early modern Britain had been explored; and most of the essential concepts of modern political thinking – religious liberty and political obedience, absolute sovereignty and constitutional government, customary rights and natural law – had been vigorously debated and voluminously documented. Confusions and aporias remained – the terms and concepts of 'law, right, authority, liberty, and power' still being, deliberately or not, equivocal and interchangeable. None the less, under Elizabeth, while the full depths of political division and national tragedy were yet to be faced, the extremes of political life had been glimpsed and touched on by particular groups, and words had been found to express these problems and paradoxes.

[89] Greenblatt, *Shakespearean Negotiations* (Berkeley, 1988). It is impossible here to do more than suggest the important contributions made by the self-styled 'new historicism' to political thought; but see Kevin Sharpe and Stephen Zwicker (eds.), *Politics of Discourse* (Berkeley, 1987); and the discussions by Jean Howard, 'The New Historicism in Renaissance Studies', *English Literary Renaissance*, 16 (1986), 5–12, also in A. Kinney and D. Collins, *Renaissance Historicism* (Amherst, 1987); James Holstun, 'Ranting at the New Historicism', *English Literary Renaissance*, 19 (1989), 189–225; the entire issue of *New Literary History*, 21 (1990), 'New Historicism, New Histories, and Others'; and the reviews by David Harris Sacks in *Journal of British Studies*, 26 (1987), Kevin Sharpe in *History*, 71 (1986), 235–47, and Jonathan Goldberg *English Literary History*, 49 (1982), 514–42.

[90] A large subject, but see now D. R. Woolf, *The Idea of History in Early Stuart England* (Toronto, 1990).

3   Kingship, counsel and law in early Stuart Britain

Linda Levy Peck

When Queen Elizabeth I died on 24 March 1603, her secretary of state, Sir Robert Cecil, devised a makeshift great council to proclaim James VI of Scotland King of England. Made up of the now defunct Elizabethan privy council and three noblemen on hand in London, this unlikely body issued the first political text of the new reign.[1] Claiming to speak in the name of the lords temporal and spiritual, the privy councillors, the principal gentlemen of the kingdom, the lord mayor, aldermen and citizens of London, and the commons of the realm, the proclamation declared that James 'by law, lineal succession, and undoubted right is now become the only sovereign lord and king of these imperial crowns'.[2]

Cecil drafted the proclamation of the first foreign monarch since William the Conqueror before the queen's death and, in secret correspondence with King James, secured approval 'for musicke that soneth so sueitely' before it was issued.[3] The prudence of crafting such a text was made plain by the actions of Henry Percy, the earl of Northumberland, who, along with Lord Cobham and Lord Thomas Howard, was asked to take part in privy council deliberations. While Northumberland had agreed to support the Scottish king's title, he appeared with a retinue of 100 men, challenged the privy councillors whose authority had lapsed with the queen's death and asserted the privileges of the old nobility.[4] Cecil plastered over the crack in authority and soothed noble

I am grateful to John Pocock, John Guy and Lois Schwoerer for their very helpful comments on earlier drafts of this essay.

[1] Samuel Rawson Gardiner, *A History of England, 1603–1640* (10 vols; London, 1884), I, pp. 85–6. 'The Councell of state and nobility caused at one instance the Queen's death and the King's proclamation of his infallible right to be ... published'. John Hawarde, *Les Reportes del Cases in Camera Stellata, 1593–1609* (London, 1894), p. 179.

[2] STC 8297, 24 March, 1603. *Stuart Royal Proclamations*, eds. James F. Larkin and Paul L. Hughes (2 vols., Oxford, 1973), I, pp. 1–4.

[3] Hatfield House, Salisbury Mss. 99/43. John Bruce (ed.), *Correspondence of King James VI of Scotland with Sir Robert Cecil and Others*, Camden Society, o.s. 78 (1861), p. 47.

[4] Bruce (ed.), *Correspondence of King James VI of Scotland with Sir Robert Cecil and Others in England*, pp. 1, 55, 74–5.

sensibilities by casting James' accession in the language of legitimacy and history. The proclamation thus avoided the language of conquest, describing instead James' inheritance of the crown by descent from Margaret, daughter of the founder of the Tudor dynasty, Henry VII.

Nevertheless, the proclamation of the new king spoke with other voices too. A great council, however hastily constituted, suggested the language of baronial homage, fealty and, implicitly, revolt, for according to feudal law a vassal might withdraw his allegiance from a lord who did not protect his rights. Medieval texts issued in the name of the community of the realm such as the Provisions of Oxford of 1258 and the Ordinances of 1311 had called on English kings to live by the law. Such baronial language was repeatedly invoked in thirteenth-, fourteenth- and fifteenth-century England to limit royal power and to remove five monarchs.

Finally, the language of law and history on which the proclamation relied formed part of the discourse of the 'ancient constitution', and articulated both the powers of the king and the privileges claimed by parliament. The ritual of accession and coronation thus framed the complex relationship of kingship and law. In addition, it posed the question of counsel. Who were to be the king's advisors? His councillors, his nobility, his clergy, his judges, his parliament?

In his coronation on 25 July 1603, King James continued to stress his house's continuity with the Tudors by using the traditional ceremonial, the *Liber Regalis*, as had every English monarch since 1307, while making a few changes in the service.[5] Reassuring his Protestant sub-jects, he took communion in both kinds. Most important, the monarch, who had sought to anglicize the Scots language, had the service translated from Latin into English.[6] But this political act, designed to win support, had unexpected long-term political consequences.

It was customary for English monarchs to take a coronation oath swearing to keep the peace of the church, to see that justice was done and to maintain the law. The Latin oath had been ambiguous as to the origin of these laws: the phrase *quas vulgus elegerit* might mean either the laws that the people 'shall choose' or those they 'have chosen', suggesting perhaps the role of parliament in creating law. The new English translation adopted by James I referred to 'the laws the people have',

---

[5] *Liber Regalis*, Roxburgh Club (London, 1870); the fourteenth century manuscript was annotated over the centuries with marginal notes in the hands, among others, of William Cecil, Lord Burghley, and Archbishop William Sancroft.

[6] John Wickham Legg, *The Coronation Order of King James I* (London, 1902), pp. 35, 40, 41.

omitting any reference to their role in making law.[7] Secondly, the electoral element in the service, the point at which the people had traditionally been asked if they agreed to the king's election, may have been dropped, and the king simply presented to shouts of 'God Save the King'. This was certainly the case at Charles I's coronation. Thirdly, the king's promise to uphold the laws was embellished in English, as it had not been in Latin, to include a reference to the royal prerogative.[8]

These changes in language were to become crucial in English political debate. To begin with, the notion embedded in the coronation oath that the king, instituted by God, was the protector of law and judgements, was at least as old as tenth-century Anglo-Saxon texts. But how should the king's oath be construed? Sir John Fortescue had argued in the middle of the fifteenth century that in taking the coronation oath the English monarch bound himself before God to observe the law. As King of Scots, James had claimed that such an oath was not a contract between king and subjects but a promise to God. Even if it were a contract, according to the civil law neither party to the contract could judge if it had been abrogated; only God could judge if the promise had been broken.[9] Finally, James argued, only the king could judge which laws were 'lowable'.

Moreover, references to the 'imperial crowns' in the accession proclamation provided no definition of the relationship between the two kingdoms of which James was now singular head or of his relationship to the laws of either. Within two months James proclaimed his intention to secure the Union of England and Scotland through parliamentary enactment. His plan for the union was clear: his imperial crowns did not mean one king ruling over separate realms, but rather a unified kingdom. Until the king with the advice of parliament could establish the Union, he commanded his subjects to hold 'the two realms as presently united, and as one realm and kingdom, and the subjects of both the realms as one people, brethren and members of one body'.[10] Celebrating his accession, his first coin declared him Emperor of Britain.[11]

Two different models of early Stuart political thought have been

[7] Robert S. Hoyt, 'The Coronation Oath of 1308', *English Historical Review*, 71 (1956), 353–83.

[8] Percy Schramm, *A History of the English Coronation* (Oxford, 1937), pp. 99–100; F. G. W. Legg, *English Coronation Records* (Westminster, 1901), pp. 240–1, prints Henry VIII's own revision of the oath but there is no evidence that it was ever used. He stated that the oath's promises were 'not prejudicial to his Crown or imperial jurisdiction'.

[9] James I, *The Trew Law of Free Monarchies* in *The Political Works of James I*, ed. C. H. McIlwain (New York, 1965), p. 68. James asserted that 'this oath in the coronation is the clearest, civil and fundamental law, whereby the king's office is properly defined', p. 55.

[10] *Stuart Royal Proclamations*, eds. Larkin and Hughes, I, pp. 18–19, 19 May 1603.

[11] B.M. Department of Coins and Medals, James I, 1603–1625, no. 1.

offered recently. On the one hand, J. P. Kenyon, Conrad Russell and others argue that amongst the English political elite 'everyone spoke the same language'.[12] Everyone agreed that government was instituted by God, all claimed to proceed by the rule of law, all appealed for legitimacy to the ancient constitution. In a society based on consensus it was not possible, some have argued, for a different political theory to exist.[13] On the other hand, Johann Sommerville finds three divergent and competing theories of the origin and the powers of government in the early seventeenth century which he denotes as royal absolutism, the ancient constitution and social contract.[14]

Neither model is wholly satisfactory because the first overlooks nuance in the search for consensus while the second imposes rigid categories on what was a fluid political discourse. Instead, we have much to learn from analyzing the choices contemporaries made from the different vocabularies of political discourse available to them. Otherwise, we are at a loss to explain how it was possible for those who believed in the divine right of kings – nearly everyone – and those who believed in the rule of law – nearly everyone – to articulate why, legitimately, they could kill each other and, ultimately, the king.

If it is anachronistic to ascribe absolutism to the Stuart monarchy in the 1620s, neither can we read back to that time the more moderate attitudes of parliamentarians of the Long Parliament who, sometimes with reluctance, supported the crown when the need to choose between king and parliament was thrust upon them. Moreover, in his Answer to the Nineteen Propositions in 1642, Charles I and members of parliament who supported him crafted a political language carefully based on the ancient constitution and the rule of law in which limitations on the power of every estate were recognized and in which the king took for himself the position of protector of the law against the illegal actions of the House of Commons and the Lords. But that was not the dominant, that is, the most widely circulated, description of the powers of the early Stuart monarchy. This essay examines the language in which the crown claimed authority in the early seventeenth century and the challenge articulated by some of its subjects.[15]

---

[12] J. P. Kenyon (ed.), *The Stuart Constitution* (Cambridge, 1966), p. 10.
[13] See, for example, Mark Kishlansky, *Parliamentary Selection* (Cambridge, 1986); Kevin Sharpe (ed.), *Faction and Parliament* (Oxford, 1978).
[14] J. P. Sommerville, *Politics and Ideology in Early Stuart England* (London, 1987).
[15] For recent approaches to the study of political thought, see J. G. A. Pocock, 'Texts as Events', in *Politics of Discourse*, ed. Kevin Sharpe and Stephen Zwicker (Los Angeles, 1988), pp. 21–34; Roger Chartier, *Cultural History: Between Practices and Representations*, trans. Lydia G. Cochrane (Ithaca, NY, 1988); Sean Wilentz, *Rites of Power* (Philadelphia, 1985); Clifford Geertz, *The Interpretation of Cultures* (New York, 1973); Quentin Skinner, 'Meaning and Understanding in the History of Ideas', *History and Theory*, 8 (1969), pp. 3–53.

I

As king of Scotland, James VI wrote two notable books on the nature of kingship, *The Trew Law of Free Monarchies* and *Basilikon Doron*. Later, as King of England, he participated in a long quarrel in print over the nature of kingship and obedience with Catholic controversialists such as Cardinal Robert Bellarmine, Jacob Gretser and others. In speeches to parliament and to the judges, James laid out his own views of the power of kings and the duties of subjects.[16] He promoted a clerical hierarchy to propagate his views both at home at abroad whose influence continued to shape theory and practice in the Caroline period.[17]

The religious controversies of sixteenth-century Europe provided the theoretical context of the *Trew Law* written in 1598. Catholics, Lutherans and Calvinists developed theories of resistance to secular authority in the aftermath of the Reformation to argue that while the church was instituted by God, secular government arose out of the state of nature. Therefore, a heretical king could be deposed.[18] In response to such arguments contemporary French theorists, especially Jean Bodin, shaped the notion of sovereignty.

In Scotland, the Calvinist George Buchanan posited in *The Right of the Kingdom in Scotland* that in the state of nature 'the whole body of the people' came together to create a political society based on a covenant that they made with the ruler they designated. Bolstering his argument from natural law theory with Boece's fictional forty early Scottish kings, Buchanan argued that the ruler was not a sovereign but rather an administrator. The people 'prescribe to their king the form of his *Imperium*' to ensure that 'he acts like a guardian of the public accounts'.[19] Described by Quentin Skinner as 'the most radical of all

---

[16] For recent and differing views on James VI and I's political thought, see Jenny Wormald, 'James VI and I, *Basilikon Doron* and *The Trew Law of Free Monarchies*'; Johann Sommerville, 'James I and the Divine Right of Kings: English Policy and Continental Theory'; and Paul Christianson, 'Royal and Parliamentary Voices on the Ancient Constitution, *c.* 1604–1621', in *The Mental World of the Jacobean Court*, ed. Linda Levy Peck (Cambridge, 1991), pp. 36–95.

[17] Kenneth Fincham, *Prelate as Pastor: The Episcopate of James I* (Oxford, 1990); Peter Lake and Kenneth Fincham, 'The Ecclesiastical Policy of King James I', *Journal of British Studies*, 25 (1985), 169–207. Nicholas Tyacke, *Anti-Calvinists: The Rise of English Arminianism* (Oxford, 1987).

[18] Sommerville, *Politics and Ideology in Early Seventeenth Century England*, pp. 35; *passim*; Sommerville, 'Richard Hooker, Hadrian Saravia, and the Advent of the Divine Right of Kings', *History of Political Thought*, 4 (1983), 229–245; Richard Tuck, *Natural Law Theories* (Cambridge, 1979).

[19] Quoted in Quentin Skinner, *The Foundations of Modern Political Thought*, 2 vols. (Cambridge, 1978), II, p. 342.

the Calvinist revolutionaries', Buchanan argued that 'whatever rights the populace may have granted to anyone, they can with equal justice rescind'. This right inhered in 'every individual citizen'. Because Buchanan was James VI's tutor, the king was thoroughly familiar with resistance theory, which he hated and sought to counter.[20]

The immediate political context in which James wrote also marked the young king's assertion of power over the kirk and over aristocratic factions, which together had overpowered his mother Mary, Queen of Scots. Moreover, in 1594 the Catholic writer, Robert Parsons, argued in his *Conference about the Next Succession to the Crown of England* that, as a heretic, James VI of Scotland could not succeed Elizabeth and that the right of succession belonged to the Spanish Infanta. James' *The Trew Law of Free Monarchies* responded to both secular and religious rebellion, to seditious preachers in Scotland and on the continent.

James clearly defined his vision of the godly prince responsible to God for the welfare of both church and state, claimed the inalienable right of kings to rule and denied the right of resistance. 'Kings are called Gods by the prophetical King David, because they sit upon God his throne in the earth, and have the count of their administration to give unto him.' According to both patriarchal and corporeal analogies, the king was father of his people and the head of the body politic, his duty 'the virtuous government of his children'. James argued that nothing could free subjects from their allegiance; their birthright was not inalienable rights but unquestioning obedience to the king.[21]

The Stuarts were kings of Britain *de jure* not *de facto*. Drawing on natural law and history, James argued that the British polity was created by conquest even though his own succession was based on legitimacy. The allegiance owed to the king grew out of 'the first manner of establishing the laws and form of government among us'. Although 'those that pride themselves to be the scourges of Tyrants' (perhaps a dig at Buchanan) claimed that some societies elected their kings, 'our Kingdom and divers other Monarchies are not in that case, but had their beginning in a far contrary fashion'.

By his conquest of Scotland, King Fergus, who came from Ireland, 'a

---

[20] On resistance theory, see Skinner, *Foundations of Modern Political Thought*, II, pp. 302–48.

[21] '[N]o objection either of heresie, or whatsoever private statute or law may free the people from their oath-giving to their king, and his succession, established by the old fundamentall laws of the kingdome ... he is their heritable over-lord, and so by birth, not by any right in the coronation, commeth to his crown ...' (James I, *Trew Law*, in *Political Works*, ed. McIlwain, p. 69).

wise king coming in among barbares', established 'the estate and forme of gouvernement'. Kings in Scotland were 'before any estates . . . before any Parliaments were holden, or laws made: and by them was the land distributed (which at first was whole theirs) . . . and forms of government devised and established: And so it follows of necessity, that the kings were the authors and makers of the laws, and not the laws of the kings.'[22]

Because 'the health of the commonwealth' had to be his guide the king had the right to mitigate and suspend parliamentary statute. James put it in brief: 'a good king will frame all his actions to be according to the Law; yet is he not bound thereto but of his good will, and for example-giving to his subjects'.[23] James did not deny that there could be wicked princes, but their punishment must be left to God who might raise up a scourge against them.

England too was a free monarchy. William the Conqueror 'gave the law and took none, changed the Laws, inverted the order of government, set down the strangers his followers in many of the old possessors rooms'. Language denoted political power: James declared of the English that 'their old Laws, which to this day they are fueled by, are written in his language, and not in theirs. And yet his successors have with great happiness enjoyed the Crown to this day'.[24] Thus kings of England and Scotland were not only the original authors of the laws but the framers of government and owners of all property in their kingdoms.

Historians disagree on whether James had intended his writings to remain private. In *The Trew Law of Free Monarchies*, published in 1598, James wrote 'my intention is to instruct' and self-consciously committed his message to print. When first published anonymously in 1599, *Basilikon Doron* was printed not in Scots but in English. Yet James had only seven copies printed which he gave to leading officials.[25] Whatever the King's original intentions, as Elizabeth was dying in 1603, London and Edinburgh printers rushed to get out copies of the book. James himself prepared a copy for the press because, he claimed, false copies were circulating.[26] 'I know the greatest part of the people of this whole Isle, have been very curious for a sight thereof . . . since books are vive

---

[22] James I, *Trew Law*, in *Political Works*, ed. McIlwain, p. 62. See also Arthur Williamson, *Scottish National Consciousness in the Age of James VI* (Edinburgh, 1979).
[23] James I, *Trew Law*, in *Political Works*, ed. McIlwain, p. 69.
[24] *Ibid.*, p. 63.
[25] *Ibid.*, p. 53; Craigie, *The Basilikon Doron of James I*; Jenny Wormald, 'James VI and I, *Basilikon Doron* and *The Trew Law of Free Monarchies*: The Scottish Context and the English Translation', in *The Mental World of the Jacobean Court*, ed. Peck, pp. 36–54.
[26] James I, *Basilikon Doron*, in *Political Works*, ed. McIlwain, p. 11.

Ideas of the authors.'[27] Peter Blayney argues that printers in London turned out 10,000 copies in three weeks.[28] The English quickly knew the political thought of their new monarch at first hand.

James' political texts generate different readings because he intentionally created a tension between theory and practice. He emphasized the difference between good kings and tyrants and between the origin of kingship and the behaviour of kings in settled kingdoms who acted according to their law.[29] This tension was played out when the king confronted new political problems in England, where he encountered a different tradition of political theory, law, and parliamentary procedure.

II

In 1606, after the discovery of the Gunpowder Plot, the crown crafted an oath of allegiance that spoke directly to contemporary Catholic resistance theory. The oath taker had to 'sweare that I doe from my heart abhorre, detest and abiure as impious and Hereticall, this damnable doctrine and position: That Princes which be excommunicated or deprived by the Pope, may be deposed or murthered by their Subjects or any other whatsoever'.[30] James dedicated his treatise in support of this oath to the Emperor Rudolf and to all the kings of Europe in the name of their common interest.[31]

In the same year, Convocation drafted and passed canons upholding royal power. Canon II denied the Aristotelian and Ciceronian explanations of the origin of political power in the state of nature adopted by Catholic and Protestant resistance theorists; any claim that 'civil power, jurisdiction, and authority, was first derived from the people ... is originally still in them, or else is deduced by their consents ... and is not God's ordinance originally descending from Him' was a great error.[32]

Yet a collision between doctrine and statecraft led James to suppress

[27] *Ibid.*, p. 9.
[28] Peter Blayney, 'The Printing History of *Basilikon Doron*', paper presented to Folger seminar, 'Kings, Courtiers and Judges: Political Thought in Early Stuart England', Folger Center for the History of British Political Thought, February, 1988. *Basilikon Doron* was published in French in 1603 and a Spanish translation exists in manuscript. Craigie, *Basilikon Doron*, II, p. 63.
[29] See Paul Christianson, 'Royal and Parliamentary Voices on the Ancient Constitution, *c.* 1604–1621', in *The Mental World of the Jacobean Court*, ed. Peck, pp. 71–95.
[30] James I, *Triplici Nodo, Triplex Cuneus. Or An Apologie for the Oath of Allegiance* in *Political Works*, ed. McIlwain, p. 74.
[31] I am grateful to Lenore Thomas for this point.
[32] *The Convocation Book of MDCVI commonly called Bishop Overall's Convocation Book concerning the Government of God's Catholic Church and the Kingdoms of the Whole World* (Oxford, 1844), p. 3.

these canons. In their zeal to condemn rebellion, Convocation had also denounced invasions by 'bordering kings', and revolt against a *de facto* ruler, even one whose own rule had originated in rebellion. James' legitimist views recoiled. He reminded them first that he was 'the next heir ... the crown is mine by all rights but that of conquest'. Secondly he had invited them to justify his support for the Dutch in their rebellion against the king of Spain, which he admitted to be a difficult position.

[T]he honour of the nation will not suffer the Hollanders to be abandoned, especially after so much money and men spent in their quarrel. Therefore I was of the mind to call my clergy together, to satisfy, not so much me, as the world about us, of the justice of my owning the Hollanders at this time ... you force me to say I wish I had not.

Convocation had misread James' political message and 'dipped too deep into what all kings reserve among the *arcana imperii*'.[33] He acted similarly when John Cowell, Regius Professor of Civil Law and Master of Trinity Hall at Cambridge, published *The Interpreter*, a legal dictionary, in 1607[34], and it was attacked in the parliamentary session of 1610. Cowell reflected James' own views when he wrote that there was no aspect of regality 'that belonged to the most absolute Prince in the world which doth not also belong to our King'. In time of war, the king 'useth aboslute power, in that his word goeth for law'.[35] The 'prince of his absolute power might make law of himself', but chose to accept the consent of the Lords and Commons in parliament to enhance the law's effectiveness. Cowell like other civil lawyers easily altered the meaning of sovereignty from 'autonomous', i.e. free from outside interference, to 'legally unrestricted'.[36] Although Cowell had enjoyed the king's patronage, James agreed to suppress the book. The reason was clear: Robert Cecil was in the midst of unsuccessfully negotiating the Great Contract and the privy council sought to soothe the House of Commons. In silencing Cowell for practical political reasons, and later in obliging John Selden to apologize for offending the clergy by his *Historie of Tithes* in 1618, James maintained his right to control the language in which his

---

[33] *The Convocation Book of MDCVI*, p. 51, VI–IX. 'Mr Solicitor [Sir Francis Bacon] has sufficiently expressed my own thoughts concerning the nature of kingship in general, ... and I believe you were all of his opinion.'

[34] Brian Levack, *The Civil Lawyers* (Oxford, 1973), pp. 52, 221.

[35] Quoted in *ibid.*, pp. 97, 101.

[36] *Ibid.*, pp. 97, 103–106. S. B. Chrimes, 'The Constitutional Ideas of Dr John Cowell', *English Historical Review*, 44 (1949), 461–87. James Daly, 'The Idea of Absolute Monarchy in Seventeenth Century England', *Historical Journal*, 21 (1978), 227–50.

subjects discussed not only *arcana imperii* and the extent of royal power, but other matters of controversy in church and state.[37]

King James' Bible, the major publishing event of his reign, was designed to shape the vocabulary of contemporary political and ecclesiastical discourse. Although Archbishop Bancroft worried that there 'would be no end of translating', the king, responding to a request made at the Hampton Court Conference, vigorously backed the project and ensured that the leading scholars in Hebrew and Greek would be involved.

His Majesty wished that some especial pains should be taken . . . for one uniform translation (professing that he could never, yet, see a bible well translated in English; but the worst of all, his Majesty thought the Geneva to be) . . . no marginal notes should be added, having found in them which are annexed to the Geneva translations . . . some notes very partial, untrue, seditious, and savouring too much of dangerous and traitorous conceits.[38]

The King James version, undertaken by six teams of scholars working at London, Oxford and Cambridge, operated under fifteen rules devised by the king and his episcopacy. These required 'the old ecclesiastical words to be kept, viz. the word church not to be translated congregation' and 'no marginal notes at all to be affixed, but only for the explanation of the Hebrew or Greek words which cannot . . . briefly and fitly be expressed in the text'.[39] Such rules distinguished the King James version from the Geneva Bible, whose notes, some by Calvin, focused on

---

[37] See John Cowell, *The Interpreter* (Cambridge, 1607); Elizabeth Read Foster, *Proceedings in Parliament*, 2 vols. (New Haven, 1966), I, pp.185–9; Levack, *The Civil Lawyers*, pp. 4, 97–106. On Selden, see Edith Bershadsky, 'Controlling the Terms of Debate: John Selden and the Tithes Controversy', in Gordon J. Schochet (ed.), *Law, Literature and the Settlement of Regimes* (Proceedings of the Folger Institute Center for the History of British Political Thought, II), p. 27 (Washington, DC, The Folger Shakespeare Library, 1990), pp. 187–220.

[38] Quoted in Ward Allen (ed.), *Translating for King James* (Kingsport, 1969), p. 4 and B. F. Westcott, *A General History of The English Bible*, 3rd ed. rev. by W. A. Wright (London, 1905), pp. 108–9. See William Barlow, *The Summe and Substance of the Conference* (London, 1604). The English church in 1408 had declared it heretical for one to 'translate on his own authority any text of holy scripture in the English tongue'. The Rhemes-Douay Catholic translation of the Bible attacked Protestant 'liberty in translating'. *The Cambridge History of the Bible*, ed. S. L. Greenslade (Cambridge, 1963), III, p. 162. Alfred W. Pollard, *Records of the English Bible* (Oxford, 1911); quoted in A. S. Herbert, *Historical Catalogue of Printed Editions of the English Bible, 1525–1961* (London, 1968), p. xxix. *The Cambridge History of the Bible*, ed. Greenslade, III, pp. 158–64. Archbishop William Laud was accused of trying to prevent the introduction of Geneva Bibles printed abroad. In August 1645, parliament prohibited the sale of imported Bibles until sanctioned by the Assembly of Divines. Herbert, *Historical Catalogue of Printed Editions of the English Bible, 1525–1961*, p. 182. Westcott, *A General View of the History of the English Bible*, pp. 120–1.

[39] Alfred W. Pollard, *Records of the English Bible* (Oxford, 1911), pp. lxii–lxiii and 37–64. One rule stated: 'His Majesty is very careful in this point', pp. 53–54.

justification by faith alone, frequently attacked the papacy and, in general, provided extensive commentary on the Biblical text.

This was not an attempt to suppress the Geneva Bible but to supplant it with a version that announced its authority not only by royal command but by ostensibly eschewing Reformation controversies.[40] The preface claimed to have 'on the one side avoided the scrupulositie of the Puritans, who leave the old Ecclesiastical words, and betake them to other, as when they put washing for baptism, and congregation instead of church; as also on the other side we have shunned the obscurity of the papists, in their azimes, tunike, rathional, holocausts, praepuce, pasche and a number of such like, whereof their late translation is full'.[41]

The importance of omitting the marginalia can be seen in two examples that James had used in *The Trew Law*. James had insisted that the language of 1 Samuel supported the absolute authority of kings. The marginal note to 1 Samuel 11 in the Geneva Bible stated emphatically 'Not that kings have this authority by their office, but such as reign in God's wrath should usurp this over their brethren contrary to the law'. Similarly the marginal note to Jeremiah 29 argued that 'The Prophet speaketh not this for the affection that he bare to the tyrant, but that . . . they might with more patience and less grief wait for the time of their deliverance which God had appointed . . . when these tyrants should be destroyed'. In sum, the Geneva marginalia undermined the scriptural examples James relied on to define kingship.

Originally published in folio, the Authorized Version was published in octavo and quarto the next year. But the Geneva Bible continued in private use and had 140 editions up to 1644. Even as King James promoted anti-Calvinists to bishoprics, the King's Printer, Robert Barker, who had the patent to print both Bibles, published them side by side throughout the period.[42] The preface to the King James version emphasized the power of the godly prince with references to Constantine, Justinian, David and Solomon. To this the translators joined language more often found in parliamentary debate, as in the Apology of

[40] Despite his harsh words, the Geneva Bible had been cited by King James in his theoretical works, used by Miles Smith in his preface to the Authorized Version, and cited in sermons by Lancelot Andrewes and even by Archbishop Laud. See *The Cambridge History of The Bible*, ed. Greenslade, III, pp. 168, 168n.

[41] *STC* 2216.

[42] The John Rylands Library, Manchester, *Catalogue of an Exhibition Illustrating the History of the Transmission of the Bible* (Manchester, 1935). An Irish New Testament was published in 1602 and The Book of Common Prayer was printed in Irish in 1608–1609. The Bible and Book of Common Prayer were translated into Welsh by 1588 and its text made consistent with the Authorized Version in 1630. There was no translation of the Bible into Scottish Gaelic until 1767. *The Cambridge History of the Bible*, ed. S. L. Greenslade, III; P. M. Handover, *Printing in London* (1960), ch. 3.

1604, than in royal propaganda. Recognizing that the translation might encounter resistance, the authors admitted 'he that meddleth with men's Religion in any part, meddleth with their custom, nay with their freehold'.[43] The English claimed their most important liberties, whether parliamentary privilege or religious belief, in the language of the common law, the language of land tenure, which was to become the language of property.

III

Indeed, the king's power over his subjects' property was a critical issue in early modern political thought. James argued in *The Trew Law* that all his subjects held their lands from the king as their overlord. By conquest, Fergus became the owner of the universal fee of Scotland and William the Conqueror of England. But how was the king to use this universal fee, a feudal term meaning ownership divided between lord and vassal, which Fortescue had argued the king held in trust for his people? The answer differed in James' several kingdoms.

J. G. A. Pocock's *The Ancient Constitution and The Feudal Law* contended that the dominant political language in early Stuart England was that of the ancient constitution.[44] More recently, Glenn Burgess has argued that 'the Englishmen of the early seventeenth century were typically, if to varying degrees, possessors of common-law minds'. He suggests that James I himself admitted that his power was controlled by the English common law, that his absolute power was only interstitial, filling the cracks, as it were, of the edifice of the common law.[45] However, this formulation may overstate James I's 'common-law mind' if not his practice.

Moreover, the common law mind was only one influence on British political thought, albeit an important one. The English political elite were not as insular as sometimes supposed.[46] John Selden and Sir John Davies, leading common lawyers, were fully familiar with natural law

---

[43] Quoted in Pollard, *Records*, pp. 342–5.

[44] J. G. A. Pocock, *The Ancient Constitution and the Feudal Law, A Reissue with a Retrospect*, 2nd edn (Cambridge, 1988).

[45] Glenn Burgess, 'Common Law and Political Theory in Early Stuart England', *Political Science*, 40 (July, 1988), 4–17; *The Politics of the Ancient Constitution, passim*.

[46] Education at Oxford and Cambridge continued the humanist agenda, the English eagerly received news and information from abroad and, despite the focus on the English book trade, sixteenth-century English libraries were made up primarily of continental books. See Richard Cust, 'News and Politics in Early Seventeenth-Century England', *Past and Present*, 112 (1986), 60–90. F. J. Levy, 'How Information Spread Amongst the Gentry', *Journal of British Studies*, 21 (1982), 11–34. Elizabeth Leedham-Green, *Books in Cambridge Inventories*, 2 vols. (Cambridge, 1986).

theory and civil law and drew on both in their writings. While he used common law patterns of vocabulary and discourse in parliament, in *Mare Clausum* Selden used natural law theory to claim that King James controlled the seas. Similarly, Sir John Davies, Attorney General of Ireland, used the maxims of the civil law to justify the Crown's conquest of Ireland while continuing to maintain that the common law was the common custom of the realm, spun out of English experience, 'as the silkworm spinneth out of her self only'.[47]

In Ireland, the crown used conquest theory to justify the expropriation of land from Gaelic and Old English communities to establish the plantation of Ulster. The Irish responded with resistance literature written both in English and Gaelic, and later with revolt.[48] The issue of property was not as clear in Scotland. There James claimed that the king had better right 'to take the land from his lieges, as overlord of the whole, and do with it as pleaseth him ... [than] the people might unmake the king, and put another in his room. But either of them as unlawful, and against the ordinance of God, ought to be alike odious to be thought, much less put into practice.'[49]

In England, however, the relationship of the king to property was hedged by judicial decision, parliamentary custom, charter and statute. Parliament had gained the right to levy taxes in the Confirmation of the Charters in 1297 in which Edward I had granted 'for us and our heirs ... that on no account will we henceforth take from our kingdom such aids, taxes, and prises, except by the common assent of the whole kingdom and for the common benefit of the same kingdom, saving the ancient aids and prises due and accustomed'.[50] By the beginning of the seventeenth century it was established custom that the crown could not call together other assemblies than parliament to grant taxes. Benevolences or free

---

[47] Paul Christianson, 'Young John Selden and the Ancient Constitution, *c.* 1610–1618', *Proceedings of the American Philosophical Society*, 128 (1984), 271–315; 'John Selden, the Five Knights Case, and Discretionary Imprisonment in Early Stuart England', *Criminal Justice History*, 6 (1985), 65–87. Hans Pawlisch, *Sir John Davies and the Conquest of Ireland* (Cambridge, 1985). Pocock, *The Ancient Constitution and the Feudal Law*, pp. 32–35.

[48] Pawlisch, *Sir John Davies and the Conquest of Ireland*; Michael Perceval-Maxwell, *The Scottish Migration to Ulster in the Reign of James I* (London, 1973). T. W. Moody, F. X. Martin and F. J. Byrne, *A New History of Ireland*, vol. 3 (Oxford, 1976); Steven G. Ellis, *Reform and Revival, English Government in Ireland, 1470–1534* (Royal Historical Society, Woodbridge, 1986); Aidan Clarke, *The Old English in Ireland* (London, 1966); Brendan Bradshaw, *The Irish Constitutional Revolution of the Sixteenth Century* (Cambridge, 1979). K. R. Andrews, N. P. Canny and P. E. H. Hair, *The Westward Enterprise* (Liverpool, 1978); Nicholas Canny, 'Literature, Politics and the Making of the Gaelic Mind', *Past and Present*, no. 95 (1982), 91–116.

[49] James I, *Trew Law*, in *Political Works*, ed. McIlwain, p. 62.

[50] *Confirmatio Cartarum.*

gifts, forced loans and local levies such as ship money from coastal towns formed a grey area and continued to be collected.

When, in 1606, John Bate, who imported currants from Venice, challenged the king's right to impose a new customs duty, the court of exchequer upheld the king's right to levy impositions. Although he decided for the crown, Chief Baron Thomas Fleming's analysis of the royal prerogative differed from that of King James since he did not assert that the king was the owner either theoretically or in actuality of his subjects' property. Moreover, he examined the purpose of the king's power, not its origins, to determine its limits.

The king's power is double, ordinary and absolute ... the ordinary is for the profit of particular subjects ... and this is exercised by equity and justice in ordinary courts, and by the civilians is nominated *jus privatum*, and with us Common Law: and these laws cannot be changed without Parliament ... The absolute power of the King is not that which is converted or executed to private use, to the benefit of any particular person, but is only that which is applied to the general benefit of the people ... and this power ... is most properly named policy and government.[51]

Bate's case turned on the issue of whether impositions were taxes or regulations of foreign policy. As part of international commerce, customs, like war, peace and treaties, were made by the absolute power of the king. Fleming found that the imposition was not on Bate as a subject but as an importer of foreign goods.

The issue was thus raised of how the king's undoubted power to regulate external dealings stood in relation to the law of *meum et tuum* and the subject's right to its protection. The hundreds of impositions levied by the crown in the wake of Bate's case evoked major debates and memorable expressions of ancient constitution and common law doctrine in the parliamentary sessions of 1610 and 1614.[52] When parliamentary efforts to reconstruct the crown's finances by a 'great contract', trading the crown's feudal rights of wardship and marriage and ancient perquisites of purveyance for a fixed annual income, proved unsuccessful,[53] the crown turned with renewed energy to projects for revenue. As a result, monopolies for the importation of new technology and regulation of the economy, joined impositions as a grievance. Although

---

51 Quoted in Kenyon (ed.), *The Stuart Constitution*, pp. 62–4. On Bate's case, see Pauline Croft, 'Fresh Light on Bate's Case', *Historical Journal*, 30 (1987), 523–39.

52 See Christianson, 'Royal and Parliamentary Voices on the Ancient Constitution, *c.* 1604–1621', in *The Mental World of the Jacobean Court*, ed. Peck, pp. 71–95.

53 Pauline Croft (ed.), 'A Collection of Several Speeches and Treatises of the Late Lord Treasurer Cecil', *Cambridge Miscellany*, 39 (1987); A. G. R. Smith, 'Crown, Parliament and Finance: The Great Contract of 1610', in *The English Commonwealth*, ed. P. Clark, A. G. R. Smith and N. Tyacke (Leicester, 1979); Joel Hurstfield, *Freedom, Corruption and Government* (Cambridge, MA, 1973).

monopolies were severely restricted by the statute first proposed in parliament in 1621 and passed in a campaign led by Sir Edward Coke in 1624, loopholes in the law allowed their continuance.[54] But the religious wars in Europe and parliament's support for war with Spain at the request of Charles and the Duke of Buckingham brought the issues of prerogative and property to the fore as Charles I came to the throne in 1625.[55] James I had other troubles with parliament which require examination.

IV

It has been strongly argued in recent years that parliament was an occasion, not an institution.[56] It met irregularly, was called together and dispersed entirely at the will of the monarch.[57] Between 1603 and 1640 parliament passed little legislation; members were much more focused on private bills than public policy. Innovations in the committee system, ascribed to the early seventeenth century by Wallace Notestein, date back to the Elizabethan period. While the House of Lords has until recently been overlooked, it played a significant role in the meetings of parliament throughout the period. In short, the notion that the House of Commons seized the initiative from the crown from 1607 has fallen from favour among early Stuart historians.[58]

Despite this revisionist analysis, however, parliament in the first decade of the seventeenth century denied King James's desire for a union of his kingdoms; opposed efforts to rationalize royal finances and repeatedly challenged the decision in Bate's case allowing impositions. By 1615 Lord Chancellor Ellesmere bitterly denounced the contrariness of the first parliament of James' reign.[59]

That sessions' wrangling was captured in the House of Commons Apology of 1604 which sought to secure the parliamentary privileges

---

[54] See Joan Thirsk, *Economic Policy and Projects: The Development of a Consumer Society in Early Modern England* (Oxford, 1979).

[55] See Thomas Cogswell, *The Blessed Revolution: English Politics and The Coming of War, 1621–1624* (Cambridge, 1989); Conrad Russell, *Parliaments and English Politics, 1621–1629* (Oxford, 1979).

[56] See Russell, *Parliaments and English Politics.*

[57] James called no parliament between 1614 and 1621 and the truncated 'Addled Parliament' may not have been legally a parliament at all. See Pauline Croft, 'Annual Parliaments and the Long Parliament', *Bulletin of the Institute of Historical Research*, 59 (1986), 155–71.

[58] See Sheila Lambert, 'Procedure in the House of Commons in the Early Stuart Period', *English Historical Review*, 95 (1980), 753–81; Jennifer Loades, *Parliament under the Tudors* (Oxford, 1991); Wallace Notestein, 'The Winning of the Initiative by the House of Commons', *Proceedings of the British Academy*, 11 (1924–5), 125–75.

[59] See Louis Knafla, *Law and Politics in Jacobean England: The Tracts of Lord Ellesmere* (Cambridge, 1976).

asserted in Tudor parliaments, freedom from arrest, freedom of speech and freedom of election. The Apology clearly stated the need to keep the constitution in balance: 'the power of princes do daily grow; the rights and privileges of the people are forever at a stand' and could easily be lost. The people inherited parliamentary privilege as much as they inherited their lands or the king inherited his crown. We need not see the Apology as 'the high road to civil war'[60] to find this language significant. Drawing on medieval history and law, Members of Parliament shaped a discourse by the late 1620s that differed in important ways from that of the crown and asserted limits to a vocabulary of royal power put forward by the early Stuarts. Their aim was not to take power from the king but to return to the balance of what they envisioned as the 'ancient constitution'.

Historians disagree about the political implications of English antiquarianism. On the one hand, Christopher Hill argues that both in personnel and issues the antiquarian movement of the 1580s and 90s was connected to the parliamentary opposition of the 1610s and 1620s and Civil War tracts that attacked the 'Norman Yoke' imposed on the English by its monarchs. Despite radically different conclusions, John Adamson asserts that baronial arguments mounted on behalf of the third Earl of Essex, the parliamentary general in the 1640s, can be traced back to the antiquarian clients of his father in the 1590s.[61] Yet the ancient constitution provided language to shore up arguments for the powers of the crown as well as parliament.[62] G. L. Harriss convincingly argues that English parliamentarians saw themselves as part of a political continuum stretching back to the medieval period and drew on medieval precedent out of a sense of a shared culture,[63] a culture they shared, of course, with the crown.

The Elizabethan Society of Antiquaries displays the several voices of English antiquarianism, its centrality to seventeenth-century political discourse and James' own wariness toward historical investigation.

---

[60] On the Apology, see J. H. Hexter, 'The Apology of 1604', in *For Veronica Wedgwood These*, ed. Richard Ollard and Pamela Tudor-Craig (London, 1986), pp. 13–44; G. R. Elton, 'A High Road to Civil War?' in *From the Renaissance to the Counter-Reformation: Essays in Honor of Garrett Mattingly*, ed. Charles C. Carter (New York, 1965), pp. 325–47.

[61] Christopher Hill, 'The Norman Yoke', in *Puritanism and Revolution* (London, 1958), pp. 50–122. J. S. Adamson, 'The Baronial Context of the English Civil War', *Transactions of the Royal Historical Society*, 5th ser. 40 (1990), 93–120. See also Mark Kishlansky, '"Saye No More"', *Journal of British Studies*, 30 (1991), 399–449.

[62] See Christianson, 'Royal and Parliamentary Voices on the Ancient Constitution', in *The Mental World of the Jacobean Court*, ed. Peck, pp. 71–95.

[63] G. L. Harriss, 'Medieval Doctrines in the Debates on Supply, 1610–1629', in *Faction and Parliament*, ed. Sharpe, pp. 73–103.

Founded about 1587, the society took up the issue of the origins, authority and privileges of parliament at the beginning of James I's reign.[64] Most members of the Society had professional connections to the court. These lawyers, antiquaries and country gentlemen disagreed on when parliament had begun, and what its powers were. Most thought its functions had been performed by earlier British and Anglo-Saxon councils. Drawing on the *Modus Tenendi Parliamentum*, a legal tract drafted in the reign of Edward II, and widely circulated in manuscript, which some members such as Sir William Hakewill and Sir Robert Cotton owned, several antiquaries located parliament before the Conquest. Sir Edward Coke traced its origins to the reign of Edward the Confessor, Sir John Dodderidge to communal assemblies among the Druids and the Britons. While the antiquaries recognized that parliament's procedures and composition were now different from that described in the *Modus* – the lower clergy were no longer called and the definition of barons called to parliament had changed – they did not quarrel with one of the central points of the *Modus*: parliament could be held without the Lords but not without the Commons.[65] Dodderidge, later Solicitor-General and Judge of King's Bench, drew on the *Modus* (although he does not cite it directly) to argue that the House of Commons was the key component of parliament: even without the secular or ecclesiastical lords, parliament had authority to pass statutes.[66]

In contrast, William Camden, whose *Britannia* served as a paradigm for the Society, stressed that though there had been assemblies prior to the conquest, 'after the Norman Conquest, the two first kings reigned

---

[64] On the Society of Antiquaries, see Linda Van Nordern, 'The Elizabethan Society of Antiquaries', PhD dissertation, UCLA, 1946; Kevin Sharpe, *Sir Robert Cotton, 1586–1631* (Oxford, 1979); Joan Evans, *A History of the Society of Antiquaries* (Oxford, 1956); Peck, *Northampton*, pp. 101–21. Many of the papers presented to the Society of Antiquaries are brought together in *A Collection of Curious Discourses*, ed. Thomas Hearne, 2 vols, (London, 1775). On history and antiquarianism in the sixteenth and seventeenth centuries, see D. R. Woolf, *The Idea of History in Early Stuart England* (Toronto, 1990); F. J. Levy, *Tudor Historical Thought* (San Marino, 1967).

[65] The effort to see the *Modus* as strictly a baronial document is in error. See Adamson, 'The Baronial Context of the English Civil War', pp. 97–9 and 97n. While Adamson emphasizes the section of the *Modus* dealing with the twenty-five barons who will be called on in case of a dispute with the king, he ignores the paragraph about the importance of the Commons, which was as significant to seventeenth-century parliamentarians as the other. The lawyer and antiquarian MP, William Hakewill, drafted an account of the procedure of the House of Commons in 1610 which he preceded with a translation of the *Modus*. Nicholas Pronay and John Taylor, *Parliamentary Texts in the Later Middle Ages* (Oxford, 1980), pp. 54 and 54n.

[66] Hearne (ed.), *Curious Discourses*, I, pp. 281–93. Pronay and Taylor, *Parliamentary Texts in the Later Middle Ages*, err in saying that the Society of Antiquaries was formed in 1572 and that members were associated with the parliamentary 'opposition'.

with their swords in their hands, absolutely of themselves ... not admitting of themselves any general assemblies of the states of the realm'.[67] Arthur Agarde, however, exalted statute: 'of such force is an act of parliament here in the governance of the state of the realm, that it is deemed as an oracle from heaven, and resteth onely in the kings and queens power to qualifie and mitigate the severity thereof'.[68] Like the canons of 1606, such antiquarian speculations were suspect; despite their court connections and support for the king the antiquaries were discouraged from resuming their meetings in 1614 by King James himself.[69]

James I had every reason to believe that his subjects would welcome a peaceful union with Scotland with which it had warred for centuries and tried to amalgamate by marriage under the Tudors. He reckoned without both the House of Commons led by Sir Edwin Sandys and the judges. For Sandys adopting the name of Great Britain would extinguish the rights and liberties enjoyed by Englishmen both under the English common law and the king's coronation oath. 'The King cannot preserve the fundamental laws by uniting no more than a goldsmith two crowns ...'[70] Privy councillors who attempted to counter with the example of other multiple kingdoms were brought up short when the judges consulted by James decided that the adoption of the new name by parliamentary statute would indeed abrogate the laws of England unless their laws were united first.[71] When in 1616 James gave instructions to the judges about to set out on circuit, he plaintively recalled his intentions about the Union.

For the Common Law ... I never pressed alteration of it in Parliament ... when I endeavoured most an Union reall, as was already in my person, my desire was to conforme the Lawes of *Scotland* to the Law of *England*, and not the Law of *England* to the Law of *Scotland* ... It was a foolish Querke of some Judges, who held that the Parliament of *England* could not unite *Scotland* and *England* by the name of *Great Britaine*, but that it would make an alteration of the Lawes, though I am since come to that knowledge, that an Acte of Parliament can doe greater wonders ... I was sworne to maintaine the Law of the Land, and therefore I had beene periured if I had altered it.

[67] Hearne (ed.), *A Collection of Curious Discourses*, I, p. 304.
[68] *Ibid.*, pp. 298–299. Francis Tate wrote that to ensure knowledge of the law 'we use printing of the acts; so before printing, all the ordinances affirmed by royal assent were recorded, ... published under the great seal of England ... and proclaimed in every shire'.
[69] Sharpe, *Sir Robert Cotton*, p. 36.
[70] Quoted in Brian Levack, *The Formation of the British State* (Oxford, 1987), p. 39. See further Roger Mason (ed.), *Scots and Britons: Scottish Political Thought and the Union of 1603* (Cambridge, 1994).
[71] Levack, *British State*, pp. 38–39; Peck, *Northampton*, pp. 186–92; Bruce Galloway, *The Union of England and Scotland, 1603–1608* (Atlantic Highlands, NJ, 1986).

Nevertheless, the king concluded, the common law should be 'kept within her owne limits'. The common law was the law of inheritance in England but there were other, older laws, the law civil and canon, which he was also pledged to uphold. He would maintain 'all the points of mine Oath, especially in Lawes, and of Lawes, especially the Common Law'.[72] His language was sullen and ambiguous; he had lost a round but there were others to come.

VI

We turn from the debate over the extent of royal power to the language of counsel and the question of who should serve as the king's advisors. Many competed for the post. From at least the 1570s some members of the House of Commons claimed that they were not simply representatives of their localities but public officials and advisors to the monarch. Both houses of parliament, Lords and Commons, not only claimed to be advisors but asserted their right to rid the government of corrupt ministers and, by 1641, their right to name the king's ministers. If such claims were new in the mouth of the Commons, they were ancient in the mouth of the English nobility.

For centuries English monarchs had been reminded both by political tract and political violence that their natural advisors were the nobiilty. Baronial revolt in thirteenth and fourteenth century England had identified the nobility with 'the community of the realm'. At moments of political crisis, such as the 1260s, the 1320s and the 1380s, some peers had claimed that the Lord High Steward, the Lord Constable and the Earl Marshal possessed the right to govern in peace and war, to remove evil councillors, to try peers and even execute them.[73] In *Basilikon Doron* James had urged his son to keep the nobility under control while recognizing their important role in counselling the king. Counsel was a right and a duty; it could also be an evil.

Advice to Princes was a traditional mode of political discourse in Britain. One of the earliest books printed in Scotland was a *Buke of Gude Counsale to the King* of 1508.[74] Renaissance literature on the

---

[72] James I, *Political Works*, ed. McIlwain, pp. 329–31.
[73] M. V. Clarke, *Medieval Representation and Consent* (repr. New York, 1964); Pronay and Taylor, *Parliamentary Texts of the Later Middle Ages*; L. W. Vernon Harcourt, *His Grace the Steward and Trial of Peers* (London, 1907). Adamson, 'The Baronial Context of the English Civil War', pp. 93–120.
[74] Harry G. Aldis, *A List of Books Printed in Scotland Before 1700* (Edinburgh, 1970). Written in Scots verse, it drew on a Latin manuscript 'De regimine principium bonum consilium'. R. W. Henning and David Rosand(eds.), *Castiglione, the Ideal and the Real in Renaissance Culture* (Yale, 1983). Frank Whiggam, *Ambition and Privilege* (California, 1984).

education of the courtier, such as Castiglione's *Il Libro del Cortegiano* and Machiavelli's *Il Principe*, found reflection in Thomas Elyot's *Boke of the Governor* and in Sir Thomas Hoby's translation of Castiglione which went through four editions between 1561 and 1603. The discourse of counsel was reflected in the *Essays* of Sir Francis Bacon and made immediate in his advice to George Villiers, later Duke of Buckingham and the king's favourite. Even by the early seventeenth century, English government still remained intensely personal. King James VI, used to the more personal access and operation of the Scottish monarchy, brought with him the habits of a lifetime and made his Bedchamber a centre of politics through a series of favourites of whom Buckingham was the last.[75]

Favourites, whose power was based on the personal affection of the monarch, played an important role in the medieval and early modern court, insulating the monarch from incessant demands and substituting for a nobility whose institutional power made them a greater threat to the monarch than a favourite, who was his 'creature'. Of James it was said in 1626 after the parliamentary attack on Buckingham that he 'therefore strengthened himself ever with some favorite, whom he might better trust than many of the nobility tainted with this desire of oligarchy'.[76]

The ideal of the courtier had an unsavoury side, expressed both in baronial attacks on evil counsellors or parliamentary debates on impeachment, and in such Tacitean condemnations of the courts of the first century Roman Emperors as Ben Jonson's *Sejanus*. Tacitean pessimism found a home in circles around the second Earl of Essex and Prince Henry.[77] Then, in 1614, one of the greatest scandals of the century was uncovered. Jacobean revenge tragedy seemed to come to life with Sir Thomas Overbury's death in the Tower and the conviction of the king's favourite, Robert Carr, Earl of Somerset, for his murder. As news spread throughout the kingdom, salacious lyrics and tracts dramatized the evils of the court.[78]

---

[75] See Neil Cuddy, 'The Revival of the Entourage: the Bedchamber of James I, 1603–1625', in *The English Court*, ed. David Starkey (London, 1987), pp. 173–225.

[76] Quoted in Richard Cust, *The Forced Loan* (Oxford, 1987), p. 21. For an extended discussion of the discourse of favourites from 1558 to 1640, see Robert Shepherd, 'Royal Favorites in the Political Discourse of Tudor and Stuart England', PhD thesis, Claremont, California, 1985.

[77] J. H. Salmon, 'Seneca and Tacitus in Jacobean England', in *The Mental World of the Jacobean Court*, ed. Peck, pp. 169–188; 'Cicero and Tacitus in Sixteenth Century France', *American Historical Review*, 85 (1980), 307–71.

[78] See Sir Walter Davenport's Commonplace book, Chester Record Office, CR/63/2/1 which contains material on the Essex divorce and Overbury murder, scurrilous verses on Carr and Buckingham; I am grateful to Richard Cust for this reference.

In *The Vision of Sir Thomas Overbury's Ghost*, Richard Niccols, editor of *The Mirror for Magistrates*, equated Somerset with Piers Gaveston, Edward II's favourite. Even as he distinguished James I from Edward II who was deposed and murdered, he suggested dangerous similarities between the two monarchs who both had male favorites. Another tract on the Overbury murder, *The Bloody Downfall of Adultery, Murder, Ambition*, examining 'the customs of this age', portrayed the contradiction of the courtier who was comely without, but 'within nothing but rotten bones and corrupt practices'.[79] Such was the dark side of the great imagery of counsel in Renaissance kingship. Any favourite who monopolized patronage and access to the king might be cast in the role of evil counsellor and over-mighty subject. Buckingham's hegemony and his remarkable success in transferring himself to the role of favourite to Charles I, complicated Caroline politics by introducing the image of power beyond the control of royal majesty or common law.

The protean figure of Sir Francis Bacon cannot be contained within simple categories. As a major philosopher he exceeds the boundaries of English political discourse.[80] As James I's Attorney General, he addressed issues of kingship, law, parliament, empire and property.[81] As an advisor on reason of state, his advice to Buckingham on how to be a favourite combined the language of humanist counsel, the realism of Machiavelli and Tacitus, and those English histories that chronicled the rise and fall of favourites. He found space within Jacobean political discourse for ministerial accountability, of a sort.

It is no new thing for Kings and Princes to have their privadoes, their favourites ... remember then what your true condition is. The King himself is above the reach of his people, but cannot be above their censures; and you are his shadow, if either he commit an error and is loath to avow it, but excuses it upon his Ministers, of which you are the first in the eye, or you commit the fault, or have willingly permitted it, and must suffer for it; so perhaps you may be offered as a sacrifice to appease the multitude.[82]

Bacon pointed out the important difference between ruling by divine right and royal absolutism: 'Kings are stiled Gods upon Earth, not

---

[79] Richard Niccols, *Sir Thomas Overburies Vision* (London, 1616); the *Bloody Downfall of Adultery, Murder, Ambition*, HEH 60225, Printed at London for R.H. and are to be sold at his shop ... (1616).

[80] For recent work on Bacon, see Julian Martin, *Francis Bacon, the State, and the Reform of Natural Philosophy* (Cambridge, 1992); Ian Box, *The Social Thought of Francis Bacon* (Lewiston, NY, 1989); Antonio Perez-Ramos, *Francis Bacon's Idea of Science* (Oxford, 1988); Charles Whitney, *Francis Bacon and Modernity* (New Haven, CT, 1986).

[81] James Spedding (ed.), *The Life and Letters of Francis Bacon*, 7 vols. (London, 1861–74). On the Union, for instance, see III, pp. 89–99, 217–47.

[82] *Ibid.*, VI, p. 14.

absolute . . . and they shall die like men . . . They commit trusts to their ministers.' While kings were answerable only to God, their ministers were 'answerable to God and man, for the breach of their duties'. As part of his advice, Bacon provided a language in which to encompass both kingship and laws: 'if they be rightly administered, they are the best, the equallest in the world between the Prince and People; by which the King hath the justest Prerogative, and the People the best liberty.' This ambiguous formula was echoed in Charles I's answer to the Petition of Right in 1628; but unlike Charles, Bacon spelled out his meaning in a way that stressed the antiquity of the law, the role of parliament and the need for settled procedure.

In the Laws we have a native interest, it is our birth-right and our inheritance, and I think the whole Kingdom will always continue that mind which once the two Houses of Parliament publicly professed . . . under a Law we must live, and under a known law, and not under an arbitrary law is our happiness that we do live.[83]

The language of corruption became an increasingly effective way in which to attack early Stuart officials and policies.[84] Whether in the form of Tacitean cynicism about courts, religious criticism of laymen's greed, or baronial motifs of the rise and fall of base-born advisors, the English had ready to hand a discourse in which to frame criticism of the king's policies and his advisors. In 1621, the House of Commons revived the fourteenth-century procedure of impeachment to condemn Sir Giles Mompesson, the notorious patentee of alehouses, and forged an ideology that lived comfortably alongside the legal fiction that the king could do no wrong. King James acknowledged as much when he allowed parliament to impeach Bacon, now lord chancellor, and other civil law judges in 1621, and his lord treasurer, Lionel Cranfield, in 1624, on charges of venality.

But when Charles I refused in 1626 to permit parliament to impeach Buckingham on charges of high crimes and misdemeanours, which included several practices that were not against the law, such as ennobling his family or helping the king to sell titles, John Pym in a powerful indictment used the language which exposed corruption to expand the reach of parliamentary power. Although there were no positive laws controlling royal bounty to such a favourite,

this is the fittest law to insist upon in a court of parliament where the proceedings are not limited either by civil or common laws, but matters are judged according

---

[83] *Ibid.*, VI, pp. 15, 18, 19.
[84] Peck, *Court Patronage and Corruption in Early Stuart England*, pp. 161–207.

as they stand in opposition or conformity with that which is *suprema lex, salus populi.*[85]

Pym's language ominously declared that since a favourite's power stood above the law, parliament might impeach him on charges unknown to the law. This action was taken against Strafford fifteen years later, with results more catastrophic than any dreamed of in 1626.

V

Charles I was neither a political theorist nor a sponsor of Europe-wide propaganda battles such as James had undertaken over the Venetian Interdict or the Oath of Allegiance between 1606 and 1619. His attitudes and those of the Caroline court toward royal power must be sought in his policies, answers to parliamentary petitions, officially sanctioned sermons, judicial decisions, and tracts by favour seekers who reflected what they took to be the regime's political views.

The political discourses of the Jacobean court continued during his son's reign with one significant change: a vocabulary developed to deal with papal and Presbyterian resistance theory was now also directed against domestic political challengers. Sir Robert Filmer's *Patriarcha*, which draws heavily on James VI and I's *Trew Law of Free Monarchies*, displays this shift in concern, turning from countering resistance theory in Book I to taking up the challenge of parliament in the Petition of Right in Book III.

In *The Causes of the English Civil War*, Conrad Russell argues that both sides in the English Civil War claimed to be acting pursuant to the rule of law and declares his inability to find supporters of royal absolutism in early Stuart England. He demonstrates that several Members of Parliament, who in the 1620s and 1630s challenged royal policy over the forced loan and ship money, became royalists in the 1640s. He claims, therefore, that English politics and the political nation did not differ over political theory which was only an occasional adjunct to political issues such as taxation. But the issue of taxation, the king's power over his subjects' property, was central to contemporary political theory. Moreover, by dismissing concern about the origins of political power Russell takes away one of the vital preoccupations of contemporary writers. Finally, to find absolutists in Caroline England we need only look to some clergy, civilians and favour-seekers.

Patriarchalism in particular came increasingly to the fore in Caroline

---

[85] Hampshire Record Office, Jervoise Mss 07, ff. 3–5. I am grateful to Conrad Russell for this reference.

theory.[86] It found its most powerful expression in Robert Filmer's *Patriarcha*, first written between 1628 and 1632.[87] When Charles I came to the throne the most pressing issue was war with Spain, which parliament had agreed to wage in the session of 1624. The new king tried to finance the war by traditional means but his requests went unheeded in the parliaments of 1625 and 1626 as the House of Commons wrangled over war policy and subsidies.[88] As a result the king turned to two familiar solutions: the benevolence and the forced loan. A benevolence was, by definition, given freely, but when the crown tried to raise the forced loan, royal chaplains insisted on the necessity of compliance.[89] Roger Maynwaring preached two sermons before Charles I on religion and allegiance in July 1627. After Maynwaring was impeached by parliament in 1628, Charles promoted him. Russell suggests that lay royalists did not accept arguments such as Maynwaring's.[90] Charles I did, and so did Filmer, Sir Francis Kynaston and less remarkable Caroline favour seekers.

What did Maynwaring say? He differentiated between earthly laws and the divine law which the king's commandments embodied, noted explicitly that the king could not be bound by any law other than God's and insisted on the king's right to his subjects' monies based on the biblical injunction to render unto Caesar that which was Caesar's. Maynwaring's sermon, of course, was drafted specifically to reinforce the king's right to the forced loan of 1626.[91]

Using language similar to James I's, Maynwaring explicitly rejected any notion of community consent or any ascending notion of power. The power of the king was supra-human. 'That sublime power therefore which resides in earthly Potentates, is not a Derivation, or Collection of humane power scattered among many, but a participation of Gods owne Omnipotency.' Maynwaring adopted what Gordon Schochet has called

---

[86] On patriarchalism, see Gordon Schochet, *Patriarchalism in Political Thought* (Oxford, 1975).

[87] See Richard Tuck, 'A New Date for Filmer's Patriarcha', *Historical Journal*, 29 (1986), 183–6. Johann Sommerville (ed.), *Sir Robert Filmer, Patriarcha and Other Writings* (Cambridge, 1991), pp. xxxii–xxxiv.

[88] Historians differ, as did contemporaries, as to what parliament agreed to in 1624; see Russell, *Parliaments and English Politics*; Cogswell, *The Blessed Revolution*; Michael B. Young, 'Buckingham, War and Parliament: Revisionism Gone Too Far', *Parliamentary History*, 4 (1985), 45–69.

[89] See Richard Cust, *The Forced Loan* (Oxford, 1987). Elton, *Tudor Constitution*, p. 44. Benevolences had been raised by James I in 1614 after the dissolution of the Addled Parliament. Kenyon, *Stuart Constitution*, p. 81.

[90] Russell, *The Causes of the English Civil War*, pp. 131–160.

[91] Maynwaring, *Religion and Allegiance* (London, 1627); Russell does not discuss Maynwaring, Sibthorpe or Filmer in *The Causes of the English Civil War*.

the genetic form of patriarchalism, Adamite dominion.[92] In this formulation there was little room for parliament, or any limitation of the royal will through law. Maynwaring's omissions are significant: he says nothing of the exchange of benefits between king and subject that James VI had written about in *Trew Law*, neither does he discuss, as James had done, the importance of kings in settled kingdoms following the laws that they themselves have given. If the king commanded anything that was not contrary 'to the originall Lawes of God, Nature, Nations, and the Gospell', even if it did not correspond to national and municipal laws, 'nothing can be denied (without manifest and sinful violation of Law and Conscience) that may answer their Royall state and Excellency'.[93] Obedience should be voluntary; but whether voluntary or coerced, obedience was owed to the king.

Maynwaring applied this theory of royal absolutism to the practice of collecting the forced loan. Although parliaments were 'sacred and honorable and necessary also for those ends to which they were at first instituted', they were called into session not to question taxation 'but for the more equall Imposing, and more easie Exacting of that, which unto Kings doth appertaine, by Naturall and Originall Law, and Justice; as their proper Inheritance annexed to their Imperiall Crownes, from their very births'.[94] Addressing the immediate circumstances of the forced loan, he argued that parliament had agreed 'to give supplie to those Warres, which, the Resolutions of his Subjects represented in the high Court of Parliament, caused him to undertake'.[95] With Maynwaring's sermons, the discourse crafted to deny resistance theory was deployed to enforce royal taxation with doubtful regard to parliamentary consent.

The Petition of Right was the most important parliamentary text of the early Stuart period: the climactic attempt to use ancient constitution argument to bind the crown by agreement to act according to fundamental and immemorial law. It rehearsed the doctrine of successive confirmations of the laws of England from before the Conquest, culminating in Magna Carta, of which it claimed to be the re-enactment and whose authority it claimed to possess. It shaped future parliamentary action, but it provoked responses restating the nature of royal power, one of

---

[92] Maynwaring, *Religion and Allegiance*, pp. 10–11. 'For Adam had Dominion setled in him, before ever there was either Pope, or People: neither Popes nor Populous Multitudes have any right to give, or take, in this case' (p. 13). See Schochet, *Patriarchalism.*

[93] Maynwaring, *Religion and Allegiance*, pp. 20–1.

[94] *Ibid.*, p. 26.

[95] See also Robert Sibthrope's sermon urging the payment of the forced loan: *Apostolike Obedience Shewing the Duty of Subjects to pay Tribyute and Taxes to their Princes, according to the Word of God* (London, 1627).

which appears to have been Filmer's *Patriarcha*. The debate over the Petition of Right moved parliamentary discourse from concern over individual liberties to liberty more generally and brought to centre stage claims that a fundamental law, guaranteeing to each free man security and due process of law in his lands and goods, shaped the polity of which the king was only a part. The Commons and Lords yearned for an answer that would speak to their claims of law and liberties and the ancient constitution; the king and his councillors focused on the necessities created by waging war.[96]

The Petition was directed at the forced loan, refusal of *habeas corpus* to forced loan protesters, billeting of troops and imposition of martial law. The Confirmation of the Charters of 1297 had required all taxes to be assented to by parliament: 'your subjects have inherited this freedom, that they should not be compelled to contribute to any tax . . . not set by common consent in Parliament'. Magna Carta had declared that 'no freeman may be taken or imprisoned or be disseised of his freehold or liberties . . . but by the lawful judgement of his peers or by the law of the land'. Yet the king's subjects had been imprisoned without cause shown. When those imprisoned sued for deliverance by the writ of *habeas corpus*, 'no cause was certified, but that they were detained by your Majesty's special command signified by the Lords of your Privy Council'. Troops had been billeted in homes and suffered 'to sojourn against the laws and customs of this realm and to the great grievance and vexation of the people'. Finally, Magna Carta and the laws of Edward III required that 'no man ought to be adjudged to death but by the laws established in this your realm'. Yet the king had issued commissions of martial law. The Petition urged the king to eschew arbitrary taxation, arbitrary imprisonment, billeting and martial law. Echoing the language of the Apology of 1604 the Petition claimed 'their rights and liberties according to the laws and statutes of this realm', and insisted that the practices they condemned not be used as precedents. They asked the king to respond by declaring that his officials would serve 'according to the laws and statutes of this realm'.[97]

---

[96] J. G. A. Pocock, 'Propriety, Liberty and Valour; Ideology, Rhetoric and Speech in the 1628 Debates', unpublished paper prepared for a conference on the Petition of Right, Washington University, 20–1 October 1978.

[97] Sir William Fleetwood, Justice of the Peace for Buckinghamshire, wrote to the Privy Council of the order to billet troops that 'he had never read that word in any of our lawes, and knew not what it meant . . . I did not know that any of our lawes had ordeined it to be an offence for any man to refuse to yield thereto, neither had I any authority as a Justice of the Peace to punish it who was sworn to do right to all men according to the lawes of the land.' PRO SP 16/92/69, 8 February 1628.

Charles provided two answers to the Petition of Right. In the first, of June 2, he did not give his assent to the Petition: instead,

The King willeth that right be done according to the laws and customs of the realm, and that the statutes be put in due execution, that the subject may have no just cause to complain of any wrong or oppression contrary to their rights and just liberties, to the preservation whereof he holds himself in conscience as well obliged as of his prerogative.

In the Commons the response was silence, then uproar, and a move for a Remonstrance. Five days later, on 7 June, Charles I came to the House of Lords, had the Petition of Right read and pronounced *Soit droit fait comme est desire*, the form of assent to a private bill. The king then said: 'I know you cannot hurt my prerogative and as it is your maxim that my prerogative cannot stand without your liberties, so it is my maxim that your liberties cannot subsist without my prerogative. I have done my part and if the parliament do not end happily it shall not be my fault but your sin.'[98] This ambiguous statement was met with joy by the Lords and Commons, who were then let down when the king continued to collect tonnage and poundage without parliamentary consent. When the Petition of Right was printed in 1629 the king appended his first answer of 2 June and the speech, but not the assent, of 7 June.[99]

VII

The Petition thus failed to achieve the consensus at which its drafters thought they were aiming, and left a legacy of mistrust aimed, after Buckingham's assassination, at the increasing 'Arminianism' of the higher clergy and the crown's 'illegal' taxation which led to the violent disruption of the session of 1629. There followed eleven years of Personal Rule, during which we can see ideas of kingship rising to a height to which the epithet 'absolutism' seems hard to deny.

Robert Filmer's *Patriarcha*, perhaps the most powerful political statement of royal absolutism in the seventeenth century, prompted John Lock's response fifty years later in his *Two Treatises on Civil Government*. But *Patriarcha* derives from a context different from that of the Exclusion Crisis of 1679–81 during which it was published.[100] While

---

98 Mary Frear Keeler, Maija Jansson Cole and William B. Bidwell, *Commons Debates 1628*, 6 vols (New Haven, CT, 1978), IV, 193.
99 Russell, *Parliaments and English Politics*, pp. 374–83; Elizabeth Read Foster, 'Printing the Petition of Right', *Huntington Library Quarterly*, 38 (1974), 81–3; Frances Relf, *The Petition of Right* (Minneapolis, 1917).
100 On Filmer's *Patriarcha*, see Sommerville (ed.), *Sir Robert Filmer, Patriarcha and Other Writings*; Schochet, *Patriarchalism*; James Daly, *Sir Robert Filmer and English Political Thought* (Toronto, 1979); Peter Laslett, *Patriarcha and Other Political Works of Sir Robert Filmer* (Oxford, 1949).

Filmer continued to revise it, it was most probably written sometime before 8 February 1632 when Filmer asked that 'A Discourse . . . of Government and in praise of Royaltie' be licensed for publication.[101] That Charles I refused it license suggests that we should be cautious in ascribing Filmer's political views to the king himself. But Filmer's arguments are part of the strand of monarchical thought in the early Stuart period that reaches from James I, echoed and reconceptualized by Maynwaring and disseminated in court sermons and petitions of favor seekers. Filmer himself moved in the ambit of the court, he was married to the daughter of a bishop, his brother was part of the king's household.[102] He melded the diverse political vocabularies of scripture, Aristotle and Bodin, history and law in the construction of *Patriarcha*, which must be placed in the context of the debate over the *Petition of Right*.

Like many contemporary writers Filmer rejected scholastic and Calvinist theories of popular sovereignty which held that political power originated in the people who then designated their ruler. Filmer located the authority of monarchical government in the power God granted Adam over his family at the Creation. It was 'the only fountain of all regall authority, by the ordination of God himself'.[103] Political power and patriarchal power were identical in origin and extent. It did not matter how a particular king came by his power: his authority was the 'natural authority of a supreme father'.[104] Moreover Filmer shared the early Stuarts' focus on legitimacy by stressing that there was always one legitimate heir. In case of want of heirs, power did not revert to the multitude or the magistracy but 'to the prime and independent heads of families' who could confer 'sovereign authority on whom they please'. But the person selected received his power from God, not as a donation from the people.[105] Filmer read Bracton to say the king 'is under none but God only'. Bracton's most famous statement, that the king was under God and the law, was ignored. Kings, Filmer argued, existed before laws and 'for a long time the word of the king was the only law'.[106]

[101] Before 8 February 1632 Filmer brought 'a Discourse . . . of Government and in praise of Royaltie' to Charles I's Secretary to request licensing to which the king responded negatively, Sommerville (ed.), *Patriarcha*, p. viii. On the dating of *Patriarcha* also see: John M. Wallace, 'The Date of Sir Robert Filmer's *Patriarcha*', *Historical Journal*, 23 (1980), 155–65; James Daly, 'Some Problems in the Authorship of Sir Robert Filmer's Works', *English Historical Review*, 98 (1983), 737–62; Richard Tuck, 'A New Date for Filmer's Patriarcha', *Historical Journal*, 29 (1986), pp. 183–6.

[102] Sommerville (ed.), *Patriarcha*, pp. x, xv–xx. Sir Francis Kynaston, another member of the King's Household wrote in a similar vein in 1629. *Ibid.*, pp. 2–3.

[103] *Ibid.*, p. 7.   [104] Quoted in *ibid.*, pp. xxii, 11.   [105] *Ibid.*, p. 11.

[106] *Ibid.*, p. 35; quoting from James's *Trew Law of Free Monarchies*, he cited James' reading of the First Book of Samuel to spell out the powers of kings.

Filmer denied that there was 'any place for such imaginary pactions between kings and their people as many dream of'.[107] Drawing on James I's *Trew Law of Free Monarchies* he argued that even were such a contract made either originally or at the coronation, only God could judge if the king had broken it.[108] The coronation oath required the king 'to keep no laws but such as in his judgement are upright, and those not literally always, but according to the equity of his conscience joined with mercy'.[109] Yet James had taught that a king governing in a settled kingdom became a tyrant when he did not rule by his own laws. Filmer blended this notion with patriarchalism. Thus all kings were bound 'to preserve the lands, goods, liberties and lives of all their subjects, not by any municipal law of the land, but by the natural law of a father, which binds them to ratify the acts of their forefathers and predecessors in things necessary for the public good of their subjects'.[110]

Citing Bodin, Filmer placed indivisible sovereignty, the power of law-making, in the hands of the king. He rejected the notion of a mixed polity by saying, 'if a king but once admit the people to be his companions, he leaves to be a king, and the state becomes a democracy. That which giveth the very being to a king is the power to give laws'.[111] Consultant assemblies only advised the king on the making of public law; they did not share sovereignty with him. He was also, *contra* Coke, the interpreter of the laws. He had, Filmer suggested, anciently sat with his judges in court and now was 'still representatively present in all courts'.[112] Magna Carta's limits on royal power dealt only with 'ordinary jurisdiction in common causes', and could not restrain his 'absolute authority' in those rare cases which the king could hear with his council.[113] Both common law and statute were subject to the king who was their 'sole immediate author, corrector and moderator'. Neither could diminish 'that natural power which kings have over their people by right of fatherhood'.[114]

Filmer's treatment of Bodin is highly significant for it points to a marked change in the possible readings of that author. Bodin wrote that the royal monarch, while sovereign, did not have power over the

---

[107] *Ibid.*, p. 7. This sentence is not in the Chicago manuscript of *Patriarcha*, Regenstein Library, University of Chicago, Codex Ms. 413, which Sommerville dates before 1632, but in Cambridge University Library Ms. Add 7078, dated between 1635 and 1642.

[108] *Ibid.*, p. 32.

[109] *Ibid.*, p. 42. These were those laws that James had called 'lowable'.

[110] *Ibid.*, p. 42.

[111] *Ibid.*, pp. 32, 44. He cited Ulpian's rule of civil law that 'the prince is not bound by the law' (p. 45).

[112] *Ibid.*, p. 47.   [113] *Ibid.*, pp. 49–50.   [114] *Ibid.*, p. 52.

property of his subjects.[115] One Englishman in the late sixteenth century had argued that Bodin's theory of royal monarchy left room for the power of parliament in which the king had only a negative voice – a remarkable amalgam with Hooker – and required consent to taxation.[116] By the early seventeenth century, with the continuing struggles over impositions, benevolences, forced loans and ship money, Bodin was read by some royalists to mean that a monarch had a right to his subject's property. Certainly, that was how Filmer read Bodin.

Subjects were bound to provide revenues for the crown. Filmer glossed the New Testament text, 'render unto Caesar that which is Caesar's', in language that recalled the debates in parliament in 1626 and 1628:

> When the Jews asked our blessed Saviour whether they should pay tribute, He did not first demand what the law of the land was, or whether there was any statute against it, nor enquired whether the tribute were given by act of parliament, nor advised them to stay their payment until a parliament should grant it.[117]

Filmer also explicitly located *Patriarcha* in contemporary politics. 'The prerogative of a king is to be above all laws, for the good only of them that are under the laws, and to defend the people's liberties – as his majesty graciously affirmed in his speech after his last answer to the Petition of Right.'[118]

For Filmer, parliament was the place in which the king listened to his subjects' petitions and ordained laws to deal with their grievances.[119] Parliament in its present form was not immemorial but dated from the reign of Henry I. Parliamentary privileges – freedom of speech, authority over their members, access to the king – were not natural rights but the bounty of the monarch. Magna Carta and other charters were granted under the Great Seal; statutes were adopted with the formula *Le roi se veult*; and 'originally the difference was not great between a proclamation and a statute'. Great councils existed alongside parliaments, and parliament had often turned to the judges for advice. Filmer concluded 'the king's council hath guided and ruled the judges, and the judges guided the parliament'.[120]

While Filmer claimed to eschew 'the mysteries of the present state',

---

[115] Unlike the tyrannical or feudal monarch: see Jean Bodin, *Six Books of the Commonweale*, trans. Knolles (London, 1606), Book II.

[116] See Peck, 'The Mentality of a Jacobean Grandee', in *The Mental World of the Jacobean Court*, ed. Peck, pp. 148–68.

[117] Sommerville (ed.), *Patriarcha*, p. 39.   [118] *Ibid.*, p. 44.

[119] *Ibid.*, pp. 52–3.   [120] *Ibid.*, p. 63.

Patriarcha seems firmly rooted in the political battles over law, taxation and parliamentary privilege in the late 1620s.[121] He denied that 'men may examine their own charters, deeds, or evidences by which they claim and hold the inheritance or freehold of their liberties', a claim made by members of the House of Commons in the Apology of 1604 and in the Petition of Right. Hoping that the people would enjoy 'ample privileges', he argued that 'the greatest liberty in the world (if it be duly considered) is for people to live under a monarch. It is the Magna Carta of this kingdom.'[122] Filmer's *Patriarcha* can be located squarely in the aftermath of the parliamentary debates of the 1620s; controversy over ship money generated similar royalist responses.

VIII

In the 1630s, fears sparked by the Thirty Years War and long-standing concerns about the financing of the royal navy led Attorney General William Noy to suggest the use of a fourteenth-century levy on coastal towns to support a fleet in the English Channel to protect the coasts. 'Ship money' was levied to build and maintain the fleet from 1633 on.[123] At the outset the duty was imposed on coastal towns. By 1634 it was imposed throughout the kingdom and became the most effective tax in the royal arsenal. Up to the decision in the famous ship money case, *Rex v. Hampden*, in 1638, close to 80 per cent of assessments were paid. Oliver St John, one of Hampden's counsel, did not deny that the king controlled defence, that in a case of necessity his prerogative allowed him to act to protect the safety of the kingdom and that subjects could be impelled to pay for that defence. Instead, he argued, no emergency had

---

[121] See for instance his reference to 'The new coined distinction of subjects into royalists and patriots is most unnatural'. Sommerville (ed.), *Patriarcha*, p. xxxiv, notes that 'royalist' is first used in the 1620s.

[122] *Ibid.*, p. 4.

[123] On ship money, see Kenneth Fincham, 'The Judges Decision on Ship Money in Feburary 1637: The Reaction in Kent', *Bulletin of the Institute of Historical Research*, 57 (1984), 230–7; Peter Lake, 'The Collection of Ship Money in Cheshire during the Sixteen-Thirties', *Northern History*, 17 (1981), 44–71; R. J. W. Swales, 'The Ship Money Levy of 1628', *Bulletin of the Institute of Historical Research*, 50 (1977), 164–76; N. P. Bard, 'The Ship Money Case and William Fiennes, Viscount Saye and Sele', *Bulletin of the Institute of Historical Research*, 50 (1977), 177–84; Elaine Marcotte, 'Shrieval Administrations of Ship Money in Cheshire, 1637', *Bulletin of the John Rylands University Library*, 58 (1975), 137–72. For later reactions to the ship money decision, see Michael Mendle, 'The Ship Money Case, *The Case of Shipmony*, and the Development of Henry Parker's Parliamentary Absolutism', *Historical Journal*, 32 (1989), 513–36; William Palmer, 'Oliver St. John and the Legal Language of Revolution in England, 1640–1642', *Historian*, 57 (1989), 263–82.

required the levy year after year, and the king had not followed the proper form, that of a parliamentary statute.

Procedure was as much a part of the rule of law to seventeenth-century Englishmen as appeal to law – giving or law-making. It is here that the English political nation parted company: was the following of such procedure a gracious condescension by the sovereign or was it central to authority and legitimacy? The judges split 7 to 5. Sir Robert Berkeley articulated the majority's position in language shared by contemporaries in parliament. The people were 'freemen, not villeins to be taxed *de alto et basso* . . . Subjects have in their goods a propriety, a peculiar interest . . . a birthright in the laws of the kingdom.' No laws could be imposed or altered 'without common consent in parliament'. But the king had a right to 'impose a charge' for defence, only he could judge whether an emergency existed and consent to taxation was not fundamental to government. Indeed, the king himself was 'a living, speaking and acting law'.[124] It was this procedural judgement, according to Clarendon, which convinced the proprietors of England that the protection of the law was being denied them in the courts.

In the late 1630s a certain Robert Chiver proposed a project to increase production of corn, beef, mutton, butter, cheese and all other provisions in England, Wales and Ireland. He asked for 'free liberty to enter and improve any man's lands he finds meet to be improved without interruption of the owners'. The owners of the lands would be given a third of the profits after the charges were deducted, the king a third and the projector a third. The king could compel his subjects to use their lands beneficially because 'the king was the owner of the universal fee of his kingdom'.

The projector made a traditional distinction between the king's private inheritance in which he had 'both the property and use in his royal person' and the public in which he had only the property and not the use'. Significantly, however, Chiver argued the right to private profit from the king's public inheritance which Chief Baron Fleming had explicitly denied in Bate's Case. Furthermore, he insisted that the king's prerogative allowed, indeed impelled him, to undertake the project.

The king as *pater patriae* is bound to procure [it] . . . A statute is needless, and the decree of a court of justice is impertinent where the whole kingdom cannot be made parties. Only the royal prerogative warranted by common law is sufficient as being the proper and principal subject of authority, the foundation of wisdom . . . an act of this public nature, is to declare itself to be absolute without

---

[124] Kenyon (ed.), *The Stuart Constitution*, p. 113. See Margaret Judson, *The Crisis of the Constitution* (New Brunswick, 1949), p. 272.

dependency, potent without infirmity, sovereign without superiority above it.[125]

John Cusacke, an Irish gentleman and projector, sought to support a patent of monopoly for land development, probably Chiver's, in 1637 or 1639. In doing so Cusacke argued, like Filmer and Sir Francis Kynaston, that the king was the lawgiver. Moreover, he put forward a peculiar notion of the relationship of the king and parliament. He reconceptualized the common law as the law the king made for the common good and distinguished between common law, custom and statute; the first had to do with the general good, the latter two with individual good. The king's obligation to look after the common good allowed, indeed impelled, him to force landowners to improve their lands for the common good, from which they, as well as the king and the projector, would benefit financially. Cusacke argued that in England there were two parliaments, one made up of lords and clergy who agreed to ordinances of common law that the king made, and another, which included the commons, who apparently did little but petition.

To doubt whether the king may produce or exercise the proper and perfect acts of his royal prerogative without the assent of the Commons in parliament is to turn monarchy into democracy and to make him the servant of the people instead of being a divine viceregent and their master; and to expose common law to the judgement of the Commons is to cast a pearl before swine. For however they are by accident learned they are in the concept of law unlearned; and they are not with their profane hands to touch the sacred and inviolable bounds of common law to which the king himself is also subject *per vim directivam*.

As Filmer had located *Patriarcha* in the context of debate over the Petition of Right, Cusacke argued from the decision in the ship money case. 'He knows not either what common law or king is who doubts of the free and absolute exercise of the royal prerogative in this particular act concerning the public good of the kingdom which is the chief ground of his challenge of ship money now allowed by common law; and he who denies the one must also deny the other by plain consequence'. Thus *Rex v. Hampden* had wide-ranging implications not only for the king's right to tax but to regulate and accrue benefits on the crown's behalf and that of its clients from subjects' 'propertie'. Citing Bracton, Cusacke insisted that

---

[125] Bodleian Library, Bankes MSS. 48/22, c. 1637–1639. 'It plainly appears that the King may by his royal prerogative by common law in this case raise a permanent revenue to himself and to his servant whom he shall employ in procuring a permanent improvement of lands in kingdom for the public good'. On projects generally, see Joan Thirsk, *Economic Policy and Projects: The Development of a Consumer Society in Early Modern England* (Oxford, 1979).

the king makes the laws of England, and to admit any other lawmaker in England is high treason ... The king who is by the rules of common law to compel his subjects to live according to virtue, is to compel them by the same common law to give way to any his discovery or design concerning the public object of *beata vita* in the preservation of man's life *in genere* with the necessary fruits of the earth, and to dispose of their lands and tenements to that end; and who shall wilfully disobey the king therein is a traitor by this definition of high treason in common law.[126]

With this radical reconceptualization of the meaning of common law, Cusacke demonstrates the need for us to rethink what we mean by the pervasiveness of the common law mind.

Even if we can dismiss Cusacke, a Dublin merchant who had enjoyed royal favour, as merely a projector from a conquered kingdom,[127] it is evident that some remarkable reconceptualizations of common law were afloat in the last years of the Personal Rule. But this evidence from the papers of Attorney General Bankes, who helped shape the crown's collection of ship money in the 1630s, cannot be easily dismissed as the fantasies of favour seekers. For on 10 March 1640, Chiver got his grant 'for the sole practice of a new way by him invented for improving and manuring of land'. The king's share was increased to half and any inconvenience in the project was to be determined not at common law but by the king or the council.[128]

IX

Whether the theology of the early Stuart church sustained a Calvinist orientation adopted with the Elizabethan settlement, maintained the middle way between Catholicism and Presbyterianism or continued Catholic traditions that still remain in the High Church tradition is currently hotly debated. There is no doubt, however, that some bishops appointed by James I, such as Richard Neile, Lancelot Andrewes, John Buckeridge and William Laud, increasingly stressed 'the beauty of holiness', with a renewed emphasis on ceremony and sacraments. The insistence of some Laudians that Protestant churches lacking bishops lay outside the apostolic succession, whereas the Church of Rome although

---

[126] Oxford, Bodleian MS. Bankes MSS. 48/13, *c.* 1637–40. I am grateful to Johann Sommerville for discussion of Cusacke's petition.

[127] Cusacke claimed to be the great-nephew of Sir Thomas Cusacke who had served as Lord Chancellor of Ireland under Edward VI and been rewarded with monastic lands. Sir Thomas had urged the Duke of Northumberland to extend English law to every part of Ireland and to extinguish the ancient jurisdictions. See *Calendar of State Papers Ireland 1625–32*, pp. 149, 152, 460, 638, 639; *Acts of the Privy Council 1629–1630*, p. 379; Bradshaw, *The Irish Constitutional Revolution of the Sixteenth Century*, pp. 190–1, 194.

[128] *CSPD 1639–40*, p. 532.

corrupt was a true church of Christ, raised fears of a crypto-Catholic conspiracy which would make the Church of England an enemy to king and parliament alike. Charles I's own support for such clergy only increased the perceived danger.[129]

Such views were reenforced when, in their effort to make uniform the language and belief systems of subjects in all three kingdoms Charles I and Archbishop Laud embarked on the misadventure of imposing the English Book of Common Prayer on the Presbyterian Scots. The result was the two Bishops Wars, in which the Scots defeated the English with the tacit support of many of them. Conrad Russell has persuasively argued that it was the challenge to this imperial crown in the form of war with the Scots and the Irish rebellion that led to the fall of the British monarchies.[130]

In November 1640, the Long Parliament set out to purge what many saw as a popish conspiracy and attack on fundamental law associated with the policies of the Personal Rule and especially with Charles's privy councillors Strafford and Laud. Strafford was impeached and attainted, not as a royal favourite – Dublin was too far from the king's person – but as an evil counsellor who had advised the king to subvert the fundamental laws and use one kingdom (Ireland) to destroy the liberties of the others. At the York assizes he was alleged to have said that 'the King's little finger should be heavier than the loins of the law' and in Dublin to have declared that 'Ireland was a conquered nation, and that the king might do with them what he pleased ... their charters were nothing worth, and did bind the king no further than he pleased.' Further, Strafford was accused of urging the king to make war on the Scots and, with the help of Archbishop Laud, procuring the dissolution of the Short Parliament, advising King Charles 'that having tried the affections of his people, he was loosed and absolved from all rules of government ... that he had an army in Ireland ... which he might employ to reduce this kingdom'. At his trial in January 1644, Laud was

---

[129] For recent work on these issues, see Peter Lake, 'Lancelot Andrewes, John Buckeridge, and Avant-Garde Conformity at the Court of James I', in *The Mental World of the Jacobean Court*, ed. Peck, pp.113–33; Lake, *Anglicans and Puritans? Presbyterianism and English Conformist Thought from Whitgift to Hooker*, (London, 1988); Lake, 'Calvinism and the English Church, 1570–1635', *Past & Present*, 114 (1987), 32–76; Lake, 'The Laudians and the Argument from Authority', in Bonnelyn Kunze and Dwight Brautigam (eds.), *Court, Country, and Culture: Essays on Early Modern British History in Honor of Perez Zagorin* (Rochester, 1992), pp. 149–76; Nicholas Tyacke, *Anti-Calvinists: The Rise of English Arminianism* (Oxford, 1987); Sheila Lambert, 'Richard Montagu, Arminianism and Censorship', *Past & Present*, 124 (1989), 36–68. Caroline Hibbard, *Charles I and The Popish Plot* (Chapel Hill, 1983); W. M. Lamont, *Marginal Prynne* 1600–1669 (London, 1963).

[130] Conrad Russell, *The Fall of the British Monarchies* (Oxford, 1991).

said to have deliberately changed Charles's coronation oath to deny a role to parliament in the making of law. Although he pleaded that he had relied on the Jacobean texts of the coronation ceremony, this charge was one of those on which he was condemned to death.[131]

In the Nineteen Propositions and the Militia Ordinance the Long Parliament claimed to control the power of the sword and nominate the king's counsellors, acting as 'the great council of the kingdom', a role at once baronial and revolutionary.[132] After his failure to arrest the Five Members on the floor of the House of Commons, Charles I withdrew from London, the capital into which his father had made triumphal entry thirty-nine years before.

When Charles I raised his standard in 1642 the English were plunged into a battle for political supremacy not seen since the Wars of the Roses. The outbreak of civil war, however, marked the breakdown of the effort to sustain what were logically impossible if not historically improbable corollaries: a divinely empowered king whose word was law but who was simultaneously bound by laws passed by his parliament; a baronage who sat at his right hand as pillars of his regime but claimed to counsel him against favourites and foreigners; humanist and Protestant obedience to a godly prince that became problematic when that prince showed signs of following the wrong god; privilege, liberties and franchises that existed within an undivided sovereignty. Historians may disagree whether the English Civil Wars were the last wars of religion (Morrill), the last wars of the baronage (Adamson), the struggle for liberty and property (Whigs), the struggle for economic ascendancy (Marxists), or no war at all (revisionists), but most agree that the fundamental political vocabulary of the English would now be deployed in new ways. The War of the Three Kingdoms put an end to the political culture of court and counsel with which this book has so far been concerned.

---

[131] Quoted in J. P. Kenyon, *The Stuart Constitution* (Cambridge, 1966), pp. 206–210. Laud claimed that his purpose was 'to mend many slips of the pen, to make sense in some places and good English in other. And the Book [of King James I Coronation] being trusted with me, I had reason to do it with my own hand, but openly at the committee.' Schramm, *A History of The English Coronation*, p. 100. One significant change did not appear in the proceedings against Laud: the king's traditional promise to guarantee the laws of Edward the Confessor to the people was truncated to refer only to the clergy. Legg, *English Coronation Records* pp. 250–1.

[132] Michael Mendle, *Dangerous Positions: Mixed Government, The Estates of the Realm, and the Making of an Answer to the XIX Propositions* (Alabama, 1985); Corinne Weston and Janelle Renfrew Greenburg, *Subjects and Sovereigns: The Grand Controversy over Legal Sovereignty in Stuart England* (Cambridge, 1981); Mendle, 'The Great Council of Parliament and the First Ordinances: The Constitutional Theory of the Civil War', *Journal of British Studies*, 31 (1992), 133–62.

Part II

Dissolution, restoration and revolution

4 The Puritan revolution: a historiographical essay

William M. Lamont

> How the purer spirit is united to this clod is a knot too hard for fallen
> humanity to untie. How should a thought be united to a marble-statue
> or a sunbeam to a lump of clay!
>
> (Joseph Glanvill)

Glanvill's question must touch a sensitive nerve in all who write about
the English Revolution of the mid seventeenth century. There was a
time when it seemed as if the momentous, if not enduring, changes
introduced in those years – the regicide, the collapse of censorship, the
removal of bishops and lords, the establishment of a republic – could be
referred *in a direct way* to the ideological conflicts of preceding generations. This is not an easy position to sustain in the light of recent
research, with its emphasis on the *agreements* of aim between crown and
parliament, the falseness of 'court' and 'country' polarities, and the
conservatism of English puritans. It has now become easier to explain
why the Civil War should never have happened than why it did.

But perhaps this recent research is wrong? If we look at the problem in
microcosm – in the career of the puritan revolutionary, William Prynne
– we can at once see that revisionism has indeed come up with the right
answers to the question whether there is 'a high road to Civil War' but to
no other. Prynne saw no conflict in aims between king and parliament
(that is to say right up to a year before he was writing the officially
commissioned Civil War case for parliament against king). He was a
consistent critic of certain court activities in the 1630s, it is true, but this
was from a reformist perspective. And his puritanism was backward-
looking, not forward: it took the form of a sentimentally idealized
Elizabethanism. No 'high road to the Civil War' here!

But there are low roads as well as high ones, and *culs de sac* which are
themselves worth exploring. The revisionists' answers are right; it is
their question which has been badly put. To the idea that Prynne's
championship of parliament in the Civil War is an *inevitable* condition-
ing of his faith (Calvinism) or his profession (the lawyer from Lincoln's
Inn) there can only be a negative response. But put the question more

diffidently – is there no relationship between the actions of the later generation and the thought of the previous generation? – and the revisionist answers no longer seem to satisfy. Prynne may have had staggeringly little to say about the constitutional and legal conflicts of the 1630s – and this is a phenomenon itself to be investigated – but the little he had to say (a lecture on the Petition of Right buried in manuscript, a treatise on Ship Money, itself not published until 1641) underwrites a thesis of conflict, not consensus. It is true that Prynne had not given up on Charles I simply because he had the misfortune to have a popish wife, but performances in court masques, however reprehensible, were for him (as for other Protestants in the 1630s) a different order of challenge from that posed in 1641 by suspected complicity in an Irish Catholic rebellion. Finally, the true conservatism of his religious convictions was shot through, from the outset, with chiliastic intimations. The way in which a millenarianism rooted in Foxe and Jewel could give way in 1641 to headier brews from Revelation – centrifugal millenarianism replacing centripetal millenarianism – is one that is now beginning to be properly understood. Elizabethanism and a New Jerusalem were complementary, not contradictory, models; until 1641, at least, that is true.

To make the English Revolution the deliberate focus for the discussion of what preceded it is not, therefore, to perpetrate some historiographical jacobitism. There is no going back to those days – not so very far away – when puritan sermons were ransacked in the 1620s and 1630s for the odd whiff of resistance theory. Into the dunghill of loyalism the historian dipped, and triumphantly plucked out the odd pearl of resistance: a Burton here, a Downing there! It is not in that spirit that this essay will discuss our three themes, Arminianism, Calvinism and the 'world turned upside down', even though it is not possible to discuss either of the first two in the 1620s and 1630s without at least touching on their relevance to the coming of the Civil War, whilst the third is seen (perhaps too confidently) as the simple consequence of what had already happened in 1642. Other reasons governed the selection of what must still seem to be arbitrary areas to focus upon. Let us examine these reasons in each case.

Arminianism has become a football in the revisionist debate: it is worth for that reason alone taking stock of the controversy so far. But two other considerations justify its inclusion in this volume. It has a major place in 'Anglican' political thought, although that term is not a little anachronistic when read backwards to Richard Hooker and even further back still to ambiguities in the origins of the Protestant Reformation itself. Read forward, however, Arminianism can be related to latitudinarianism in post-Restoration England, and to the Socinian and unitarian movements in the late seventeenth century and the latter half of the eighteenth. That is its *English* dimension. But there is also a continental dimension, and the great names here are Erasmus and Grotius. The willingness of historians in this period to move outside the confines of the nation state has already had important consequences. The rehabilitation of James I's kingship owes as much to a new awareness of what he did in Scotland as it does to a revisionist reading of his English constitutional problems.[1] Caroline Hibbard has put anti-Catholicism on the map *by putting it on the map*: by recognizing the European dimensions of an English phobia.[2] Conrad Russell has produced an elegant statement of the thesis that the English Civil War origins are a *British* problem.[3]

Calvinism would seem to require less justification as the choice for our second theme. After all, in its English form, it has been credited – among other associations – with the rise of capitalism, the creation of a modernizing ideology and even the development of a new concept of matrimony. How recent controversies cast light on all three assumptions will be discussed in what follows; more contentious will be the decision to pick up this theme, less in its own right, than as a *defensive* response to the Arminian provocation, and this too will have to be justified.

The third of our themes, that of a 'world turned upside down', sometimes seems to have sprung unbid from the fertile mind of Christopher Hill. The phenomenon of mid seventeenth-century radicalism is powerfully linked to the explosion of the printed word: with the Thomason Tracts in the British Library, with all those Leveller, Digger, Ranter, Muggletonian outpourings. Enough, of course, was known in general about them to inspire the loathing for 'enthusiasm' which is so prominent a theme in succeeding chapters in this volume: England now had its own Münster monster. But the detailed recovery of the texts was another matter. Catharine Macaulay and Carlyle were pioneers in the field. We had to await the deciphering of William Clarke's shorthand, and the editorship of his papers by Sir Charles Firth, before the Putney Debates became accessible to us. Notoriously, Marx and Engels missed Winstanley.

In the past twenty years, however, the position has been redressed, and it is the overwhelming achievement of Christopher Hill and others

---

[1] Gordon Donaldson, *Scotland: James V–VII* (Edinburgh, 1965); Jenny Wormald, 'James VI and I: Two Kings or One?', *History*, 68, 223 (June 1983), 187–209; Christina Larner, 'James VI and I and Witchcraft', in A. G. R. Smith (ed.), *The Reign of James VI and I* (London, 1973), pp. 74–90.

[2] Caroline Hibbard, *Charles I and the Popish Plot* (Chapel Hill, 1983).

[3] Conrad Russell, 'The British Problem and the English Civil War', *History*, 72, 236 (1987), 395–415; *The Fall of the British Monarchies 1637–1642* (Oxford, 1991).

to have made the existence of a proletarian 'third culture' in our period the object of scholarly debate.[4] But debate it still is, while at least three questions remain to be answered. First, given the importance in this movement of the printed word, what do we know of its reception? The specialists in this field provide humbling information about the persisting depth of our ignorance on such crucial matters as the numbers of copies produced in editions, the circumstances of production, the pressures of censorship, the contribution of the printer to the text, even the significance of the types of print used, and so on.[5] Second: how do we give proper weighting to a very unequal development? There is the sudden influx of the printed word when Thomason begins collecting, to be set against the erratic restrictions of the 1630s market. There is the imbalance of the prevalence of the printed word in our period against the relative drying-up of private sources.[6] It is easy in such circumstances to overemphasize both the novelty and the importance of this material. Third, is Hill's methodology the right way, indeed the only way, to read 'the world turned upside down'? By his methodology I mean a 'horizontal' approach to his texts (a term that will be explained later) which, when applied to writers as seemingly diverse as Hobbes and Winstanley, may yield some rewarding insights. Does the method overreach itself, on the other hand, when a writer as complex as Milton is seen in relationship to a radical underground 'third culture'? To see the writer in the context of his time seems to those of us who have contributed to this volume one of the most difficult, but rewarding, tasks the intellectual historian can engage in. This is how Quentin Skinner made us revalue (not reduce) Hobbes by placing *Leviathan* in the *de facto* controversies provoked by the Engagement Controversy.[7] J. M. Wallace put Marvell's *Horatian Ode* in a similar context.[8] J. G. A. Pocock related Harrington's *Oceana* to the debates in the second Protectorate parliament.[9] The present writer tried to set Baxter's *Christian Directory* against a particular crisis in post-Restoration nonconformity.[10] However, in all

---

[4] William Lamont, 'The Left and its Past: Revisiting the 1650's', *History Workshop*, 23 (1987), 141–54, discusses the losses as well as the gains of this emphasis.

[5] Like other contributors to this volume I am indebted to Elizabeth Eisenstein and Peter Blayney for the generous way they shared their expertise with us on this theme, so important to political thought, in discussions in the Folger Library.

[6] The profusion of printed material in this period has to be set against 'the great dearth of archives (extending even to private estate documents)': Conrad Russell, 'Losers', *London Review of Books*, 6, 18 (1984), 20–2.

[7] Quentin Skinner, 'Conquest and Consent: Thomas Hobbes and the Engagement Controversy', in G. E. Aylmer (ed.), *The Interregnum* (London, 1972), pp. 79–98.

[8] J. M. Wallace, *Destiny his Choice, The Loyalism of Andrew Marvell* (Cambridge, 1968).

[9] J. G. A. Pocock, 'James Harrington and the Good Old Cause', *Journal of British Studies*, 10, 1 (1970), 30–48.

[10] William Lamont, *Richard Baxter and the Millennium* (London, 1979).

these cases, a text was being set against a specific political circumstance. Hill's *Milton* is more ambitious: it is nothing less than to set an entire career against a particular set of political priorities. The gains and the losses of such a venture need to be weighed.

I

The first controversial area we have chosen for comment seems, at first sight, a classic example of how the introduction of a continental dimension has transformed our understanding of the subject. Nicholas Tyacke had turned upside down previous perceptions of Calvinism as a destabilizing ideology, Arminianism as a creed for conservatives.[11] That interpretation, however, has now been challenged by Peter White. For he does not simply argue back (against Tyacke) that Calvinism does inflame, Arminianism does stabilize. He argues something much more interesting: that the 'two sides' are themselves myths, that Arminianism understood properly is an offshoot of the Calvinist or reformed tradition of thought.[12] In other words, like other scholars of the new wave, White is calling on Europe (mainly on Holland and France) to redress English insularity; he is drawing upon excellent work on continental theologians (notably by B. G. Armstrong and C. H. Bangs);[13] he is using this material to debunk the idea of two ideologically armed camps moving towards 1642; his conclusion, therefore, is that the rise of Arminianism was 'a puritan alibi', not a cause of the Civil War.

This analysis of ecclesiastical conflict chimes agreeably with recent political and constitutional revisionism.[14] Historians, sensitive to the power of popular pelagianism, see nothing traumatic in its manifestation in courtly circles at the time of Archbishop Laud: for them, the aberration at Canterbury was Abbot. But anti-revisionist historians such as Christopher Hill found here surprising common ground with his opponents: he, as much as they, bridled at the idea of Laud as an aberration. Indeed, Hill's perception of Laud's place in the history of the English church is not unlike A. J. P. Taylor's perception of Hitler's

---

[11] Nicholas Tyacke, *Anti-Calvinists: The Rise of English Arminianism* c. *1590–1640* (Oxford, 1987).

[12] Peter White, 'The Rise of Arminianism Reconsidered', *Past and Present*, 101 (1983), 34–54. See also Sheila Lambert, 'Richard Montagu, Arminianism and Censorship', *Past and Present*, 124 (1989), 36–48.

[13] B. G. Armstrong, *Calvinism and the Amyraut Heresy; Protestant Scholasticism and Humanism in Seventeenth-Century France* (Madison, 1969); C. Bangs, *Arminius; A Study in the Dutch Reformation* (Nashville, 1971).

[14] Christopher Haigh, 'The Church of England, the Catholics and the People', in Christopher Haigh (ed.), *The Reign of Elizabeth I* (London, 1984), pp. 195–220.

place in German history: a little worse than his predecessors, but not so very different from them.[15]

However, two historiographical problems present themselves at once with White's thesis. He seeks to deny 'any doctrinal high road to civil war' with a discussion which itself ends in 1629: a reasonable terminal date for the rise of Arminianism (the subject of his paper) but not for the religious origins of the Civil War. If the rise of Arminianism before 1629 was as innocent of ideological calculation as he argues, and if the imposed truce between 1629 and 1640 was as even-handed as he implies[16] – both dubious propositions – it still would not follow that a sincere (if now shown to be mistaken) perception of a doctrinal counter-revolution in the minds of Laud's opponents was a factor that could thus be discounted by historians explaining the origins of the Civil War. A word like 'alibi' confuses intentionality with effect.

Closely related to this point is the demonstration of false polarities. Peter Lake, replying to White,[17] drew attention to the valuable article by Stuart Clark (who has written equally acutely on James I, witchcraft and the millennium) in which he pointed out how important it was in this period for Englishmen to see the world in terms of binary oppositions and inversions.[18] Political and religious polemic thrived on the assimilation of one's opponent to a discredited polarity: popery versus puritanism, pelagianism versus antinomianism. The claim made for oneself was the ability to hit upon a golden mean between two extremes: one fruit of the Aristotelian revival of late sixteenth-century England. Contemporaries saw through the humbug. Richard Baxter once said:

I never thought that when ever men differ, it is my duty to go in a middle between both (for so that middle will be next taken for an extream, and men must seek out another middle to avoyd that).

[15] Christopher Hill, 'Archbishop Laud and the English Revolution', in Gordon J. Schochet (ed.), *Religion, Resistance and Civil War*, Proceedings of the Folger Institute Center for the History of British Political Thoughts, vol. 3 (Washington D.C., 1990), pp. 127–50. Laud is less of an aberration, of course, if figures such as Bancroft and Andrewes can already be seen as anti-Calvinists. Tyacke (*Anti-Calvinists*, p. 17) argues against this for Bancroft, however, and Peter Lake similarly for Andrewes; see Lake, 'Lancelot Andrewes, John Buckeridge and Avant-garde Conformity at the Court of James I', in *The Mental World of the Jacobean Court*, ed. Linda Levy Peck (Cambridge, 1991), pp. 113–33.

[16] For an interpretation strikingly different from White's, of the nature of the 'truce' of the 1630s, see Dewey D. Wallace Jr., *Puritans and Predestination: Grace in English Protestant Theology, 1525–1695* (Chapel Hill, 1982), pp. 83–104. Even more devastating (when it is published) will be Anthony Milton, 'The Laudians and the Church of Rome, 1625–1640', unpublished PhD thesis, University of Cambridge, 1989.

[17] Peter Lake, 'Calvinism and the English Church, 1570–1635', *Past and Present*, 114 (1987), 32–76.

[18] Stuart Clark, 'Inversion, Misrule and the Meaning of Witchcraft', *Past and Present*, 87 (1980), 98–127.

Yet in the very tract where he wrote those wise words, *Confession of his Faith* (1655), he proceeded to draw up a number of pages into three columns, and labelled them 'antinomian', 'truth' and 'papist'. The fact that 'papist', not 'Arminian', is seen as the opposite of 'antinomian' tells us where he found his 'truth' in 1655.[19]

To see Arminianism developing out of continental Calvinism is one thing; to see the Laudian supremacy in England between 1629 and 1640 in the same light is another. Because, whatever else it was, Laudianism was not a celebration of intellectual endeavour; it was (*pace* White) a period when one side stifled the views of the other. Thus, when Richard Baxter in 1655 is genuinely trying to recover an Arminian tradition, where does he turn to? As one might have expected from Armstrong's illuminating study, to Cameron, to Amyraut and (in England) to Davenant – the exponents of 'hypothetical universalism'. Apart from Davenant (a victim, not a beneficiary, of the Laudian take-over), Baxter has to go back in time to the 'practical preachers' of the 1620s for inspiration – Sibbes, Gouge, Dod, Preston, Bolton – not forward to the Laudians of the 1630s. The disputes at Cambridge in 1595/6 and the aftermath of the Synod of Dort had ensured that there were two sides: as Lake reminds us, if contemporaries perceived two sides, their perceptions have to be integrated into our account.

Nor was it mistaken for contemporaries to perceive two sides. It is the greatest single merit of Tyacke's scrupulously documented work to show how one group of clergymen wrested control of the Church of England from another. Similarities between Laud and all his predecessors pale beside this one towering dissimilarity: Laud was the first anti-Calvinist ever to become Archbishop of Canterbury. It is a measure of Tyacke's confidence that he can afford to leave the best joke about Arminianism to the last page of his book, but he has good reason for doing so. Bishop Morley was asked what the Arminians held. He replied that 'they held all the best bishoprics and deaneries in England'. It is a very good joke, and a very English one. There is something healthily non-ideological about it; it chimes with the protestations of Laud and his controversial supporter, Montague, that they had never actually *read* Arminius. That is precisely the case that cannot be made now in the light of Tyacke's careful researches into continental influences, correspondence across the waters, the control of doctoral theses and the like. The Morley anecdote did not come from a neutral source. It came from Clarendon who had his own reasons for arguing that the rot set in for the Church of England with Abbot's indolence, not Laud's intemperance.

[19] Richard Baxter, *Confession of his Faith* (London, 1655), preface.

The negative use to which the Laudians put their power says more about their intellectual limitations than about any absence of ideological conviction. The wrong people took up the right cause: that is the theme of Hugh Trevor-Roper's recent *Catholics, Anglicans and Puritans* when he returns, after a lifetime of scholarship, to his first study, Archbishop Laud.[20] Nobody has better than he – in his *Religion, the Reformation and Social Change*, most notably – put 'the Pyrrhonist crisis' of the earlier seventeenth century in its continental dimension. Erasmus, Hooker, Grotius – these were the mind-enhancing influences which became straitjacketed into Neile's and Laud's narrow programmes of church reform – and this gave the story of English Arminianism its 'tragic' overtones. Blair Worden reviewing Trevor-Roper's analysis sympathetically comments: 'It was not Arminianism that brought down Charles I, but Charles I who brought down Arminianism'.[21] This was very much what Baxter had written to a friend in 1653:

And doubtless, one reason why they [the Arminians] were so bad in England was, that the godly being first entered into another schoole, and so running one way (much by the force of example and affection and much by divine grace) the others were temporizers that took up the opinions for worldly respects.[22]

Thus Arminianism and impiety were *contingently*, not *causally*, related. This was what he said in 1653, but not what he had said of Arminianism earlier and not what he would ever say about antinomianism.

This did not mean that Baxter, in recovering the Arminian tradition, was not himself affected by the Pyrrhonist crisis. It led to his discussion, in *Catholick Theologie*, of the nature of truth, to an emphasis on *probability*, not *certainty*, as the antidote to fear, and to his separation of 'objective certainty' from 'subjective certainty': 'men may be *uncertain* of that which is certain in itself'. In Baxter's case, the Pyrrhonist crisis led him back to the 'practical preachers' of the 1620s whose no-nonsense casuistry he so much admired.[23]

The rehabilitation of the importance of Arminian doctrine does not reduce the problem from which this chapter started; in some ways, it worsens it. The more seriously we take the theory, the more divergent it seems from the practice. John Selden, as usual, was there first. He spoke of puritans 'who will allow no free will, but God does all'. Then he pointed out the incongruity of these same people allowing 'the subject his liberty to do or not to do, notwithstanding the king, the God upon

[20] Hugh Trevor-Roper, *Catholics, Anglicans and Puritans* (London, 1987), esp. pp. 40–120, 'Laudianism and Political Power'.
[21] Blair Worden, 'Intellectual Liberation', *London Review of Books*, 10, 2 (1988).
[22] William Lamont, *Richard Baxter and the Millennium* (London, 1979), p. 127.
[23] William Lamont, 'The Rise of Arminianism Reconsidered', *Past and Present*, 107 (1985), 229–30.

earth'. But worse was to follow: 'The Arminians, who hold we have free-will, yet say, when we come to the king there must be all obedience, and no liberty must be stood for.[24] How indeed to unite a thought with a marble statue, a sunbeam to a lump of clay? Or to put it another way, why *should* freedom have become associated with a bunch of high-flying, absolutist clergymen? They were not even then the only Arminians in England. Tyacke has one footnote allusion to the Arminian General Baptists in his entire book, and that seems miserly in view of their influence on the Arminians of the 1650s: Baxter (as we have already seen), Milton, John Goodwin, George Fox and the Quakers. It is not the case that Tyacke is unaware of the wider philosophical currents, as is evident in an earlier piece which he wrote in 1981 on 'Arminianism and English Culture'.[25] But though interesting cross-references between Arminians and *libertins* are drawn there, they are not associated (nor could they be) with a conscious programme initiated from the top by Arminians in office (which was the subject of his book). Baxter, recovering the doctrine of freedom in the 1650s for his fellow puritans, lamented (as Trevor-Roper was to do, from another angle) the difficulty in detaching the term 'Arminian' from its unfortunate, but contingent, association with Laudian clergymen. The Laudians, we now know, perpetrated the self-fulfilling prophecy that all Calvinists were puritans; it would take a later generation to discover, with Baxter, the truth that not all puritans were Calvinists.

II

We needed to reevaluate Arminianism before we could reevaluate English Calvinism. Once we understood its essentially defensive nature, other findings fell into place. That an English Calvinist, like William Prynne, could (up to 1641, that is) offer as the summit of his ambitions a return to the Elizabethan church, no longer surprises. That he would support Archbishop Whitgift ('an arrant Puritane') against the Eliza-bethan Presbyterian, Cartwright ('an opposite') is similarly intelligible. And so, too, with his invocation of the Lambeth Articles and the Synod of Dort against new-fangled 'Copernican' doctrinal innovations, and even his attacks on 'the Prelates Intollerable Usurpations Upon the King's Prerogative' (to quote from part of his lengthy title of 1637).[26]

---

[24] John Selden, *Table Talk*, ed. S. Reynolds (Oxford, 1892), p. 71.
[25] Nicholas Tyacke, 'Arminianism and English Culture', in A. C. Duke and C. A. Tamse (eds.), *Britain and the Netherlands* (The Hague, 1981), VII, pp. 94–117.
[26] William Prynne, *A Breviate of the Prelates Intollerable Usurpations* ... (London, 1637), p. 123.

This was the profile of a man who would have no truck with 'root and branch', who would be won to the chances of a 'reduced episcopacy' on the lines set out by Ussher, and who would rally to the compromise leadership of a bishop like John Williams. Except that Prynne (like many other English Protestants) did none of these things in 1641, and instead threw in his lot with 'root and branch'.

To understand the *mentalité* of the English Calvinist in 1641 covert comparisons with Victorian nonconformity must be rejected. Keith Thomas' *Religion and the Decline of Magic* is one key to a world where witches fly at night, women give birth to monsters, the Jesuits peddle lies and the Book of Revelation conveys truths. The world which anthropology has opened up for us – and which has enhanced our understanding of popular culture, charivari, witchcraft, lunacy, crime, marriage, and many other aspects of our social history[27] – has at the same time closed other doors, most notably the assimilation of seventeenth-century puritanism with Victorian nonconformity. No scholar has taken us into the early modern Protestant mind with greater penetration than has Patrick Collinson; in his Ford Lectures he has stripped away nineteenth-century preconceptions about his subject (and it is significant that his recent collection of essays should contain, in the introduction, acknowledgement of his primary debt to Thomas' 'giant of a book').[28] The nineteenth-century preconceptions often derive from a 'vertical' reading of history, particularly to be found in denominational histories. In a seminal essay, Collinson contrasted the 'vertical' approach with the 'horizontal' approach, which has characterized more recent religious history written deliberately outside a denominational perspective.[29] There are losses as well as gains in this shift in historiography, as we shall see later; Collinson's is far from being an unequivocal endorsement of the 'horizontal' approach. Where that approach works, however, with telling effect is shown, for example, in the rehabilitation of John Foxe as a major intellectual influence. Victorian nonconformity gobbled up Foxe's *Book of Martyrs* in edition after edition as an arsenal of anti-Catholic bigotry. Scholars such as Yates, Haller, Olsen and others have taught us to honour the design of the author of *Acts and Monuments*, whose anti-Catholicism is to be placed in an eschatological

---

[27] The best recent summary of these developments is to be found in Keith Wrightson, *English Society 1580–1680* (London, 1982).

[28] Patrick Collinson, *The Religion of Protestants* (Oxford, 1982); *Godly People* (London, 1983).

[29] Patrick Collinson, 'Towards a Broader Understanding of the Early Dissenting Tradition', in R. C. Cole and M. E. Moody (eds.), *The Dissenting Tradition: Essays for Leland H. Carlson* (Ohio, 1975), pp. 3–38.

framework.[30] Caroline Hibbard, in her study of Charles I and the Popish Plot, has shown how embarrassed and confused S. R. Gardiner, greatest of all Victorian interpreters of English Puritanism, became when confronted with the depth of anti-Catholicism in men whom he saw as his ancestors. The irony is that the decent, humane Foxe who fought to save Edmund Campion and Dutch Anabaptists from execution had more in common with Gardiner than with those contemporaries of Gardiner who most identified with the historian of Protestant martyrs. The history of anti-Catholicism is being rewritten by Hibbard, Anthony Fletcher (in his account of the coming of the Civil War) and Robin Clifton (in his doctoral dissertation and his later book on the Monmouth Rising): the effect of their researches, and those of others in the field, is to put anti-Catholicism in the centre, not periphery, of events, and show it belonging not so much to psychopathology as to eschatology.[31]

If 'root and branch' won converts in 1641 as much by anti-Catholic fears as by millennial hopes (and the two were often, of course, inseparably intertwined) there were contemporaries like Clarendon (and after them, historians like Trevor-Roper) swift to denounce the bad faith of their opponents. Conrad Russell has already demonstrated how Pym's career was built on the premature (in 1624, that is) identification of 'Arminianism' as *the* issue and *the* enemy.[32] The subsequent elision of 'Arminianism' with 'Popery', and the demonstration of Irish Rebellion as the fulfilment of prophecy, were Pym's master-cards in converting many of his countrymen, non-resisters in their bones, to the need for recourse to arms. It is easy for others besides Clarendon to see this as the triumph of calculation and perhaps, as Michael Finlayson does too readily, to equate Pym's career with that of Shaftesbury later. In Finlayson's hands 'anti-Catholicism' becomes a catch-all explanatory system throughout the century, without his showing the sensitivity of Hibbard and Clifton to the *particular* event and time which made the concept grip the imagination of men and women, on whom its hold was

---

[30] Frances Yates, *Astraea: The Imperial Theme in the Sixteenth Century* (London, 1975); William Haller, *Foxe's Book of Martyrs and the Elect Nation* (London, 1963); V. N. Olsen, *John Foxe and the Elizabethan Church* (California, 1973).

[31] Caroline Hibbard, *Charles I and the Popish Plot*; Anthony Fletcher, *The Outbreak of the English Civil War* (London, 1981); Robin Clifton: 'The Fear of Catholics in England, 1637–45', unpublished DPhil thesis, University of Oxford, 1964; *The Last Popular Rebellion* (London, 1984); 'Lessons and Consequences of the Rebellion of 1685', Schochet (ed.), *Religion, Resistance and Civil War*, pp. 115–26.

[32] Conrad Russell, 'Parliamentary Career of John Pym 1621–1629', in *English Commonwealth, 1547–1640: Essays in Politics and Society Presented to Joel Hurstfield*, ed. P. Clark et al. (Leicester, 1979), esp. pp. 159–62.

tenuous in other circumstances.[33] Hibbard used her command of court sources to document Catholic intrigue at the Court of Charles I from the late 1630s to the outbreak of Civil War. She does not believe that there was a single 'papist' conspiracy at court which provoked the Civil War. On the other hand, she distinguishes skilfully all the complicated intrigues around the court which inspired the rumours which made such beliefs plausible, not simply, *pace* Clarendon, to men and women of bad faith. Many of these intrigues were self-contradictory. Most, but not all of them, centred around Charles I's Catholic wife, Henrietta Maria. Charles I still awaits the biographer to explain to our satisfaction his relationship to his wife and to these intrigues. Ominously for him, by 1641 a significant number of Charles I's subjects thought that they had such an explanation. The people at court who fuelled their suspicions were a motley crew – Henrietta Maria herself, Scottish Catholics, the mission of George Con, Montagu, Digby, Jesuits, seculars, anti-Richelieu exiles, Spanish sympathizers and others. Hibbard's strength is to place these intrigues in the context of the Thirty Years' War. It is the restoration of an European dimension to the problem – so evident in contemporary sources – which makes the threat to England posed by the numerically insignificant Catholics one not of illusion but of substance.

In such a context the Irish Rebellion of October 1641 becomes the logical, as well as chronological, prelude to civil war in 1642. And the Antrim Commission – linking Crown with rebellion – becomes a key document.[34] Who was the Earl of Antrim? He was the Irish Catholic, Randall MacDonnell, who had married Katherine, the widow of the Duke of Buckingham and herself a Catholic convert. Until moving to Ireland late in 1638 with her new husband, the Duchess occasionally carried messages between Laud and the papal agent at Henrietta Maria's court, George Con. Antrim had, as early as the beginning of 1638, presented to Charles I and Henrietta Maria a plan to take an army of his Ulster clansmen (he claimed to be able to raise 10,000) to Scotland to crush Protestant rebellion. When the king needed his help in May 1639 Antrim was then not able to honour his promises. But later? He was one of the leaders of the Irish Catholic Rebellion of October 1641. He was a personal friend of the leader of the rebels, Phelim O'Neill. After the Restoration the scandalous claim was made that Charles I had given

[33] Michael Finlayson, *Historians, Puritanism, and the English Revolution: The Religious Factor in English Politics before and after the Interregnum* (Toronto, 1983).
[34] Conrad Russell, 'The British Background to the Irish Rebellion of 1641', *Historical Research*, 61, 145 (1988), pp. 166–82, shows the historical (as opposed to mythical) unimportance of this belief. See now Jane Ohlmeyer, *Civil War and Restoration in the Three Stuart Kingdoms: The Career of Randal MacDonnell, Marquis of Antrim, 1609–1683* (Cambridge, 1993).

backing to Antrim in his actions in the Irish Rebellion (beginning in the 1641 rising, continuing in the king's support for Antrim's revival of the 1638 project in the spring of 1643, and culminating in his approval of Antrim's alliance with Montrose's Highlanders between 1644 and 1645). Worse still was alleged: that Charles II recognized the validity of the understanding between the Earl and his father – the notorious Antrim Commission – when he pardoned him at the Restoration. The present writer has traced the story of the Antrim Commission in a study of Baxter, and has argued its (concealed) importance in persuading Baxter to side with parliament; Fletcher has shown the importance of such suspicions of the crown in the origins of the Civil War; both hypotheses have been given an extra boost in Paul Seaver's fascinating later study of a London artisan, *Wallington's World*, where we see the same forces at work.[35]

Baxter, Pym's 'root and branchers', Wallington: none may be presumed to be Paisleyites *avant la lettre* in their conviction of the reality of a Royalist 'Popish Plot' in 1641. What Clifton's doctoral research showed is that anti-Catholicism was not a constant tap, to be switched on and off, at the whim of a demagogue. He revealed, for instance, how Plymouth was seriously damaged by its Great Fire of 1637 without unleashing a violent anti-Catholic *pogrom*. Yet his study also demonstrated the fragility of the peace: how *potential* anti-Catholicism could become *actual* and violent when it was linked with doubts about the crown's position. Hence, the traumatic shock of the Irish Catholic Rebellion and the significance (the Antrim Commission) of the rebels' claims – only half-heartedly contested – to be fighting with the crown's approval. Thus on the fifth of November 1641 (a happy date) Pym could urge on his colleagues – no need for the equivocations of his Short Parliament speech in April 1640: 'Wee must not look on a Papist as he is in himselfe *but as he is in the body of the Church*'[36] – the importance of sending in the Scottish Army to fight the rebels in Northern Ireland, and the need for 'ill councillors' to be removed before parliament took further steps to relieve Ireland: itself the pretext for the Militia Ordinance, which caused the final breach between king and parliament.

It is not wholly true, as is sometimes alleged, that the Protestant imperialists had no political texts to justify rebellion – setting aside the discredited Knox, Goodman, Buchanan, Ponet. They had Bilson, Grotius and Barclay (and Baxter was one who invoked all three retrospec-

---

[35] William Lamont, *Richard Baxter and the Millennium*, pp. 76–88; Paul Seaver, *Wallington's World: A Puritan Artisan in Seventeenth-Century London* (Stanford, 1985).
[36] Quoted by K. Lindley, 'The Part Played by the Catholics', in B. Manning (ed.), *Politics, Religion and the English Civil War* (London, 1973), p. 173.

tively): in their varying ways, each recognized that a king who went mad, invaded his own realm, and subordinated his authority to the pope, ceased to have authority over his subjects. To the Protestant, this was a logical extension of imperialist theory, not its refutation: Baxter thus called Bilson a teacher of *obedience*.[37] In constitutional matters, Baxter preferred to follow George Lawson,[38] who argued that the quarrel over the militia had led to the dissolution of government, than to heed Henry Parker who argued, in such circumstances, that the king should be recognised only as *singulis maior, universis minor*. Baxter attributed that dreadful maxim to Richard Hooker: 'As bad as Hooker!' was his dismissal of a contemporary who was rash enough to quote it, in a letter to him.[39]

Protestant Englishmen were not (either in theory or practice) therefore without remedy when faced with a king mad enough to throw his imperial crown at the pope's feet. The solution was no more republican in its implications than were the traditional constitutional arguments: the king was in need of rescue, not only from evil counsellors who had advised him to impose Ship Money, but equally from his papist would-be captors. It was not until as late as 1643 that Prynne, for instance, saw Charles I as an accomplice, rather than the dupe, of papist designs; Prynne's *Popish Royall Favourite* would, in turn, have a profound effect on Baxter. When Henry Parker, John Sadler and Thomas May published *The King's Cabinet Opened* (1645), after the capture of the king's papers at Naseby, the suspicions raised by the Antrim Commission were at last confirmed.

The time-lag, though, tells its own story, as does Baxter's revulsion from Hooker's populism. His reason for this reaction underlines the formidable strengths, in the war of words, which still lay with the crown: 'rebellion is so heynous a sin, that we have 100 times more reason to cry it down . . . than to tell the people when they may resist.'[40] John Morrill makes the important point that between the Grand Remonstrance in December 1641 and the King's *Answer to the XIX Propositions* in June 1642 each side responded directly to the other within days. The silence after the *Answer* is deafening, as Morrill points out: the Houses made no further declaration for six weeks.[41]

[37] For the curiously varied seventeenth-century reception of Bilson, see William Lamont, 'The Rise and Fall of Bishop Bilson', *The Journal of British Studies*, 5, 2 (1966), 22–32.
[38] Conal Condren, 'Statement and Resistance Reconsidered: An Aporetic Reading of Lawson's *Politica*', in Schochet (ed.), *Religion, Resistance and Civil War*, pp. 201–21.
[39] Richard Hooker, *Of the Laws of Ecclesiastical Polity*, ed. A. S. McGrade (Cambridge, 1989), p. 143. Baxter's rebuke was to his friend John Humfrey (*A Case of Conscience*, (1669)) in a private letter: (Dr Williams' Library) *Baxter Correspondence*, III, fos. 11ᵛ–12.
[40] (Dr Williams' Library) *Baxter Treatises*, VI, fol. 293.
[41] John Morrill, 'Rhetoric and Action: Charles I, Tyranny, and the English Revolution', Schochet (ed.), *Religion, Resistance and Civil War*, pp. 91–114.

Instead it would be outside Parliament that the most emphatic repudiation of its thesis would come: Henry Parker's *Observations upon some of his majesties late answers and expresses* of June 1642. Parker is an under-researched figure. Though Michael Mendle's expected reinterpretation will fill in much that has hitherto been obscured (particularly on Parker's relationship with his uncle, Lord Saye and Sele) it is not likely to dislodge the accepted view (expressed by Margaret Judson)[42] that Parker is the earliest, and most important, exponent of the defence of parliamentary sovereignty. That dubious crown should have been William Prynne's: in 1643, parliament had commissioned him to write, under that title, the official defence of its actions. Prynne knew enough Bodin to quote him and even to part-understand him; there are passages in Prynne's work which echo Parker in the claims made for parliament's sovereignty over the laws of the land and over Magna Carta; but, unlike Parker, he gets bogged down in precedents and self-contradictions and, in truth, his work belongs to that genre of *post hoc* justifications for actions taken and debating replies to points raised by opponents, which Morrill saw as characteristic of the exchanges between Crown and Parliament up to the King's reply to the Nineteen Propositions.[43] But it may be with Henry Parker as with other seventeenth-century figures: that commentators have over-secularized their man. For all their differences in verbal sophistication, Parker inhabits the same universe as Prynne. 'The main Engineers in this Civill Warre are Papists, the most poysonous, serpentine, Jesuited Papists of the world': this was said, not by Prynne, but by Parker.[44] And in another pamphlet Parker said in 1645 what Prynne had been saying repeatedly in the 1630s: that the Laudians' major crime was not to exalt the Royal Supremacy but to emasculate it by *iure divino* pretensions for episcopacy.[45] If in an earlier pamphlet, *The Oath of Pacification*, he sneered at Prynne's predilections for plots and conspiracies[46], it was on grounds of the weakness of the material produced, not on the soundness of the thesis. Parker did not need to believe in the existence of *a* Popish Plot (particularly when it came bedecked in Prynne's lurid colours) to be convinced of the existence of *the* Popish Plot.

Michael Walzer is an historian who has reminded his colleagues of the need to keep the seventeenth-century's own preoccupations at the centre

---

[42] Margaret Judson, *The Crisis of the Constitution* (New Brunswick, 1949); Michael Mendle, 'Henry Parker: The Public's Privado', Schochet (ed.), *Religion, Resistance and Civil War*, pp. 151–78.

[43] William Lamont, *Marginal Prynne* (London, 1963), pp. 85–119.

[44] Henry Parker, *The Contra-Replicant* (London, 1643), p. 9.

[45] Henry Parker, *Ius Regum* (London, 1645), pp. 26–7.

[46] Henry Parker, *The Oath of Pacification* (London, 1643), p. 23.

of the stage.[47] He remarks with some scorn: 'in the Marxist world of economic reason, beggars are duly whipped, witches untouched by the flame'. It cannot be said that his own counter-model has been convincing: the attempt to portray mainstream puritans, not the fringe sects, as the vehicles of modernization, 'the revolution of the saints'. This is because he has not followed his own advice. By omitting Foxe and distorting Jewel (who becomes an implausible internal exile), by reifying puritanism and obliterating refinements of distinction in time and place, by failing to recognize the dependence of the English Calvinist on the godly magistrate, he imposes false twentieth-century presuppositions on his own early-modern man. But that does not disqualify him as a witness against other scholars who have written on the Protestant ethic.

R. H. Tawney cannot be said to hold the field; but, though published as long ago as 1926, his *Religion and the Rise of Capitalism* still commands an influence – its themes are developed explicitly by Christopher Hill and R. B. Schlatter and indirectly by C. B. Macpherson[48] – which is itself a tribute to the importance of the issues it raises. Baxter was a key text in Tawney's work; for Walzer, he is, contrariwise, an example of the barrier which could not be crossed between the seventeenth-century puritan and the modern capitalist spirit. Walzer quotes from Baxter's own autobiography his boast that 'in his Kidderminster parish the enforcement of the new moral order was made possible by "the zeal and diligence of the godly people of the place who thirsted after the salvation of their neighbours and were in private my assistants"'. To Walzer, this is the spirit of the covenant ('institutionalises suspicion and mutual surveillance') as against that of the contract ('assumes trust, a mutual recognition of economic rationality and even of good will'). Walzer goes on to speak of the Puritans' 'almost Manichean warfare against Satan and his worldly allies, their nervous lust for systematic repression and control' as being 'not compatible with liberal thinking or with entrepreneurial activity'. Instead, Walzer claims, 'they point directly to the revolution, when the struggle against Antichrist would be acted out and, for a brief moment, the repressive Holy Commonwealth established'.[49]

---

[47] Michael Walzer, *The Revolution of the Saints* (London, 1966) and also his 'Puritanism as a Revolutionary Ideology', *History and Theory*, 3 (1963–4), 59–90.

[48] Christopher Hill, *The World Turned Upside Down* (London, 1972); R. B. Schlatter, *The Social Ideas of Religious Leaders, 1660–1688* (New York, 1971); C. B. Macpherson, *The Political Theory of Possessive Individualism* (Oxford, 1962).

[49] Walzer, 'Puritanism as a Revolutionary Ideology', pp. 63–5. We now have a brilliant recreation of one 'repressive Holy Commonwealth', in John White's Dorchester; see David Underdown, *Fire from Heaven: Life in an English Town in the Seventeenth Century* (London, 1992).

Here we have, neatly encapsulated, the strengths and weaknesses of Walzer. He shrewdly relates Baxter to struggles against Antichrist, and the building of repressive Holy Commonwealths. Moreover, Walzer emphasizes the gap between the suspicion that cements the covenant and the mutual forbearance that governs the market exchange. It was a gap that would concern Blair Worden when he wrote about religious toleration. That 'Victorian subject, a monument to Victorian liberalism' was not the proper point of entry for Calvinist scruples about liberty of conscience.[50] And the weaknesses? First, Walzer's claim that these qualities 'point directly to the revolution'; they always do, in Walzer's reconstructions. Second, that Baxter's commitment to a clerical spy system (so antithetical to the rise of modern capitalism) is not drawn from Baxter's writings or practice, but from *remembered* practice in memoirs written after the Restoration, although not published posthumously until 1696. This would seem inferior to the voluminous quotations from Baxter's *Christian Directory* in Tawney, Schlatter and Hill. Yet more detailed research once more corroborates Walzer's hunch: the recovery of Baxter's last treatise, *The Poor Husbandman's Advocate*, shows how far Baxter was from endorsement of the Protestant ethic; the record of his activities in the Commonwealth supports the claims that he would make in his memoirs later; *Christian Directory* is an interim statement of aims (for a specific polemical purpose) which is contradicted by both earlier and later testaments.[51]

For these reasons, Walzer penetrates the seventeenth-century mind in a way that Christopher Hill does not. Hill, for instance, quotes from *Reliquiae Baxterianae*: '"The rich will rule in the world", sighed the well-to-do Richard Baxter philosophically, "and few rich men will be saints".' The 'well-to-do' is irrelevant, the philosophical sighs invented. The context of the quoted passage is an exchange between two men, Baxter and Eliot, who had been caught up in the 1650s with the millennial excitements opened up by missionary work among the heathen. Eliot retained that excitement in New England and thus even in 1663 could write to Baxter of his hopes of a universal language and the imminent prospect of the world becoming a Divine College. The excerpt is taken from Baxter's chastened reply of 30 November 1663; a cautionary word to a valued fellow activist is some distance from a smug acceptance of the society of his day.

More telling for the identification of the early modern puritan with the

---

[50] Blair Worden, 'Toleration and the Cromwellian Protectorate', in W. J. Sheils (ed.), *Studies in Church History* (1984), pp. 199–233.

[51] These points are developed at length in Lamont, *Richard Baxter and the Millennium*, pp. 309–19.

Protestant ethic is Christopher Hill's quotation from Baxter's *Christian Directory*:

Whensoever the preservation of life is not in open probability like to be more serviceable to the common good than the violation of property will be hurtful, the taking of another man's goods is sinful, though it be to save the taker's life . . . Therefore ordinarily it is a duty rather to die than to take another man's goods against his will.

Hill also quotes this from Baxter's *Holy Commonwealth*: 'Were not this multitude restrained they would presently have the blood of the godly.'[52]

The quotations cannot be taken (as Hill would have it) as an absolute defence of property. Both are good statements of Baxter's totalitarianism. Instead of narrowing the gap between the seventeenth-century puritan and the later liberal nonconformist, they *widen* it. This is the 'horizontal' Baxter, not the 'vertical' Baxter of denominational piety: no democrat, no respecter of individual lives, certainly no 'liberal' spokesman for a balanced constitution. This was the man who would have obeyed Nero, because even bad government was better than no government. However, the key phrase in the longer extract is service to 'the common good', which is the ultimate arbiter of whether life or property should be preserved. Baxter is never so chillingly removed from 'liberal' preconceptions than when, for instance, in his *Christian Directory* he weighs the lives of some men against others:

But yet it must be confessed, that some few Persons may be of so much worth and use to the Commonwealth (as Kings and Magistrates) and some of so little; that the maintaining of the honours and succours of the former, may be more necessary than the saving of the lives of the latter.

But the criterion is still 'worth and use to the Commonwealth' which is not necessarily simply equated with property. Indeed, in a pamphlet in 1681 he defended breaking the law to save the lives of the poor (a policy fleshed out in his *Poor Husbandman's Advocate* when he did not flinch from equations with 'Levellers' and 'Quakers' in this respect). And he appealed to the authority of Selden and Hale for a view of 'the common welfare' as 'so essentially the *Terminus* of the Policie, that to exclude it is to dissolve all the Policie, Kingdom and State'.[53]

---

[52] Hill, *The World Turned Upside Down*, pp. 283, 266, 280.
[53] Richard Baxter, *A Christian Directory* (London, 1673), pp. 725–36; *An Apology for the Nonconformist Ministry* (London, 1681), pp. 47–8; *The Reverend Richard Baxter's Last Treatise*, ed. F. J. Powicke (Manchester, 1926), p. 53. Though the latter treatise (*The Poor Husbandman's Advocate*) which Baxter wrote in 1691 is the most swingeing of attacks on rack-renting landlords, Christopher Hill notes of it only that Baxter 'felt he had to disavow levelling when he criticised the extravagance of the rich' (*World Turned Upside Down*, p. 305 n. 57). But cf. Baxter's comment in 1675: 'Levelling hath not

The word 'property' is, in any case, a word loaded with anachronistic connotations. Interesting research has been recently carried out to question the premise in older works that 'property' had for seventeenth-century contemporaries the meaning which it has for us.[54] J. G. A. Pocock has argued, in opposition to C. B. Macpherson, that descriptions of a bourgeois market society emerge not with Hobbes, Harrington, Locke and the Levellers but with Harrington's critic, the younger Matthew Wren.[55] Margaret Sampson takes a different tack: she follows Quentin Skinner in shifting interest away from the Tawney/Macpherson exploitation of political theorists as *witnesses* to social change towards a Weberian attention to the arguments used to *legitimize* social change.[56] With particular reference to the tithes controversies of the 1650s she shows how divines tried (but failed) to develop a counter-attack against the confidence and assurance of the laity that it held absolute individualized rights of property created and guaranteed by the common law.

Our interim findings are, therefore, that recent controversy has not strengthened the case for equating Calvinism either with modernization theory or the Protestant ethic. But what of a third claim: that it helped to sponsor the 'companionate marriage' and transformed the position of women? There has been an increasing amount of research in this field[57] – although, to date, no single scholar has done for early modern England what Natalie Davis has done for early modern France[58] – but, here too, the findings are on the whole negative. Puritan attitudes to marriage and the role of women were both intellectually derivative and heavily patriarchal. Even so, there is more to be done, and one very interesting line of inquiry has recently been advanced by Peter Lake. He has taken a single piece of unpromising evidence – a funeral sermon on the life of

---

destroyed one soul for ten thousand that an inordinate love of Propriety hath destroyed' (Baxter, *A Treatise of Self-Denial*, p. 333).

[54] Especially G. E. Aylmer, 'The Meaning and Definition of "Property" in 17th Century England', *Past and Present*, 86 (1980), 87–97; James Tully, *A Discourse on Property: John Locke and his Adversaries* (Cambridge, 1980); Andrew Reeve, 'The Treatment of Property by some English Economic Legal and Social Writers between 1600 and 1700', unpublished DPhil thesis, University of Oxford, 1980; Richard Tuck, *Natural Rights Theories* (Cambridge, 1979).

[55] J. G. A. Pocock (ed.), *The Political Works of James Harrington* (Cambridge, 1977), 'Historical Introduction'.

[56] Margaret Sampson, '"Property" in Seventeenth-Century English Political Thought', Schochet (ed.), *Religion, Resistance and Civil War*, pp. 259–76.

[57] The valuable bibliographical guide, Olwen Hufton, 'Women in History', *Past and Present*, 101 (1983), 125–141, needs now to be updated; there are a number of illuminating essays relating to this theme in: Mary Prior (ed.), *Women in English Society, 1500–1800* (London, 1985).

[58] Natalie Z. Davis, *Society and Culture in Early Modern France* (London, 1975).

Mrs Jane Ratcliffe by her puritan minister, John Ley – and by a sensitive exploration, not merely of the language, but of the silences, omissions and divergences from the norm, opened up new ways of understanding how women in this period 'could and did take up and use a puritan style of godliness for their own, at least partially, emancipatory purposes'.[59]

III

We have already seen that Margaret Sampson was attempting to use contemporary sources for the arguments they employed to legitimise social change, rather than as witnesses to social change which had already been delineated. J. C. Davis' recent work, *Fear, Myth and History: The Ranters and their Historians*, addresses the problem of the Ranters with the same methodological approach which Margaret Sampson brings to her study of property.[60] This would not be apparent from the initial reception of Davis' thesis. This has ranged from the mildly sceptical (Aylmer) to the courteous denial (Hill) to the discourteous denial (Thompson).[61] For this, Davis himself is not free from blame. It is not enough for Davis to expose how dependent upon dubious sources were Hill, A. L. Morton and Norman Cohn – who incorporated Ranter material in an unconvincing epilogue to his *The Pursuit of the Millennium* – in their endeavours to identify the existence of Ranters; upon sources mainly the propaganda of their enemies. Nor even has it been enough for Davis to go further and to deny that they ever had existence at all except in the eyes of opponents. He has had to go further still (and spoil an elegant argument) by insisting that it had to be the Marxist background of Morton and Hill which led to their credulity about the sources. He makes great play with their membership of the Communist Party Historians' Group between 1946 and 1956, and E. P. Thompson's *The Making of the English Working Class* becomes circumstantially linked to a common purpose to impose a false English cultural tradition on popular movements. This may explain, but not excuse, Thompson's counterblast. Like the critics of Alan Macfarlane's thesis on English

[59] Peter Lake, 'Feminine Piety and Personal Potency: The "Emancipation" of Mrs Jane Ratcliffe', *The Seventeenth Century*, 2, 2 (1987), 143–65.

[60] J. C. Davis, *Fear, Myth and History: The Ranters and their Historians* (Cambridge, 1986).

[61] G. E. Aylmer, 'Did the Ranters Exist?', *Past and Present*, 117 (1987), 208–19; Christopher Hill, 'The Lost Ranters? A Critique of J. C. Davis', *History Workshop*, 24 (Autumn 1987), 134–40; E. P. Thompson, 'On the Rant', in G. Eley and W. Hunt (eds.), *Reviving the English Revolution: Reflections and Elaborations on the Work of Christopher Hill* (London, 1988), pp. 153–60. The controversy is fully ventilated, and his position reasserted, in J. C. Davis, 'Fear, Myth and Furore: Reappraising the "Ranters"', *Past and Present*, 129 (November 1990), 79–103.

individualism, who (G. R. Elton noted) combined the difficult positions of saying both that the argument was wrong and that everybody knew it anyway, Thompson simultaneously asserts both that Morton and Hill knew the fragility of their sources and that the phenomenon was widely understood and deep-rooted in time. But the latter he achieves by a long exposition on antinomianism, taking us back to St Paul. And this is grievously to misstate Davis' position, who did not deny that 'Ranterism' existed, or that individuals identified people whom they called 'Ranters'. What he denied was that a kernel of Ranter writings, outside this circumstantial dross, could be identified. He did this by a careful examination of the writings of those who have been generally identified as Ranters: Coppe, Clarkson, Salmon and Bauthumley (and it is something of a historical scandal that it should only have been as late as 1983 that Nigel Smith brought their collected writings into one volume).[62] Davis' cool analysis of these works led him to deny that there was a serious, identifiable common platform that could be discerned. It was the same admirable logic which he had brought to his analysis of the Christian contribution to Leveller thinking, particularly the conceptual importance of 'equity'.[63] It seems to me that neither Hill nor Aylmer meets this primary intellectual objection, although at least they do not, like Thompson, see in Davis' study 'the encroaching thatcherism of the upwardly-mobile historical mind'.

However, Davis' high-class investigative approach can be extended to his own attempt to see the problem in Cold War dimensions. It has become clear so far in this chapter that much of the interesting work which is now being done in political thought is precisely in listening to the language of contemporaries without interposing our own preoccupations (Marxist or anti-Marxist) into the process. The great mid twentieth-century Marxist historiographical conspiracy may have much the same reality, and lack of it, as the great mid seventeenth-century Ranter movement.

We may not listen attentively enough to what the seventeenth-century source is saying, because we feel that we have already caught the drift. If what he or she is saying seems actually contradictory, that too can be accommodated to an established 'set'. William Haller was a scholar attuned with peculiar sensitivity to the puritan mind. As early as 1938 that had led him to the conclusion that 'Prynne is another figure of the Puritan Revolution who deserves closer critical study than he has so far

---

[62] Nigel Smith (ed.), *A Collection of Ranter Writing from the Seventeenth Century* (London, 1983).
[63] J. C. Davis, 'The Levellers and Christianity', in B. Manning (ed.), *Politics, Religion and the English Civil War* (London, 1973), pp. 225–50.

received'; it had not, however, prevented him from an assessment which made more or less clear why such a study would hardly be worth the effort: 'just the kind of person to turn the doctrines of the preachers into reckless assault upon the existing order .. His avowed aim could be construed only as the overthrow of everything established in the church'.[64] We have already seen that neither judgement tallies with what Prynne actually said, nor (thanks to the considerable weight of recent scholarship) does it tally with the views of those puritans and parliamentarians whom he claimed (with, it now seems, some justice) to represent.

For historians of political thought in this period the liberation now seems to consist therefore in escaping the tyranny of what we have seen described as a 'vertical' approach to history (and Marxists have no monopoly on such an approach). The tendency to read history backwards from a denominational perspective, to see constitutional conflicts in terms of a 'high road' to civil war, to see puritanism in terms of the nonconformity which came after it: these are some of the ghosts that are now being exorcised by historians, anxious to see their seventeenth-century figures 'horizontally', and in the process re-creating the demons (sometimes literally so) which possessed them. And yet the historian who has best underlined the dangers of 'vertical' history has been at pains to stress its compensatory strengths. Patrick Collinson notes that 'those who write from within the tradition with theological awareness and spiritual sensitivity, have much the better chance of getting it right'.[65] This is a salutary caution. A 'horizontal' approach to Baxter can, as we have already seen, cancel the image of the spokesman for the Protestant ethic, for the balanced constitution, for liberalism and for democracy. These are gains, but what they do not cancel out are the spiritual insights offered by Geoffrey Nuttall's *Richard Baxter and Philip Doddridge*. This 1951 gem of a lecture is subtitled 'A Study in a Tradition', and one could hardly get more 'vertical' than that.[66]

In this light we should reevaluate Davis' work on the Ranters. Its value lay not in correcting a Marxist-inspired 'vertical' approach (even if that was how he himself saw it), but actually in refining the crudities of a 'horizontal' approach. The discovery of 'sameness' in contemporaries is one of the rewards of 'horizontal' history, but also one of its perils. The zest which Christopher Hill brought to the task of tracing affinities in groups hitherto thought beneath the historian's attention has rightly been celebrated, but there are dangers in that process (not least, for instance, in reifying a 'third culture', to which Milton may or may not

---

[64] Haller, *The Rise of Puritanism*, pp. 219, 393.
[65] Collinson, 'The Early Dissenting Tradition', p. 26.
[66] G. F. Nuttall, *Richard Baxter and Philip Doddridge* (Oxford, 1951).

belong). Davis' unwillingness to lump together Coppe, Clarkson, Salmon, Bauthumley, but instead to discriminate between them, is here a healthy corrective. The 'horizontal' historian as much as the 'vertical' historian may find that his preoccupations make him deaf to nuances in the tone of voice.

Which is why we should be prepared to see, in the unexpected windfall of the recovery of the eighty-eight volumes of Muggletonian manuscripts, a chance to savour the advantages of 'vertical' history. The Muggletonians have suffered hitherto (inevitably, given the history of the source material) from being studied for the value of their inter-connections with other radical groupings of 'the world turned upside down'. Thanks to the recovery of the papers it is possible for the first time to appreciate the ideas that were significant to later generations of believers. We can give these ideas intrinsic weighting, not merely for their extrinsic value in corroborating or not the interests of contempor-ary groupings. The interest of eighteenth-century Muggletonians in Hobbes, the affinities with Deism, the nineteenth-century revisionism of Thomas Robinson – these are some of the unexpected offshoots of a 'vertical' reading of Muggletonianism.[67]

The 'horizontal' approach has never been applied more daringly by Christopher Hill than when he seeks to relate Milton to the under-ground 'third culture'.[68] How far does he succeed? His book, *Milton and the English Revolution*, was an answer to W. R. Parker's influential study, *Milton's Contemporary Reputation*, which had conditioned its readers to a view of Milton as the 'aloof scholar'. If that were all that he was attempting the book could be acclaimed as a total success: to have done for Milton what other scholars have done for Hobbes, Harrington and Marvell. Nor would it have been a new departure in Milton studies: arguably A. E. Barker and Don Wolfe before him had also related Milton's writings to their historical context.[69] But it is at this point we see what *is* new in Hill's approach, and the subsidiary thesis which he is smuggling into the main one: that Milton enjoyed particularly fruitful relationships with radical political groups not only occasionally but at all times. In the studies of both Barker and Wolfe we get a sense of vertical movement in Milton's development in the 1640s: we understand the

---

[67] William Lamont, 'The Muggletonians, 1652–1979: A "Vertical" Approach', *Past and Present*, 99 (1983), 22–40 (and debate between Lamont and Hill in *Past and Present*, 104 (1984), 153–63).

[68] Christopher Hill, *Milton and the English Revolution* (London, 1977). For a recent alternative view, see H. R. Trevor-Roper, *Catholics, Anglicans and Puritans* (London, 1987), pp. 231–283: 'Milton in Politics'.

[69] A. E. Barker, *Milton and the Puritan Dilemma* (Toronto, 1942); D. M. Wolfe, *Milton in the Puritan Revolution* (New York, 1941).

process by which Milton painfully attains the insight that new presbyter is but old priest writ large. In both of these studies we see Milton growing both towards, and away from, revolutionary movements that were themselves in a state of evolution. But such a 'vertical' approach blunts the force of Hill's 'horizontal' revisionism. He wants to show a Milton as radical in the 1630s as he was in the 1640s. When Milton wrote *Of Reformation Touching Church Discipline in England* in 1641 he knew the force of the 'Pope-in-every-Parish' objection that was being mounted at the time to Presbyterianism, and rejected it. The famous question he asked in *Areopagitica* in 1644: 'who shall be the rectors of our daily rioting?' sprang not from new discoveries about the nature of the Presbyterian beast, but from new self-discoveries about the nature of man. Hill plays down the significance of Milton's Arminian evolution, just as he plays down the significance of the Laudians' divergence from the Church's Calvinist past. Hill minimises the change it made in Milton to give up Calvinism and to give up Presbyterianism: the process was 'natural and inevitable'; initial advocacy of Presbyterianism and later rejection 'both sprang from his own self-esteem'; and even – least plausible of all – 'Milton's brief period of support for Presbyterianism sprang perhaps from the idea that because Presbyterians opposed Laud they also shared Milton's hatred for ecclesiastical interference with freedom of expression, whether religious or literary'. Thus, Milton's attraction to Presbyterianism in 1641 is accommodated within his already established radical position; moreover, his rejection of Constantine in the same period shows that he is 'aligning himself with this [the really radical] tradition, as against middle-of-the-road men who followed Foxe'.[70] The latter point is strained. All sorts of 'middle-of-the-road men', not least among them Prynne and Pym, were being forced to repudiate the traditions of Foxe and Constantine in 1641 against opponents, led by such anti-Laudians as John Williams, who sought to use their prestige to bolster up a discredited church.

Hill saw the Civil War as a clash of two cultures – 'aristocratic Laudianism versus middle-class Puritanism' – and Milton not as spokesman for a third culture ('the underground Familist tradition') but 'living in a state of permanent dialogue with radical views which he could not wholly accept, yet some of which greatly attracted him.' Or, as he put it more pithily (and crudely): 'I see Milton as a two-and-a-half culture man'.[71] It is not easy to see how such a hypothesis can be falsified; a critic who discovers elitism in the younger Milton can be seen

---

[70] Hill, *English Revolution*, pp. 159, 255, 64, 84.
[71] Hill, 'Milton the Radical', *Times Literary Supplement*, 29 November 1974, pp. 1330–2.

off with the defence that that is the half missing in the equation. But there are times when it is clear that Hill does not see this as an adequate defence. Even with a score of two-and-a-half out of three (which would seem to leave room for manoeuvre) Milton's alleged elitism could put him outside the club. And so Hill shows that his elitism is spurious, even in *Of Education* which he wrote in 1644. In a hasty, embarrassed discussion of no more than four pages, he is at pains to show its affinities with the plans of the Hartlib group, thinks that the radical educationist William Dell 'may well have read Milton', believes that his later writings in the 1650s show progressive tendencies, and sees his ideas as anticipating the eighteenth-century dissenting academies. Most disingenuous of all, since his book has been written in part out of the conviction that W. R. Parker got Milton wrong because of his fear of radicalism, Hill presses Parker's claims that Milton's educational ideas were 'basically rebellious and revolutionary' into the argument. But more honestly at later parts in the book he concedes that *Of Education* is an elitist tract, and in the course of an illuminating discussion of Biblical criticism writes that Milton was 'highly elitist, had little but contempt for the uneducated, at least from the mid-forties'.[72]

This chapter has interrupted what is otherwise a continuous history of British political thought. It has given itself up entirely to a discussion of where numbers of historians stand in relation to the puritan revolution. To make sense of what happened in those twenty or so years became, as we now know, the supreme challenge to the English political imagination for subsequent generations: it is a theme which will be developed in the following chapters. As the prelude to the chapters of this book which deal with the aftermath of revolution this essay therefore needs no justification.

The effort to ascribe the momentous events of the mid seventeenth-century to equally momentous ideological clashes in the preceding generation has been made with most *panache* by Christopher Hill. And yet in the three areas we chose to examine – the relationship of the Arminian controversy to long-standing problems in church and state, the significance of Calvinism as the motor for modernization, and the relationship of the greatest poet of the seventeenth century to a discrete radical underground movement – it has to be said that his thesis is hard to sustain. And yet the opposing revisionist case can itself slide into some form of ideological nihilism. J. J. Scarisbrick, reacting intelligibly against a mechanistic interpretation of the English Reformation as the response

---

[72] Hill, *English Revolution*, pp. 146–149, 201, 248, 336.

to clerical abuses, is almost driven to the claim that the assault on the church came suddenly out of a blue sky.[73] It is the language of Clarendon trying to relate (and failing in the attempt to do so) the halcyon days of the 1630s to the convulsions that followed. It is, equally significantly, the language of C. H. George, one of the acutest critics of a school of thought which emphasizes simple continuities from pre-Elizabethan puritanism to its civil war manifestations: from Lollard-to-Leveller. The correct emphasis in his analysis on *discontinuity* leads however to the incorrect emphasis on *cataclysm*: 'Now suddenly and mysteriously all religious perceptions seemed to respond to the previous generations of change in the structure of English society and to the related cultural explosion which culminated in the extraordinary creativity of parliament, press and army in the 1640s – blasting all former piety into competing fanaticisms'; and again: 'the heady vapours of Reformation theology [were] blown apart in the crises of civil and class war'.[74] What we have seen, in each of the three areas under discussion, is that there *is* a mystery in the relation between thought and action, that previous attempts to explain away that mystery no longer satisfy, that to leave it as a mystery is equally unsatisfactory, and that the challenge for the next generation of scholars is to approach that mystery with a different set of questions.[75] In the meantime we would seem to have ended where we began: with Glanvill's recognition that sunbeam and lump of clay remain mockingly, obdurately, as far apart as ever they were.

This may be too gloomy a conclusion. Perhaps all along our focus has been too narrow: too insular, too short a range of time. And, if there is to be a way out of the impasse, perhaps it will come from marrying the seventeenth-century insights of James Harrington with the twentieth-century insights of Conrad Russell.[76]

Hugh Kearney has recently imaginatively retold the story of the British Isles as a 'history of four nations'.[77] When Russell applies this

[73] Only slightly caricaturing (I hope) views to be found in J. J. Scarisbrick, *The Reformation and the English People* (Oxford, 1984); C. Haigh, 'The English Reformation: A Premature Birth, a Difficult Labour and a Sickly Child', *The Historical Journal*, 33, 2 (1990), 449–59.

[74] C. H. George, 'Puritanism as History and Historiography', *Past and Present*, 41 (1968), 86, 83.

[75] See my response to George's article, *Past and Present*, 44 (1969), 113–46; and also Kevin Sharpe, 'Ideas and Politics in Early Stuart England', *History Today* (January 1988), pp. 45–51 (with a useful bibliographical guide to some of the most interesting recent constructive responses to our present impasse).

[76] I first advanced this suggestion in reviewing Professor Russell's Ford Lectures, 'The Civil War as Optical Illusion', *Times Literary Supplement*, 25 January 1991, p. 10.

[77] H. F. Kearney, *The British Isles: A History of Four Nations* (Cambridge, 1989).

perspective to the English Revolution, familiar contours dissolve.[78] The English Civil War becomes a misnomer; rather we should see a series of British wars (the 'Wars of the Three Kingdoms') beginning in 1637 and ending at Worcester in 1651. Thus it would be Oliver Cromwell, certainly not Charles I, who succeeded in imposing English hegemony over the British Isles. What 1688–9 did was to confer sovereignty on English parliaments. The story of the next 200 years is of the extension of that sovereignty with the acquisition of an empire; a process which only began to unwind with the 1931 Statute of Westminster. The loss of an empire, and now the challenge of Europe, have exposed the durability of the multiple-kingdom problem. They have also made highly desirable a re-reading of James Harrington.

In one sense Harrington has never gone away. The boldness of his analysis had inspired the semi-Marxist readings of Tawney and Hill no less than the anti-Marxist readings of Trevor-Roper. But in hailing the insights of his analysis there was also a tendency to skip over the shortcomings of his solutions. Harrington as prophet of the American Constitution? Yes, but hardly of the British Constitution, as it evolved over the next 200 years. Nevertheless, Harrington's prescriptions derived from that famed analysis, and suddenly those very prescriptions have acquired a new resonance. The political journalist, Neil Ascherson, without ever mentioning the name 'Harrington', has recently argued that the European Community is developing on what we would see as Harringtonian lines.[79] Harrington had argued that monarchy and aristocracy were relics of the feudal system. He saw a republic as the natural embodiment of post-feudal values, but buttressed by a written constitution, a separation of powers (executive, legislative, judiciary), a rotating office of president, and bicameralism. The Rome Treaty and the 1985 Single Act represent that written constitution, the Strasbourg parliament that legislature (at least in embryonic form), the Commission that executive, the European Court at Luxembourg that judiciary. Those who now resist these tendencies as incompatible with English parliamentary sovereignty indubitably have seventeenth-century history on their side. The terrible price, however, exacted by that concept is the real theme, it may not be too fanciful to argue, of the English puritan revolution.

---

[78] Conrad Russell, *The Causes of the English Civil War*, and *The Fall of the British Monarchies, 1637–1642* (both Oxford, 1991).
[79] Neal Ascherson, 'The Spectre of Popular Sovereignty looms over Greater England', *The Independent on Sunday*, 18 November 1990, p. 23.

5 Interregnum and Restoration

J. G. A. Pocock and Gordon J. Schochet

That the execution of Charles Stuart was extraordinary and momentous hardly needs restating. Kings had been killed before, but only as a result of baronial rebellions or dynastic feuds. Such disputes were little more than power-struggles that were *internal* to the institution of monarchy. Charges of 'misrule' and 'tyranny', when they were heard at all, were a kind of ideological and rhetorical window-dressing that was generally intended to add weight to the more frequent and substantial claims of 'usurpation'. Never before had a reigning sovereign been officially, and proclaimedly legally, *executed* for apparent reasons of state. None the less, the regicide of 1649 was carried out in a deeply monarchical political culture, and it can almost be said that it could have been carried out in no other. Whereas Louis XVI a century and a half afterwards was killed for being a king by revolutionaries some of whom were bent on destroying the institution itself, Charles I was killed for failing to be one: for failing to bring peace to his subjects, for persistently frustrating their endeavours to make peace with him, and most of all for launching the second civil war in 1648. Yet he could not with any plausibility be tried and executed unless it were charged that he had all along plotted to make war on his subjects, or without involving the abolition of monarchy itself in the act of 'cutting off the King's head with the crown upon it'.[1] The dreadful paradox of these events called forth Andrew Marvell's *Horatian Ode*, the greatest poem on the ambiguities of politics in the English language,[2] and more immediately *Eikon Basilike* – probably written

---

[1] Algernon Sidney claimed to have heard Cromwell use these words. See Jonathan Scott, *Algernon Sidney and the English Republic* (Cambridge, 1988), p. 92. Like others of the Protector's most striking sayings, this rests on the authority of a none-too-friendly witness.

[2] See Blair Worden, 'Andrew Marvell, Oliver Cromwell, and the Horatian Ode', in Kevin Sharpe and Steven M. Zwicker (eds.), *The Politics of Discourse: The Literature and History of Seventeenth-Century England* (Berkeley, 1987), pp. 147–80; and further J. A. Mazzeo, *Renaissance and Seventeenth-Century Studies* (New York, 1964); David Norbrook, 'Is Marvell's "Horatian Ode" a Horatian Ode?' in Gordon J. Schochet (ed.), *Religion, Resistance, and Civil War*, Proceedings of the Folger Institute Center for the History of British Political Thought, vol. 3 (Washington D.C., 1990); John M. Wallace,

with Charles' connivance and ready for distribution as he stood on the
scaffold – which, by a propaganda triumph greater than any achieved by
the radical press, created his martyrdom in the hour of his execution.[3]
The charge that Charles I had been false to the duties of monarchy
had much to be said for it but must lead to the less plausible historical
allegation that the monarchy itself had always been hostile to the
liberties of Englishmen: a charge unsupported by any coherent set of
republican doctrines and put forward with a visible lack of conviction in
the very act that declared the monarchy abolished. Using much of the
same rhetoric that had sustained the parliamentary cause during the civil
wars and appealing to the liberty of the 'people' and its right to chose its
own governors, the act that established a kind of representative council
in place of the monarchy on 17 March 1649 declared that

it hath been found by experience that the office of king in this nation and Ireland
... is unnecessary, burdensome and dangerous to the liberty, safety and public
interest of the people, and that for the most part use hath been made of the regal
power and prerogative to oppress and impoverish and enslave the subject, and
that usually and naturally any one person in such power makes it his interest to
encroach upon the just freedom and liberty of the people, and promote the
setting up of his own will and power above the laws ...
... by the abolition of the kingly office provided for in this act a most happy way
is made for this nation (if God see it good) to return to its just and ancient right of
being governed by its own Representatives or National Meetings in Council,
from time to time chosen and entrusted for that purpose by the people ...[4]

Such language was neither familiar nor persuasive. It can plausibly be
argued that English republican theory was far more the effect than the
cause of the execution of the king in 1649. Such theory as there was had
been compounded from baronial and humanist sources; great magnates
in earlier centuries had known how to put kings in tutelage and the
crown itself in commission. Those of them who had read Tacitus in
more recent times could see themselves as senators rather than counsel-

Destiny His Choice: The Loyalism of Andrew Marvell (Cambridge, 1968); and Christopher Wortham, 'Marvell's Cromwellian Poems: An Accidental Triptych', in Conal Condren and A. D. Cousins (eds.), *The Political Identity of Andrew Marvell* (London, 1990).
3   Philip A. Knachel (ed.), *Eikon Basilike: The Portraiture of His Sacred Majesty in His Solitudes and Sufferings* (Ithaca, 1966). See also Lois Potter, 'Royal Martyr as Royal Actor', in Gordon J. Schochet (ed.), *Restoration, Ideology, and Revolution*, Proceedings of the Folger Institute Center for the History of British Political Thought, vol. 4 (Washington, D. C., 1990).
4   'An act for Abolishing the Kingly Office in England and Ireland, 17 March 1649', as reprinted in J. P. Kenyon (ed.), *The Stuart Constitution, 1603–1688: Documents and Commentary*, 2nd edn (Cambridge, 1986), p. 306. The text is also available in Samuel R. Gardiner (ed.), *The Constitutional Documents of the Puritan Revolution, 1625–1660*, 3rd edn (Oxford, 1906), pp. 384–7.

lors and barons, and could imagine the English kingship as rather a Venetian dogeship than what it historically was. Yet the execution of Charles was far different from the deposition of Richard II, and – as James Harrington was to point out – the English Civil War differed as deeply from any rebellion of barons (even if, as is now contended, it contained a baronial component).[5] The discourse of regicide was therefore two-faced, carrying on the one hand a thesis of royal accountability and on the other an exploration of the dissolution of government. The republican theory that necessarily emerged was an important by-product, and the profoundly innovative political philosophy that appeared at the same time can be seen as a response to the appalling questions posed when the natural order of government was subverted and God seemed to have turned away his face. It was the collapse of sovereignty that had caused both civil war and regicide, and the political thought of the Interregnum was an attempt to fill the vacuum.

Charles I's death at the hands of parliament defied all previous practice. The implications were nothing less than that kings were answerable for their conduct, that they could be disciplined, and that there was within the constitutional structure of the civil society a legitimate, institutional means for calling them to account. In extreme cases, that means included the execution of a king and the abolition of the monarchy itself. This assertion of superiority of parliament over the monarchy – the regicide was nothing less than the claim of legislative supremacy – was an unusual constitutional doctrine. For a time at least, it operationally resolved the conflicts that were inherent in the political fiction that the government of England was conducted by the king-in-parliament.

An early step on the road that led from parliament's Grand Remonstrance to Charles Stuart's scaffold was taken by the king himself in his 'Answer' to the Long Parliament's 'Nineteen Propositions'. Those 'Propositions', presented to Charles in June 1642, before the first Civil War had erupted, called upon the king to recognize the entitlement of both Houses to oversee appointments to and the activities of the privy council (Propositions 1 and 2), demanded 'that such a Reformation be made in the Church-Government and Liturgy, as both Houses of Parliament shall advise' (Proposition 8), insisted that the military command be brought under greater parliamentary scrutiny (Propositions 15 and 16), and called for passage of a bill restraining newly created peers 'from sitting or voting in Parliament, unless they be admitted

---

[5] J. S. A. Adamson, 'The English Nobility and the Projected Settlement of 1647', *Historical Journal*, 30 (1987), 567–602.

thereunto by the Consent of both Houses of Parliament' (Proposition 19).[6]

Charles – or whoever put his name to the words of the *Answer to the Nineteen Propositions* – appreciated the danger to the crown. Not only has Parliament attempted 'to weaken our just Authority and due Esteem' among the people, the *Answer* contended, it has 'broached new Doctrine, That we are obliged to pass all Laws that shall be offer'd to us by both Houses (howsoever our own Judgment and Conscience shall be unsatisfied with them), a Point of Policy as proper for their present Business, as destructive to all our Rights of Parliament'.[7]

Instead of responding with a doctrine of monarchical sovereignty, the king's *Answer* said that the government of England was a 'Mixture' of 'Absolute Monarchy, Aristocracy, and Democracy'. The monarchy was one of the three 'estates' of the realm – the other two were the lords temporal and the commons[8] – that jointly shared in the government, and this form of government, according to the *Answer*, gave 'to this Kingdom (as far as humane Prudence can provide) the Conveniences of all three, without the Inconveniences of any one, as long as the Ballance hangs even between the three Estates'.[9] It was on that basis and in order to preserve the 'Ballance' that the king refused to grant parliament's demands for what he regarded as legislative supremacy.

The *Answer to the Nineteen Propositions* is thus a crucial document in the history of English constitutional and political theory. On the one hand, it performed the fatal move, long regretted by royalists, of reducing the king to an estate of his own realm and permitting the two

---

[6] 'The Nineteen Propositions', as published in John Rushworth, *Historical Collections: The Third Part*, (London, 1721), IV, pp. 722–4. (The text is reprinted in Gardiner (ed.), *Constitutional Documents*, pp. 249–54.)

[7] Charles I, *His Majesty's Answer to the Nineteen Propositions of both Houses of Parliament, Tending Towards a Peace*, in Rushworth, *Historical Collections*, IV, pp. 725–35, quotation from p. 725.

[8] On one view, the three estates were the Lords Temporal, the Lords Spiritual (that is the bishops), and the Commons, with the king presiding over them all. The doctrine of Charles' *Answer* was not entirely innovative, for the claims that England was a 'mixed government' and that the monarchy was one of the estates went back at least to the Elizabethan period. However, it seems not to have been the source of constitutional struggle until the 1640s. See Michael Mendle, *Dangerous Positions: Mixed Government, the Estates of the Realm, and the 'Answer to the xix Propositions'* (University, Alabama, 1985), chs. 2 and 3. There are also interesting discussions in Perez Zagorin, *A History of Political Thought in the English Revolution* (London, 1954), pp. 190–6; and Austin Woolrych, 'Political Theory and Political Practice', in *The Age of Milton: Backgrounds to Seventeenth-Century Literature*, ed. C. A. Patrides and Raymond B. Waddington (Manchester, 1980), pp. 35–6. For the earlier lineage of the doctrine, see James M. Blyth, *Ideal Governments and the Mixed Constitution in the Middle Ages* (Princeton, 1992).

[9] Charles I, *Answer*, Rushworth, *Historical Collections*, IV, p. 731.

houses of parliament to represent their acts as necessary to maintain a balance in which they were of equal weight with him. The king might thus become a 'duke of Venice', incidental and conceivably unnecessary to the maintenance of balance and stability. Out of this step a new and much more coherent republican theory in due course emerged but this was far from anyone's recorded thoughts in 1642. On the other hand, the *Answer*, presenting sovereignty as conjointly exercised by a self-balancing trinity-in-unity, warned all the king's realms that sovereignty was indivisible – in the sense that, however it was lodged in the king-in-parliament, there it now resided – and that any breach between the conjoined parties must be a drawing of the sword and a dissolution of the government.[10] But what the *Answer* warned against had already begun to happen.[11] Following the fatal attempt on the five members, the king withdrew from Westminster, from London and above all from parliament.

After further negotiations failed, he set up his standard in the midlands, by processes still little understood found men to fight for him, and proclaimed the (by now pretended) parliament in a state of rebellion. The parliamentary leaders accepted the challenge and began a civil war in which the two sides fought over the means to a common end, that of bringing the king back to his parliament and the head back to unity with the body. The objective was realized and appallingly parodied when the king was brought into London to face trial and decapitation outside his own palace in 1649. The monarchy was then abolished for failure to unite its own realm; the question remained whether the realm could exist without it. The political thought of the Interregnum, from as early as 1647 through 1660, was concerned with the replacement of a sovereignty that had collapsed; and the political thought of the remainder of the period covered in this volume was concerned with ensuring that this problem should never again recur.

Sovereignty is about power and authority as a coherent and *legal*

---

[10] The best modern studies of the *Answer to the Nineteen Propositions* bring out the duality of its character. See Corinne C. Weston, *English Constitutional Theory and the House of Lords* (London, 1965), and with Janelle R. Greenberg, *Subjects and Sovereigns: The Grand Debate over Legal Sovereignty in Stuart England* (Cambridge, 1981); and Mendle, *Dangerous Positions*. For its role as a seedbed of republican theory, see further J. G. A. Pocock, *The Machiavellian Moment: Florentine Political Thought and the Atlantic Republican Tradition* (Princeton, 1975), pp. 361–5, and *The Political Works of James Harrington* (Cambridge, 1977), pp. 19–22.

[11] See, in general, Michael Mendle, 'The Great Council of Parliament and the First Ordinances: The Constitutional Theory of the Civil War', *Journal of British Studies*, 31 (1992), 133–62. David Wootton, 'From Rebellion to Revolution: The Crisis of the Winter of 1642/43 and the Origins of Civil War Radicalism', *English Historical Review*, 105 (1990), 654–69, argues that a significant number of parliamentary supporters were committed to revolution almost from the start.

singularity. As Bodin – the author to whose name the theory is most frequently linked – said, sovereignty is 'the most high, absolute, and perpetual power ouer the citizens and subjects in a Commonweale, . . . that is to say, The greatest power to commaund'. The 'principall point of soueraigne maiestie, and absolute power' consists 'in giuing laws vnto the subjects in generall, without their consent'.[12] In that – its modern – form, the doctrine of sovereignty developed in France in the context of and in response to the problems inherent in 'estates' theory. It was a codification of historical experience and emerging practices as well as a prescription for resolving existing conflicts and preventing the rise of others in the future.

In a monarchical context, of course, the doctrine bears a close affinity to absolutism. But it was always inappropriate, for however incoherent and theoretically fictitious the doctrine of king-in-parliament may have been, it was a correct *description* of the accommodation by which English politics actually proceeded. Although James I seems to have been the first English ruler to have *proclaimed* royal absolutism – and he certainly seems to have taken it seriously – it was not until the accommodation itself came apart in the 1640s that the inherent problems in that practice were altogether revealed. Ironically – if not paradoxically – it was Charles' endorsement of the view that the government of England was actually a mixture of monarchy and republicanism that paved the way for an insistence by parliamentary apologists that king-in-parliament be replaced by genuine and undivided sovereignty exercised by the parliament as the institution that represented the true owners of sovereign entitlement, the people.

From this point, the issue of sovereignty encompassed more than the location of the ultimate legislative authority. It could always be agreed that the authority to enact statutes lay with the king, lords, and commons in parliament; and even when the two houses claimed that their ordinances were binding without the king's consent, they were at pains to deny that these were statutes altering the common law. They were rather acts of 'the great council of the kingdom', performed at a time when the king was unable to play his proper role – because, it would soon be argued, he had been misled and seduced by the evil counsellors who had drawn him, as head, away from the body of the realm. The issue of sovereignty thus became that of what was lawfully to be done in such circumstances, and transcended the mere location of the legislative power. Bodinian language continued to be used, but in the context of

---

[12] Jean Bodin, *The Six Bookes of a Commonweale*, trans. Richard Knolles (London, 1606), facsimile reprint, ed. with an Introduction by Kenneth D. McRae (Cambridge, MA, 1962), I, viii, pp. 84 and 98).

civil war – in which context Bodin himself had written – it subsumed the problem defined by the various tracts that appeared under such titles as 'the grand case of allegiance truly stated'. What was the subject's duty when head and body were at war, when an 'unnatural' conflict had led king and parliament, equally legitimate and inherent in one another, to draw the sword and make conflicting demands on his allegiance? Was this merely a problem in casuistry, a 'case' of unprecedented difficulty that could be resolved only by following one's conscience and submitting to the judgement of heaven, or was there some legal, moral, or political principle which, with ultimate authority, commanded one's allegiance?

In his *Observations upon some of His Majesties Late Answers and Expresses* – published barely a month after the king's *Answer* was issued – Henry Parker implicitly recognized the dilemma implicit in a mixed constitution, noting that 'two supreames cannot bee in the same sence and respect'. 'Power', he said, 'is originally inherent in the people', who had entrusted it to their rulers.[13] Monarchical authority was not held absolutely but 'subject to some conditions . . . That the saftie of the people is to bee valued above any right of his . . .'[14] The guardians of that trust were the people themselves and, in some cases, the parliament.

Endorsing Bodin's conception of sovereignty without mentioning his name, Parker said, 'There is an Arbitrary power in every State somewhere . . . If the State intrusts this to one man, or few, there may be danger in it; but the Parliament is neither one nor few, it is indeed the State itself.' It followed then that 'in matters of Law and State, where Ambiguity is, some determination must be supream . . . and there can be nothing said against the Arbitrary supremacy of Parliaments, &c.',[15] Parker stopped short of endorsing the absolute sovereignty of parliament, preferring the advantage of 'popular and mixt government' and proclaiming himself to be 'as zealously addicted to Monarchy, as any

---

[13] [Henry Parker], *Observations upon some of His Majesties Late Answers and Expresses*, 2nd edn (n.p., n.d. [London, 1642]), pp. 8 and 1. Thomason's copy of the first edition is dated 2 July 1642. The second edition was reprinted in facsimile preserving the original pagination in William Haller (ed.), *Tracts on Liberty in the Puritan Revolution*, 3 vols. (New York, 1936), II, pp. 167–213. On Parker in general, see Michael Mendle, 'Henry Parker, the Public's Privado', in Schochet (ed.), *Religion, Resistance, and Civil War*, and 'Parliamentary Sovereignty: A Very English Absolutism', in Nicholas Phillipson and Quentin Skinner (eds.), *Political Discourse in Early Modern Britain* (Cambridge, 1992). Mendle has superseded the older work of W. K. Jordan, *Men of Substance: A Study of Two English Revolutionaries, Henry Parker and Henry Robinson* (Chicago, 1942). Still useful, however, is Margaret Atwood Judson, 'Henry Parker and the Theory of Parliamentary Sovereignty', in Carl Wittke (ed.), *Essays in History and Political Theory in Honor of Charles Howard McIlwain* (Cambridge, MA, 1936).

[14] [Parker], *Observations*, p. 8.   [15] *Ibid.*, pp. 34 and 36.

man can, without dotage'.[16] In the end, however, he insisted that the
king must bend to the judgement of the kingdom or incur disobedience:
'in all irregular acts where no personall force is, Kings may be dis-
obeyed, their unjust commands may be neglected, not only by communities, but also by single men sometimes'.[17] But all he could bring
himself to say about resolving conflicts that placed the king and
parliament absolutely at loggerheads – short of proclaiming 'Civill
Warre, and . . . blow[ing] the Trumpet of generall confusion' – was that
'we must retire to ordinary justice', and if that does not work, 'We must
retire to the principles of Nature'.[18] There was, presumably, no
question in his mind which side justice and nature would favour; but the
concept of a dissolution of government had appeared.

In declaring the parliament 'the state itself', Parker had gone beyond
the thesis of mixed government (while continuing to recognize an
'ambiguity' in relations between 'law and state'). Philip Hunton's *A
Treatise of Monarchy*, published in May, 1643, nine months into the
armed conflict of the First Civil War, reverted to the language of the
Answer to the Nineteen Propositions and squarely faced its consequences.
Hunton endorsed the *Answer*'s view of the English government as 'a
Monarchy mixed with Aristocracy in the House of Peers, and a
Democracy in the House of Commons' and held that the monarchy was
limited by the mixture as well as by the laws. When those limits were
exceeded, he held that it was permissible to use 'positive and forcible
resistance' against the 'inferriour Officers and Instruments advising to,
or executing the illegal commands'. But 'force ought not to be used
against the person of the Soveraign, on any pretense whatever by any or
all his subjects; even in limited and mixed Monarchies'. 'Without such
power of resistance in the hands of subjects', he continued, 'all distinction and limitation of Government is vain; and all forms resolve into
Absolute and Arbitrary'.[19]

---

[16] *Ibid.*, pp. 40 and 41.
[17] *Ibid.*, p. 44. See also p. 16, where Parker had asserted the entitlement of the people to act
in their own defence: 'if the King will not joyne with the people, the people may without
disloyalty save themselves . . .'
[18] *Ibid.*, pp. 43 and 44.
[19] [Philip Hunton], *A Treatise of Monarchy* (1643), reprinted (London, 1689), pp. 32, 40,
and 42 (chs. 3 and 5). (This printing also includes portions of Hunton's 1644 *A
Vindication of the Treatise of Monarchy*.) For more general discussions of Hunton, see
Julian Franklin, *John Locke and the Theory of Sovereignty: Mixed Monarchy and the
Right of Resistance in the Political Thought of the English Revolution* (Cambridge, 1978),
pp. 39–49; C. H. McIlwain, 'A Forgotten Worthy, Philip Hunton, and the Sovereignty
of the King-in-Parliament', in his *Constitutionalism and the Changing World: Collected
Papers* (Cambridge, 1939), ch. 9 (originally published in *Politica*, February, 1935); and
Pocock, *Political Works of James Harrington*, pp. 22–4, and *Machiavellian Moment*, pp.
364–70.

What this amounted to was a reassertion of their original power by the people who had conditionally entrusted it to the monarch. Hunton agreed with Parker (and others of this stripe) that the people 'have a vertual, radical Power, by publick Consent and Contract to constitute this or that form of Government, and resign up themselves to a condition of subjection on *Terms*, and after a form of their own constitution'.[20] Failing other remedies, it was the prerogative of the people themselves to enforce the conditions of their grant, and to do it by force if necessary:

In case the Fundamental Rights of either of the three Estates be invaded by one or both the rest, the wronged may lawfully assume force for its own defence; because else it were not free, but dependent on the pleasure of the other. Also the suppression of either of them, or the diminishing of their Fundamental Rights, carries with it the dissolution of the Government: And therefore those grounds which justifie force to preserve its Being, allows this case, which is a direct innovation of its Being and Frame.[21]

On one level, this notion of dissolution – which would assume great importance in Locke's theory of revolution[22] – was a virtual *invitation* to civil war, for Hunton's penultimate chapter was entitled 'Where the Legal Power of Final judging in these cases doth reside, in case the Three Estates differ about the same?' As he admitted:

this final utmost controversie arising betwixt the three Legislative Estates, can have no legal, constituted Judge in a mixed government . . . I take it to be an evident truth, that in a mixed government, no power is to be attributed to either Estate, which directly, or by necessary consequence, destroys the liberty of the other.[23]

It was on this ground that Sir Robert Filmer, a devoted follower of Bodin, charged that 'instead of a treatise of *monarchy*, he [Hunton] hath brought forth a treatise of *anarchy*'.[24]

The language of mixed government, intended to warn the realm against actions leading to civil war, had proved capable within its limits of predicting and explaining, but not of resolving, that war. From this terrifyingly open-ended predicament many consequences could flow, ranging from the absolute sovereignty of the king or of the parliament –

---

[20] [Hunton], *Treatise*, pp. 50 and 52 (ch. 5).   [21] *Ibid.*, p. 55 (ch. 6).

[22] On the larger significance of the 'dissolution' theory of resistance, see Franklin, *John Locke*, esp. chs. 2 and 3; and Conal Condren, *George Lawson's 'Politica' and the English Revolution* (Cambridge, 1989), pp. 153–68.

[23] [Hunton], *Treatise*, p. 57 (ch. 7).

[24] Sir Robert Filmer, *The Anarchy of a Limited or Mixed Monarchy* (1648), reprinted in his *Patriarcha and Other Writings*, ed. Johann P. Sommerville (Cambridge Texts in the History of Political Thought; Cambridge, 1991), p. 150. All subsequent references to Filmer will be to this edition.

each indicating by the sword its claim to be the exclusive representative of the realm – to the radical proposition that the historic balance of king, lords, and commons had failed to maintain itself and must be replaced by a republic. Even the great, but brief, explosion of quasi-democratic programmes we associate with the Army's manifestoes, the Leveller *Agreement of the People*, and the Putney debates,[25] belongs in this context of dissolution of government and appeal to heaven. The Lord was speaking terribly to his people, and all former covenants were dissolved. What came to the surface was both the Fifth Monarchist expectation of the return of Christ in an actual rule of the saints and millennium and the even more dramatic and subversive identification of Christ with 'the great spirit reason', which could lead Gerrard Winstanley to the utopia of *The Law of Freedom in a Platform*.

But the World Turned Upside Down found no permanent base, and the only radical sects to survive were the Quakers and the Muggletonians,[26] both of which found their paths to quietism and only the former to a role in subsequent history as well. Lilburne died a Quaker; Walwyn, Winstanley and even Abiezer Coppe the Ranter lived out their lives in private contemplation and practice, as indeed did Lodowick Muggleton. We must remain alert for a persistent radicalism styled that of the Good Old Cause; but its historical context is that of a resolute conservatism, as old as the events to which it responded. The dissolution of government was experienced and remembered as the worst disaster England had ever endured, and the collapse of authority not as a revolutionary opportunity but as a catastrophe which had imposed on the subject the appalling obligation to reconstitute authority out of his own naked being.

The collapse of authority in what Parker called 'law and state' was

---

[25] The most recent works on this subject are Mark A. Kishlansky, *The Rise of the New Model Army* (Cambridge, 1979); Austin F. Woolrych, *Soldiers and Statesmen: The Army Council and its Debates, 1647–48* (Oxford, 1987); and Ian Gentles, *The New Model Army in England, Ireland, and Scotland* (Oxford, 1992). The most recent study of Leveller political thought is David Wootton, 'Leveller Democracy and the Puritan Revolution', in J. H. Burns (ed. with the assistance of Mark Goldie), *The Cambridge History of Political Thought, 1450–1700* (Cambridge, 1991), pp. 412–42. See also, for one of the most interesting of the Leveller theorists, William Walwyn, *The Writings*, ed. with an introduction by Jack R. McMichael and Barbara Taft (Athens, GA, 1989).

[26] Christopher Hill, *The World Turned Upside Down: Radical Ideas During the English Revolution* (New York, 1973); Hill, *Milton and the English Revolution* (London, 1977); Hill, William M. Lamont and Barry Reay, *The World of the Muggletonians* (London, 1983); and J. C. Davis, *Fear, Myth, and History: The Ranters and Their Historians* (Cambridge, 1986).

accompanied, and in many eyes surpassed, by a collapse of authority in crown and church. Historians have been slow to recognize the central significance of the Church of England's temporary disestablishment and underground survival. They have preferred – for very good reasons – to study the failure of puritanism to solve the problem of 'godly rule', to reconcile the liberty of the Christian spirit with the demands for authority in church and state. The puritan impulse is reduced to the vanishing point, to be replaced in 1660–2 by a resurgent Anglicanism as suddenly presented as it has been previously unexplained. Attention is at last focusing on the phenomena of the established church's not altogether unpopular survival; we are conscious that Charles I's immediate request to Cornet Joyce, when the latter took charge of his person at Holmby House, was that he might have the company of Gilbert Sheldon and Henry Hammond, the two divines more active than any bishop in keeping the Church of England alive in the wilderness of the following years.[27] Joyce made no objection to the king's request, and the Anglican divines were much in his society at Carisbrooke Castle, as (interestingly) was James Harrington, present there and at Holmby in the un-republican role of a gentleman of the king's bedchamber. It was from the Isle of Wight that Charles helped launch the Second Civil War, the direct occasion of his arraignment; but it was also at Carisbrooke that he came closest to an agreement with English and Scots Presbyterians, so that the image of an 'Isle of Wight kingship' haunted Anglican memories thereafter.[28] In the year after his death, his son took the Covenant with the Scots (infuriated by the English execution of a king who was also theirs) and inaugurated the long and uneasy period during which the Church of England could not quite trust its own supreme head and governor.

Perhaps this is why Charles I is said to have taken an interest in Robert Sanderson's preachings on the obligations of conscience, which won their author a reputation as the chief of English casuists. The Army had debated when a covenant with the Lord might be held annulled by

---

[27] John W. Packer, *The Transformation of Anglicanism, 1643–1660: With Special Reference to Henry Hammond* (Manchester, 1969), provides a full and pro-Anglican account of the church's fortunes during the Interregnum years; his perspective, however, is that of the old-fashioned church historian. John Spurr, *The Restoration Church of England, 1646–1689* (New Haven, 1991), ch. 1, is a much more even-handed discussion – albeit certainly sympathetic to Anglicanism – as well as one that has a broader point of departure. See also C. N. Lettinga, 'Covenant Theology and the Transformation of Anglicanism', unpub. PhD dissertation, Johns Hopkins University, 1987.

[28] See Mark Goldie, 'Danby, the Bishops and the Whigs', in Tim Harris, Paul Seaward, and Mark Goldie (eds.), *The Politics of Religion in Restoration England* (Oxford, 1990), pp. 77–8.

divine action; problems of conscience and obligation in the 'dangerous or doubtful times' of 'confusions and revolutions in government' forced themselves on the highest in the land, not excluding the king himself, and continued after the regicide to supply the context of all political reflection. Even those amorally ready to change allegiance sought for a justifying authority. Marchamont Nedham,[29] transferring from the royal to the parliamentary service, argued that in the event of civil war among the members of a mixed government, the judgement of heaven invested the victor with the authority of a conqueror. To Charles I's claim that his judges in the High Court were exercising the mere power of the sword, one of a sufficiently strong stomach might retort that it was by the *jus conquestus*, recognized by natural and divine law, that he was indeed being judged. Few had the nerve for this, and we have now to deal less with the justification of regicide itself – a task carried out by John Milton[30] – than with the enduring, and philosophically perhaps more interesting, problem of the terms on which the subject might or might not give his obedience to a government that had little legitimacy to claim. The abolition of the monarchy could be vindicated by asserting the original liberties of the people of England, but these were not the grounds on which every male subject was soon after required to engage himself to 'the government as it is now established, without a king or house of Lords'.[31] The minimalist language betrays the lack of a revolutionary programme or principle, and what historians call 'the Engagement controversy' – one of a series of debates about '*de facto* authority' – revolved around the questions whether the subject was obliged to obey any government rather than none, and what authority for doing so he might discover where the government itself could claim none. His original liberty, if he had any, presented not a revolutionary opportunity but a dreadful choice, and there were those who saw that civil liberty consisted precisely in freedom from this choice. The regime's claim was that as the established and effective government of England – whatever its origins – the Commonwealth was entitled to the loyalty and obedience of its members, who, accordingly, were obliged to

---

[29] Joseph Frank, *Cromwell's Press Agent: A Critical Biography of Marchamont Nedham, 1620–1678* (Washington, 1982); Enrico Nuzzo, *La Superiorità degli Stati Liberi: i republicani inglesi, 1649–1722* (Naples, 1984).

[30] Martin Dzelzainis (ed.), *Milton: Political Writings*, (Cambridge Texts in the History of Political Thought; Cambridge, 1991), contains *The Tenure of Kings and Magistrates* and a translation of *Defensio Populi Anglicani*.

[31] 'An Act for Subscribing the Engagement', 2 January 1650, from Kenyon (ed.), *Stuart Constitution*, p. 307. The Engagement was not widely subscribed and apparently not strongly enforced (see Kenyon, p. 297), but it was intensely debated. A major study of the controversy and its aftermath is Wallace, *Destiny His Choice*.

take the Engagement.[32] Even the unblinking royalist Sir Robert Filmer could accept this reasoning; as he said in 1652, echoing the sentiments of Thomas Hobbes, '*protection* and *subjection* are reciprocal, so that where the first fails, the latter ceaseth'.[33] Or, as Hobbes himself put it, the unequivocal 'designe' of the *Leviathan* was 'to set before mens eyes the mutuall Relation between Protection and Obedience'.[34]

Hobbes and Filmer were certainly not apologists for the Commonwealth.[35] Much more representative of the Engagement writers and a far better and more influential representative of the interests of the Commonwealth was that former royalist Marchamont Nedham, whose *Case of the Commonwealth* (1650) defended the proposition 'That the Power of the Sword Is, and Ever Hath Been, the Foundation of All Titles to Government',[36] and asserted:

That those whose title is supposed unlawful and founded merely upon force, yet being possessed of authority, may lawfully be obeyed. Nor *may* they only, but they *must*;[37] else by judgment of civilians such as refuse may be punished as seditious and traitorous, the victors being ever allowed, *jure gentium*, to use all means for securing what they have gotten and to exercise a right of dominion over the conquered party. Whosoever therefore shall refuse submission to an established government upon pretense of conscience in regard of former allegiances, oaths, and covenants, or upon supposition that it is by the sword

[32] As John M. Wallace observes, 'The mark of an Engager was his willingness to lend his passive support to a usurper who commanded lawful things, regardless of the usurper's claim to legitimacy. He obeyed for the sake of peace, to prevent further bloodshed, and he did so on the understanding that illegal government would continue only for an interim period, until a more stable constitution could be formed.' 'The Engagement Controversy, 1649–1652: An Annotated List of Pamphlets', *Bulletin of the New York Public Library*, 68 (1964), 384–405, at pp. 386–7.

[33] Filmer, *Directions for Obedience to Government in Dangerous or Doubtful Times* (1652), reprinted in *Patriarcha and Other Works*, ed. Sommerville, p. 285.

[34] Thomas Hobbes, *Leviathan, or The Matter, Forme, & Power of a Commonwealth Ecclesiastical of Civill* (1651), ed. Richard Tuck (Cambridge Texts in the History of Political Thought; Cambridge, 1991), p. 491 ('Review, and Conclusion'). All references to *Leviathan* will be to this edition, cited by chapter and page.

[35] Hobbes has been read as if he were an Engagement writer, originally by Quentin Skinner, who subsequently altered his interpretation. See his 'The Ideological Context of Hobbes's Political Thought', *Historical Journal*, 8 (1965), 151–78 (revised as 'Conquest and Consent: Thomas Hobbes and the Engagement Controversy', in *The Interregnum: The Quest for Settlement, 1646–1660*, ed. G. E. Aylmer (London, 1972), ch. 3), and 'Thomas Hobbes on the Proper Signification of Liberty', *Transactions of the Royal Historical Society*, 5th ser., 40 (1990), 121–51, at pp. 144–6 and refs. Cf. Glenn Burgess, 'Usurpation, Obligation, and Obedience in the Thought of the Engagement Controversy', *Historical Journal*, 29 (1986), 515–36, and Gordon J. Schochet, 'Intending (Political) Obligation: Hobbes and the Voluntary Basis of Society', in Mary D. Dietz (ed.), *Thomas Hobbes and Political Theory* (Lawrence, KS, 1990), ch. 4.

[36] Marchamont Nedham, *The Case of the Commonwealth of England Stated* (1650), ed. Philip A. Knachel, Folger Documents of Tudor and Stuart Civilization (Charlottesville, 1969), p. 13 (ch. title). All references are to this edition.

[37] Marginal reference to Grotius, *De Jure Belli et Pacis*, III, 15.

unlawfully erected, deserves none but the character of peevish, and a man obstinate against the reason and custom of the whole world. Let his pretense be what it will, resistance, in the eye of the law of nations, is treason; and if he will needs perish in the face of his own phrenetic zeal, he can at best be reckoned but the madman's saint and the fool's martyr.[38]

Nedham defended 'the Excellency of a Free State above a Kingly Government' and argued that the 'prudent toleration of opinions in matter[s] of religion . . . can be no way destructive of public peace'.[39] The second edition of his book concluded with an appendix of quotations from Salmasius' *Defensio Regia pro Carlo I* and Hobbes' *De Corpore Politico*,[40] works that, according to Nedham, enjoyed 'great reputation' among 'the two parties, presbyterian and royal', that were antagonistic to the Commonwealth. His purpose was 'to determine the point of power in general and of submission and obedience to such a power, though it had been unlawfully gained'.[41] It is unlikely that Nedham intended to endorse the overall perspective of either writer,[42] neither of whom was particularly friendly toward the Commonwealth. Salmasius' defence of the executed king – written at the behest of Charles II and published in 1649[43] – was answered by Milton in his *Pro Populo Anglicano Defensio* (1651) and defended by Filmer in his *Observations concerning the Originall of Government* (1652). Hobbes too was believed to harbour royalist sympathies, and the unyielding absolutism of his political tracts was hardly supportive of rule by popular representative assemblies.

The peculiar importance of Nedham, however, is that his writings show how the debate over submission to a *de facto* government – which outlasted the Engagement controversy properly so called – could both involve the earlier writings of Hobbes in ways that point to the context in which *Leviathan* was to make its impact, and appeal to Machiavellian doctrine in ways that led to the theoretical establishment of a true republic (never to be realized in the actual England). What is worth emphasizing here is that *Leviathan* appeared in April 1651, and was

[38] Nedham, *Case of the Commonwealth*, pp. 28–9.   [39] *Ibid.*, pp. 110 (ch. title), 123.
[40] Thomason acquired his copy of *De Corpore Politico* on 4 May 1650, four days earlier than the first edition of Nedham's *Case of the Commonwealth*.
[41] Nedham, *Case of the Commonwealth*, pp. 129–30.
[42] Cf. Knachel, Introduction to his edition of Nedham, *Case of the Commonwealth*, p. xxxv, who suggests, following Skinner's original argument, that Nedham's quotations from Hobbes revealed rather more of an endorsement than his own somewhat ironic explanation might indicate.
[43] Thomason's copy is dated 11 May, but the work must have been available in England long before, for the Council of State requested Milton to prepare his answer to Salmasius on January 8, 1650. See Milton, *Complete Prose Works*, IV, Part I, 1650–1655, ed. Don M. Wolfe (New Haven, CT, 1966), p. 285 and refs.

therefore first read during the Scottish invasion we term the Third Civil War, terminated by the 'crowning mercy' of the battle of Worcester on 3 September. A reader of the outlook of an Anthony Ascham[44] might recognize that Hobbes offered little advice – and indeed there was none to offer – on what to do when two contenders for the role of Leviathan were in the field, each demanding the subject's allegiance at the point of the sword. Hobbes did not return to England until this danger was at an end.

Nedham, now the editor of the government journal *Mercurius Politicus*, kept it supplied during the year between Dunbar and Worcester with homilies excerpted from his previously published *Case of the Commonwealth*, arguing the case for submission to the conqueror, i.e., the existing government of England. Two weeks after Worcester, however, with the fear of further conquests and civil wars removed from the board, a change of editorial tone occurred and Nedham began to print editorials which he later published as his republican classic *The Excellency of a Free State*.[45] The conqueror to whom he advocated submission was now identified as the democratic component of the former mixed government, and further identified with the army rather than the House of Commons. Nedham invited it to act not merely as conqueror but as legislator in the manner of Lycurgus, using the authority of the sword to found a new mode of government in which it would render its rule legitimate and permanent; it was a programme as close to being that of a revolution as the early-modern intellect was capable of constructing. He was still no democrat in the sense that he rejected the Levellers and held that the democratic power should include itself within a larger polity; but he expressed very bitter opposition to the survival of any kind of hereditary or 'kingly' power, whether that of a 'Norman' king or peerage in England or that of magnates, chiefs, or lairds in Scotland. His republic is to have no nobles or patricians, and the bearer of the sword is to be his own master.

Blair Worden has suggested[46] that the appearance of these doctrines in *Mercurius Politicus* indicates an upsurge in post-Leveller radical sentiment after the defeat of Charles II at Worcester and that Nedham may at this time have been associated with a group of republicans in

---

[44] For Ascham, author of a *Discourse Wherein Is Examined What Is Particularly Lawfull during the Confusions and Revolutions of Government* (1648) and *The Bounds and Bonds of Politique Obedience* (1649), see Wallace, *Destiny His Choice*, generally. He was dead by 1651, having been murdered by royalists at Madrid.

[45] For details, see Pocock (ed.), *Political Works of James Harrington* (hereafter *PW*), pp. 13–14, 33–7.

[46] Blair Worden, *The Rump Parliament, 1648–1653* (Cambridge, 1974). In general, see Austin Woolrych, *Commonwealth to Protectorate* (Oxford, 1982).

some sense of the term, headed by Henry Marten, Thomas Chaloner and Henry Neville. However that may be, there are not too many signs of a republican programme between 1652, when the last of Nedham's republican writings appeared in *Mercurius Politicus*, and 1656, when *The Excellency of a Free State* and Harrington's *The Commonwealth of Oceana* appeared as printed books. The intervening years are those of the successive failures of the Rump and the Parliament of Saints, and the transition from commonwealth to protectorate. They were years that semi-revolutionary idealists in the reign of George III[47] were to see as marking a lost opportunity, when England might have been, but was not, transformed by philosophical republicans 'who called Milton friend'.

In Hobbes, we meet the first genuine political *philosopher* encountered in this volume devoted to British political *thought*. His *Leviathan* has been called 'the greatest, perhaps the sole, masterpiece of political philosophy written in the English language'.[48] And for that very reason, Hobbes does not need and cannot be given exhaustive treatment here. While political philosophy is an integral part of political discourse, the history of political philosophy deserves separate treatment. *Leviathan* was intended to form part of a canon of philosophical writings, which should follow Bacon in replacing Aristotle with a *novum organon*, and certainly Hobbes had a political agenda in constructing this canon. He made clear his belief that the ancient error of Greek metaphysics, which permitted the invention of false substances and real essences, had for centuries permitted papists and rebels to appeal to these non-entities against the authority of the civil sovereign. Nevertheless, it would be one thing to trace the history of his thinking in the context of his relations with Descartes, Mersenne and Gassendi, when he withdrew to Paris on the eve of the English Civil War; another, which is our primary intention here, to trace it in that of the English political context in which *Leviathan* was read, and the English political discourse with which it interacted, causing such a stir.

His standing as a proponent of absolute sovereignty is well known and, indeed, is part of what distinguished him from contemporaries who shared his belief in *de facto* legitimacy. One of the most significant things about Hobbes' version of that doctrine is that it was grounded in a thoroughly naturalistic conception of human nature and civil society. Hobbes' transformation of the opposition ideology of rights and liberty into the basis of absolute authority is among the most remarkable but

---

[47] See below, pp. 255, 309.
[48] Michael Oakeshott's characterization in the Introduction to his edition of *Leviathan*, Blackwell's Political Texts (Oxford, 1957), p. viii.

least noted of his accomplishments. He did not merely point out the weaknesses of these doctrines and argue that they gave rise to anarchy, as had some of his contemporaries: Dudley Digges, Bishop John Maxwell, Filmer,[49] and even Nedham.[50] He retained the juridical or legalistic vocabulary of rights and liberties and preserved the natural law and natural rights theories, from which he moved to absolutism rather than to the more conventional insistence upon *constitutionalist* limitations on political power. For this, Hobbes earned the mixed praise of Filmer, who fully appreciated what he was up to:

> With no small content I read Mr Hobbes' book *De Cive*, and his *Leviathan*, about the rights of sovereignty, which no man, that I know, hath so amply and judiciously handled. I consent with him about rights of exercising government, but I cannot agree to his means of acquiring it. It may seem strange I should praise his building and yet mislike his foundation, but so it is, his *jus naturae*, and his *regnum institutivum*, will not down with me, they appear full of contradiction and impossibilities.[51]

Filmer might be said to have anticipated the Church of England's response to Hobbes, if that had not, as we shall see, taken shape from the moment *Leviathan* appeared; the clergy were always to see him as a supporter more dangerous than any enemy. Filmer's point here, as in *Patriarcha*, is that the Book of Genesis makes a better foundation for kingship than does natural law, which grounds sovereign absolutism on radical individualism. Hobbes moved from nature to authority *through* liberty, not by abandoning or rejecting it. Freedom itself was merely a description of a human condition. 'According to the proper signification of the word', he said, it means 'the absence of externall Impediments'.[52] It was not 'good', or a standard to which political institutions should aspire (as it was for the Levellers) or even something to be reconceptualized along humanist, republican lines (which may have been what Nedham and James Harrington were about).[53] Hobbes saw that freedom could be dangerous and that its expression must be politically muted if government was to be stable. In this manner, Hobbes was able to transform a discourse of resistance into a discourse of authority.

Hobbes' sensitivity to language was manifest throughout the *Leviathan* and is one of the leitmotifs of that great work, much of which

[49] See Gordon J. Schochet, *The Authoritarian Family and Political Attitudes in 17th-Century England: Patriarchalism in Political Thought*, 2nd edn (New Brunswick, 1988), pp. 102–12.

[50] See *Case of the Commonwealth*, pp. 31–2, which invites comparison with *Leviathan*, ch. 29.

[51] Filmer, *Observations*, in *Patriarcha and Other Works*, ed. Sommerville, pp. 184–5.

[52] Hobbes, *Leviathan*, ch. 14 (p. 91).

[53] And is surely what Rousseau was to contend for 100 years later.

consists of precise definitions. Speech, he said, was 'the most noble and profitable invention of all other ... without which, there had been amongst men, neither Common-wealth, nor Society, nor Contract, nor Peace, no more than amongst Lyons, Bears, and Wolves'.[54] Hobbes urged 'any man that aspires to true Knowledge, to examine the Definitions of former Authors; and either to correct them, where they are negligently set down; or to make them himself'.[55] He then, in his initial discussion of natural law, warned against what he suggested was a standard confusion of *lex* and *jus* and, in fact, *stipulated* a pair of meanings that broke from his predecessors and accorded with his own political purposes:

For though they that speak of this subject [i.e., natural law], use to confound *Jus*, and *Lex*, *Right* and *Law*; yet they ought to be distinguished; because RIGHT, consisteth in liberty to do, or to forbeare; Whereas LAW, determineth, and bindeth to one of them: that Law, and Right, differ as much, as Obligation, and Liberty; which in one and the same matter are inconsistent.[56]

Modern scholarship is at last learning to confront Hobbes' views on religion,[57] an aspect of his doctrine which, perhaps more than any other, attracted notice in his own day.[58] Attention has recently been drawn to an important shift in his attitudes toward the ecclesiastical hierarchy that was evident in the publication of the *Leviathan*.[59] In 1642, in *De Cive*, apparently siding with the Church of England in its dispute with the Presbyterians, Hobbes said, 'It is apparent therefore by the custome of the Primitive *Church* under the *Apostles*, that the *ordination*, or *consecration* of all Church-men, which is done by *prayer*, and *imposition of hands*, belonged to the *Apostles* and *Doctors*; but the *Election* of those who were to be consecrated, *to the Church*'.[60] Nine years later, he had

---

[54] Hobbes, *Leviathan*, ch. 4 (p. 24).   [55] *Ibid.*, ch. 4 (p. 28).

[56] *Ibid.*, ch. 14 (p. 91).

[57] See J. G. A. Pocock, 'Time, History, and Eschatology in the Thought of Thomas Hobbes', in his *Politics, Language, and Time: Essays on Political Thought and History* (New York, 1971, Chicago, 1985), ch. 5; Arrigo Pacchi, 'Hobbes and the Problem of God', in G. A. J. Rogers and Alan Ryan (eds.), *Perspectives on Thomas Hobbes* (Oxford, 1988), ch. 8; Glenn Burgess, 'Contexts for the Writing and Publication of Hobbes's *Leviathan*', *History of Political Thought*, 11 (1990), 675–702; and especially Richard Tuck, 'The Civil Religion of Thomas Hobbes', in Phillipson and Skinner (eds.), *Political Discourse*, and his *Hobbes*, Past Masters (Oxford, 1989), pp. 76–91.

[58] See Samuel I. Mintz, *The Hunting of Leviathan: Seventeenth-Century Reactions to the Materialism and Moral Philosophy of Thomas Hobbes* (Cambridge, 1962), and Schochet, *Authoritarian Family*, pp. 179–84.

[59] Tuck, *Hobbes*, pp. 86–91.

[60] Thomas Hobbes, *De Cive* (1642), translated (not by Hobbes) as *Philosophicall Rudiments concerning Government and Society* (1651), XVII, xxiv, reprinted in a critical edition as *De Cive: The English Version*, ed. Howard Warrender, The Clarendon Edition of the Philosophical Works of Thomas Hobbes, III (Oxford, 1983), p. 239.

altered his opinion. Collapsing the distinction between the 'ordination' and 'election' of the clergy, Hobbes said in a passage in the *Leviathan* labelled '*Ordination of Teachers*', 'As the Apostles . . . were not made by our Saviour himself, but were elected by the Church, that is, by the Assembly of Christians . . . so were also the *Presbyters*, and *Pastors* in other Cities, elected by the Churches of those Cities'.[61] He followed that assertion with a relatively brief review of Hebrew and early Christian ordination practices and concluded:

> if there had been then any Christian, that had had the Power of Teaching before [the first investment of teachers]; the Baptizing him, that is, the making him a Christian, had given him no new Power, but had onely caused him to preach true Doctrine, that is, to use his Power aright; and therefore the Imposition of Hands had been unnecessary; Baptisme it selfe had been sufficient. But every Soveraign, before Christianity, had the Power of Teaching, and Ordaining Teachers; and therefore Christianity gave them no new Right, but only directed them in the way of teaching Truth; and consequently they needed no Imposition of Hands (besides that which is done in Baptisme) to authorize them to exercise any part of the Pastorall Function, as namely, to Baptize, and Consecrate.[62]

This new position had the theoretical advantage of bringing Hobbes' conception of religious organization into line with his doctrine of sovereign absolutism by making the church a thoroughly Erastian institution.[63] On the other hand, with this argument, Hobbes entered into a whirl of controversies that would dominate religious politics for the next forty years. In 1651, his position inevitably and irrevocably alienated the remaining Anglican clergy, many of whom had been among his associates ten years earlier. Other passages in *Leviathan* made it clear that he was willing to accept a religious settlement in which neither bishops nor ordained ministers exercised any *jure divino* authority, and a diversity of congregations was 'reduced to the Independency of the Primitive Christians to follow Paul, or Cephas, or Apollos, every man as he liketh best' under the overriding authority of the civil sovereign.[64] It was this abandonment of the royal, apostolic and episcopal church which was never to be forgotten or forgiven and in whose light Hobbes' philosophy and physics were to be read for the rest of his long life and after. His materialist philosophy, whether atomistic or holistic, was perceived as what indeed it was, a means of exiling spirit from the universe of being and thus depriving the restless mind of any means of making claims against the sovereign based on a communion

---

[61] Hobbes, *Leviathan*, ch. 42 (pp. 365–6).   [62] *Ibid.*, ch. 42 (p. 377).
[63] Which Tuck suggests may have been part of the reason for this change. *Hobbes*, p. 86.
[64] *Leviathan*, ch. 47 (p. 479).

beyond his reach. Those striving to maintain the apparently disestab-
lished Church of England could never accept this strategy; there must be
a realm of the spirit exercising Christ's authority transmitted through
the apostles and bishops, and the royal authority by which the Church
was governed must be part of it.

Hobbes' physics and metaphysics drew less immediate fire than his
account of the ordinations, or rather elections, of the first deacons and
presbyters of the apostles. In a vigorous reply, Henry Hammond
expounded the differences between ordination and election, and showed
how the laying on of hands maintained the apostolic succession.[65] This
question was to prove crucial in later years. Symon Patrick, who would
serve as Bishop of Ely in 1690, recorded that his original ordination by
presbyters 'afterwards troubled me very much'. He and several friends
sought out John Hall, the former Bishop of Norwich, who 'ordained us
in his own parlour at Higham [to which he had retired], about a mile
from Norwich, April 5th, 1645'.[66] Throughout the Restoration, investiture would constitute one of the principal obstacles to Anglican-
Presbyterian reconciliation;[67] and in this perspective, it was plain that
Hobbes was an upholder of Independency so drastically Erastian as to
be irreligious, opposed to both episcopacy and Presbyterianism, in
which the *jus divinum* of the clergy was maintained.

A not dissimilar anti-clericalism prevails in the writings of the second
great intellectual innovator of the Interregnum, otherwise a humanist
and historian where Hobbes was a philosopher and a republican where
Leviathan was a king. James Harrington, attendant on Charles I to the
eve of his execution, vanished from sight until 1656, when he reappeared
as the author of *The Commonwealth of Oceana*, in which we find the
remark that the English monarchy, 'the most indulgent to, and least
invasive for many ages upon, the liberty of a people that the world hath
known', has nevertheless 'fallen with such horror as hath been a
spectacle of astonishment unto the whole earth'.[68] Harrington wrote
both to explain how this had happened – so that his book is a
reconstruction of history designed to account for the *de facto* situation –
and to explain why a republic was the only possible replacement
for monarchy and in some ways preferable to it. His trajectory there-

---

[65] Henry Hammond, *A Letter of Resolution to Six Quaeres, of Present Use in the Church of England* (London, 1653), pp. 384–409.

[66] Symon Patrick, *The Auto-Biography* (Oxford, 1839), pp. 23–4.

[67] For general discussions of attitudes toward the episcopacy, see Packer, *Transformation*, ch. 5; Spurr, *Restoration Church*, pp. 132–65; and J. A. I. Champion, *The Pillars of Priestcraft Shaken: The Church of England and Its Enemies, 1660–1730* (Cambridge, 1992), ch. 3.

[68] *PW*, p. 235.

fore in some ways resembles Marchamont Nedham's; but we need to understand the circumstances in which both writers published their books.

1656 was a late year in the history of the short-lived English revolution and may display it already in decline. Oliver Cromwell had only two years to live, and his increasingly conservative protectorate was under double pressure, both from army officers discontented with their roles as servants of a quasi-prince and from a parliamentary gentry who disliked the whole phenomenon of the army as an instrument of government. It has been argued that *The Commonwealth of Oceana*, *The Excellency of a Free State*, and Sir Henry Vane's *A Healing Question*[69] were all published in 1656 as challenges to the regime to reintegrate itself with the army and its ideals, and more recently that the publication of *Oceana* can be connected with the failure of apocalyptic hopes associated with the 'Western design', the defeat at Havana and the conquest of Jamaica in the previous year.[70] There exists a text[71] in which Harrington is shown explaining to Restoration inquisitors how he came to write his book; and he recounts that some of Cromwell's officers spoke to the Protector about a commonwealth and were told that they did not know what one was and neither did he. This suggests the discontent of colonels like Okey, Alured and Saunders in 1654, the year in which Harrington seems to have begun writing his book. This is such evidence as we have for thinking of *Oceana* as a product of 'the good old cause',[72] and points to an 'old cause' very different from that of the Rumper Algernon Sidney, who was to remain all his life a proponent of an ideal parliamentary supremacy.[73] Sidney's republicanism was aristocratic to the point of being baronial; Harrington's was based on the belief that the English nobility had fallen and dragged their king down with them, an arresting reinterpretation of English history that gives him his place within it.

Harrington's book is both a blueprint for an English republic, embodying a new union between liberty and the conquering sword, and a historical explanation of why the monarchy had fallen and a republic must take its place. It is in the latter capacity that it marks a new

---

[69] Margaret Judson, *The Political Thought of Sir Henry Vane the Younger* (Philadelphia, 1969). *PW*, pp. 12–14.

[70] David Armitage, 'The British Empire and the Civic Tradition, 1656–1742', unpub. PhD dissertation, University of Cambridge, 1991, ch. 2.

[71] *The Examination of James Harrington*, *PW*, pp. 855–59.

[72] J. G. A. Pocock, 'James Harrington and the Good Old Cause: A Study of the Ideological Context of his Writings', *Journal of British Studies*, 10 (1970), 30–48.

[73] Scott, *Algernon Sidney and the English Republic, 1623–1677* and *Algernon Sidney and the Restoration Crisis, 1677–1683* (Cambridge, 1991). Also Alan Houston, *Algernon Sidney and the Republican Heritage in England and America* (Princeton, 1991).

departure in the history of English political discourse, since it introduces an altogether new style in the writing of English history and the use of historical explanation. Harrington picks up[74] a suggestion made by Francis Bacon, in his *History of King Henry VII* a generation earlier, to the effect that legislation after 1485 emancipated tenants from military obligations to their lords and provided the realm with an improved infantry. Harrington elaborates Bacon's point into the thesis that this explains why civil war in 1642 could no longer be a feudal conflict between barons and their king. There was now an independent people, owning their land, their weapons, and themselves, and since the sword was the root of all public action, these could not but act for themselves in politics, rendering both crown and baronage historically obsolete. A republic – the self-government of an armed citizenry – was thus inevitable, and the problem was to devise the institutions whereby this new 'king people'[75] could rule themselves in the act of wielding the sword.

Harrington's new history has been defined as 'a Machiavellian meditation upon feudalism',[76] linking the civic humanism of the Florentines with the political economy of the eighteenth-century Scots. One reward of reading him in this way is that it enables us to stress that his thought was so far humanist as almost to lack a juristic dimension; he was interested in property in so far as it provided the individual with autonomy and the capacity for civic virtue, hardly at all because it provided him with rights which were embodied in law and defended either by or against the sovereign. Though this distinction has become both momentous and contentious in the interpretation of Anglo-American political discourse, it concerns us less immediately than the discovery that Harrington both remodelled the writing of history in England and pioneered the historical explanation of the causes of the Civil War. He did not sole-handedly invent, but he imposed upon his Whig and Scottish successors, a reading of Western and British history that stressed the decline of the Roman republic, the feudalization of the later empire, and a period of feudal, 'Gothic' or medieval history lasting until the end of the fifteenth century. The Tudors were the unwitting gravediggers of English feudalism, and the crisis of Charles I's reign was the crisis of a post-feudal monarchy and aristocracy. Harrington had no conception of the bourgeoisie as a class, and his revolutionary class is a 'king people' of gentlemen, yeomen, Londoners and freeholders. Nevertheless, his Civil War is a revolution in the modern sense, the

---

[74] *PW*, pp. 157–8, 197–8.   [75] *Ibid.*, p. 229.
[76] J. G. A. Pocock, *The Ancient Constitution and the Feudal Law* (Cambridge, 1957, 1987), p. 147, and ch. 6 generally.

collapse and transformation of a political structure under stresses originating in the changing nature of property. The long-term, social-change explanations of the Civil War which post-modern historians strive to undo originated in perceptions contemporary with the civil wars themselves.

Alongside the historicist component in Harrington's thought there is another, utopian, Platonist and even millenarian. His reading of Western history culminates at the moment when Oceana becomes what Rome once was, a commonwealth of armed equals capable of sustaining a republic; but this is also the moment when the proprietors cease being the subjects of their lords and become their own masters. They now leave the domain of 'the goods of fortune' and enter that of 'the goods of the mind';[77] they become materially capable of ruling themselves, which is to say of exercising a self-determining intellect in an otherwise material world. 'The heaven, *even* the heavens, *are* the Lord's; but the earth hath he given unto the children of men.'[78] When property becomes the precondition of intellect, men become the creatures of God, created by him in his own image; and when the exercise of intellect is seen to be the government of selves by selves, we see that the political capacity is what is godlike in men. Property becomes the mode whereby the divine is present in human society; Oceana is at one point not far from being the Bride of Christ.[79] Harrington is the Gerrard Winstanley of the gentry, making of property what Winstanley had made of community.

Harrington's republican humanism here gives form to his hatred of priests.[80] The citizen, free to determine his own being, is to determine, through civic and political action, his own relation with God, and for any profession to claim special authority in the conduct of that relation is to rob the republic of that which is its own. But it is not easy to keep this civic relation Christian. If Christ is not to be the author of a church which derogates from the republic, he must be the author of the republic, and that must be his body; but a Christ who comes merely to restore the political to men is not the equal of his Father and stands closer to Jethro the Midianite than Moses the Hebrew (if Hebrew indeed he was). Like Milton and Hobbes, though for other reasons, Harrington

---

[77] *PW*, pp. 163, 169–70.   [78] Psalms 115, 16; a text Harrington often quotes.
[79] *PW*, p. 333.
[80] Mark Goldie, 'The Civil Religion of James Harrington', in Anthony Pagden (ed.), *The Languages of Political Theory in Early Modern Europe* (Cambridge, 1987), pp. 197–222. Champion, *Pillars of Priestcraft Shaken*, is a thorough analysis of attacks on the Church of England by republicans and radical freethinkers from the Restoration through the early eighteenth century.

here became caught up with the Socinianism of the Interregnum, so very different from the Socinianism of the eighteenth century. This is the issue which emerges from a study of his dealings with his controversial opponents, most of whom were (or he took to be) clerics. The most persistent of these was Matthew Wren, a layman but son of the imprisoned Laudian bishop of Ely. He attacked[81] Harrington's ideal of a stabilized republic founded on the equal distribution of land between numerous proprietors, and laid emphasis on the importance of trade and moveable goods. Harrington had no antipathy whatsoever to this component in the economy of his republic, but held that it must be contained within a structure of landed property; artisans could not be spared for long periods of military service in the way that farmers could, and an economy of moveable goods could not produce a stable citizen body. The difference between him and Wren at this point, however, lay in their perceptions of human nature and government. Wren's commercial man was driven by his interests and passions, which conflicted with those of others, and needed to be governed by a strong, probably an absolute, monarchy, itself defended not by a militia but by a force of guards. Though neither he nor Harrington can be said to have anticipated the true 'standing army' maintained by the fiscal structure of the state, which the Cromwellian army never quite succeeded in becoming and which emerged in English history only some thirty years after the Protectorate, Wren is visibly closer to envisaging a military force maintained by taxation of land and goods; and in all these respects it is he, not Harrington, who may be termed a 'possessive individualist' in the sense used by C. B. Macpherson. His possessive individualism made him an advocate of absolute monarchy, in a king or a protector.

Wren had been encouraged to read and criticize *Oceana* by John Wilkins[82] of Wadham College, Oxford, successively Cromwell's brother-in-law and bishop of Chester at the Restoration. Wilkins was also a founding member of the group later known as latitudinarians, whose members had been able to accept office under the Presbyterian-Independent ordinances of the Protectorate but were to find no difficulty in conforming to episcopacy in 1660–2. Their view of episcopacy was 'low' in the sense that it was open to *jure humano* interpretations of the bishop's office, but Harrington could see that they would be instrumental in bringing back a clergy with 'high' claims to *jure divino*

[81] In *Considerations upon Mr Harrington's Commonwealth of Oceana, Restrained to the First Part of the Preliminaries* (London, 1657) and *Monarchy Asserted, or the State of Monarchical and Popular Government in Vindication of the Considerations upon Mr Harrington's Oceana* (Oxford, 1659).
[82] Barbara Shapiro, *John Wilkins, 1614–72: An Intellectual Biography* (Berkeley and Los Angeles, 1969).

authority. His replies to Wren (and Wilkins) are therefore joined with attacks on Henry Hammond and the Presbyterian Lazarus Seaman; these take the form of a debate about the nature of ordination in the apostolic church. On this Hammond had attacked Hobbes, and in 1658–9 Harrington retorted to Hammond on every issue, point by point, on which he could come to Hobbes' defence.[83] His insistence that the first ordinations had been performed by a show of hands (*chirotonia*) rather than a laying on of hands (*chirothesia*) of course presents an image of republican voting in the first congregations, whereas Hobbes is concerned to present the ordinations as civil actions subject to the authority of the civil magistrate, and ultimately the civil sovereign. Similarly, Harrington had depicted ancient Israel as a republic[84] in which sacred charges were performed by citizens (the Levites were a problem here), whereas for Hobbes it had been a theocratic monarchy ruled by Moses and his successors as God's representatives, in which they had played the role of Leviathan more effectively than the Davidic kings ever did.[85] But these differences were secondary. What mattered overwhelmingly to both Hobbes and Harrington was that both the first and the second Israel should have been civil societies conducting their own relations with God, so that no kind of priesthood, rabbinate or clergy could possibly claim that their office and authority came to them from God in ways which set them apart from the civil structure. The monarchy of Leviathan was one way of saying this, the republic of Oceana was another, and Matthew Wren – whether speaking with his father's voice or John Wilkins' – could see that there was not much difference between the two.[86] The enemy was not monarchism so much as clericalism.

Thomas Hobbes, it should be recalled, had his own quarrel with the Oxford circle, on issues immediately mathematical, in the year of the publication of *Oceana*.[87] Harrington and Hobbes were now aligned against both the groups who were to figure in the doctrinal politics of the Restoration Church of England: the resisters like Hammond who

---

[83] *Prerogative of Popular Government*, Book II, *passim*.
[84] At length in *The Art of Lawgiving in Three Books* (1659), Book II.
[85] For detailed references, see Pocock, *Politics, Language, and Time*, pp. 170–3.
[86] Wren, *Considerations*, p. 14: 'Leviathan and Oceana (whose names might seem to promise a better agreement) . . .'
[87] Thomas Hobbes, *Six Lessons to the Professors of the Mathematics . . . in the Chairs set up by the Noble and Learned Sir Henry Saville in the University of Oxford* (London, 1656). This work was seen by some as part of a growing attack on the universities and a continuation of the criticism that Hobbes had launched in the *Leviathan*. Among Hobbes' opponents in this context were men who would become some of the founders of the Royal Society. Thus, it should not be altogether surprising that, despite his Baconian sympathies toward the 'new science', Hobbes was never elected to the Society. See Noel Malcolm, 'Hobbes and the Royal Society', in Rogers and Ryan (eds.), *Perspectives on Thomas Hobbes*, esp. pp. 54–6.

upheld divinely sanctioned episcopacy and the apostolic succession, and the trimmers like Wilkins who were to found the Royal Society and return to the church as latitudinarians. Hobbes attacked the Oxford mathematicians because he believed geometry could bring the sovereign and subject to assured knowledge, and distrusted the probabilism and experimentalism through which counsellors and clerics might creep back to power; his materialism was to become part of this polemic.[88] Harrington derided political 'mathematicians'[89] – by whom he meant Wilkins and never Hobbes – for substituting a calculus of forces for the presence of God in the forms of government which presented man in God's image. In the last analysis, there is that in Harrington – as there certainly is not in Hobbes – which is Platonic. 'The contemplation of form is astonishing to man, and has a kind of trouble or impulse accompanying it, that exalts his soul to God. As the form of a man is the image of God, so the form of a government is the image of man.'[90] It was this kind of Platonism which Coleridge later believed had been driven underground by Baconian philosophy at the Restoration, and by Lockean and Newtonian philosophy after the Revolution;[91] what happened to Hobbes at the same time is not as simple a question as Coleridge may have supposed, but Platonism both occasioned and limited Harrington's messianism. It ensured that he would have nothing to do with those who, like Vane in the *Healing Question* of 1656 and Milton in the *Readie and Easie Way* of 1660, saw the republic as a rule of the saints or spiritual elite; he repeatedly insisted that a rule of the saints would be an oligarchy – and a clerical oligarchy at that – in which a few claimed civil authority on the grounds that they possessed spiritual gifts.[92] If the nature of man was political, this claim must be false. It was the opposite of the danger, which Milton as clearly perceived, that if the nature of Englishmen was not transformed by new orders remaking them as either saints or citizens, they must revert to their second nature given them by custom, 'chusing them a captain back for Egypt', and restore the ancient constitution of king, lords and commons.[93]

[88] The fullest account of the Hobbes polemic remains Mintz, *Hunting of Leviathan*.
[89] E.g., *PW*, p. 431; probably the first attack on quantitative methods in political science.
[90] *A System of Politics*, the last of his compositions; *PW*, p. 837.
[91] See John Morrow, *Coleridge's Political Thought: Property, Morality and the Limits of Traditional Discourse* (New York, 1990) for a valuable study of Coleridge in the mainstream of British political thought.
[92] *PW*, pp. 108–9, 111–13, 118.
[93] The quoted phrase is Milton's in *The Readie and Easie Way to Establish a Free Commonwealth*, 2nd edn (1660), from John Milton, *Complete Prose Works, VII, 1659–1660*, revised edn, ed. Robert W. Ayers (New Haven, 1980), p. 463. For Harrington's response, see *PW*, pp. 728, 762–3, 794, 797–8.

Harrington and Milton were agreeing on this, though wrangling about everything else, as the English republic, which had been an experiment in *de facto* government rather than in revolution, fell apart in 1660.

The ancient constitution, and the balance of government in which the House of Lords served as 'screen or bank', were now restored, with wild popular applause, to the muffled but interminable thunder of the ancient–constitutionalist prose of William Prynne,[94] while George Lawson, last of the great *de facto* theorists, lived out his life as a churchman too 'low' to attract the preferment he probably never sought.[95] The monarchy was restored in parliament and the republican experiment rejected for ever, though parliament willingly conceded to the king the control of the armed forces and the freedom to choose his advisors for which his father had fought in 1642. This restoration was the work of Presbyterians, heirs to the peace party that had always sought a compromise and had suffered fifteen years in the political wilderness, but the Church of England was about to return unforgiving from a harder exile.[96] Abroad with Hyde (now Clarendon) or at home with Hammond, there were those who saw the wars as fought to maintain the unity of crown with church, without which the realm of England was neither sacred nor secure. To them a compromise with presbytery presaged a surrender to popery, and since Charles I had negotiated with the Scots and Charles II taken the Covenant they had known in their hearts that the Church might not be able to trust its crowned head. A complex series of failed negotiations meant that Presbyterians (to say nothing of sectarians) would not be comprehended within the Church of England, and in 1662 a further Restoration was consummated which drew the battle lines of English politics for the next 170 years.[97]

---

[94] William M. Lamont, *Marginal Prynne, 1600–1669* (London, 1963); and Pocock, *Ancient Constitution*, pp. 155–62 and 355–7.

[95] Condren, *George Lawson's 'Politica'*.

[96] The process of the Church's restoration continues to be studied in detail. Spurr's *Restoration Church* was preceded by R. S. Bosher, *The Making of the Restoration Settlement: The Influence of the Laudians, 1649–1662* (Oxford, 1951); I. M. Greene, *The Re-Establishment of the Church of England, 1660–63* (Oxford, 1978); and, from the Presbyterian perspective, George R. Abernathy, Jr., *The English Presbyterians and the Stuart Restoration, 1648–1663*, American Philosphical Society, *Transactions*, n.s., 55, part 2 (1965).

[97] See further, Ronald Hutton, *The Restoration: A Political and Religious History of England and Wales, 1658–1667* (Oxford, 1985, 1987); J. R. Jones (ed.), *The Restored Monarchy, 1660–1688* (London, 1979); Michael G. Finlayson, *Historians, Puritans, and the English Revolution: The Religious Factor in English Politics before and after the Interregnum* (Toronto, 1983); and Harris, Seaward, and Goldie (eds.), *Politics of*

Throughout the Interregnum, remnants of the Laudian church – men like Hammond, Sheldon, and even Patrick – had been keeping Anglican faith and practices alive as best they could against the day when the old establishment would be restored. But the context of that restoration when it finally occurred was a profusion of religious sects unlike any England had previously known. In April, 1660, in his famous Breda Declaration issued just before he returned to England, Charles, recognized and, with some qualifications, accepted that sectarianism in his promise of 'a liberty to tender consciences'. 'No man shall be disquieted or called into question for differences of opinion in matter of religion which do not disturb the peace of the kingdom', he declared, and affirmed his readiness 'to consent to such an Act of Parliament as upon mature deliberation shall be offered to us for the full granting that indulgence'.[98] Parliament and the church both proved recalcitrant, and the immediate responses to the king's defence of 'tender consciences' were a reopening of the debate on *adiaphora* and the conditions under which religious practices could legitimately be coerced, the Clarendon Code, and the subsequent persecution of religious dissenters. Thus, as the ghost of the previous two decades was not put to rest after 1660, their spawn were hardly eradicated either. The Restoration was haunted by the spectre of the Regicide and by the fear that the religious, political, and social upheavals of the Commonwealth and Protectorate might well return.

Nowhere were these concerns more evident than in the restored church and the politics that emanated from and surrounded it. As always, religion provided a convenient cover and locale – to say nothing of excuse – for politics. Behind the Clarendon Code, and especially its first and primary constituent, the Act of Uniformity, was the desire to establish – or reestablish – what we increasingly think of as a 'confessional state'. But this was hardly an unmixed *religious* objective, for also behind the Clarendon Code, in particular in the Corporation Act, was the aim of establishing Anglican domination of the English state from top to bottom. It was equally a reflection of a continuing concern about the preservation of order lest the world once again be turned upside down and populated by those 'masterlesse men' who so troubled

Religion. Although D. T. Witcombe, *Charles II and the Cavalier House of Commons, 1663–1674* (Manchester, 1966) remains useful, much of it has been superseded by Paul Seaward, *The Cavalier Parliament and the Reconstruction of the Old Regime, 1661–1667* (Cambridge, 1988); see also, more generally, Seaward's *The Restoration, 1660–1688* (New York, 1991). The classic survey of post-revolutionary English history as dominated by the Anglican ascendancy is now J. C. D. Clark, *English Society, 1688–1830* (Cambridge, 1986).

[98] The text is available in Kenyon (ed.), *Stuart Constitution*, pp. 331–2.

Hobbes.[99] Hardly less significant were the growing political struggle between king and parliament and the battle within the church itself between relatively permissive Latitudinarians and High Church advocates of rigid uniformity. Blended in with all this were a profound animus against allegedly king-killing Presbyterians and conflicting attitudes toward Roman Catholics. In these struggles, theology shared a place with politics. The central issue was not whether England was to be or remain a confessional polity but how wide that confession should be and the status and entitlement of those who stood outside it.

It was in these terms that Restoration debates moved between the poles of comprehension for Presbyterians and toleration (or 'indulgence') for non-conforming Protestants, on the one hand, and persecution of all who dissented from the establishment on the other. The official and persistent policy remained persecutorial, and its *public* objectives seem to have been to eliminate schism by coercing dissenters into joining the church and to preserve social order by punishing those who obstinately refused to re-enter the Anglican communion. Mixed with and scarcely masked by those appearances was a refusal to share power and status with their former enemies. The Independents (to say nothing of the Quakers and the Baptists) had made clear their unwillingness to participate in a national church, preferring instead their voluntary 'gathered churches'. The Presbyterians, however, were eager to rejoin the established church but insisted upon alterations in Anglican practices and rituals as the conditions for reunification and balked at all calls for reordination. This inflexibility made it a simple matter for their enemies to see that the Presbyterians remained excluded from the church. Vigorous debate over religious and theological concerns revealed the obstinate non-co-operativeness of the Presbyterians.[100]

---

[99] Hobbes, *Leviathan*, chs. 18 (p. 128) and 21 (p. 149). See also Gordon J. Schochet, 'The English Revolution in the History of Political Thought', in Dwight Brautigam and Bonnie Kunze (eds.), *Country and Court: Essays on Early-Modern History for Perez Zagorin* (Rochester, 1992).

[100] For a fuller discussion of the politics and political bases of the Restoration debates over comprehension and toleration, see Gordon J. Schochet, 'From Persecution to 'Toleration''', in J. R. Jones (ed.), *Liberty Secured? Britain before and after 1688* (Stanford, CA, 1992); for the various comprehension and toleration proposals, see John Spurr, 'The Church of England, Comprehension and the Toleration Act of 1689', *English Historical Review*, 104 (1989), 927–46. Roger Thomas, 'Comprehension and Indulgence', in Geoffrey F. Nuttall and Owen Chadwick (eds.), *From Uniformity to Unity, 1662–1962* (London, 1962) remains the best account of the Presbyterian and Independent perspectives.

There was at least an irony, if not a series of deep contradictions, inherent in the dominant (non-Latitudinarian) establishment position. The continuing exclusion of dissenters meant that a substantial number of people, who were generally regarded as disruptive trouble-makers, were cut off from the discipline of the church. It was clear that these people would not simply cease to exist. (In fact, they flourished and grew, encouraged and abetted both by inconsistent and often indifferent enforcement of the Clarendon Code[101] and by the various indulgences granted by Charles and James.[102]) If persecution did not drive them back into the Establishment by giving them material reasons for surrendering their dissenting principles, England would remain a divided, schismatic, and partially undisciplined nation, and the integrity of its political institutions would be protected *legally* – if at all – by the strictures of the Test and Corporation Acts. On the other hand, should the non-conformists rejoin the church, they would be entitled to all the benefits of membership, which was undoubtedly among the interests of the Presbyterians and which the High Church party fully understood. Enactment of toleration would accomplish the former, and comprehension (or overly successful persecution) would bring about the latter. In the end, of course, it was toleration without comprehension that was adopted, and England – subsequently Britain – was forced to come to terms with an irreducible and ineliminable religious pluralism. But even that issue was not altogether resolved until the Test and Corporation Acts were finally repealed in 1828.[103]

The authority of the church was restored as much by nobility and gentry in Parliament as by an often uncertain episcopate and divided clergy; those Presbyterians and congregationalists who could not accept the church's demands withdrew to form a 'dissenting interest', and a brutal persecution of Quakers and other sectarians continued for some years. The church thus restored must insist on its apostolic character as

---

[101] See, e.g., Anthony Fletcher, 'The Enforcement of the Conventicle Acts, 1664–1679', in *Persecution and Toleration*, ed. W. J. Sheils, *Studies in Church History*, 21 (1984), 235–46.

[102] For which see, generally, Frank Bate, *The Declaration of Indulgence, 1672: A Study in the Rise of Organized Dissent* (London, 1908); Richard Boyer, *English Declarations of Indulgence, 1687 and 1688* (The Hague, 1968); Douglass Lacey, *Dissent and Parliamentary Politics in England, 1661–1688: A Study in the Perpetuation and Tempering of Parliamentarianism* (New Brunswick, NJ, 1969), pp. 64–70, 180–5, 209–13 *passim*; Thomas, 'Comprehension and Indulgence'; and Schochet, 'From Persecution to "Toleration"'.

[103] See Clark, *English Society*, pp. 393–408. For an excellent account of the eighteenth-century political and religious controversies leading up to those repeals, see R. K. Webb, 'From Toleration to Religious Liberty', in Jones (ed.), *Liberty Secured?*, pp. 158–98.

Christ's continuing presence,[104] and on the sacred character of the monarchy which was its supreme governor; but it was very early apparent that the crown itself was not altogether reconciled to its role. The cult of Charles the Martyr kept alive in vivid colours the Anglican ideal of monarchy, but the martyr's sons were not wholly reliable witnesses to the church for which he was supposed to have died. They were interested in a policy of indulgence towards at least the Presbyterian forms of nonconformity, and their motives may have been as benign as their characters allowed. But to indulge that which the church condemned weakened the unity of the church and crown; and the known Catholic leanings, acquired abroad by the princes restored in 1660, kept alive – and founded in reality – the fear that surrender to presbytery might bode surrender to popery. Alternatively there was the spectre of an altogether *politique* monarchy, indifferent to religion except as a prop to power and thus weakening the church's essential support of authority; cynical, indifferent, materialist and atheist. Here, the spectre of Hobbes (sometimes tutor to Charles II) began to loom large; it was his breach with the church in *Leviathan* that made him a figure in Restoration discourse.

The episcopal and lay champions of the Church of England faced their own versions of these dilemmas. If they gave their support to a sovereign too strong for the church, were they not Hobbists? If they responded by proclaiming the church stronger than the monarchy, were they not engaging in that 'priestcraft' of which the most perfect expression was 'popery'? They must incessantly condemn the doctrines of resistance and rebellion which might be laid at the nonconformists' door, while steering a very delicate course in defining the authority that might not be resisted. These were the circumstances in which it became important that a proportion of the leading clergy were men like Wilkins, who had officiated in the headless ecclesiastical order of the Protectorate but had conformed to episcopacy – and accepted episcopal re-ordination – at the Restoration of the crown and the church. Such figures – who were not necessarily latitudinarians[105] – might take the lead in formulat-

---

[104] Which was among the primary obstacles to reunion with the Presbyterians, whose ministers would have been compelled to submit to ecclesiastical reordination as a condition of comprehension. It is certainly plausible to suggest that the anti-Presbyterian party in the re-established church as well as in parliament insisted upon this as much – if not more – to block comprehension as it did as a matter of church principle. See Anne Whiteman, 'The Restoration of the Church of England', and especially E. C. Ratcliff, 'The Savoy Conference and the Revision of the Book of Common Prayer', both in Nuttall and Chadwick (eds.), *From Uniformity to Unity*.

[105] See John Marshall, 'The Ecclesiology of the Latitude-Men, 1660–1689: Stillingfleet, Tillotson, Hobbesism', *Journal of Ecclesiastical History*, 36 (1985), 407–27, and John

ing doctrines of conformity and obedience which avoided the perils that arose when authority was too precisely defined; since the days of Cranmer it had been close to the heart of the Church of England to avoid such precision.

Alongside popery and Hobbism there loomed the spectre of 'enthusiasm', that dangerous conviction that the spirit was speaking in, to and through one that could lead men to kill their king and turn the world upside down. As far back as 1656 we can trace the beginnings of a polemic against enthusiasm that was to dominate discourse both religious and skeptical throughout the eighteenth century; Meric Casaubon and Henry More[106] had diagnosed it as a disease of the intellect, which filled the mind with fantasies and false ideas and inhibited the recognition that the mind itself had generated them, so that the sufferer thought his own ideas the promptings of the spirit or the very voice of God. More wrote as a Platonist, one of a group to whom the epithet 'Cambridge Platonist' was in due time to become attached.[107] They held that reason, a knowledge of the universe implanted in man by God, was that spirit which was the candle of the Lord and searched out the innermost secrets of the body; by attending to it patiently and devoutly, one could hope to avoid the melancholy and hysteria which were the symptoms or causes of enthusiasm. But it was dangerous for churchmen to rely on a spirit identical with reason which pervaded the universe and was immanent in the body; that was all too like 'the great spirit Reason' in whose name Gerrard Winstanley (probably a reader of Jacob Boehme) had proclaimed a pantheistic communism that denied all distinctions between spirit and matter, between God and man. In 1666 Samuel Parker (a sometime Presbyterian, now the hardest of persecuting Anglicans) launched, partly against More, a savage attack against Platonic and neo-Platonist philosophy,[108] in whose idealism and mysticism he found the sources of both priestcraft (ultimately the belief that Christ could be present in the sacraments) and enthusiasm (the belief that the Holy Spirit could be present in the congregation or the worshipper). It was better, Parker proclaimed, to follow the philosophy of Bacon and the Royal Society, realizing that the nature of things could

---

Spurr, 'Latitudinarianism and the Restoration Church', *Historical Journal*, 31 (1988), 61–82.

[106] Meric Casaubon, *A Treatise concerning Enthusiasm* (London, 1656), facsimile reprint, ed. Paul J. Korshin (Gainesville, 1970); and Henry Moore, *Enthusiasmus Triumphatus* (London, 1662), facsimile reprint, Augustan Reprint Society (Los Angeles, 1966).

[107] C. A. Patrides (ed.), *The Cambridge Platonists* (Cambridge, MA, 1970).

[108] *A Free and Impartial Censure of the Platonick Philosophie* (Oxford, 1666). For Parker, see further Gordon J. Schochet, 'Between Lambeth and Leviathan: Samuel Parker on Natural Law and the Church of England', in Phillipson and Skinner (eds.), *Political Discourse*, pp. 189–208.

never be known, but only their behaviour observed and sometimes predicted. We think of Bacon as the prophet of an instrumental control over the natural world, but for the churchmen who founded the Royal Society his philosophy taught caution, moderation and obedience; if essences could never be known, the conduct of experiments taught us to accept the authority of what knowledge was available to us.[109] In a few decades, Locke's *Essay Concerning Human Understanding* was to subvert the authority of some kinds of churchmen while reinforcing that of others.[110]

But if intellect could never comprehend essences, where was the spirit in the universe and where was the Logos in Flesh? Was this not a Hobbesian universe, and was not the Incarnation (and thereby the church) threatened by the philosophy that men such as Parker were advocating? There was the danger of a mechanistic atheism which presented the universe as governed by the blind laws or mere chances controlling the free fall of atoms; but there was already, and increasing as the philosophy of Spinoza became known or misunderstood in England, the danger that materialism itself might become a new kind of enthusiasm. If mind and God were reduced to infinitely tenuous material substances, neither of them distinct from the universe itself, would not mind be of the same substance as God – the very error which lay at the heart of all enthusiasm? It has been shown how Thomas Hobbes and Robert Boyle, advocates of the plenum and the vacuum respectively, accused one another of enthusiasm: of creating at the heart of the universe a space filled by substance from which the mind could not separate itself.[111] Ralph Cudworth, in *The True Intellectual System of the Universe* (1678), sought to show that Platonic theology was compatible with a divine mind that directed the fall of atoms and with a vision of Trinity that presaged the Incarnation. He was engaged on a voyage among deeply threatening possibilities; among them, it was not clear how Christ could be both God and Man if the Spirit was to be always subject to the civil magistrate, or how the doctrine that he was both could be the matter of personal experience rather than of submission to

---

[109] Margaret C. Jacob, *The Newtonians and the English Revolution, 1689–1720* (Ithaca, 1976); Michael Hunter, *Science and Society in Restoration England* (Cambridge, 1981); J. R. Jacob, *Robert Boyle and the English Revolution* (New York, 1977), and *Henry Stubbe: Radical Protestantism and the Early Enlightenment* (Cambridge, 1983).

[110] On Bacon and Locke, see Neal Wood, 'The Baconian Character of Locke's *Essay*', *Studies in the History and Philosophy of Science*, 6 (1975), 43–84, and, more broadly, his *The Politics of Locke's Philosophy: A Social Study of 'An Essay Concerning Human Understanding'* (Berkeley and Los Angeles, 1983).

[111] Steven Shapin and Simon Shaffer, *Leviathan and the Airpump: Hobbes, Boyle, and the Experimental Life* (Princeton, 1985); and J. G. A. Pocock, 'Thomas Hobbes, Atheist or Enthusiast? His Place in a Restoration Debate', *History of Political Thought*, 11 (1990), 737–49.

authority. The church among its many dilemmas was tempted to reduce religion from a communion to a discipline and a practice; it needed to be – though it still can be[112] – defended against the charge that it saw 'the whole duty of man' as the discharge of obligations reinforced by the hope of rewards (and the fear of punishments) hereafter. The politics of church and monarchy in the Restoration were to be characterized, though never dominated or controlled, by the advent of latitudinarianism and the beginnings of an English (preceding a Scottish) Enlightenment.

[112] Spurr, *The Restoration Church*, pp. 390–401.

6   The later Stuart age

Howard Nenner

I

In 1985 J. G. A. Pocock remarked that no comprehensive history of British political thought in the early modern period has ever been successfully written.[1] The failure, although regrettable, is also easily understood. Given the extraordinary volume and variety of discourse in the three-century bridge from the medieval to the modern state, the task of writing its history has been nothing less than daunting. But if the lack of a panoramic treatment of political thought for the entire period from 1500 to 1800 is conspicuous, even more striking is that a much smaller segment of that epoch, the second part of the seventeenth century, has been neglected almost entirely – at least in any book-length exploration. Whereas there have been a number of more narrowly focused studies, an all-embracing history of the post-Interregnum era has still to be undertaken.

In contrast, the first part of the century has been remarkably well served. Among those works dealing comprehensively with early Stuart political thought are the contributions of J. W. Allen and Margaret Judson, and more recently of J. P. Sommerville.[2] For 1645 to 1660

In writing this essay I have drawn generously and gratefully on the contributions of the regulars and guests in my seminar in 1986 at the Folger Institute Center for the History of British Political Thought. My debt to the participants will be most obvious from my citations to Gordon J. Schochet (ed.), *Restoration, Ideology, and Revolution*, Proceedings of the Folger Institute Center for the History of British Political Thought, Vol. 4 (Washington DC, 1990), in which much of their work appears.

[1] J. G. A. Pocock, 'The History of British Political Thought: The Creation of a Center', *Journal of British Studies*, 24 (July 1985), 283.

[2] J. W. Allen, *English Political Thought, 1603–1644* (1938; repr. Hamden, CT, 1967); J. P. Sommerville, *Politics and Ideology in England, 1603–1640* (London, 1986); Margaret Atwood Judson, *The Crisis of the Constitution: An Essay in Constitutional and Political Thought in England, 1603–1645* (1949; repr. New York, 1964). In later life Professor Judson produced two addenda for the years 1649–56. Margaret A. Judson, *The Political Thought of Sir Henry Vane the Younger* (Philadelphia, 1969); *From Tradition to Political Reality: A Study of the Ideas Set Forth in Support of the Commonwealth Government in England, 1649–1653* (Hamden, CT, 1980).

there is the work of Perez Zagorin.[3] None of the four, however, ventures past the end of the republic. The result is that once we get to 1660 and to that fundamentally important political era stretching from the Restoration through the Revolution, there are no general histories of political thought to be found.

Why this should be so is by no means clear. One possibility, the notion that all the important political ideas of the century had been generated before and especially during the mid-century upheavals, and that, Locke excepted, 1660–90 offered no more than minor variations on earlier themes, has never seemed particularly persuasive. In the four decades following 1660 the constitutional uncertainties that arose from questions about monarchical succession, establishment and nonconformity, peacetime standing armies, the dispensing and suspending powers, political parties, and the location of sovereignty, surfaced with such visibility as to produce a torrent of political discourse, much of it rushing onto previously untouched ground. The evidence will not support Christopher Hill's assertion that after 1660 'there was "a king with plenty of holy oil about him" but no risk of absolutism'.[4] If anything, the risk was greater[5] and the discourse, accordingly, took a noticeably more urgent turn.

In the second half of the century the word 'absolute' itself lost much of its earlier meaning of 'complete' or 'perfect', as absolute monarchy came to be identified increasingly with arbitrary rule alone.[6] An absolute monarch was to be feared because, as George Lawson warned in 1660, he 'hath a full power over his subjects' goods and persons'.[7] It is in fact certain that James II was undone not simply because he was a Catholic, but because he was believed to be moving toward absolute rule. Nor, after James' first three years of expanding his prerogative, was this belief substantially misplaced.[8] By 1688 the king was seen to be holding firm

---

[3] Perez Zagorin, *A History of Political Thought in the English Revolution* (London, 1954). A useful anthology and introduction is that of Andrew Sharp, *Political Ideas of the English Civil Wars* (London, 1983).

[4] Christopher Hill, 'A Bourgeois Revolution?', in J. G. A. Pocock (ed.), *Three British Revolutions: 1641, 1688, 1776* (Princeton, 1980), p. 121.

[5] A case can be made that after the Revolution of 1688–89, owing to the growth of the army and the increased centralization of the state, the risk of absolutism was greater still. John Brewer, *The Sinews of Power: War, Money, and the English State, 1688–1783* (New York, 1989).

[6] James Daly, 'The Idea of Absolute Monarchy in Seventeenth-Century England', *Historical Journal*, 21, 2 (1978), 227–50.

[7] George Lawson, *Politica Sacra & Civilis*, 2nd edn (London, 1689), p. 133.

[8] For another view, see John Miller, 'The Potential for "Absolutism" in Later Stuart England', *History*, 69 (1984), 187–207. Miller argues that James' 'concern was not to establish an absolute monarchy but to secure full liberty and civil equality for Catholics', p. 207.

to his right to suspend the penal laws against dissenters and Catholics, and although that right remained legally and politically questionable, the use of the monarchical dispensing power had already been settled convincingly in James' favour.

It was of little moment in 1686 that the legal mind and reputation of Chief Justice Edward Herbert were thought to be no match for those of his more illustrious predecessor, Edward Coke. Of greater practical importance was that in the two years before the Revolution Coke's claim for the supremacy of the common law would prove to be no match for Herbert's dictum in *Godden v. Hales* that 'the Lawes of England are the Kings Laws' and that the dispensing power is their 'inseparable Prerogative'.[9] A comfortable fiction had given way to a harsher reality. Instead of the law being sovereign, it was a sovereign king who was in control of the law. This is not to suggest that James II denied or discarded the rule of law. It is rather that after 1686 he had effectively turned that rule to his decided advantage.[10] The result was the prospect of a legal absolutism, but the fact that it was legal made it that much more menacing.

The comparative neglect of later Stuart political thought may also be owed to the preference in intellectual taste for passion over pragmatism. The arresting rhetoric of the mid-century was distinguished by an apocalyptic zeal for political and religious liberty, while the discourse from the Restoration through the Revolution was more often expressed in an idiom of religious conservatism and political restraint. The reason for the shift was that a powerful fear of another civil war operated through the remainder of the century to temper the language of opposition. A characteristic of virtually all the literature of political dissent after 1660 was that it retreated conspicuously from allegations of Charles I's tyranny. Opposition was necessarily framed in a discourse of denial, muted by the need to distance itself from any imputation of regicide, republicanism, or religious excess.

The historiographical result has been striking: the 1640s, in thought as well as in action, continue in many quarters to be celebrated for having wrought a real revolution, while the 1680s, until only recently, have been commended principally for their political and ideological moderation.[11] Given the imprint of an intellectual tradition which

---

[9] BL, Add. MS 5540, f. 45; Harley MS 4139, f. 106ᵛ.
[10] Howard Nenner, *By Colour of Law: Legal Culture and Constitutional Politics in England, 1660–1689* (Chicago, 1977), ch. 4, especially pp. 99–101.
[11] For further musings on the same question, see Blair Worden, 'The Revolution of 1688–9 and the English Republican Tradition', in Jonathan I. Israel (ed.), *The Anglo-Dutch*

extolled 1688–9 for 'a revolution, not made, but prevented',[12] it could hardly have been otherwise. Even disinterested foreigners at a remove from Anglo-American Whig history lent authority to the idea of the later Stuart triumph of forbearance, attributing it specifically to the conservative English mind. 'The English intellect', according to von Ranke, was 'as far removed from the keen dialectic of the French as from the world-embracing ideology of the Germans; it has a narrow horizon; but it knows how to comprehend and satisfy the requirements of the moment with circumspection and great practical sense.'[13] Little wonder, then, that historians have for so long looked elsewhere in the seventeenth century for dynamic political ideas.

This relegating of the later Stuart age to a lesser position in the history of seventeenth-century English political thought has yet another dimension, one that may have been best expressed by J. P. Kenyon more than a decade ago. In 1981 Kenyon observed that 'there is still a lingering idea abroad that the 1642 (or 1649) Revolution was about liberty, which is a "hurrah" word . . . [whereas] the 1688 Revolution was about property, which is emphatically not'.[14] But as Kenyon appreciated, the distinction is a false one. Every seventeenth-century commentator understood that liberty and property were not discrete categories easily disengaged. As rhetorical weapons in the arsenal of theorists and polemicists of all political persuasions, liberty and property were inseparable. In his scaffold speech, Charles I recognized that the security of one's property was a fundamental component of English liberty. The people's 'liberty and freedom', he said, 'consist in having of government those laws by which their life and their goods may be most their own'.[15] The idea could also be expressed with equal force in reverse, as it was by those after 1660 who insisted that all men had a property in their liberty as well as in their estates. And forty years after Charles' execution, the Revolution of 1688–9 would be celebrated in much the same way, specifically for its having secured the liberty and property of all. Liberty, therefore, like property, although it could and did mean different things to

Moment: Essays on the Glorious Revolution and its World Impact (Cambridge, 1991), pp. 241–77. Worden supposes that one possible explanation might be that in the twentieth century 'so many historians of stature – Tawney, Trevor-Roper, Stone, Hexter, Hill . . . – were drawn to the earlier conflict' (p. 277).

[12] Edmund Burke, 'Speech on the Army Estimates, 1790', in *The Works of Edmund Burke* (New York, 1837), I, p. 454.

[13] Leopold von Ranke, *A History of England, Principally in the Seventeenth Century* (Oxford, 1875), IV, p. 500.

[14] J. P. Kenyon, 'The Great Rebellion and its Results', *Times Literary Supplement* (March 6, 1981), p. 261.

[15] Roger Lockyer (ed.), *The Trial of Charles I* (London, 1974), p. 135.

different people, was as much a part of the later discourse of the seventeenth century as it had been of the earlier.[16]

The suggestion, therefore, that Restoration and Revolution political thought offered little that was as new or as important as what had come in the half century before, can no longer be sustained. As a corollary of the suggestion that 1688–9 was merely an echo of 1641–2, it is an idea that does not survive close scrutiny. Even J. C. D. Clark, whose work has been focused on the similarities he finds between the best revisionist studies of the early Stuart era and his own understanding of the Hanoverian period – thereby subordinating once again, if only unintentionally, the value of all that lies between – does not disdain the importance of later Stuart political thought.[17] For Clark, however, it is not the undercurrents of late seventeenth-century radicalism, but the dominant and neglected discourse of Tories and Anglicans, that he would like to see retrieved.[18]

This revisionist belief in an uninterrupted English confessional state is consonant with John Kenyon's finding that in political thought after the Revolution 'the dogma of divine right and non-resistance still applied with its old rigour, and the innate conservatism of the nation and the church was affirmed'.[19] It is also in keeping with the renewal of scholarly interest in Jacobitism[20] and with recent work demonstrating the continuing vitality of Anglican political discourse.[21] That, however, is not the same as denying the importance of the Revolution itself. It is one thing to contend for the confessional state persevering beyond 1689, but quite another to insist that in the aftermath of the Revolution nothing very much had changed and the ruling triumvirate of monarchy,

---

[16] On the conjunction of the ideas of liberty and property in the later Stuart age, see Howard Nenner, 'Liberty, Law, and Property: The Constitution in Retrospect from 1689', in J. R. Jones (ed.), *Liberty Secured? Britain Before and After 1688* (Stanford, 1992), pp. 88–121; Tim Harris, ' "Lives, Liberties and Estates": Rhetorics of Liberty in the Reign of Charles II', in Tim Harris, Paul Seaward and Mark Goldie (eds.), *The Politics of Religion in Restoration England* (Oxford, 1990), pp. 217–41; H. T. Dickinson, *Liberty and Property: Political Ideology in Eighteenth-Century Britain* (London, 1977).

[17] J. C. D. Clark, *Revolution and Rebellion: State and Society in England in the Seventeenth and Eighteenth Centuries* (Cambridge, 1986).

[18] Mark Goldie's forthcoming study, *The Tory Ideology: Politics, Religion and Ideas in Restoration England* (to be published by Cambridge University Press), should go a long way toward addressing that plea. See also J. A. I. Champion, *The Pillars of Priestcraft Shaken: The Church of England and its Enemies, 1660–1730* (Cambridge, 1992).

[19] J. P. Kenyon, *Revolution Principles: The Politics of Party, 1689–1720* (Cambridge, 1977), p. 200.

[20] See, for example, Paul Kleber Monod, *Jacobitism and the English People, 1688–1788* (Cambridge, 1990).

[21] Mark Goldie, 'The Political Thought of the Anglican Revolution', in Robert Beddard (ed.), *The Revolutions of 1688* (Oxford, 1991), pp. 102–36.

aristocracy, and church remained gloriously unaffected and essentially undisturbed.

II

Despite the Anglican triumph of the 1660s, sectarian politics and polemics persisted throughout the later Stuart era, even to the point of precipitating constitutional crisis as arguments against Catholic rule became the logical extension of the denial of rights to Catholics at large. But papists were not alone in being deprived because of their religious persuasion. Dissenting Protestants were similarly dispossessed, and this raised the broader question of how far the magistrate might go in curtailing, or for that matter extending, a freedom of conscience. Hobbes' early response to that issue is instructive in that it laid out some of the important contours of the Restoration debate. Hobbes's secular view of the world afforded him little persuasive authority among his contemporaries, but his arguments nonetheless captured the prevailing political mood: religious diversity was to be resisted because it undermined political stability. Hobbes, of course, went further. In matters of religion he was prepared to concede the existence of God, but denied that the author of the universe had anything to do with editing it. Human beings had been left to their own devices, victims of their passions and subject to the exploitation of each other in a perpetual contest for power. And if God was uninterested in his creatures or, more precisely, if his interest in them was unknowable, there was no justification for a mediating clergy pretending to specialist credentials for interpreting his will. A society that allowed its clergy to compete with the civil authority for power would put itself in the way of anarchy.[22]

Much of the ecclesiastical discourse of the period centred on the issue of how a stable order could be maintained in a religiously permissive society. The experience of two civil wars and a republican interregnum seemed to suggest that it could not. In respect of public opinion at large it was relatively easy to justify denying toleration to Catholics, but arresting the march towards toleration of Protestant nonconformists was an infinitely more complex and difficult matter. Gordon Schochet observes that toleration, 'so called, was simply the next means at hand to control and contain Protestant nonconformity. Comprehension had proved impossible to achieve; persecution had not worked; and genuine

[22] James R. Jacob, ' "By an Orphean Charm" Science and the Two Cultures in Seventeenth-Century England', in Phyllis Mack and Margaret C. Jacob (eds.), *Politics and Culture in Early Modern Europe: Essays in Honour of H. G. Koenigsberger* (Cambridge, 1987), pp. 231–49.

toleration was unacceptable'.[23] What was conceded by statute in 1689 was far less than Charles II or James II had promised by way of their respective Declarations of Indulgence. Certainly it was not religious liberty in any sense that recognized the 'right' of all Christians – even if that meant only Protestant Christians – to act freely on their own theological beliefs.

The problem of religious dissent cut deeply into the fabric of Restoration politics. Notwithstanding the illusion of restoration, the reality in 1660 was ironically once again a world turned upside down. The restored monarchy was real enough, but not so the supposed restoration of the early Stuart constitution. In the new political order, the natural and accustomed alliance of church and crown was to fail almost from the start. Whereas the civil wars of the mid-century were traceable in large measure to the breach between parliament and the established church, the early strength of the Restoration Parliament was to be found in the formidable alliance of Anglicans and Cavaliers. Now it was the monarchy's turn to support rather than to suppress religious dissent – whether from a sincere commitment to widespread toleration; a calculated manoeuvre to relieve Catholics of their legal disabilities; or a misguided belief in religious uniformity being politically less useful than the rewarding of Presbyterians for their assistance in restoring the king to his throne.

In respect of political thought the problem went further. Once Charles II began to explore ways of undermining the 1662 Act of Uniformity, he effectively joined issue with church and parliament on more than the issue of toleration. At stake in the emerging debate on the exercise of royal supremacy in matters ecclesiastical was the viability of royal absolutism, and on this issue first Charles, and then James, alienated not only parliament, but also the established church. It has been suggested and may be true that for the royal brothers and for James, particularly, absolutism was a means and not an end.[24] It is certainly true that for the church absolutism as an abstraction was tolerable whereas toleration as a practice was not. As long as king and church were of the same intolerant mind on Catholic recusancy and Protestant dissent, the church could accept the Erastian leadership of its supreme governor. But as soon as Restoration monarchy claimed the

---

[23] Gordon Schochet, 'The "Tyranny of a Popish Successor" and the Politics of Religious Toleration', in Schochet, *Restoration, Ideology, and Revolution*, pp. 83–103.

[24] Miller, 'Potential for Absolutism', p. 197. For the opposite view that 'Charles II, like James II after him, was no disinterested advocate of religious toleration, but a monarch bent on making much of monarchy', see R. A. Beddard, 'The Restoration Church', in J. R. Jones (ed.), *The Restored Monarchy, 1660–1688* (London, 1979), p. 161.

right to indulge the consciences of all its subjects, Anglican ecclesiology took a different turn.

At first the church found itself in the curious position of seeking protection from parliament rather than from the king. After 1662, churchmen, acting from necessity, had little choice but to be drawn to a limited defence of parliamentary supremacy. If statutory law was to be the principal bulwark of Anglican privilege and exclusivity, it would be incumbent upon the church to align itself with the principal guardians of statute. As R. A. Beddard has noted, the Act of Uniformity

allowed them to assert the rule of law against even the King. Henceforth Archbishop Sheldon ruled the Church with a rod of iron, declaring, regardless of the vagaries of royal policy, that 'His Majesty's sense is no otherwise known than by his public laws, and by them, therefore, we are only to be guided in our duties'.[25]

The position was born of expediency rather than principle, but it remained an attractive argument against kings who were striving for independence and who, in the exercise of their prerogative, were working to break free of both secular and ecclesiastical constraints.

In this regard there is a line in Anglican political thought running directly from Sheldon to Sancroft. When Archbishop Sancroft and his six episcopal co-defendants petitioned James II to be excused from reading the king's Declaration of Indulgence from their pulpits, and were therefore charged with seditious libel, they defended themselves effectively by calling the suspending power into question. James had hoped to make their trial at common law a forum for exposing the intolerance of the church, thereby driving a deeper wedge between Anglicans and Dissenters. The bishops, however, refused the bait. In their petition they may well have been disingenuous in protesting a concern for the plight of Protestant dissenters, but they were convincingly straightforward in objecting to an Indulgence 'founded upon such a dispensing power as hath often been declared illegal in Parliament'.[26] And on that ground they were popularly understood to have won. Despite the judges' forbearing from rendering a decision on the legality of the suspending power and the case having turned instead on narrower issues of fact, the acquittal of the bishops was seen by the nation as a vindication of the rule of law. In the words of the dissenter Roger Morrice, reminiscent of those of Sheldon a generation earlier, it had

[25] Beddard, 'Restoration Church', pp. 170–1.
[26] Roger Thomas, 'The Seven Bishops and their Petition, 18 May 1688', *Journal of Ecclesiastical History*, 12 (1961), 64–5.

been a contest of wills, the 'prince's private will and pleasure against his legal and incontrovertible will', the law as enacted in parliament.[27]

The church, of course, was no more prepared to abandon all control of ecclesiastical matters to king-in-parliament than it was to the king alone. We need to be reminded that in 1680 there was concern that parliament Whigs might have more than one item on their legislative agenda. The Anglican hierarchy feared that the Whigs would press for some form of toleration as well as for exclusion in order to provide for a solid Protestant front against the perceived incursions of popery.[28] If, then, neither king nor parliament could be trusted in the end to preserve uniformity, Anglican political theology would need to fall back to a more basic line of defence. Accordingly, it invoked the imperatives of conscience in order that it might put its own interpretation on the meaning of fundamental law. In this regard, churchmen could readily agree that there was a distinction to be drawn between *malum prohibitum* and *malum in se*, and whereas the king might dispense with proscriptions against the one, he was enjoined from any action against the other. Seen in this perspective, the Test Acts and the penal laws could be claimed as security for the true faith, defences against the intrinsic evils of popery and schism.

It might be said that Chief Justice Herbert dealt Anglican doctrine two crushing blows, one direct and the other by way of foreshadowing what was soon to come. The first, delivered from the bench in *Godden v. Hales*, was to the effect that the 1673 Test Act could be dispensed with by James II because it was not in the category of fundamental moral law. What that portended in 1686 was a church deprived of its position and power. It was now bereft of the support of the king; parliament, even if inclined, was powerless to protect it; and the courts had torn away its shield of fundamental law. Within two years, however, Herbert had taken a near about-face, though one that signalled only partial relief for the church. Reflecting on the matter in 1688, he concluded that 'the dark learning . . . of dispensations, should receive some light from a determination in parliament, that the judges for time to come, may judge by more certain rules which Acts of Parliament the king may, and which he may not dispense with'.[29] This, in theory, would have been of some comfort to Anglicans, but only if parliament could be relied upon to

---

[27] *Ibid.*, p. 62, quoting Morrice's *Entry Book*, II, p. 258.
[28] Mark Goldie, 'Danby, the Bishops and the Whigs', in Harris, *et al.*, *Politics of Religion*, p. 80.
[29] Edward Herbert, *A Short Account of the Authorities in Law, upon which Judgement was given in Sir Edw. Hales his Case. Written by Sir Edw. Herbert, Chief Justice of the Common Pleas, In Vindication of Himself* (London, 1689), p. 37.

protect their privileges in the way that the king had not. That, as we know, was not to happen.

III

Moving in a direction contrary to both Whig consensualism and Tory revisionism, recent scholarship has come to focus increasingly on the importance of several kinds of radicalism in the 1680s.[30] A significant result of that focus is the work of neo-Whig historians who now insist that the threat of Stuart absolutism was met and defeated by a political nation moving forward to change its constitution rather than backward to preserve it. Whether the agent of change was the Revolution or the settlement that began in 1689 and was completed in the dozen years that followed, the outcome is seen to have been the same. The new Whigs, rejecting Macaulay's vision of revolutionary glory residing in a constitution that was *restored*, believe instead that we have been distracted for too long by the mirage of the ancient constitution.[31] They are persuaded that there was a real revolution precisely because between 1689 and 1701 the constitution had been radically altered. As Lois Schwoerer would have it, the results were even more immediate: the Revolution and its central document, the Bill of Rights, established not merely a new king on the throne, but also a new kingship.[32]

It is not necessary, however, to be convinced of the radical results of the Revolution in order to be persuaded of the importance of radical thought and activity in the period after 1660. Jonathan Scott, who has recently completed a two-volume study of Algernon Sidney,[33] has reclaimed Sidney from the pantheon of Whig martyrs to constitutionalism, and has located him instead among those who would have readily

---

[30] Richard Ashcraft, *Revolutionary Politics and Locke's 'Two Treatises of Government'* (Princeton, 1986); Jonathan Scott, *Algernon Sidney and the Restoration Crisis, 1677–1683* (Cambridge, 1991); Richard L. Greaves, *Make My Enemies Turn: British Radicals from the Popish Plot to the Revolution of 1688–89* (forthcoming from Stanford University Press). Manuel Schonhorn, focusing on Defoe, takes the opposite tack. Challenging the conventional view of Defoe as a radical and an opportunist, Schonhorn is struck instead by the 'conservative-royalist thread in the complex weave of his [Defoe's] political imagination'. Manuel Schonhorn, *Defoe's Politics: Parliament, Power, Kingship and Robinson Crusoe* (Cambridge, 1991), p. 8.

[31] One such historian, Janelle Greenberg, goes so far as to see in the 'ancient constitution' the roots rather than the antithesis of seventeenth-century radicalism. Janelle Greenberg, 'The Confessor's Laws and the Radical Face of the Ancient Constitution'. *English Historical Review*, 104, 412, (July 1989), 611–37.

[32] Lois G. Schwoerer, *The Declaration of Rights, 1689* (Baltimore and London, 1981). Also see the discussion below, n 77.

[33] Jonathan Scott, *Algernon Sidney and the English Republic, 1623–1677* (Cambridge, 1989); *Algernon Sidney and the Restoration Crisis, 1677–1683* (Cambridge, 1991).

welcomed another civil war and the renewed opportunity for destroying monarchy by the sword. Sidney was a radical republican who, had he lived into 1689, would have deplored the victory of limited monarchy in general and in particular of William of Orange, the man Sidney regarded as his and republicanism's 'most hated enemy'.[34] In a similar vein, John Pocock, taking Burke as his point of reference, has focused on the Glorious Revolution as England's fourth civil war, albeit one that never came to battle because James II chose not to fight and fled instead to France. As Pocock observes, 'it was only the subsequent series of events occurring in 1689 which gave a constitutional meaning to those of 1688'.[35] In Burke's view, it was only because the radical political revolution of 1688 had been mooted by James' flight that the conservative constitutional revolution of 1689 had been able to succeed. This reading accords as well with Pocock's understanding of Locke. 'There is', he maintains, 'no way of reading Locke's scenario of appeal to heaven, dissolution of government, and reversion of power to the people, except as a scenario of civil war'.[36]

We have, of course, accepted for some time that the *Two Treatises* were written nearly a decade earlier than originally supposed, and that they are to be understood properly as a product of the Exclusion era rather than of the Revolution.[37] The effect of this understanding has been to make Locke more of an extremist, underpinning Pocock's assertion that the *Treatises* were a radical call to revolt rather than a liberal rendering of a respectable settlement.[38] Consistent with this view is an historical Locke who, as Richard Ashcraft has argued, was part of 'a radical movement comprised of Dissenters, Whigs, and Republicans that emerged between 1670 and 1690'.[39] Whether or not

---

[34] Scott, *Sidney and the English Republic*, p. 2.

[35] J. G. A. Pocock, 'The Fourth English Civil War: Dissolution, Desertion and Alternative Histories in the Glorious Revolution', *Government and Opposition*, 23, 2 (1988), 154; reprinted in Lois G. Schwoerer (ed.), *The Revolution of 1688–1689: Changing Perspectives* (Cambridge, 1992), p. 54.

[36] *Ibid.*, p. 162.

[37] Peter Laslett, 'The English Revolution and Locke's *Two Treatises of Government*', *Cambridge Historical Journal*, 12 (1956), 40–55.

[38] Possibly it was neither. Both the writing and the later publication of the *Two Treatises* may have been intended as a cautionary tale, first for Charles II and then for William III, reminding each that political power was ultimately based on consent. Charles D. Tarlton, ' "The Rulers Now on Earth": Locke's *Two Treatises* and the Revolution of 1688', *Historical Journal*, 28 (1985), 279–98.

[39] Richard Ashcraft, 'John Locke, Religious Dissent, and the Origins of Liberalism', in Schochet (ed.), *Restoration, Ideology, and Revolution*, p. 149. See also Ashcraft, *Revolutionary Politics*, and his earlier article, 'Revolutionary Politics and Locke's *Two Treatises Of Government*: Radicalism and Lockean Political Theory', *Political Theory*, 8 (1980), 429–86.

such a movement actually existed is uncertain,[40] and whether Locke fits into a unified and progressive plan of Exclusion, Rye House Plot, and Monmouth's Rebellion, is at best problematic; but that Locke, as a client of Shaftesbury, moved in a circle in which rebellion would have been discussed with some seriousness is scarcely open to question. Nor, as Blair Worden and Jonathan Scott have shown, is there much question about Sidney's *Discourses Concerning Government*, which effectively advocated the overthrow of Charles II, having been written in the 'period following the collapse of parliamentary Whiggism in March 1681 when Whig polemicists moved into radical territory'.[41]

Still, it is of more than passing significance that the *Two Treatises of Government* were not published until 1689, then only anonymously, and that they called forth no replies until 1703.[42] Nor should the limited impact of Locke's message on his contemporaries be wholly surprising. Of the variety of political languages available to seventeenth-century writers, secular rationalism was employed considerably less often and with far less effect than the dominant idioms of religion and the law. Law, in fact, was likely the most politically compelling of what Pocock has called the 'institutional languages' of the day.[43] The reality of Restoration and Revolution politics is that no argument advanced without the support of legal and historical precedent was likely to gain much currency or to be accorded persuasive authority. Indeed, to the extent that we can with any confidence characterize the late seventeenth-century political mind, it seems to have run most comfortably in channels cut by the common law.

Chief Justice Matthew Hale, possessed of arguably the best judicial intellect in a century that is marked by the contributions of Sir Edward Coke, Sir John Holt, and the first earl of Nottingham, offered what may be the most trenchant statement of the contemporary distrust of political theory. In a repudiation of Hobbes that also served as a clear adumbration of later reactions to Locke, Hale exhorted the common law bench to be 'governed by the analogy of the law' and not to be seduced by 'reason at large'. Hale insisted that the judges'

---

[40] In this regard see Lois G. Schwoerer, 'The Trial of Lord William Russell (1683): Judicial Murder?', *The Journal of Legal History*, 9 (1988), 142–68.

[41] Blair Worden, 'The Commonwealth Kidney of Algernon Sidney', *Journal of British Studies*, 24 (1985), 15; Scott, *Sidney and the Restoration Crisis*, pp. 201–64.

[42] Martyn Thompson, 'The Reception of Locke's *Two Treatises of Government*, 1690–1705', *Political Studies*, 24 (1976), 184–91; J. P. Kenyon, *Revolution Principles*; Richard Ashcraft and M. M. Goldsmith, 'Locke, Revolution Principles, and the Formation of Whig Ideology', *Historical Journal*, 26 (1983), 773–800.

[43] J. G. A. Pocock, 'Texts as Events: Reflections on the History of Political Thought', in Kevin Sharpe and Steven N. Zwicker, *Politics of Discourse: The Literature and History of Seventeenth-Century England* (Berkeley and Los Angeles, 1989), p. 27.

experience and observation and reading gives them a far greater advantage of judgment, than the airy speculations, and notions, and consequences and deductions from certain preconceived systems of politicks and lawes of some that call themselves philosophers; which, though they may please the authors in the contemplation, yet, when they come to practice and use, vanish into smoak and nothing.[44]

Despite Hale's warning, Locke's 'system' did not 'vanish into smoak and nothing'. Lockean ideas were critical to radical thought throughout the 1680s and afterwards, even if they were to leave surprisingly few traces in the debates of the Convention and almost none in the Revolution settlement.[45] Yet as to his main point, the contemporary suspicion of a discourse divorced from law and history, Hale was plainly on the mark.

To understand the contemporary preference for a politics of experience over a politics of reason requires an appreciation of the persuasive power of law and history on which Hale relied. We need to recognize that constitutional innovation was largely unacceptable to the later Stuart political mind. For that reason radical opinion could rarely be expected to advertise itself boldly and chose instead the safe haven of constitutional precedent. Every position on the political spectrum, whether in speeches, tracts, or pamphlets, tended therefore to be painted in muted and conservative tones. So it should not surprise us when we find, as Richard Ashcraft does, 'that throughout the 1670s and 1680s the radicals saw themselves as the defenders of the English constitution *against* a conspiracy to subvert it'.[46] Whigs and Tories alone, as well as the publicists who supported them, perceived themselves to be holding fast against the encroachments of a new and threatening order. All that was certain, and what imparted a characteristic voice to seventeenth-century discourse, was that political virtue resided in preserving the constitution, not in changing it. As Worden reminds us, even when 'the Revolution, by laying the foundations of constitutional monarchy, made republicanism redundant', a more respectable post-Revolution republicanism continued to look to the past. 'It came to hope, not for a novel system of government, but for the purification of the ancient one'.[47]

Much of this evokes the familiar theme of the ancient constitution, the idea 'that the common law, and with it the constitution, had always been

---

[44] One of several extant versions of Hale's *Reflections on Hobbes's Dialogue of the Law*. BL, Hargrave MS 96, fols. 46ᵛ–47.

[45] For the presence of Locke's ideas at the time of the Revolution, see Lois G. Schwoerer, 'Locke, Lockean Ideas, and the Glorious Revolution', *Journal of the History of Ideas*, 51, 4 (1990), 531–48.

[46] Ashcraft, 'John Locke, Religious Dissent, and the Origins of Liberalism', p. 152.

[47] Worden, 'The Revolution of 1688–9 and the English Republican Tradition', pp. 241–2.

exactly what they were ... that they were immemorial'.[48] That theme was sounded continually through the century, but by the later Stuart era, when the idea of legislative sovereignty came to be recognized as a growing reality, the emphasis on immemorial custom began to seem functionally out of place. Corinne Weston argues that seventeenth-century advocates of an ancient constitution early on saw parliament in its role as lawmaker and were as taken 'with a legislating parliament as with the idea of a fundamental common law'.[49] And J. G. A. Pocock, in the much expanded new edition of his *Ancient Constitution and the Feudal Law: A Reissue with a Retrospect* (1987), has rephrased some of his earlier analyses to make it clear that he has all along been persuaded that immemorial law was an argument in favour of legislative sovereignty and not against it.

It is, in fact, an irony of seventeenth-century discourse that fundamental law managed to lead an exceedingly protean life all the while that it stood as a monument to immutability.[50] Charles I and the High Court of Justice that tried him resorted to the refuge of fundamental law and a fundamental constitution as polemical shields against each other. Later on in the controversy over Exclusion there was an extensive debate in parliament and the press on the question of the Duke of York's legal standing in the line of succession. No one doubted that James was the next in blood to his brother and that he had a presumptive hereditary expectation of receiving Charles' throne. Yet whether James had a vested right to the succession and, if he did, whether he could legally be divested of that right, were questions that turned as much on one's political perspective as on one's reading of the law. From 1679 to 1681 it was the proponents of monarchical right, the Tories, who rushed to appropriate fundamental law arguments. Their concern, and Charles', was to break a gathering radical momentum that threatened to turn England into an elective monarchy or, what was worse, a republic. They argued that hereditary succession was legally an unalterable succession and that an exclusion bill, even if it should pass into law, would be null and void.[51] The result was that those who had grown accustomed to

[48] J. G. A. Pocock, *The Ancient Constitution and the Feudal Law: A Study of English Historical Thought in the Seventeenth Century* (Cambridge, 1957, 1987), p. 36.
[49] Corinne C. Weston, ' "Holy Edward's Laws": The Cult of the Confessor and the Ancient Constitution', in Schochet (ed.), *Restoration, Ideology, and Revolution*, p. 318.
[50] Martyn P. Thompson, 'The History of Fundamental Law in Political Thought from the French Wars of Religion to the American Revolution', *American Historical Review*, 91 (1986), 1103–28.
[51] Howard Nenner, 'Ideas of Monarchical Succession in the Debate on Exclusion', in Schochet (ed.), *Restoration, Ideology, and Revolution*, pp. 445–60.

invoking the authority of fundamental law against the king now found that the authority could be put to an opposing and equally effective political use. Yet within ten years the game would return to the Whigs, and the same marvellously adaptable fundamental law that had been raised as a shield during Exclusion to protect James as heir presumptive would at the Revolution be directed against James as king – only this time as a bludgeon. The Commons' Resolution of 28 January 1689, finding James guilty of 'having violated the fundamental laws', held the king in consequence to have abdicated, or vacated, but somehow to have forfeited his throne.[52]

Still, the incongruity remains between a law and a constitution regarded as fundamental and the periodic assertions, especially in time of crisis, of an omnicompetent king-in-parliament. The resolution of this issue, where sovereign power was to be located in the later seventeenth-century English state, proved elusive to contemporaries, and has been almost as much of a problem for historians. Pocock had it right thirty-five years ago, and appears still to have it right today. 'One of the underlying themes in the history of seventeenth-century political thought', he wrote in 1957,

is the trend from the claim that there is a fundamental law, with parliament as its guardian, to the claim that parliament is sovereign. Books are still being written in the attempt to decide how far this transition was carried and at what times; but it seems to be fairly well agreed that it was both incomplete and largely unrealized.[53]

That trend, of course, was not Whiggishly progressive. It did not proceed in a straight or even a discernible line over the course of the century. If anything, there was both overlap and inconsistency. Two clear themes to emerge from Charles I's trial were parliament as keeper of the fundamental law and parliament as sovereign; and no one appeared much troubled by the possible contradictions between the two. Parliament, specifically the Commons, unabashedly asserted its supremacy in 1649, and although that assertion seemed to die unceremoniously eleven years later, the more limited and less threatening claim of a sovereign king-in-parliament was periodically revived. Most conspicuously, the issue of what parliament might and might not be privileged to do re-emerged during Exclusion, at the Revolution, and again in 1696 in the debate over Fenwick's attainder – and in all three

---

[52] Particularly useful for the role of fundamental law and its obvious connection to the development of parliamentary sovereignty in the politics of the seventeenth century is J. W. Gough, *Fundamental Law in English Constitutional History* (Oxford, 1955).

[53] Pocock (1987 edn), p. 49.

instances the point and counterpoint of parliamentary sovereignty and fundamental law were clearly to be heard.[54]

The reality is that by 1660 antinomian enthusiasm had totally expended its remaining credit; but even if voices calling for republicanism and a godly commonwealth had been quieted, there were others to take up the cry of political protest – and a growing popular audience to receive them.[55] With the Restoration came the vigorous revival of ideas freshly appropriate to new circumstances. The earlier parliamentary rhetoric that was constitutionalist rather than republican, and that remained as a persistent undercurrent through the Commonwealth and Protectorate, was no less vital for being constitutionalist. That rhetoric quickened in 1660 and moved through the Restoration and Revolution in ways that were at once familiar and more complex. The necessary frequency and permissible duration of parliaments, the proper exercise of the royal supremacy in matters ecclesiastical, and the appropriate use of the king's dispensing power, became the new focal points for a developing opposition politics. It was of little consequence that, quantitatively, republican ideas merely flickered in the discourse of the seventies and eighties, making no significant appearance in parliamentary debate. The effective departure of republicanism did not leave a polemical void, nor did it eliminate the ideological edge of Stuart political thought.

IV

During the second half of the Stuart century political discourse focused increasingly, as it had to, on the issue of monarchical legitimacy. By what warrant did a king achieve and exercise his right to rule? Even more basic, from the trial of Charles I through the eleven-year Interregnum, was the question of the legitimacy of the monarchy itself – or for that matter, of any form of government. Monarchs had been deposed and murdered before, but 1649 bore witness to the first suggestion of a king's treason. The principle upon which Charles' trial was conducted was that of a sovereign people through its representative, the Commons, bringing its governor to justice. Arthur Heselrige's retrospective analysis of the

---

[54] See Robert J. Frankle, 'Parliament's Right to Do Wrong: The Parliamentary Debate on the Bill of Attainder against Sir John Fenwick, 1696', *Parliamentary History*, 4 (1985), 71–85.

[55] Carolyn A. Edie, 'Reading Popular Pamphlets: A Question of Meanings', in Schochet (ed.), *Restoration, Ideology, and Revolution*, pp. 287–306. Despite the marked increase in polemical literature it is still difficult to judge the nature and extent of the readership. See further Tim Harris, *London Crowds In The Reign of Charles II: Propaganda and Politics from the Restoration until the Exclusion Crisis* (Cambridge, 1987).

trial captured its essence and underscored an important turn that had taken place in political discourse. 'God never made such a creature to govern men, and not to be accountable to men', he said.[56] It was a radical vision in 1649 when Charles was executed, in 1659 when Heselrige offered his analysis, and again in 1688–9 when James II was deposed; and through the four decades between Charles I having 'traitorously and maliciously levyed war against. . . parliament and the people' and James II 'having endeavoured to subvert the constitution', the possibility of a king's treason was to be an important subtext in the development of English political thought.

Underpinning this view was Bracton's thirteenth-century pronouncement that the king is under the law, a dictum that in the middle years of the Stuart century was to be renewed and affirmed. This, however, did not mean the rejection of the common law maxim, 'the king can do no wrong'. That maxim survived, even if implicitly it had been turned on its head. Because everyone knew that a true king was incapable of doing wrong, the maxim would ingeniously become the test of a king's legitimacy: if Charles was guilty of doing wrong it was likely that he was not, or should not be, king. The stunning result was that the crown could now be considered forfeitable at law. That was the constitutional lesson for Charles I in 1649.[57] It was to be repudiated in 1660,[58] but within a generation the lesson was to be repeated for his son. Despite the one element of restraint in the Convention's resolution of January 1689, the fiction that what James II had done was 'by the advice of Jesuits and other wicked persons', the monarch himself would be held to account. The second Earl of Nottingham had seen it coming. He warned that in place of the constitution's rightful protection of the king they were substituting the common law rule of *respondeat superior* – for the crimes of the servant the master must answer. Few would admit that Nottingham was right. They chose instead to nurture the pretense of the sovereign's immunity at law. But for the second time in forty years the king who could do no wrong had been seen to forfeit his crown.

This inverted idea of treason, the notion that kings might be perpetrators of the crime as well as its victims, was only infrequently articulated

---

[56] J. T. Rutt (ed.), *Diary of Thomas Burton* (London, 1828), III, pp. 96–7.

[57] Howard Nenner, 'The Trial of Charles I and the Failed Search for a Bounded Monarchy', in Schochet (ed.), *Restoration, Ideology, and Revolution*, pp. 1–21.

[58] 'The king can do no wrong; it is a rule of law . . . If he can do no wrong, he cannot be punished for any wrong. The king hath the infirmities and weaknesses of a man, but he cannot do any injury, at least not considerable in person. He must do it by ministers, agents and instruments . . . He is not to be touched' (*The Judgment of Sir Orlando Bridgman, declared in his Charge to the Jury at the Arraignment of the Twenty-nine Regicides* (London, 1660)). *Somers Tracts*, 2nd edn (London, 1813), VII, p. 457.

during the period between the Regicide and the Revolution, but not so the premise upon which it was based. The concept of monarchical power being held in trust had originally been regarded as offering no threat to the exercise of monarchical sovereignty. Kings by divine right received their power from God and were accountable to him for any abuse of that power. But the accountability was clearly to God alone. In 1649, the Commons, sitting in judgement on Charles I, redefined the parties to the trust and thereby appropriated the trust construction to a radically different political purpose. The king was still the trustee, the people were still the beneficiaries, but instead of God being the grantor of the trust, the trust was now understood to have originated with the people themselves. In the vocabulary of the law, which was increasingly the coin of political discourse, the people were the 'settlors' of a revocable trust. Acting on that interpretation, Charles' judges affirmed the army's view that a king who had been 'trusted with a limited power to rule according to laws' could, by his malfeasance, 'forfeit all that trust and power he had'.[59] The result was that government returned to the people and became theirs to re-entrust as they saw fit.

This most powerful idea of 1648–9 ran underground until the time of the Revolution, and obviously while there enjoyed a rich subterranean life. John Locke's *Two Treatises* are ample testimony to that. Locke's rational and pragmatic view of government was that it was instituted by the people 'to provide for their own safety and security, which is the end for which they are in society'. Both the legislative and the executive were capable of abusing their fiduciary responsibilities, in which case the trust could be concluded. 'By this breach of Trust', Locke wrote, 'they *forfeit the Power*, the People had put into their hands, for quite contrary ends, and it devolves to the People'.[60]

There can be no doubt about the contextual radicalism of this idea.[61] To suggest, as Locke did, that government was dissolved upon the forfeiture of the legislative or executive trust, and that power thereupon returned to the people, was wholly out of keeping with the constitution, either as preliminarily repaired in the 1650s, or as fully restored after 1660. Singularly striking in this regard was the refusal of the political nation in 1688–9 to follow through on the implications of the Commons' January 28th finding of monarchical subversion of the constitution, breach of the original contract, violation of the fundamental laws, and

[59] Army's Remonstrance (November 1648). William Cobbett, *Parliamentary History of England* (London, 1808), III, p. 1092.
[60] Peter Laslett (ed.), *John Locke: Two Treatises of Government* (Cambridge, 1960), *Second Treatise*, ch. XIX, section 222.
[61] Julian H. Franklin, *John Locke and the Theory of Sovereignty: Mixed Monarchy and the Right of Resistance in the Political Thought of the English Revolution* (Cambridge, 1978).

abdication of the government. For that reason Locke's thinking has always been something of an anomaly on the political landscape. Tied as it was for so long to a justification of the Revolution, it had curiously limited relevance to that event. The Revolution was not conceived as an overt appeal to heaven, there was no dissolution of government, power did not devolve to the people, and even the Convention's construction of a contract between king and people was not drawn from the Lockean model. Little wonder then that the *Two Treatises* received such scant attention when first published.

We know that Locke hoped the Convention would not hastily declare itself a parliament. That it lost no time in doing so reminds us that the ancient constitution was always more than a convenient rhetorical tool. It was a central ornament of the seventeenth-century political mind, and even in the waning years of the century so much an integrated part of that mind that the idea of a fundamental constitution continued to inhibit the advance toward full parliamentary sovereignty. To understand this is to appreciate part of the reason at least for the Convention's reluctance to move beyond a consentient statement of existing law and a necessary settling of the crown. For most Englishmen in 1689, a sovereign parliament without a king would have been unthinkable. It would have meant, as Nottingham instructed his colleagues in the Convention, 'that the ancient government was dissolved, and that their lordships were no more peers, but might be justly ranked among the plebeians'.[62] It is not surprising then that a political nation exhorted to take advantage of its unique opportunity to remake the constitution may have sensed the possibilities, but chose instead to ignore the call.[63]

V

The reality of the Revolution was ironically one of pretense. The members of the Convention pretended that James had deposed himself, that the political nation was not obliged to bear any responsibility for rebelling against its king, and that the passage of the crown to William and Mary in no way signalled a repudiation of hereditary monarchy.[64]

---

[62] *A true and impartial Narrative of the Dissenters' New Plot* (London, 1690).

[63] David Underdown has observed that even when, in 1649, Parliament did seize the opportunity to proclaim its sovereignty, it was similarly inhibited from going any further. 'It is entirely in character that, having proclaimed their own sovereignty, the revolutionaries should still have hesitated about permanently altering the constitution' (David Underdown, *Pride's Purge: Politics in the Puritan Revolution* (Oxford, 1971), p. 201).

[64] Howard Nenner, *By Colour of Law*, especially ch. 6; 'Pretense and Pragmatism: The Response to Uncertainty in the Succession Crisis of 1689', in Schwoerer (ed.), *Changing Perspectives*, ch. 5.

The transition from James II to William and Mary was therefore to be effected with a minimum of political disruption at the acceptable price of some intellectual sleight-of-hand. Englishmen, who moved comfortably in a world of useful legal fictions, were to prove in 1689 that they were capable of assimilating serviceable political fictions as well. Studiously ignored or explicitly rejected by everyone except Jacobites and extreme Whigs was the further and much more uncomfortable reality of resistance and revolution; but to admit to that reality would have been to undermine any hope of political stability and the consensus necessary to place a Dutch adventurer on the English throne.

As a result, the Revolution of 1688, in G. M. Trevelyan's characterization of the event, was to become England's 'sensible revolution',[65] and the men who made that event, as W. A. Speck has recently characterized them, its 'reluctant revolutionaries'.[66] Despite the rhetoric of original contract, fundamental law, abdication, and a vacant throne, the progress of the Revolution spoke more in the end to constitutional circumspection than to constitutional change. Even the offer of the crown to William and Mary, which Trevelyan saw as having been made only on condition that the new monarchs accept the law as stated in the Declaration of Rights,[67] has latterly come to be seen not as a condition at all, but only as an anxious hope.[68]

Equally important is that the political thought that came out of the

---

[65] G. M. Trevelyan, *The English Revolution, 1688–1689* (Oxford, 1938), p. 3. John Morrill, in a recent overview of 1688–9, undertakes to measure Trevelyan's classic Whig interpretation of the Revolution against a significant sample of the research done on the subject over the past half century. Morrill finds Trevelyan on most counts to have been intuitively right to appreciate what that research has confirmed; that despite some far-reaching, although unintended, consequences, the Revolution was essentially conservative, and that Trevelyan's characterization of the event as a 'sensible revolution' still has much to commend it. John Morrill, 'The Sensible Revolution', in Israel (ed.), *The Anglo-Dutch Moment*, pp. 73–104.

[66] W. A. Speck, *Reluctant Revolutionaries: Englishmen and the Revolution of 1688* (Oxford, 1988).

[67] Trevelyan, *The English Revolution*, p. 79.

[68] Howard Nenner, 'Constitutional Uncertainty and the Declaration of Rights', in Barbara J. Malament (ed.), *After the Reformation: Essays in Honor of J. H. Hexter* (Philadelphia, 1981), pp. 291–308, especially p. 303. See, too, Lucille Pinkham, *William III and the Respectable Revolution* (Cambridge, MA, 1954); J. P. Kenyon, 'The Revolution of 1688: Resistance and Contract', in Neil McKendrick (ed.), *Historical Perspectives: Studies in English Thought and Society in Honour of J. H. Plumb* (London, 1974), pp. 49–50; Robert J. Frankle, 'The Formulation of the Declaration of Rights', *Historical Journal*, XVII (1974), p. 270; Schwoerer, *The Declaration of Rights*, pp. 282–3; Speck, *Reluctant Revolutionaries*, pp. 113–14. John Morrill, who has surveyed some of the modern scholarship on this point, also appreciates that Trevelyan was too quick to see the offer of the crown as conditional. Morrill, however, is to be read with caution as he has mistakenly reversed the proponents and opponents of the case. Morrill, 'The Sensible Revolution', p. 90, n 56.

Revolution was largely influenced by the unexpected suddenness of events. No sooner had William descended upon England, it seemed, than James was gone. Much of the discourse therefore was reactive, responding to the realization, if not to the admission, of a successful deposing of the king. The effect was to narrow the issues considerably. Because James left England so quickly and abjectly the resistance to him did not at first need to be justified and the reality of that resistance could be ignored. Attention was turned to matters of constitutional settlement, principally the question of how to rationalize the path of William and Mary to James II's throne.

From the end of December 1688, when James made his second and final flight from England, it was more than likely that William would be the nation's next king; and by early February 1689 what had been likely had become certain. English political discourse first anticipated that likelihood and later responded to the certainty by examining and dissecting the various claims of monarchical right that could be, and were, advanced on William's behalf. It is a rich literature because such guidelines as there were from law, history, and the work of the Convention were overlapping, confused, inconsistent, and vague. Significantly, there was no official philosophy of succession to emerge from the 1689 settlement. The details of the crown's anticipated descent in a line from William and Mary through Anne were necessarily spelled out in the Declaration of Rights, and to make an acceptance of William and Mary more palatable to the scrupulous the new oath of allegiance omitted any explicit reference to them as 'rightful' monarchs. But that was all. These were housekeeping arrangements, not statements of constitutional principle. Unlike James I, who in 1603 announced his undoubted birthright by both proclamation and an act of parliament, William and Mary left the basis of their right to the throne unaddressed. The new monarchs, therefore, could have been understood to be king and queen by right of election, conquest, a tortuous rendering of heredity, an all-embracing and undefined notion of providence – or by some combination of the above.[69] It was an impressive variety of options made possible by unprecedented circumstances, a need for ambiguity, and, more important, by a rule of succession which for all that had happened was still uncertain.[70]

---

[69] Mark Goldie, 'The Revolution of 1689 and the Structure of Political Argument', *Bulletin of Research in the Humanities*, 83, 4 (1980), pp. 473–564; also Manuel Schonhorn, 'Saul, Monarchy, and Succession: Reflections on the Political Languages of 1689', in Schochet (ed.), *Restoration, Ideology, and Revolution*, pp. 385–417.

[70] I treat this issue at greater length in *The Right to be King: The Succession to the Crown of England, 1587–1714* (London: forthcoming).

Because historical scholarship has recently turned with an invigorated interest to the role and place of women, Mary, once neglected as a mere appendage to William, is now inviting closer attention. Her importance in the history of political thought is closely tied to questions of succession, to a female's right to inherit the crown, and to a woman's capacity for monarchical rule.[71] On one level, of course, these were matters settled in the sixteenth century by the first Mary and her sister, Elizabeth; but as testimony to the continued uncertainty about a rule of succession, it was not at all clear whether either Tudor queen's right was thought to be grounded in heredity or in the act of parliament and Henry VIII's will that placed both of Henry's 'illegitimate' daughters back in line for his throne. Furthermore, Mary II, unlike her female predecessors, came to the throne as a *feme covert*, a fortunate circumstance for those polemical analysts who were eager to see in the events of 1688–9 no significant compromise of the principle of hereditary monarchy. In their view James had abdicated, his counterfeit son was properly to be disregarded, and William was legally entitled to the use of his wife's inherited estate.

As a male, William did not need to have his capabilities either justified or explained. He was an established ruler, a warrior-prince who sensed only the need to underplay his warrior image by disavowing any intention of coming to England as a conqueror. Curiously, however, it was as king by right of conquest that he could most easily be made acceptable to an important segment of Tory opinion. Those who were unable to embrace any fiction that might fit William into a model of kingship by heritable right, who remained committed to non-resistance, and who understandably despised the idea of election, had little alternative but to adopt William as their conqueror-king. If they were not to become Jacobites the only theoretical choices open to them were an acknowledgement of the Dutchman as king *de facto*, by virtue of his having taken possession of James' throne, or an acceptance of William as rightful king for having conquered James in a just war. Hale, as if to prefigure one of the nation's options, had written some years earlier in the politically palatable vocabulary of the common law that

the conqueror is, as it were, the plaintiff, and the conquered prince is the defendant, and the claim is a claim of title to the crown; and because each of them pretends a right to the sovereignty, and there is no other competent trial of the title between them, they put themselves upon the great trial by battle.[72]

---

[71] Lois Schwoerer, 'Images of Queen Mary II, 1689–94', *Renaissance Quarterly*, 42 (1989), 717–48.
[72] Matthew Hale, *The History of the Common Law of England* (London, 1820), pp. 83–4.

The result was to reopen a body of discourse that the English experience of Cromwell had served to discredit for more than a generation, and to allow those who required more traditional theoretical comfort to hold to William as they had previously held to James, as their sovereign monarch by the grace of God.[73]

The philosophical difficulty in entertaining conquest theory was the need to be surgically precise. The conquest had to be understood as a victory *in regem* only, extinguishing James' rights but having no effect on those of anyone else. To be politically usable, William's 'conquest' needed to be differentiated from a victory *in populum*, without application to the interests, estates, and relationships of the nation. The problem, then, was the same as the one created by James's endeavouring to subvert the constitution and thus breaking the original contract. In 1689, both William's 'conquest' and James' 'treason' could have been read as dissolutions of government, but these were unacceptable interpretations, appealing to no more than a handful of radicals and rejected unceremoniously by the Convention and the political nation at large. With little distinction between Whig and Tory, those in the mainstream who applied their ideas to the progress of events, and those who subsequently offered their analyses of its meaning, were instead more uniformly mindful of preserving as much of the constitution as was possible.

The best legal minds of the Convention, ranging on both sides of the abdication and vacancy issue, were determined to reach a settlement with a minimum of constitutional disruption. Inevitably they were drawn to the idea of trust. That theme, which had grown in currency since the trial and execution of Charles I, may have been especially attractive as a way of defending the principle of hereditary monarchy. Henry Horwitz has suggested that a legal model of 'forfeitable public trust' was used by the Lords to reconcile their initial rejection of abdication and a vacant throne with their willingness to repudiate the government of James or any other 'popish prince'. In that way, they could redefine the monarchical estate as one in trust rather than in fee while continuing to view that trust as heritable.[74] Whether this analysis does, in fact, express what they were thinking is uncertain, but it is sure that Lords and Commons, Whigs and Tories, were attempting a

---

[73] Mark Goldie, 'Edmund Bohun and *Jus Gentium* in the Revolution Debate, 1689–1693', *Historical Journal*, 20 (1977), 569–86; M. P. Thompson, 'The Idea of Conquest in Controversies over the 1688 Revolution', *Journal of the History of Ideas*, 37 (1977), 33–46; Gerald Straka, 'The Final Phase of Divine Right Theory in England, 1688–1702', *English Historical Review*, 77 (1962), 638–58.

[74] Henry Horwitz, '1689 (and All That)', *Parliamentary History*, 6 (1987), 23–32.

settlement that would rid them of James while keeping the foundations of their government substantially intact.[75]

VI

Much of the political thought that pointed to the Revolution and was employed subsequently to rationalize it, focused on the problem of Catholic rule. The movement for Exclusion anticipated the danger, and the Convention in January 1689 declared that earlier foreboding to be correct: it was unthinkable for Protestant England to be governed by a popish king. The premise upon which this rejection of Catholic monarchy was based runs richly through the literature of the Restoration, and gathers particular urgency in the decade from Exclusion through Revolution. Again the theme of trust is sounded. Catholic princes are unfit to rule because they suffer from an inescapable moral infirmity. Because they are bound not to keep faith with heretics their commitments to their Protestant subjects are meaningless. Accordingly, they cannot be trusted to obey the municipal laws of England. Nor does it matter what promises they make to the contrary. Their obligations lie elsewhere. On this premise that obedience to the pope is civil rather than religious the constitutional doctrine, or dogma, of the Protestant Succession was to be founded.

In the immediate aftermath of the Revolution king-in-parliament

[75] There is a divide in current historical thinking about the *mentalité* of the Convention. On one side are those who see the settlement of 1689 as reflecting constitutional uncertainty and a resulting conservatism, the work of pragmatic but essentially reluctant revolutionaries. Speck, *Reluctant Revolutionaries*; J. P. Kenyon, 'The Revolution of 1688'; Howard Nenner, 'Constitutional Uncertainty and the Declaration of Rights', in Barbara C. Malament (ed.), *After the Reformation: Essays in honor of J. H. Hexter* (Philadelphia, 1980), pp. 291–308; John Miller, 'The Glorious Revolution: "Contract" and "Abdication" Reconsidered', *Historical Journal*, 25 (1982), 541–55. On the other side of the divide are those who are drawn instead to a Convention confidently in control of events creating a new monarch and, upon unambiguous constitutional principles, forging a new concept of kingship. Schwoerer, *The Declaration of Rights*; C. C. Weston and J. R. Greenberg, *Subjects & Sovereigns: The Grand Controversy Over Legal Sovereignty in Stuart England* (Cambridge, 1981); Thomas P. Slaughter, ' "Abdicate" and "Contract" in the Glorious Revolution', *Historical Journal*, 28 (1981), 399–403. Somewhere in between, sensible of the ambiguities in the settlement but less persuaded of those ambiguities having been a product of constitutional uncertainty, is Henry Horwitz, 'Parliament and the Glorious Revolution', *Bulletin of the Institute of Historical Research*, (1974), 36–52. A recent extended analysis by Robert Beddard, 'The Unexpected Whig Revolution of 1688', in Robert Beddard (ed.), *The Revolutions of 1688* (Oxford, 1991), pp. 11–101, adopts the position that the tone of the Convention may well have been halting and uncertain, but that it scarcely mattered. Beddard argues for a decisive dynastic revolution having been forged outside of the Convention by William and his Whig allies. In his reading of events, 'the Convention was not the parent, but the offspring of dynastic revolution' (p. 74).

dismantled a major component of the prerogative by condemning the suspending power and allowing the dispensing power to die. But for Anglicans this victory over the king was insufficient. It nullified the threat of Catholicism but not of regulated Protestant dissent. The Toleration Act did by legislation what the king had attempted to do by prerogative alone: it suspended the Test Acts and the penal laws, although only for trinitarian Protestants. At the same time that the monarch's right to dispense or suspend was being denied, the right was being convincingly appropriated by parliament. Writing to urge parliament to take that action in 1689, Sir Robert Atkyns, Chief Baron of the Exchequer and Speaker of the House of Lords while the seal was in commission, confirmed and went significantly beyond what Herbert had prefigured the year before. Arguing that dispensations 'are not law, but indeed contrary to law and destructive of it', he concluded that 'there is no just nor lawful power of dispensing with any Act of Parliament, in any other hands than in those that are the law-makers, that is, in the king and parliament in conjunction'.[76] To Atkyns' mind, the *malum prohibitum/malum in se* rule was derived from a 'trite distinction ... that hath more confounded men's judgments than rectified them'. His solution was to refer the matter to 'the supreme court to give some certain rule in it, that may regulate and guide the judgment of inferiour courts: and this is the proper work of the king and parliament'.[77] This proposition, that parliament was the nation's supreme court, having moved persuasively to the centre of Whig political thought, had clear implications for what lay ahead. Although the church might still cling to notions of divine right and fundamental law, it was parliamentary sovereignty that would ultimately win the day.

The political thought of the decade following the Revolution was rich in Anglican and Tory efforts to justify allegiance to the new regime.[78] In the rush to distance themselves from the imputations of rebellion and treason, Tories were willing to accept the fruits of the Revolution but continued to resist the embrace of its principles. Interestingly, many Whigs were no different. We know from the work of John Kenyon that 'revolution principles' were slow to take hold and that rather than being wholly discredited, theories of divine right, fundamental law, right of conquest, and *de facto* monarchy proved to be remarkably adaptable and persistent. Yet that, as Mark Goldie reminds us, is only half the story. Equal in importance to the literature rationalizing allegiance to

[76] Sir Robert Atkyns, *An Enquiry Into the Power of Dispensing with Penal Statutes* (London, 1689), p. 18.
[77] *Ibid.*, p. 14.
[78] Goldie, 'Structure of Political Argument', *passim*.

William and Mary was the discourse attempting to reconcile theories of passive obedience and non-resistance with the practical need to resist a papist king. It is what Goldie calls the 'political theology of the Anglican revolution',[79] the attempt to turn James II back to the monarchy's pro-Anglican, anti-Catholic, anti-Dissenter policies of the early 1680s.

In the hands of Tory polemicists and Anglican divines the doctrine of passive obedience and non-resistance was transmuted into a moral duty of passive resistance or, as it came to be known, 'non-assistance'.[80] Reaching back into early Reformation thought, they urged all men to commit themselves to defending the true faith while at the same time reminding them of their Christian duty to endure the temporal consequences for doing so. The distinction that allowed for this renewed emphasis upon 'civil disobedience' was the belief that 'obedience was not due to the ungodly command, but [only] to the duty to suffer the tyrannical prince's wrath'.[81] This, of course, raised the fundamental question of who was to decide which commands of the prince were 'ungodly' and therefore not to be obeyed. The church's answer, that it was a matter of conscience, was less ambiguous than it might have seemed. In the church's view, individual conscience was not to be the guide. It was the church itself, as guardian of moral and divine truth, that would decide, and the Anglican Church had decided that toleration of both Catholicism and Protestant dissent was ungodly. In specific terms, the church was repudiating the right of the king to employ his prerogative to relieve tender consciences and remove the civil and political disabilities of non-Anglicans. In general and much more sweeping ecclesiological terms, it was asserting its independence of secular authority and challenging the Erastian basis of the Restoration settlement. As the divinely appointed guarantor of the faith, the church was effectively denying that God's truth was alterable by the king alone or even by king-in-parliament.

The church–state conflict over toleration underscored the basic issue of obedience to the existing order. It was this issue as much as any other that framed and informed political thought throughout the entire period. On one level, as has already been noted, there was the continuing question of the right of resistance. Were the people, in the event of the king's breach of 'trust', 'contract', or 'fundamental law', privileged to rise up against him? For the most part, this was a question of obedience to an authority which, at its inception, was understood to be legiti-

---

[79] Mark Goldie, 'The Political Thought of the Anglican Revolution', in Beddard (ed.), *Revolutions of 1688*, p. 107.
[80] *Ibid.*, p. 116.   [81] *Ibid.*, p. 114.

mate.[82] Yet from the destruction of Charles I until the restoration of his son, and again from the accession of William and Mary, the legitimacy of rule was not to be taken for granted. For royalists, that legitimacy died with the king in 1649; for republicans, it vanished with the extinction of the Commonwealth in 1653; for non-jurors and Jacobites, it ceased in 1689. The result was the creation of a theory of political obligation by which *de facto* rule could itself be legitimated. One of the components of that theory, the idea of the *de facto* ruler as an instrument of God's providence, has already been discussed as particularly significant in 1689; but the secular dimension of the theory, owing a large intellectual debt to Hobbes, may be even more important.

What Hobbes taught, and what Englishmen of the later Stuart century understood, was the value of civil peace. Legitimacy, as a result, was turned from a concept of government based in traditional right and hereditary monarchy, to government that was anchored instead in its acceptance by the subject in return for protection. To a great extent that was what lay at the heart of the Engagement campaign of the early 1650s, specifically the polemical defence of the new republican government that was ushered in with the execution of the king.[83] To speak of this as an argument for government legitimated by the consent of the governed would not be wide of the mark. Simply put, the requirements of self-preservation urged, and from a Hobbesian point of view demanded, allegiance to any rule that established itself over time, that protected life and property, and that held the promise of continuing peace.

After 1689 the chimera of *de facto* government, in the sense of its being an illegitimate entity, slowly disappeared. It took time to die completely, but like the idea of an ancient constitution which would ultimately yield to the theory of parliamentary sovereignty, it was eventually to be traded in for a more pragmatically oriented polity. The new state to emerge was legitimated by its ability to protect and provide for its subjects' rights, and consequently had a warrant to command their allegiance. As an early eighteenth-century tract writer would observe, 'nothing but endless confusion can be expected, if people are not bound to pay their allegiance to those by whose possession they enjoy their lives, liberties and properties'.[84] Like government based on the ancient constitution, the post-Revolution state was grounded in

[82] Robert Zaller, 'The Good Old Cause and the Crisis of 1659', in Schochet (ed.), *Restoration, Ideology, and Revolution*, pp. 23–43.

[83] Quentin Skinner, 'Conquest and Consent: Thomas Hobbes and the Engagement Controversy', in G. E. Aylmer (ed.), *The Interregnum: The Quest for Settlement, 1646–1660* (London, 1972), pp. 79–98.

[84] *The Revolution and Anti-Revolution Principles Stated and Compar'd ...*, 2nd edn (London, 1714), p. 30.

prescriptive right, but unlike the ancient constitution it did not need to trace its origins to the immemorial. Time mattered, but no specified number of years was required to validate the new regime's claim to rule, no vast and venerable age was necessary to ensure its success. The test instead became one of competence and consent. It mattered less when or how this new government was instituted than that it proved capable of administering to the nation's needs.

This new thinking was hinted at during the Revolution and borne out in the years that followed. William Sherlock, at the centre of the allegiance controversy, argued simply that when princes 'are thoroughly settled in their thrones, they are invested with God's authority, and must be reverenced and obeyed by all'.[85] Other supporters of the new regime adopted a more secular stance, but all inclined to the same conclusion that William alone offered the most practicable solution to England's problems: he was a Protestant in the Stuart line of descent, he was the instrument of the nation's delivery from the Catholic James, and he was willing to postpone the claims of his own posterity to the better hereditary right of his sister-in-law, Anne. He was, in a word, the best available guarantor of the public good. Sir Richard Cocks, an idiosyncratic backbench Whig at the end of the century, caught this post-Revolution mood. 'Since we intended a monarchical government', he wrote, 'we could do no less in mere gratitude than set him upon the throne who gave us this choice'. In that remark lay something of the conventional Country Whig wisdom of the late 1690s.[86] Equally important was that it signalled something more, the pointing of English political thought toward a new age of rationalism and a renewed emphasis upon public virtue and the common good.

If political stability depended upon a settled constitution, England was not yet stable in 1689, nor would it be for some time to come. In the waning years of the Stuart dynasty, the constitution was still in search of an acceptable balance and was still more vulnerable than secure. Although politics would change as England entered a new age of patronage and party, critical problems remained. The prerogative had been trimmed but with limited effect on the residual power of the monarchical state; the place of Protestant dissenters in the political order had been suggested but had not been concluded; and there was still no settled rule of monarchical succession. The variety of theoretical arguments for and against an acceptance of William and Mary as king and

---

[85] William Sherlock, *The Case of Allegiance Due to Sovereign Powers, Stated and Resolved* ..., 2nd edn (London, 1691), p. 5.
[86] David Hayton, 'Sir Richard Cocks: The Political Anatomy of a Country Whig', *Albion*, 20 (1988), 22–46.

queen bore convincing witness to the uncertainties and divisions that continued well beyond the constitutional reconstruction effected in 1689 and again in 1701. The difference in the eighteenth century was in the growing emphasis upon a present that would work rather than upon a past that was imagined; and eventually a new discourse of utility would replace the older discourse of rights.

Twice in the seventeenth century Englishmen had acted on necessity and twice they had successfully persuaded themselves that they were acting according to law. It was a useful and attractive fiction, more so perhaps than any other could be in avoiding the implications of a wholesale national treason; but, even so, the pretense did not go unchallenged. 'It cannot be expected', one pamphleteer reasoned at the time of the Convention's deliberations in 1689, 'that we should have any particular directions from the law to authorize what has been done, or may further be done towards a settlement; but necessity neither has nor needs law'.[87] Had seventeenth-century Englishmen confessed to that reality the results of their Revolution might have been much more radical and certainly they would have been very different. But if the price of pretense was a constitution that continued to be unsettled, it also produced some of the richest political discourse that the English would ever know.

[87] *A Free Conference Concerning the Present Revolution of Affairs in England* (London, 1689), p. 13.

Part III

Commerce, empire and history

7 Politeness and politics in the reigns of Anne and the early Hanoverians

Nicholas Phillipson

What Country soever in the Universe is to be understood by the Bee-Hive represented here, it is evident from what is said of the laws and Constitution of it, the Glory, Wealth, Power and Industry of its inhabitants, that it must be a large, rich and warlike Nation, that is happily govern'd by a limited Monarchy.

(B. Mandeville, *The Fable of the Bees, Or Private Vices, Public Benefits*, The Preface)

The political thought of the reigns of Anne and of the first two Georges was an integral part of the political culture of a polity whose wealth was the product of a rapid if bumpy, expansion of overseas and domestic trade; whose power was derived from the wars of the reigns of William III and Anne and the massive extension of the fiscal and military power of the state that accompanied them, and whose civil and religious liberties were enshrined in 'revolution principles' whose meaning remained obscure and bitterly controversial.[1] The Revolution, the Revolution Settlement, the Act of Settlement, and the Anglo-Scottish Union notwithstanding, the succession remained in question from the Revolution to the Forty-Five. Fundamental questions about the relationship of the monarch to parliament, parliament to people and the Church of England to a protestant nation deeply penetrated by dissent, remained unanswered and would continue to fracture the politics of a notoriously volatile political nation. For while it was an evident and, for some non-jurors, regrettable fact of political history that Britain had become a mixed monarchy, the question of whether the mixture was to be described in terms of the *King's Answer to the Nineteen Propositions* or in terms of contracts ancient or modern was profoundly controversial. In fact, Britain was a mixed monarchy of the sort that had worried Grotius most: the separation of powers was governed neither by clear

---

[1] See particularly J. P. Kenyon, *Revolution Principles: The Politics of Party, 1689–1720* (Cambridge, 1977). H. T. Dickinson, *Liberty and Property: Political Ideology in Eighteenth Century Britain* (London, 1977).

constitutional principles nor by any general consensus. It was, he had observed, a situation which must cause 'the utmost confusion'.[2]

The most obvious and notorious symptom of Grotian confusion lay in the tendency of British politics to faction. That, of course, was a problem common to all systems of government and was generally recognized to be particularly acute in mixed monarchies. However, as that shrewd Huguenot, Paul Rapin de Thoyras, noticed, the peculiarity of party conflict in Britain was that it had as much to do with what David Hume called 'principle' as with traditional questions of 'family' or 'interest' and had indeed, acquired the power to override them.[3] These 'principles' were as old as the Reformation and Counter-Reformation and turned on classic questions of whether divine right or election provided the true basis of government and whether the obligations of subjects were founded on passive obedience or resistance. As Clarendon and Rapin had shown, during the reigns of the early Stuarts, these issues had been refreshed by what contemporaries came to think of as Arminian superstition and puritan enthusiasm, at a time when they were being marginalized elsewhere in Europe. They had been revived during the Exclusion Crisis – the seed-pod from which modern parties were generally deemed to have sprung – and had been institutionalized in the constitutional ambiguities of the Revolution Settlement. What matters here is that they acquired a new lease on life in 1701 as a result of the Act of Settlement, that flagrant Whig assault on divine and indefeasable right which unequivocally insisted on the parliamentary basis of monarchy. For the rest of our period, as long as the succession remained a matter of controversy – and Whigs and Jacobites made sure that it did so until the Forty-Five – the issues which had been raised during the exclusionist debate would continue to structure party polemic, fracturing the political culture of Britain and ensuring that the constitutional status of parties remained profoundly ambiguous.[4]

---

[2] H. Grotius, *The Rights of War and Peace in three books. Wherein are explained the Laws of Nature and Nations, and the Principal Parts relating to Government . . . to which are added all the large notes of Mr J. Barbyrac.* (London, 1738), pp. 71–2. This was incidentally, a view with which a decidedly non-Grotian thinker, Bernard Mandeville, could equally well agree. 'In mix'd constitutions [disagreement about the distribution of sovereign power] often is the cause of fatal Quarrels, more especially in this Kingdom, where worse Calamities that have befallen either King or People have been owing to this grand Dispute' (*Free Thoughts on Religion, the Church and National Happiness. By the Author of the Fable of the Bees* (London, 1723), p. 297.

[3] P. de Rapin Thoyras, *Dissertation sur les Whigs et les Torys* (London, 1717); D. Hume, 'Of Parties in General', and 'Of the Parties of Great Britain', in *Essays Moral, Political and Literary*, ed. E. F. Miller (Indianapolis, 1987), pp. 54–72.

[4] G. Holmes, *British Politics in the Age of Anne*, (London, 1967); J. A. W. Gunn, *Faction No More: Attitudes to Party in Government and Opposition in Eighteenth-century England* (London, 1972). Once again, cf. Mandeville: 'Notwithstanding the various

But in this context, 'principle' was, as Rapin recognized, little more than a euphemism for religion. What is more, in a society which enjoyed an unrivalled appreciation of Christian scepticism and Hobbesian metaphysics, it was easy for Whigs, Tories and Jacobites to see the 'principles' of their rivals as mere opinions which had their roots in the imagination, pride and love of dominion of a corrupt species. Throughout our period, no one doubted the power of church politics and priestcraft to perpetuate Exclusionist controversy. It mattered to political discourse that the Revolution had been an attempt to preserve the church as well as the constitution from popery and despotism. It was equally important that the Revolution Settlement had given birth to the Toleration Act which had called into question the very nature of the *Ecclesia Anglicana*. Was it a Calvinist church, as most Anglicans, jurors and non-jurors alike, believed; a visible church, whose authority descended from the Apostles, whose doors were only open to those who were prepared to engage in its sacraments? Or was it, as Whigs and Dissenters thought, a latitudinarian church, to be conceived in Lutheran terms, as a part of an invisible church, which was co-extensive with the nation and open to all sincere and well-affected Protestants? These questions were too emotive politically to be resolved in 1689 and remained so throughout our period. Indeed, they were only to be resolved, and then only partially, by the repeal of the Test and Corporation Acts in 1828–9. But the sense that the Church was under pressure from Whiggery and toleration continued to shape Tory-Anglican discourse throughout our period. It was the stuff of Tory politics during William's reign, when high Anglicans kept up a running attack on sectarianism, heterodoxy, and above all, occasional conformity. It provided the occasions for those two classic trials of strength between junto Whiggery and its Tory opponents, the Sacheverell Crisis of 1709 and the Bangorian Controversy of 1717, which not only showed the grass-roots strength of the Church Party, but demonstrated how tightly intertwined ecclesiological and consitutional issues were and how politically combustible they had become. In the General Election of 1710, Tories still found it worth using slogans like 'No Rump Parliament', 'No Forty Eight', 'No Presbyterian Rebellion', 'Save the Queen's White Neck' to link Whiggery to regicide. As the moderate Bishop of Bath and Wells, George Hooper, remarked, 'Original Compact had become a dangerous phrase, not to be used without a great deal of

Turns of Fate these two Doctrines [passive obedience and resistance] have undergone, and the many Mischiefs the Dispute has occasion'd, the Question remains still, and as each Party pretends to have the better Argument, the Quarrel is undecided' (*Free Thoughts on Religion* . . ., p. 299).

caution'.[5] It was a situation which demonstrated the power of opinion to erode the trust on which the authority of government depended.

It was the central paradox of Augustan politics that this neo-exclusionist politics, as we may call it, this politics of opinion, was to set the agenda for party political debate in a country which had witnessed a profound shift in the distribution of property and a massive extension of the military and fiscal resources of what, after 1692, John Brewer thinks it legitimate to describe as the British 'state'.[6] By the end of the Nine Years' War these secular transformations had already become the subject of that powerful Whig discourse which John Pocock has described as neo-Harringtonian.[7] By the Revolution, Harrington's original account of the shift of power and property which had occurred as a result of the decay of feudal tenures was being seen as a context within which the Civil War and the collapse of the monarchy could be usefully discussed. Indeed, during our period, Rapin and, more famously, Hume, were to develop sophisticated accounts of these complicated events as the result of an interplay between the shifts in property and opinion that had been brought about by the collapse of feudalism and the progress of the Reformation. By the Revolution, too, Harringtonians had adapted Harringtonian thought to accommodate the – to Harrington – unexpected Restoration of the monarchy and the nobility and the rapid progress of commerce. And with the Treaty of Ryswick, neo-Harringtonian discourse had been adapted once again, to take account of the expansion of the military resources of the Revolution state. It was a Whig discourse about the problem of maintaining a mixed and ancient constitution which was being subjected to the most profound secular pressures which were peculiar to the modern age. It recognized the existence of tensions between ancient constitutionalism and modern Whiggery, between the claims of ancient and modern prudence. And it had built into it a profound distrust of the priestcraft on which neo-exclusionist party politics throve.[8]

Although neo-Harringtonianism was a Whig language, it drew heavily on a vocabulary of country politics which was far from exclusively Whig;

---

[5] Holmes, *British Politics in the Age of Anne*, pp. 56, 92. More generally, M. A. Goldie, 'Tory Political Thought, 1689–1714', unpublished PhD dissertation, University of Cambridge, 1977, esp. parts II and III.

[6] J. Brewer, *The Sinews of Power, War, Money and the English State, 1688–1783* (London, 1988), *passim* but esp. ch. 6.

[7] J. G. A. Pocock, *The Machiavellian Moment: Florentine Political Thought and the Atlantic Republican Tradition* (Princeton, NJ, 1975), pp. 406–22.

[8] M. A. Goldie, 'The Civil Religion of James Harrington', in *Politics, Politeness and Patriotism: Papers Presented at the Folger Institute Seminar 'Politics and Politeness in the Age of Walpole' 1986*, ed. G. J. Schochet (The Folger Institute, Folger Shakespeare Library, Washington DC, 1993), pp. 31–46.

its rogue's gallery of corrupt courtiers, councillors, prelates, and that new source of corruption, the stockjobber, was as distasteful to Tories as to Whigs, and, as Swift noticed, there was nothing peculiarly Whiggish in disliking standing armies.[9] What is more, its concerns with power and property were of as much interest to Tories like Charles Davenant and Tory/Jacobites like Bolingbroke, as to junto Whigs and those opposition Whigs who were comfortable with the generally Ciceronian preoccupations of Harringtonians.[10] The story of the way in which neo-Harringtonian thought confronted neo-exclusionist party discourse has yet to be written and it is not the purpose of the present essay to attempt to do so. I do, however, want to open the subject up, by paying particular attention in what follows to a political language which served as a bridge between them. This was a language of manners which has so far received very little attention from political historians or historians of political thought. Its primary concern was with the intemperance of party polemic, with the frightening power of opinion to erode the trust on which government depended, and with the desire to demonstrate the advantage of moderation in political discourse. In this idiom, moderation was to be closely connected with the twin objectives of legitimizing the Revolution and the Revolution Settlement, and developing a language which was able to explain the political signifi-cance of the changing interests of the modern British state. It was a language which was to put pressure on the language of rights on which neo-exclusionist polemic of Anne's reign was based and on the language of virtue which enjoyed a powerful resurgence during the Walpolean era. Later on, in the hands of Hume and the historians of the Scottish Enlightenment, it was to serve as the language in which that profound investigation into the relations between opinion and property was conducted, and out of which Scottish historicism and Scottish political economy were to emerge. What follows, then, is not a comprehensive survey of the political thought of our period. It is a set of three distinct but related studies of party political discourse in the making. The first deals with the early years of Anne's reign, the second with the early years of the Robinocracy, the last with the formative years of the Scottish

9 'To be against a Standing Army in Time of Peace, was all *High-Church, Tory*, and *Tantivity*', *Examiner*, no. 43 (31 May 1711), in *The Prose Works of Jonathan Swift*, ed. H. Davis (Oxford, 1940), III, pp. 163–4. More generally, see D. Hayton, 'The "Country" Interest and the Party System, 1698–c. 1720, in *Party and Management in Parliament, 1660–1784*, ed. C. Jones (Leicester, 1984), pp. 37–85.

10 See, for example, J. G. A. Pocock, *The Machiavellian Moment*, ch. xiii. I. Kramnick, *Bolingbroke and his Circle: the Politics of Nostalgia in the Age of Walpole* (Cambridge, MA, 1968), esp. chs 3, 4, 6.

Enlightenment. And in each of these case studies, I shall pay particular attention to the history of language of manners, to which much of the work of the Folger Seminar was directed.

But there is one matter of context which has to be addressed before we continue. The party political discourse with which this essay is concerned took shape during a revolution in print culture which began with the failure of the ministry to renew licensing legislation in 1695. By Anne's reign, the press had become a powerful resource for transmitting the political opinions of London to the provinces by means of pamphlets, newspapers and essay-journals devoted to politics, morals, manners and religion. By Walpole's day, printers had begun to realize the commercial advantage of amalgamating these two types of periodical journalism, and of integrating such essays with the *reportage* that remained the backbone of the newspaper. There probably never will be adequate statistical data to show how the periodical press grew in our period. Michael Harris reckons that by 1712 London had about twenty single-sheet papers which sold 20–25,000 copies each week; by 1746 there were about twice that number with a total readership of around 500,000.[11] This huge readership and the incalculable number of those who listened to journals being read aloud in taverns and coffee-houses seem to have been drawn from the middling ranks, from shopkeepers, from artisans, and, with the founding of the *Tatler* in 1709, from women and servants. In other words, the press had not only opened up politics to the provinces but to something like a mass audience of citizens, most of whom had political opinions but not the vote. It enabled them to participate in discourse which was being shaped by the journalists of Grub Street, rather than by courtiers or parliamentarians. And it is with Grub Street discourse that this essay, like the Folger Seminar from whose proceedings it is derived, is largely concerned.[12]

---

[11] M. Harris, *London Newspapers in the Age of Walpole: A Study of the Origins of the Modern English Press* (London, [1987]), pp. 19, 190–1. Cf. the same author's 'Publishing, Print and Politics in the Age of Walpole', in *Britain in the Age of Walpole*, ed. J. Black, (London, 1984), pp. 189–210. See also H. L. Snyder, 'The Circulation of Newspapers in the Reign of Queen Anne', *The Library*, 33 (1968), 206–35. For the periodical press, see R. P. Bond, *Studies in the Early English Periodical* (Chapel Hill, 1957), pp. 3–48. For the Walpolean period, Simon Varey, 'The Growth of Capitalism and the Rise of the Press in the Age of Walpole', in *Politics, Politeness and Patriotism*, ed. Schochet, pp. 245–62. For general overviews, see J. Black, *The English Press in the Eighteenth Century* (London, 1987), and G. C. Gibbs, 'Press and Public Opinion: Prospective', in *Liberty Secured? Britain Before and After 1688*, ed. J. R. Jones (Stanford, 1992), pp. 231–64.

[12] Most of the papers presented to that seminar are now in limited circulation. See *Politics, Politeness and Patriotism*, ed. Schochet.

I

Three great Grub Street journalists were to demonstrate the power of the press to shape political discourse in the early years of Anne's reign; the country Whig, John Tutchin, the High Church Tory-cum-Jacobite, Charles Leslie, and Daniel Defoe. Leslie thought that Defoe's voice was indistinguishable from that of Tutchin, although in this period, it is better regarded as the voice of that most elusive of political creeds, Harley's country Toryism, conceived, as the latter once remarked, as an attempt to 'Graft the Whiggs on the bulk of the Church Party'.[13]

Tutchin was the first in the field with the *Observator* (1702–12), his attempt to revive a country Whiggery which was under attack from the Church party and the Junto.[14] His Whiggery was that of a True Whig, who had been out during Monmouth's rebellion.[15] The constitution was a product of 'reason and nature'.[16] It was ancient in origin, founded on contract and the express and collective consent of a free people and enshrined in the common law. What is more, 'she's as well beloved now by all true *Englishmen*, as she was by our Forefathers a Thousand Years ago'.[17] Tutchin was not much interested in the precise nature of this contract. What mattered was that it had transferred power from the people to a Parliament whose power 'is so great, that I cannot find it Circumscrib'd but by *Conscience* and *Native Right*'.[18] Regal power was thus derived from parliament, Tutchin declared, and English history had been nothing less than a continuing attempt by patriots to preserve liberties which were 'so firmly Fenc'd with *Law*, that no one can break thro' those Fences without breaking his Neck'.[19] Who these 'patriots' were and in whom the right of resistance was vested was a question about which Tutchin was conspicuously vague. Unlike Defoe, he applauded the Hungarian rebellion of 1704–5 as a vindication of the natural right of resistance which Englishmen had long been accustomed

---

[13] J. A. Downie, *Jonathan Swift. Political Writer* (London, 1984), p. 137.
[14] Tutchin has been neglected but see J. P. Kenyon, *Revolution Principles*, pp. 105–6 and *DNB*. He wrote a short, informative autobiography in the *Observator*, 22–5 August 1705.
[15] It was summarized in a series of essays published in the *Observator* between 29 September and 7 November 1705. These focussed in particular on his views about resistance and his differences with his principal adversary, Charles Leslie. He distinguished his own Whiggery from that of 'Modern Whigs' (who were 'the Objects of my Compassion, not of my Hatred') in the *Observator* of 20–3 January 1702/3 and from 'Republicans or Commonwealthmen' (who were 'wicked people') on 8–13 May 1703.
[16] *Observator*, 7–10 April 1703.
[17] *Ibid.*, 27–31 March 1703.   [18] *Ibid.*, 14–17 June 1703; Cf. 8–11 July 1702.
[19] *Ibid.*, 28 September–2 October 1706.

to exercise.[20] But Tutchin's view of resistance significantly lacked exclusionist rigour and smacked of an attempt to speak of limited resistance in terms which would be palatable to moderate Whig opinion. Thus, he invoked Grotius rather than Sidney or Locke to justify resistance to tyrants, although he did so with significantly little consistency or precision; tyrants were simply rulers who breached what he took to be the principles of the English constitution.[21] And although he declared that 'Providence and my own Inclination to the service of my Dear Country, has put me to the Publick Post of Vindicating the Revolution', his account of it was equally evasive.[22] It had been the collective act of a people which was faced with James' 'elopement'; he would, Tutchin conceded, have been 'coerc'd' if he had stayed.[23] Plenary powers had been given to the Convention to restore the ancient balance between regal and parliamentary power.[24] When seen in this light, those 'two great men, Mr Sidney and Mr Lock', appeared as the prototype of modern 'patriots' who had resisted the temptation of concocting Baconian or Harringtonian utopias and had played the nobler part of defending the principles of ancient liberty 'the one against Sir Robert Filmer, and the other against a whole Company of Slaves'.[25] So far as Locke was concerned, it was a portrait of the author of the first, not the second *Treatise of Government*, the critic of Filmerian patriarchalism and the defender of ancient constitutionalism. As we shall see, it was as an exclusionist of a different stamp that Locke was to appear to Tutchin's bitterest enemy, Charles Leslie.

What brought Tutchin's whiggery into political focus was its attack on those traditional country bogies, the kings, courtiers, placemen and prelates who had threatened the independence of the Commons; here, Clarendon's new *History of the Great Rebellion* (1702) could easily be turned to country Whig advantage. Tutchin's political targets were Dutch courtiers, the monied interest, and, above all Jacobites, Anglican priestcraft and its most articulate apostle, 'Parson Lesly'. Eclectic though Tutchin's Whiggery was, it remained firmly rooted in the world of the Exclusion crisis and in English xenophobia rather than Harringtonian republicanism as he made clear in a notorious satire, 'The

---

[20] *Ibid.*, 12–15 December 1705. Defoe's critique of the rebellion had begun on 2 September 1704 in *A Review of the Affairs of France*.
[21] Grotius is invoked in *Observator*, 15–18 September 1703 and 13–16 October 1703.
[22] *Ibid.*, 26–9 June 1704.
[23] *Ibid.*, 31 October–3 November 1705. On 8–13 July 1704, however, Tutchin had declared that James had been 'remov'd'. See also 2–6 October 1703, 23–6 October 1706.
[24] *Ibid.*, 23–6 October 1706. See also 9–13 October 1703.
[25] *Ibid.*, 14–18 September 1706. This appears to be the only reference to Locke in the journal from 1702–7, when Tutchin, who was murdered, ceased to edit it.

Foreigners' (1700). In this satire, William's Dutch courtiers, not standing armies, were identified as the true sources of modern corruption and
they were denounced in terms which provoked an even more celebrated
and indignant reply from Daniel Defoe. *The True Born Englishman*
(1701) excoriated the pride and ingratitude of the English and identified
the decay of trust between governors and people as the root cause of the
dangers which liberty now faced. As we shall see, Defoe was to look for
new discursive resources with which to address this old and menacing
problem.

Tutchin's country Whiggery had tap-roots in English political culture
which were too deep and too lusty for party politicians to be able to
ignore. Harley and Swift hoped that it could be purged of its hostility to
the Church and used to create a Toryism which recognized the legitimacy of the Revolution. In Walpole's day, Trenchard and Gordon tried
to reinvigorate it with Machiavellian republicanism. At the end of our
period, Hume still regarded it as one of the cornerstones of the political
culture of modern England, in spite of the fact that he thought it was
incapable of sustaining an adequate defence of revolution principles.[26]
What makes Tutchin's country Whiggery particularly important to the
political discourse of Anne's reign is that it served as a catalyst to the
Church party and to its most potent spokesman, Charles Leslie. Not
only did Leslie manage to expose the *Observator*'s intellectual shortcomings but he succeeded in demonstrating the difficulty of mounting
any credible defence of the Revolution which was based on natural
rights and resistance rather than on necessity or providence.[27]

Leslie's attack on Tutchin was carried out in his satire on Tutchin's
Whiggery, *Rehearsal of Observator* (1704–09, with a supplement from
1709–12). As in the *Observator*, this took the form of dialogues between
A Countryman and Mr Observator, whose Whiggery was systematically
demolished by the relentless and often brilliant iconoclasm of a companion who had been conspicuously passive in Tutchin's dialogues. At
its centre lay a devastasting and influential attack on 'the Great Lock',
'the Oracle of the Party' which 'I thought *Necessary*, as laying a

[26] D. Hume, 'Of the OriginalContract', and 'Of Passive Obedience', in *Essays Moral,
Political and Literary*, pp. 465–92.

[27] Gilbert Burnet thought that the revival of the High Church Party in Anne's reign had
much to do with the success of the *Rehearsals*. B. Frank, 'The Excellent Rehearser;
Charles Leslie and the Tory Party 1688–1714', in *Biography in the Eighteenth Century*,
ed. J. D. Browning (New York and London, 1980), p.68. Leslie himself has been
seriously neglected. But see Goldie, 'Tory Political Thought', 11. J. Champion deals
with Leslie's attack on Socinianism in *The Pillars of Priestcraft Shaken. The Church of
England and its Enemies, 1660–1730* (Cambridge, 1992), ch. 4.

Foundation.[28] Locke's *First Treatise of Government* had taken the form of a classic attack on Filmer's patriarchal defence of divine right and passive obedience which was designed to clear the ground for his own defence of resistance in the Second Treatise. Leslie now proposed a tit-for-tat. A successful attack on the Second Treatise would discredit the authority of the First Treatise and clear the ground for a restatement of Filmerian principles on terms which would demonstrate the necessity of an apostolic Anglican church for maintaining the principles of monarchy. Leslie's assault on Locke, which was set in an Augustinian framework, took the form of a sceptical attack on all theories of natural rights. These were no more than opinions, propagated by crafty politicians, which played on the imagination, pride and love of dominion of a fallen species and bred a distrust of all established authority. Indeed, when viewed in this light, such phrases as *our* Queen, *our* Country, *our* Laws, acquired new and sinister meaning.

For who made her *Queen* of ME? Even ME my *Self*! And you know, who *Makes*, can *Unmake*! The *Inherent* and *Radical* POWER is still in ME! For, as our *Oracle* [Locke] says,
I alone am the King of ME.
This *Kingdom of* ME, is scituated [sic] in what they Call *Terra Australis Incognita*. And is the only *Place* in the *World*, where Men were

> Born free, as Nature first made Man
> Ere the Base Laws of Servitude Began,
> When Wild in Woods the Noble Savage Ran.

From this *Utopia* We have taken all our *Schems* [sic] of *Government* ever since! This is true *Liberty* and *Property*, to Reduce all to the *Noble Savage* again! To make *Mobb* the *Supreme*, and *Kings* and *Queens* to *Worship* Us, and Wear OUR *Liveries*.[29]

Thus there was no such thing as a theory of limited resistance as junto Whigs had claimed. All such theories pointed towards the same anarchic end, a quasi-Hobbesian state of nature ruled by the vagaries of opinion and ripe for exploitation by politicians. This sceptical assault allowed Leslie to confirm Filmer's claim that passive obedience and divine right, sanctioned by the authority of revealed religion, was still the only available theory of political obligation that was secure and intelligible. And it gave him the opportunity of reminding Tutchin that it was a theory whose authority was underwritten by the apostolic authority of

---

[28] *Rehearsal*, 14–21 April 1705; 15–22 Dec. 1705. The critique of Locke was begun on 11 August and continued until 20 Oct. 1705.
[29] *Ibid.*, 28 October–4 November 1704.

the Anglican church. It was a political theology which pointed towards the old High Church view that the Revolution and the Prince of Orange's succession had been acts of necessity, sanctioned by providence to preserve the church from popery and despotism. It followed from this that the Hanoverian Succession could only be justified on the same providential grounds.

But I wou'd not be Mistaken, as if I were an Enemy to the Succession of the *House of Hanover*, in *God's* own Time, and when his *Providence* makes way for it, according to *Truth* and *Right*. Far be it for me to Limit PROVIDENCE![30]

Leslie's demonstration that 'The Great Lock' was a radical exclusionist was of enormous importance to eighteenth-century political culture. It ensured that Locke would be regarded as a theorist of resistance rather than as a philosopher who, as John Dunn has shown, was profoundly concerned with restoring trust between governors and governed.[31] It meant that until the 1760s, the *Second Treatise* would be regarded by Whigs as a volatile text, which was best handled gingerly, and that writers like Defoe who were interested in trust would have to look elsewhere for a language in which to articulate it. But what matters here is that Leslie's sceptical discussion of opinion enabled him to ridicule Whig accounts of Saxon constitutionalism as offering no more than a hypocritical *de facto* defence of what was in danger of becoming a Whig oligarchy. It was a problem which minsterial defenders of the Revolution would address by invoking the authority of conventional as well as natural rights to explain the principles of limited resistance, by paying attention to the problem of *perfecting* as well as preserving the Revolution Settlement, and by calling for a reformation of manners to restore trust between crown, parliament and people.

Benjamin Hoadly, the chief theorist of junto Whiggery, showed how difficult the problem of mounting a credible theory of limited resistance could be.[32] He turned to Grotius to show that political society was the result of an unconditional transfer of power from a people to a sovereign which vested a collective right of resistance in them. He turned to Stillingfleet and the English latitudinarians to show that there was no more natural form of government than that of a king in parliament and that there was no more natural form of political obligation than

---

[30] *Ibid.*, 17–24 October 1705.

[31] J. Dunn, 'The Concept of 'Trust' in the Politics of John Locke', in *Philosophy in History*, ed. R. Rorty, J. B. Schneewind and Q. Skinner (Cambridge, 1984), pp. 279–301, and *Locke* (Oxford, 1984), ch. 2.

[32] Another neglected Augustan political thinker, Hoadly is discussed by Kenyon, *Revolution Principles*, and by Dickinson, *Liberty and Property*, p. 73, and in the latter's 'Benjamin Hoadly', *History Today*, 25, 5 (May 1975), 348–55.

submsission to a monarch who was 'in actual Possession of the Throne, by Consent of the Three Estates of the Realm' and governed in the public interest.[33] In this view, the public interest consisted in defending 'the *Laws*, which are the standard of the *Publick Good* of a Country' and resistance was justified only when life and property were at risk.[34] The trouble was that in spite of its appeal to the authority of the common law, this line of argument was no longer proof against Leslie's scepticism; who after all, was to decide when the public interest had been violated and whether resistance was legitimate? Whig claims that this was the task of parliament could easily be met with the reply that parliament was a hot-bed of faction. Defoe's later claim that the right of resistance lay with a freeholder electorate was met with Leslie's withering retort, 'Are not all the People as Free as they? Are not all Freeholders?'[35] Hoadley, however, was a good latitudinarian who saw the need for a theory of resistance which encompassed a free people at large. As he told Leslie, 'Public Good is Public Good, and not the mistaken Fancy of Private Men, or the mistaken Judgement of Legislators or Governors'.[36] The public, however, was no 'natural body' but one which was 'in a much more flux Condition, continually changing its Members, and with such a Term of Years perfectly new, and different from what it was'.[37] Nevertheless, 'the Influence of government is of that universal Nature that it cannot but be sensibly felt by all, or a vast Majority of Subjects, when it is their Rights and Properties are invaded; and when it is that they are secured, and defended by their Governors'.[38] This was to invoke a conception of conventional rights founded on a collective view of the public interest. But explaining the nature of that interest was a matter of reforming the opinion of a singularly imprudent public – a task best left to a latitudinarian church committed to comprehending English protestants of all denominations. It was an unsteady line of argument that exposed Hoadly to Leslie's charge that resistance was only permissable when he said it was.[39]

[33] 'A Discourse Concerning the Unreasonableness of a New Separation', in *The Works of Edward Stillingfleet together with his Life and Character*, 6 vols. (London, 1707–10), III, p. 941; cf. p. 951.

[34] *Ibid.*, p. 941.   [35] *Rehearsal*, 6–13 January 1704/5.

[36] B. Hoadly, *The Measures of Submission to the Civil Magistrate consider'd. In a Defence of the Doctrine deliver'd in a Sermon Preached before the Rt. Hon. the Lord Mayor, Aldermen, and Citizens of London, Sept. 29 1705*, 3rd edn (London, 1710), p. xxv.

[37] *Ibid.*, p. ix.   [38] *Ibid.*, pp. 91–2.

[39] It is worth noting that for all their theological and ecclesiological differences, a High Anglican like Sherlock and a Dissenter like Dodderidge could still agree that they shared a joint responsibility for encouraging the reformation of manners. See R. E. Sullivan, 'The Transformation of Anglican Political Theology *c.* 1716–1760', in *Politics, Politeness and Patriotism*, ed. Schochet, pp. 47–58, esp. p. 51.

While Hoadly had seen the importance of a reformation of manners for generating an understanding of the public interest, it was left to Daniel Defoe and to Richard Steele and Joseph Addison to show how that reformation could be brought about by means of a reformation of language. Defoe addressed this problem in two personae.[40] In the first, he was Mr Review, the Harleyite critic of faction and priestcraft who devoted much of his *Review* to the politics of a free Protestant polity whose interests were being transformed by war, commerce and empire. In the second he wrote as 'The Author of the True-Born Englishman', the political satirist and pamphleteer who wrote the classic satire on Leslie's political thought, *Jure Divino. By the Author of The True Born Englishman* (1706). In this long philosophical poem, Defoe ridiculed a political theology which made more sense of the rude, nomadic world of the Old Testament patriarchs than of a free commercial polity. No doubt the origins of the English constitution were as ancient as Tutchin had claimed, but its principles could best be defended by drawing on Pufendorf and Harrington, and when the context was right, on Locke.[41] *Jure Divino* provided what Defoe later admitted was an ultimately Whiggish understrapping to a sustained assault on the superstition, enthusiasm and ignorance of a factious people who did not understand their country's changing interests. Throughout his career he continued to preach the virtue of moderation in the use of political language in order to create a political culture which would mitigate party zeal and legitimize revolution principles. His journalism was designed for the city where opinion was formed and where its corrosive effects would have to be controlled. The success of this project depended upon his ability to catch the ears of party men of all political persuasions, by mimicking and manipulating the political languages they spoke. Here Defoe was in his element; his linguistic skills were phenomenal. He wrote as easily as a

---

[40] P. R. Backscheider, *Daniel Defoe: his Life* (Baltimore 1989). M. P. Thompson, 'Daniel Defoe and the Formation of Early Eighteenth-Century Whig Ideology', *Politics, Politeness and Patriotism*, ed. Schochet, pp. 109–24.

[41] This interpretation stresses Defoe's eclecticism as well as his important debts to Pufendorf and Harrington and takes seriously his claim to have been more than a mouthpiece of Locke. 'I know, what Mr. *Lock, Sidney* and others have said on this head [the origins of government], and I must confess, I never thought their Systems fully answer'd. But I am arguing by my own Light, not other Mens' (*Review*, 10 September 1706). It differs somewhat from the view of Thompson (n. 40 above) and substantially from that of Backscheider who notes Defoe's frequent silent quotations and paraphrases of Locke but fails to take account of the contexts in which they are used. Backscheider, *Daniel Defoe*, pp. 168–72. On Defoe's debts to natural jurisprudence, see M. Novak's pioneering *Defoe and the Nature of Man* (Oxford, 1963). The most recent discussion of his politics is M. Schonhorn, *Defoe's Politics: Parliament, Power, Kingship and Robinson Crusoe* (Cambridge, 1991). I am particularly grateful to Katherine Penovich for discussing Defoe with me.

High Church Tory as he wrote in the different idioms of Whiggery.[42]
He could deploy a language with wit and good humour, with satire and
raillery, or even, as in his most celebrated satire on Leslie, 'The Shortest
Way with Dissenters', with an Erasmian vehemence that displayed the
pessimistic depths into which he sometimes sank. But the hallmark of
his journalism was his desire to provoke controversy and discussion
among his readers. It was this and this alone which would make them
think again about their political and religious opinions and about the
interests they shared as well as those which divided them. With luck,
these discussions would generate the spirit of candour which dissenters
and freethinkers looked on as a sign of Grace and would teach modern
Britons to realize that moderation was not only *prudent* but *honest*; only
then would the way be cleared for a new understanding of the sort of
virtue which was needed to defend the Revolution.

Defoe's faith in the power of language to generate a reformation of
manners was Ciceronian, but it was a Ciceronianism for the citizen, not
the magistrate, which identified conversation rather than oratory as the
linguistic skill which would have to be cultivated if the civic personality
was to be reformed. All of Defoe's journalism was designed to encourage
moderation in the use of language. His use of raillery, satire and
instruction to dislodge superstition, enthusiasm and ignorance; his faith
in the power of good-humoured conversation and the *common sense* of
companions to prevent raillery from turning into cynicism, involved an
appeal to an Erasmian tradition which was being revived philosohically
by Shaftesbury. His appeal to the candour and common sense of his
readers appears as an attempt to link this neo-Ciceronian idiom to the
spiritual disciplines of English nonconformity rather than to Shaftesbury's deistic neo-Platonism. But encouraging moderation in the use of
political and religious language was, as Leslie pointed out, tantamount
to advocating hypocrisy.

It's a *Catholicon* and Cures all *Diseases*! Take but a *Dose* of this, and thou mays't
Drink *Poison*, and Break all the *Ten Commandments*, without any *Offence*! It
Reconciles *Churches* or *No Churches*, *Christ* and *Belial*, *Light* and *Darkness*! It
can *Transform* a *Revel* into a *Saint*, and *Satan* to an *Angel* of *Light*! It can make a
Schismatick, a true *Friend* of the Church; and a *Whore* an *Honest Woman*.[43]

Leslie's expostulation indirectly raised the interesting question whether
it was possible to square a defence of the Revolution with the principles
of Christian virtue, a problem that was addressed directly by Richard

---

[42] Backscheider, *Daniel Defoe*, pp. 430–4. Backscheider believes that Defoe was successful
in 'diluting Mist's radical Tory voice considerably' (*ibid.*, p. 431).
[43] *Rehearsal*, 13–20 January 1704–5. Cf. 3–10 February 1705.

Steele and Joseph Addison in the middle years of Anne's reign. Both were devout Anglicans, who set out to show how the cultivation of manners, refined by the cultivation of taste and natural theology – what came to be known as politeness – could purge moderation of hypocrisy and ease the tensions between prudence, honesty and virtue which were inherent in Ciceronian ethics. Their innumerable essays on manners, morals and taste, written for the *Tatler* (1709–11), *Spectator* (1711–14) and *Guardian* (1713) were the response of two great theorists of manners and politeness to the Sacheverell crisis and the erosion of political trust that they blamed largely on the High Church party. It involved attacking not simply High Church politics but High Church morality and the 'strict' Augustinian principles on which it was founded. Defending revolution principles, in other words, was now becoming a matter of reconstructing the very foundations of English political, moral and religious culture.[44]

Addison and Steele's essays were designed to expose the manners and morals of the city to public discussion. They wrote for men and women who saw the modern city in Augustinian terms, as a monument to the self-love and pride of a fallen species. They portrayed the modern city as a theatre of dissimulation, hypocrisy and greed, a hatching-ground for the plots and cabals on which superstition and enthusiasm fed, a sump of luxury and corruption where virtue was always in danger of being reduced to prudence and taste to fashion. They set out to develop an alternative image of a post-Augustinian city founded upon mankind's latent capacity for the benevolence which Augustinians insisted was merely a cover for hypocrisy. It was a terrene world in which men and women would be able to distance themselves from the false friendships which were founded merely on interest and prudence and reigned in the worlds of business and politics. True friendship, friendship which was regulated by virtue rather than considerations of interest, was only

---

[44] The study of the three great vehicles of politeness has been greatly advanced by authoritative modern editions; *The Tatler*, ed. D. F. Bond, 3 vols. (Oxford, 1987): *The Spectator*, ed. D. F. Bond, 5 vols. (Oxford, 1965): *The Guardian*, ed. J. C. Stephens (Lexington, 1982). The connections between politeness and personality have been studied by M. Ketcham, *Transparent Designs: Reading, Performance and Form in the Spectator Papers* (Athens, GA, 1985). E. A. and L. Bloom, *Joseph Addison's Sociable Animal in the Market Place, on the Hustings, in the Pulpit* (Providence, RI, 1971) offer a rather dated study of the subject as a chapter in the history of the formation of a bourgeois culture. See also P. Gay, 'The Spectator as Actor: Addison in Perspective', *Encounter*, 24, 6 (Dec. 1967), 27–32. L. Klein places the subject in a different historical setting in his important *Shaftesbury and the Culture of Politeness* (Cambridge, 1994), and in 'The Political Significance of "Politeness" in Early Eighteenth Century Britain', in *Politics, Politeness and Patriotism*, pp. 73–108. Peter France has recently explored French politeness in *Politeness and its Discontents: Problems in French Classical Culture* (Cambridge, 1992).

possible in the leisured, private world of the tavern or coffee-house, in the company of well-chosen companions who were drawn from different walks of life. Only there could perfect trust reign, could man's natural capacity for benevolence be released and could the prospect of virtuous living be envisaged. In their essays on manners and morals they hoped to show that the modern city possessed the capacity to generate virtue as well as corrupt it; commerce would be the handmaid, not the enemy of virtue, and the 'strict' morality of the Augustinians could be shown to be more appropriate to the culture of a ruder age.

Perhaps Addison and Steele's most important contribution to the language of manners was to show precisely how the cultivation of taste could conquer hypocrisy and encourage the principles of Christian virtue, an enterprise in which Addison was particularly interested. He set out to show how the principles of conversation could be extended from the moral to the aesthetic and supernatural worlds. Literature and the fine arts provided opportunities for imaginary encounters between authors, readers and fictional heroes and heroines which enabled the reader to extend his views of human nature beyond the immediate confines of the terrene world, to worlds which were regulated by higher and more universal principles of order. As a result, their judgements of men and events would become less dependent on the casual opinions of acquaintances, more informed by general principles and more sensitive to 'the dignity of human nature' and man's undoubted capacity for perfection. Such a 'frame of mind' would help the polite citizen to discover the principles of natural theology and enable him or her to engage in that comfortable, conversational relationship with the deity which Anglicans since Hooker's day had been taught to seek.

In the Addisonian city, commerce was to be a vehicle of politeness and latitudinarian theology, the source of a culture which could be re-exported to a turbulent, rustic country which had generated the super-stition and enthusiasm on which neo-exclusionist zeal continued to thrive, and above all, to that most notorious of eighteenth-century battlegrounds, the family. For the polite, Addisonian family would be based on the principles of friendship and 'mutual confidence' which had been learned in the city, rather than on the patriarchal principles on which High Church political theology rested. If, as Mr Spectator once observed, 'the obedience of children to Parents is the basis of all Government', the polite family would in time become the source of the trust on which the future of liberty and happiness depended.[45]

For all that, Addison and Steele's enterprise was highly speculative. It

[45] *Spectator*, no. 424.

was, by definition, directed against the church party and was inevitably seen as a form of propaganda designed to create a Whig false consciousness.[46] Worse still, in spite of Addison and Steele's sorties into natural theology, the language of manners and politeness never managed to shrug off the charge that it merely encouraged dissent and hypocrisy. To those who had been branded as 'strict' moralists and others who could call on the formidable resources of Augustinian moral theology, on Machiavelli and on Hobbes, claims about the power of conversation to awaken man's natural benevolence, and to foster his sense of public and Christian duty seemed dangerously naive. Swift, who detested Leslie and had actually contributed to early numbers of the *Tatler*, was still acutely sensitive to the all-pervasive power of pride in motivating even the highest forms of saintliness and virtue.[47] But Mandeville was by far the most deadly critic of this language of manners and politeness. His attack had begun anonymously in 1709, in the *Female Tatler*, and was to develop into an all-out onslaught in the *Fable of the Bees*, first published in 1714 and greatly expanded in 1723 and 1728.[48] He was able to demonstrate, with great subtlety and wit, that claims that the principles of Spectatorial propriety rested on benevolence were spurious, and constituted 'a Vast inlet into Hypocrisy, which being once made habitual, we must not only deceive others, but likewise become altogether unknown to ourselves'. Addison and Steele had simply devised a bag of tricks like those 'made use of by the women that would teach children to be mannerly' which appealed simply because they pleased parents and gratified the self-love and pride of their children.[49]

---

[46] Thus a Tory squib, 'The Three Champions', identified the *Tatler*, the *Review* and the *Observator* as three Whig 'libellers' of the constitution. It is reproduced in R. P. Bond, *The Tatler: The Making of a Literary Journal* (Cambridge MA, and London, 1971), Illustration 7. In 1738 Swift ridiculed the notion that 'politeness is the firmest foundation upon which Loyalty can be supported' commenting 'for thus happily sings the never-too-much-to-be-admired Lord H[ervey] in his truly sublime Poem, called *Loyalty defined*,
'Who's not polite, for the Pretender, is;
A Jacobite, I know him by his Phizz'
(*A Proposal for Correcting the English Tongue. Polite Conversation, etc.*, ed. H. W. Davis and L. Landa (Oxford, 1957), p. 120).

[47] For example, *A Proposal for Correcting the English Tongue etc.*, ed. Davis and Landa, pp. 243–4.

[48] Mandeville's important contributions to the *Female Tatler*, first recognized by M. M. Goldsmith (note 49) are hard to locate and have never been fully republished. A modest selection appear in the highly edited *The Female Tatler*, ed. F. Morgan (London, 1992).

[49] Mandeville, *The Fables of the Bees*, pp. 52–3 and 331. On Mandeville as a critic of politeness, see T. A. Horne, *The Social Thought of Bernard Mandeville: Virtue and Commerce in Early Eighteenth-Century England* (London, 1978) and his 'Bernard Mandeville's Ironic History of Politeness', in *Politics, Politeness and Patriotism*, ed. Schochet, pp. 229–44. See also M. M. Goldsmith, *Private Vices, Public Benefits: Bernard Mandeville's Social and Political Thought* (Cambridge, 1985); and his 'Liberty,

It was Swift's Gulliver, however, who best characterized the scepticism with which claims about the civilizing powers of politeness were met. Like Defoe's Robinson Crusoe, Gulliver appears as the model of a prudent, civilized Englishman; enterprising, observant and intelligent, well able to adapt to the laws, customs and manners of even the oddest forms of civilization. If he had possessed the mind of Robinson, such encounters with exotic forms of civilization would have provided him with more extensive views of human nature and human benevolence and equipped him for a future life of virtue. Instead, these encounters taught him that mankind was irredeemably sunk in a depravity which had only been made tolerable by naive illusions about human rationality and capacity for virtue. He returned to England stripped of illusion and unfit for human society. Travel had taught him that he could only aspire to the life of a gentle yahoo, but had left him without the slightest idea how to do so. It was a problem which was to be close to the heart of one of his greatest admirers, David Hume.

II

High Church political theology and a corresponding concern with opinion and manners appeared to the Folger seminar to be two crucial and strangely neglected features in the cultural landscape of the politics of Anne's reign. Equally, it may be suggested that these same factors played an important part in shaping the political thought of the Walpolian era. The formative period in its development was the period of the Bangorian Controversy and the Bubble Crisis when Church and public credit both seemd to be in danger and when there was good reason to fear the spread of Jacobitism and ministerial power. Once again, the agenda for political discourse was set by the opposition rather than the ministry, in this case by two opposition Whigs, Thomas Gordon and John Trenchard, much of whose thought was set out in the *London Journal* and later collected in the *Independent Whig* and in the much-reprinted *Cato's Letters*. In their hands, opposition Whiggery developed as a language of opposition concerned with controlling ministerial corruption rather than vindicating the right of resistance. It was a republican language, which drew on Machiavellian and Harringtonian resources and centralized problems created by priestcraft and opinion which had hitherto only lain in the peripheral vision of republican political thought. And it was to demonstrate how a reformation of manners could lead to the perfection of the constitution.

The importance of priestcraft and opinion in shaping opposition whiggery is most clearly apparent in Gordon's writing. In the *Independent Whig*, the classic independent Whig virtues he commended – a distrust of placemen, courtiers, and prelates; an insistence on the need to judge issues on their merits; a belief in toleration – were used as a foil for an attack on priestcraft which was designed to support the prorogation of Convocation in 1717.[50] The bitter experience of the seventeenth century, Gordon wrote, had shown that it was necessary to keep the Church's nails 'always par'd, and their wings clipp'd'.[51] It was doubly important to do so now, at a time when it was necessary to maintain an expensive navy and standing army to defend the country from Jacobites and the French. This required high taxation and that was, as ever, the mother of popular discontent which could all too easily be inflamed by religious enthusiasm and Jacobitism. As Gordon pointed out tartly

If our High Church were but equally faithful to their oaths, and equally Friends to their Country, we should have seen neither new Troops nor Rebellions. The Army has sav'd us from the High Church. But for all that I have said, I should be sorry to see the People of England either love or fear a standing Force: To do either infers Danger.[52]

This unexpected defence of a standing army as the bastion needed to curb High Church enthusiasm is an indication of the importance of priestcraft and opinion to Gordon's Independent Whiggery. However, it was in *Cato's Letters* that he and Trenchard developed their thinking about the political framework which could be supported by Independent Whig virtue.[53]

Like Defoe, Cato assumed that although the constitution was ancient,

---

[50] The church's apostolic claims were memorably described in an equally memorably titled pamphlet as 'a vast Chain, long enough to hold ten Millions of Foxes ... one End of which is tied to the Apostles, and the other to themselves, and it reaches from Jerusalem to Lambeth, taking Rome in its was' ([T. Gordon], *An Apology for the Danger of the Church, Proving that the Church is, and ought to be always in danger: and that it would be dangerous for her to be out of Danger* (London 1719), p. 23). See also Champion, *The Pillars of Priestcraft Shaken*, pp. 174–9.

[51] [T. Gordon], *The Character of an Independent Whig* (London, 1719), p. 6.

[52] *Ibid.*, p. 17.

[53] For Cato, see C. Robbins, *The Eighteenth-Century Commonwealthman* (Cambridge, MA, 1959), pp. 115–25; Pocock, *The Machiavellian Moment*, ch. xiv. See also S. Burtt, 'Private Interest, Public Passion, and Patriot Virtue: Comments on a Classical Republican Ideal in English Political Thought', in *Politics, Politeness and Patriotism*, ed. Schochet, pp. 157–78. Her important study, *Virtue Transformed*, ch. 3, shows that egoist psychology was central to Cato's political thought but does not, in my view, take enough account of his concerns with opinion.

its principles could best be understood in terms of the philosophies of Pufendorf and Harrington and the effects of the recent progress of society on the common law. But Cato was more interested in political engineering than moral engineering and in perfecting the constitution rather than merely preserving it. He was Harringtonian in his preoccupation with power and property, in his interest in the use of legislation and rotations to maintain the balance between them and in his overriding concern with maintaining civil peace. He was neo-Harringtonian in recognizing that it was better to secure peace by perfecting the principles of a restored Saxon constitution than by undertaking utopian exercises in constitutional engineering or in redistributing property.[54] Likewise, he identified the recent growth in the military and civil powers of the crown as important threats to the balance of the constitution and recognized the value of militias in restoring the balance between power and property and releasing the citizen's capacity for civic virtue.

Yet this was Harringtonian and neo-Harringtonian thought with a difference. Unlike Swift and later Bolingbroke, Cato was not exclusively concerned with the civic virtue which was attached to landed property. In an age of commerce, he was prepared to recognize that 'companies' (provided they did not turn into monopolies) had legitimate interests which had to be accommodated politically if the balance of power and property was to be maintained.[55] Indeed, in one essay, which argued the case for a regular rotation of ministries, Trenchard went so far as to liken the relationship between a ministry and parliament to that of a board and its shareholders. There

the General Court, composed of all its Members, constitutes the Legislature, and the Consent of that Court is the sanction of their Laws; and there the Administration of their affairs is put under the Conduct of a certain Number chosen by the Whole. Here every Man concerned saw the Necessity of securing Part of their property, by putting the Persons entrusted under proper Regulations; however remiss they may be in taking care of the Whole. And if Provision had been made, That, as a Third Part of the Directors are to go out every Year, so none should stay above Three . . ..[56]

What troubled Cato more, however, was the problem of controlling opinion. It was opinion as much as shifts in the distribution of property that had been responsible for destroying the gothic constitution in the previous century. Nowadays, it was opinion that was obscuring the thinking of companies, parties and religious sects about the true nature

[54] *Cato's Letters: or Essays on Liberty, Civil and Religious and Other Important Subjects*, 5th edn, 4 vols, (London, 1748), I, p. lv.
[55] For example, *Cato's Letters*, no. 10, 3 January 1720/1.
[56] *Ibid.*, no. 60, 6 January 1721.

of their interests.[57] Opinion encouraged faction and ministerial corruption; indeed, Jacobitism and stockjobbing could now be seen as manifestations of the sort of enthusiasm which had destroyed the constitution a century before. Opinion was a new form of *fortuna* which would have to be mastered if liberty was to be preserved.

This allowed Cato to offer a new analysis of political corruption. He showed how factions manipulated parliaments and ministries in the hope of persuading them to create 'monopolies' in trade, commerce and religion. He showed how these had a tendency to exclude those in possession of property from access to political power. Frequent parliaments and frequently rotating ministries, such as those which had preserved Roman and Harringtonian liberty, would put an end to such corruption. But this would be impossible without a party system which was free from faction and purged of the opinions which distorted a true understanding of the public interest. This meant that all parties, Whig and Tory, High Church and Low Church, would have to come to an *éclaircissement* and reach an understanding that their common interest lay in preserving the present constitution.[58] This required a reformation of manners to curb the Spectatorial moderation which threatened to undermine the natural spirit of jealousy that fuelled the citizen's sense of right and obligation. Indeed, moderation was simply a new manifestation of the sort of superstition that had made Englishmen careless of their liberties in the past.[59] What was needed was a new understanding of the principles of human nature and new histories of Rome and England to teach citizen to distrust *all* ministers, as a matter of principle, even those who held office in a country which was governed by 'a wise and beneficent prince, a generous and publick-spirited Parliament and an able and disinterested Ministry'.[60] Catonic anger, properly directed to the perfection of the constitution, would leave the country with a constitution in which the balance of opinion, property and power would remain perpetually in equilibrium, and would make those *ricorsi* which had devastated England in the past redundant.

Cato's politics looked back to the early years of Anne's reign, when parliaments had been triennial rather than septennial and when the queen had lived in the hope of creating ministries of able counsellors, drawn from different parties. Bolingbroke, however, had less visionary fish to fry. By the late 1720's, when his onslaught on the ministry was at its fiercest, oligarchy was better established than it had been in Cato's

---

[57] For example, *Ibid.*, no. 16, 11 February 1720/1.
[58] *Ibid.*, no. 16, 11 February 1720/1; no. 85, 14 July 1722.   [59] *Ibid.*
[60] *Ibid.*, no. 3, 19 November 1720.

day, and the problems of mounting an effective opposition was correspondingly more acute. In trying to awaken the spirit of Catonic liberty, Cato had addressed the people at large; Bolingbroke, however, simply wanted to target freeholders. Cato wrote about the *possibility* of corruption; Bolingbroke thought he had *real* corruption to cope with. Cato had glimpsed a world in which future *ricorsi* would be unnecessary; Bolingbroke failed to see how the Robinocracy could be dislodged without one. For Bolingbroke, in other words, Cato's thought had moved too far from its Machiavellian moorings.

Bolingbroke is generally seen as a Tory who appropriated an opposition Whig theory of the constitution in order to sustain a neo-Harringtonian conception of the constitution.[61] He stressed the contractual nature of government, the antiquity of a constitution whose principles had been reaffirmed in 1688 and 1689, and the importance of the Commons in articulating the voice of the people. He continually poured scorn on exploded ideas of divine right and passive obedience. He regarded the Revolution as a genuine *ricorso* which had laid the foundations of a modern system of liberty and opened the gate to new forms of corruption. Of these, none was more important than the modern party system. This had sprung up after the Revolution in response to the growing influence of the Crown and the misgovernment of corrupt ministries – a development which he found to be analogous to the growth of parties during the reigns of the early Stuarts.[62] This was the context in which he set his celebrated case for a new *ricorso*, engineered by a new country party, to put an end to party altogether. This required a new spirit of patriotism and an appropriate reformation of manners. Much of Bolingbroke's political writing was directed to this end. Sometimes he invoked 'the true old English spirit, which prevailed in the days of our fathers' in an attempt to catch the ears of country Whigs and country Tories.[63] But he was more interested in tracing the origin of the spirit of modern patriotism which had followed the decline of feudal tenures and the rise of the gentry. Struggles for liberty in the feudal era had been merely ephemeral because they had not been based in the claims of property. Indeed, Magna Carta had been no more than the 'accidental outcome' of a quarrel between the crown and its subjects,

[61] Kramnick, *Bolingbroke and his Circle*, chs. 3, 4, 6; Pocock, *The Machiavellian Moment*, pp. 477–86; H. T. Dickinson, *Liberty and Property*, esp. pp. 177–8. Burtt, *Virtue Transformed*, ch. 4. Q. Skinner, 'The Principles and Practice of Opposition. The Case of Bolingbroke versus Walpole', in *Historical Perspectives. Studies in English Thought and Society in honour of J. H. Plumb*, ed. N. McKendrick (London, 1974), pp. 93–128 is indispensable.
[62] *The Works of Lord Bolingbroke*, 4 vols. (Philadelphia, 1841; repr. 1969), II, pp. 147–72.
[63] *Ibid.*, I, p. 295.

rather than 'the natural effect of the property and power that was lodged in the barons and clergy'.[64] In Cato's vision, the Catonic anger of the modern independent Whig would free modern parties from corruption and restore the balance of the constitution. But Bolingbroke thought that corruption had penetrated too deep into the fabric of the constitution to allow that to happen. In his more Machiavellian vision, rulers were 'the most powerful of all reformers' and a patriot king, ruling with the consent of a patriot propertied class, was needed to abolish party and to restore liberty.[65]

The ministerial reaction to Cato's and Bolingbroke's assaults on the Robinocracy is not particularly easy to analyse. Much of it was developed in the 1730s in such journals as the *London Journal* and the *Gazeteer* by writers such as James Pitt, William Arnall and Ralph de Courteville, who have only recently begun to attract the attention they deserve. In their hands, the ministry developed an often sophisticated if reactive response to the opposition, which, like Cato's Whiggery, looked back to the political world of Anne's reign.[66]

In a polemical world which was dominated by the opposition, it was inevitable that the first task of court writers would be to legitimize a ministry whose power rested on the Septennial Act, the decision to suspend Convocation and on the influence of the crown. To judge from Pitt and Arnall's writing, what is surprising is the circumspection they showed and the use they made of Cato's appeals to independent Whigs to attack Bolingbroke. Thus, the cutting edge of Pitt's vindication of the ministry was based on a Catonic defence of the party system Bolingbroke was committed to destroy. Free parties, like frequent elections and rotating ministries, he wrote, were necessary to a free constitution; indeed, 'the oftner the Power returns into the Hands of the People the more secure they are of their Liberties', adding 'but in this the Whigs themselves do not agree'.[67] Thus, the Septennial Act could be defended as an act of necessity which was necessary to preserve the constitution and the succession and, paradoxically, the party system. It also allowed him to argue, on proto-Humean grounds, that the influence of the crown

---

[64] *Ibid.*, I, p. 361.   [65] *Ibid.*, II, pp. 96, 396–7.

[66] The materials necessary for a proper study of the ministerial press are notoriously difficult to assemble. What follows here is heavily indebted to the following sources: J. A. W. Gunn, 'Court Whiggery – Justifying Innovation', in *Politics, Politeness and Patriotism*, ed. Schochet, pp. 125–56; T. A. Horne, 'Politics in a Corrupt Society: William Arnall's Defence of Robert Walpole', *Journal of the History of Ideas* 41 (1980), 601–14; M. M. Goldsmith, 'Faction Detected: Ideological Consequences of Robert Walpole's Decline and Fall', *History* 64 (1979), pp. 1–19. See also Burtt, *Virtue Transformed*, ch. 6. My discussion is to be regarded as provisional.

[67] *Daily Gazeteer*, 9 December 1736. Quoted in Gunn, 'Court Whiggery', p. 139.

could be legitimately used to counterbalance the growing wealth of the Commons which was threatening to upset the balance of the constitution.

This Catonic defence of the Robinocracy had interesting implications. In the first place, it allowed Pitt and other ministerial writers to develop a distinctive account of the place of party and interest in a free constitution. Like Cato, Pitt and Arnall understood the complexities of opinion; as the former put it, 'It requires no Art to govern by Force or mere Power, but the greatest to govern by the Management of other People's Opinions, Prejudices, Passions and different Views in Life'.[68] But where Cato had sought to free parties from the interest groups that clamoured for political attention, ministerial writers seem to have regarded this interplay of ministry, party and interest groups as the stuff of modern politics. All commercial societies were made up of 'jarring Interests, always opposite, often clashing'.[69] It was absurd to expect the public to speak with a single voice and it was the task of a prudent government to maintain an 'equilibrium' between them. As someone – possibly Henry Fielding – put it in 1734.

Where an unrestrain'd Freedom and Liberty is allow'd, Sectaries in Religion and Parties in Politicks, whose interests are as opposite as their Tenets and Opinions, will abound, and thus it is impossible for any Administration whatsoever, in such a State, so to . . . accommodate their Conduct, as to gain the Good-liking and Affection of all the different Parties. The utmost within the Compass of human Nature, in such a nice and ticklish Station, is so to maintain the *internal Balance* between the great Variety of Interests, as to preserve the Government stable upon the broadest Basis; to attach a Majority of the Nation's Strength to the governing Power, that the Constitution may never be liable to any destructive Changes and Revolutions.[70]

This argument, which identified the ministry, rather than Parliament or people, as the custodian of the public interest, could now be used to develop a defence of Walpole as a prudent minister whose task was to preserve the constitution at a time when civil order and public credit was being threatened by Jacobitism. And it enabled court writers to offer a Whig defence of the right of the king to appoint a prudent if unpopular minister who enjoyed the trust of a parliament to whom the people had delegated their powers.

It is important to notice how profoundly the political thought of

---

[68] *Daily Gazeteer*, 6 March 1736. Quoted in Gunn, 'Court Whiggery', p. 139.
[69] *Weekly Journal or British Gazette*, 15 April 1721. Quoted in Gunn, 'Court Whiggery', p. 140.
[70] Quoted in J. A. W. Gunn, *Faction No More: Attitudes to Party in Government and Opposition in Eighteenth Century England* (London 1972), p. 21.

Anne's reign and the Walpolian era had been shaped by the adversarial demands of party politics. It is even more important to notice the crucial part that High Anglican political thought had played in shaping Grub Street polemic, in its formative years during Anne's reign. Here, after all, was political thought which was firmly rooted in the authority of revealed religion, in a defence of patriarchy, the primitive church and the ancient rights and apostolic claims of the Church of England. It was on these narrow historical and theological foundations and on the defence of antiquity, that the defence of divine right and passive obedience depended.[71] It is interesting that so many of the writers we have been considering were increasingly reluctant to place so heavy a reliance on the authority of antiquity in validating their accounts of revolution principles. Defoe and Hoadly, Addison and Steele, Cato and Bolingbroke had all appealed to Grotius, Pufendorf, and Harrington in order to distance themselves from High Church defences of the English polity. They had viewed the reformation of manners as a mechanism for curbing High Church enthusiasm, and for manipulating opinion, that new manifestation of *fortuna*, which had the power to make and break constitutions and to generate new conceptions of public and private interests. Natural jurisprudence and Harringtonian and neo-Harringtonian discourse, deployed with an unabashed eclecticism, had proved to be the most favoured resources in curbing the superstition and enthusiasm which the old neo-exclusionist discourse of Anne's reign continued to generate and to rebuild parties on new foundations.

All of this added up to a highly eclectic and intellectually incoherent political culture. For example, questions about the origins of government and the nature of political obligation, about the relationship between natural and conventional rights, about the relevance of ancient and modern example for modern political conduct, had been raised without being intellectually resolved, provoking questions whether contemporary Britain was capable of developing a coherent political culture capable of sustaining the Revolution and Hanoverian succession. It is in this context that it is worth turning to Scotland and to David Hume. For it was here, in a political world that was remote from that of London and from English party political discourse, that the most serious contemporary attempts to develop a coherent and peculiarly *British* political culture were to be made. And with David Hume, Augustan Britain acquired a philosopher and historian who developed a strikingly coherent if uncomfortable defence of revolution principles and an

---

[71] On the future development of Anglican political theology, see R. E. Sullivan, 'The Transformation of Anglican Political Theology, *c.* 1716–1760', in *Politics, Politeness and Patriotism*, ed. Schochet, pp. 47–58.

equally problematic account of the problems of maintaining the liberty and prosperity of modern Britain.

III

At one level, the history of Scottish political thought is a story about the manner in which those languages of rights, virtue, and manners which were instrumental in shaping contemporary English political thought were appropriated in Scotland. However, that happened in a political world which was significantly different from that of England. In Scotland, the Revolution and revolution principles carried their own meanings and questions about the Hanoverian Succession. The growth in the influence of the crown and the progress of commerce and empire became inextricably intertwined with fundamental questions about Anglo-Scottish relations and the arguments for and against a new Union. Under these circumstances, it was scarcely surprising that the public life of this small underdeveloped polity came to revolve around questions about its 'independence', that were to be construed in a 'British' rather than an 'English' context. What is, perhaps, more surprising is that its political culture achieved a higher level of abstraction than that which we have been considering.

It is worth reflecting for a moment longer on the contexts in which the Scots set out to reconstruct their political culture. In England, the Revolution had been variously presented as a defence of an ancient constitution, a Harringtonian *ricorso* made necessary by the failure of the constitution to accommodate shifts in the distribution of power and property, or a Machiavellian *ricorso* which had returned the constitution to its fundamental principles. In Scotland, the Revolution Settlement had been far more radical than that of England, firmly eschewing toleration and placing the most severe limitations on the civil and ecclesiastical powers of the crown. In so doing, it looked back, in the most uncompromising manner, to 1638 and to the Rebellion, setting discussions about resistance in a context that most English political thinkers had studiously tried to avoid.[72] Attitudes to Scottish revolution principles were, however, to be influenced profoundly by the

---

[72] B. P. Lenman usefully discusses the lack of debate about Scottish revolution principles in 'The Poverty of Political Theory in the Scottish Revolution of 1688–90', in *The Revolution of 1688–89: Changing Perspectives*, ed. L. G. Schwoerer (Cambridge, 1992), pp. 244–59. This is not the same thing as saying that the political classes lacked ideological conviction. The Exclusion Crisis and the Revolution both badly need the attention of Scottish historians. But this needs to be set against W. Ferguson's idiosyncratic and underrated *Scotland's Relations with England: a Survey to 1707* (Edinburgh, 1977), chs. 9–10. The subject requires further investigation.

politics of the 1690s. Scottish political and religious life became faction-alized and royal government uncertain and insecure. It fertilized an anglophobia that fed on high tax demands, endemic corruption and continual English interference in Scottish politics, and it was plagued by well-founded apprehensions that the court would attempt to impose toleration on the Presbyterian kirk. Worst of all, so far from encouraging the expansion of the Scottish economy, William's wars had done little more than immiserate a country with a feudal agrarian economy and a system of overseas trade which was being devastated by the effects of international war.[73] When Scots looked back to the Revolution Settle-ment from the politically secure and economically promising plateau of the 1750s, they saw it as an attempt to secure property, religion and liberty which had conspicuously failed to curb the influence of the crown, the kirk, and a nobility whose power remained firmly rooted in a system of feudal tenures. In this broadly neo-Harringtonian view, the Act of Union of 1707 and the Hanoverian Succession had been necessary to correct and reinforce revolution principles and to lay the foundations of a system of civil liberty which would secure the 'independence' of a province of the English crown.[74]

The Scottish debate about the Act of Union, which ran from 1701 to 1707, was as important in shaping Scottish political culture as the English debate about revolution principles. Indeed, it is worth remem-bering that whereas the celebration of the tercentenary of the Glorious Revolution passed almost unnoticed in England, the Act of Union still plays a crucial part in shaping the Scottish politics of the British party system. The debate about an 'incorporating' Anglo-Scottish union was precipitated by the collapse of the Darien scheme and coincided with the Act of Settlement. The future of commerce and the Hanoverian suc-cession alerted the Scots to the importance of commerce and credit for maintaining a free polity, and it taught a poor country a lesson which a rich country only learned a generation later as a result of the Bubble Crisis. The question of the succession gave the Scots the opportunity of exacting free trade as a price for recognizing the Hanoverian Succession. That connection was made by an irascible, intelligent Scots republican member of parliament, Andrew Fletcher of Saltoun. He steered an Act

---

[73] For the political background, see P. W. J. Riley, *The Union of England and Scotland: A Study in Anglo-Scottish Politics of the Eighteenth Century* (Manchester, 1978) and the same author's, *King William and the Scottish Politicians* (Edinburgh, 1979); W. Ferguson, *Scotland: 1689 to the Present* (Edinburgh, 1968), chs. 1–4. For the economic background, see T. C. Smout, *Scottish Trade on the Eve of the Union, 1660–1707* (Edinburgh, 1963). But cf. B. P. Lenman, *An Economic History of Modern Scotland 1660–1976* (London, 1977).

[74] N. Phillipson, *Hume* (London and New York, 1989), ch. 2.

of Security through the Scots parliament in 1703 which made recognition of the Hanoverian Succession conditional on extending the radical principles of the Scottish revolution settlement and giving the Scots free access to English markets at home and overseas. Fletcher's Act of Security was a Harringtonian document, and the subtle and intelligent thought it embodied was to set the agenda for future discussion of what may be called union principles in Scotland. For Harringtonian republicanism was to play the same catalytic part in shaping political debate in Scotland as High Anglicanism did in England.[75]

Fletcher, like Trenchard, made his debut as a political thinker with a contribution to the militia controversy in 1697–8 which served as the opening chapter to a much more elaborate science of politics. Terse and elliptical, *A Discourse of Government Concerning Militias* was the most acute of all contributions to the militia controversy. However, it also contained a powerful critique of English neo-Harringtonianism. For Fletcher was a Harringtonian of a peculiarly Scottish stamp, an unashamed 'utopian' of the sort Tutchin and Trenchard had distrusted. As a Scottish patriot, he wanted to return the Scottish constitution to the fundamental principles of 1638 and 1688. This would create the conditions in which a virtuous parliament could engineer a shift in the balance of power and property by means of agrarian laws and a system of public credit. These would destroy feudal tenures and the power of a factious nobility and encourage the progress of agriculture, trade, manufactures and employment. All of Fletcher's political thinking was geared to achieving this Harringtonian end. But it was a far more complex matter than English neo-Harringtonians had realised. Placing limitations on the power of the crown would doubtless restore the independence of local communities and enable them to be governed by a virtuous gentry. But Fletcher did not believe that traditional country institutions were capable of checking the growing influence of the crown or of providing the military resources which were needed to defend the kingdom in an age of advanced military technology. Moreover, he thought that it was dangerous to discuss the libertarian virtues of militias in terms of the part they had played in the feudal age. Indeed, in writing about 'the past and present governments of Europe' he was anxious 'to disabuse those who think them the same, because they are called by the same names'. Instead, he called for an extension of Scottish revolution principles to Britain as a whole and a radical reorganization of its regional structure. This would be done by replacing the county

[75] J. Robertson, *The Scottish Enlightenment and the Militia Issue* (Edinburgh, 1985). See also my 'The Scottish Enlightenment' in *The Enlightenment in National Contexts*, ed. R. Porter and M. Teich (Cambridge, 1981), pp. 19–40.

structure of Britain with five huge militia camps which would be seats of government, commerce and culture and would provide for the defence of the nation. Like the Covenanters, he was proposing to create a British polity on Scottish terms.

I perceive now [says an interlocutor in Fletcher's utopian conversation about the future of British liberty] the tendency of all this discourse. On my conscience he has contrived the whole scheme to no other end than to set his country on an equal foot with England and the rest of the world. To tell you the truth, said I, the insuperable difficulty of making my country happy by any other way, led me insensibly to the discovery of these things which, if I mistake not, have no other tendency than to render not only my own country, but all mankind as happy as the imperfections of human nature will admit'.[76]

This, then, was a full-blown Harringtonian vision of a modern Oceana. It was a limited monarchy in which the balance of power between king and people would be underpinned by a balance of property and by a balance between court and country which would be maintained by regional parliaments and militias. It was this model to which ministerial politicians had to respond in the fascinating debate which took place between 1703 and 1707. As John Robertson has shown, that response offered a natural-jurisprudential analysis of the condition of Scotland, and, perhaps predictably, it called for a reformation of manners to create a 'friendly' relationship between two distinct nations.[77] During these debates, the case for such a reformation was set out by Defoe.[78] Therafter, the reformation of manners became closely associated with Spectatorial politeness. What is more, Scottish politeness was to become associated with a new North British patriotism which was directed to 'compleating' and perfecting the union on which the preservation of liberty and independence depended. For in Scotland, completing the Union was to become as important to preserving liberty as perfecting the Revolution in England.[79]

These Scottish concerns with manners, politeness and patriotism were to be reinforced by philosophy and here the Presbyterian kirk was all-important. The abolition of episcopacy and the restoration of

---

[76] *Fletcher of Saltoun: Selected Political Writings and Speeches*, ed. D. Daiches (Edinburgh, 1979), p. 136.

[77] J. Robertson, *The Scottish Enlightenment and the Militia Question*. The Union was the subject of a major reappraisal in the Folger Institute's Seminar 'Union, State and Empire: the Political Identities of Britain, 1688–1750', directed by John Robertson. Its proceedings are forthcoming in J. C. Robertson (ed.), *A Union for Empire: The Union of 1707 in the Context of British Political Thought* (Cambridge).

[78] See J. Robertson's suggestive comments in 'Redefining Sovereignty: The Course of the Union Debate in Scotland, 1698–1707', presented to the Folger Institute Seminar 'Union, State and Empire: the Political Identities of Britain, 1688–1750'.

[79] See my *Hume*, esp. ch. 2 and the works cited there.

Presbyterianism in 1690 – which high flyers thought of as a Third Reformation – brought about a purge of the universities of Episcopalian and non-juring professors and regents, and precipitated an inquiry into the state of the curricula. This quickly developed into a protracted and intricate dispute between orthodox and moderate Presbyterians about the principles of clerical education, which revolved around the question of whether and how the natural jurisprudence of Grotius and Pufendorf could be adapted to suit presbyterian needs. Grotius, after all was Arminian and straightforwardly heretical according to the canons of the Westminster Confession of Faith; Pufendorf was dangerously Hobbist.[80] As James Moore and others have shown, this was an operation which involved a meticulous and sophisticated re-examination of the metaphysical principles on which natural jurisprudence was founded and of the moral and political thought which was derived from it. Here, then, was an intellectual enterprise which involved exploring the intellectual foundations of the political language in which ministerial defences of revolution principles were being articulated. It was an enterprise in which Francis Hutcheson, the Scots-Irish moral theologian, was deeply involved and it is one to which David Hume was exposed as a student, philosopher and historian and it is with his political thought that the last part of this essay is concerned.[81]

Hume's interest in the legitimacy of the Revolution, the Revolution Settlement and the Hanoverian Succession was deep and longstanding.[82] He addressed the question of election and divine right, resistance and passive obedience, as a philosopher in the *Treatise of Human Nature* (1739–40) and in the *Essays Moral and Political* (1741/2/8). He addressed them as a historian in the *History of England* (1754–63). He devoted two of his *Political Discourses* (1752) to essays defending the Protestant succession and reflecting on the nature of a perfect common-

---

[80] See my 'The Pursuit of Virtue in Scottish University Education: Dugald Stewart and Scottish Moral Philosophy', in *Universities, Society and the Future*, ed. N. T. Phillipson (Edinburgh, 1983), pp. 82–100.

[81] See particularly, J. Moore, 'The Two Systems of Francis Hutcheson: Between Civic Moralism and Natural Jurisprudence', in *Politics, Politeness and Patriotism*, ed. Schochet, pp. 281–304, and the revised version 'The Two Systems of Francis Hutcheson: On the Origin of the Scottish Enlightenment', in *Studies in the Philosophy of the Scottish Enlightenment*, ed. M. A. Stewart (Oxford, 1990), pp. 37–59. But compare K. Haakonssen, 'Natural Law and Moral realism: The Scottish Synthesis', in the same volume, pp. 61–85.

[82] What follows summarizes and develops the argument in my *Hume* and 'Propriety, Property and Prudence: David Hume and the Defence of the Revolution', in *Studies in Political Discourse in Early Modern Britain*, ed. N. Phillipson and Q. Skinner (Cambridge, 1993). The first sketch of that argument was presented to the Folger Institute Seminar under the title 'Politics and Politeness in the Philosophy of David Hume; in *Politics, Politeness and Patriotism*, ed. Schochet, pp. 305–18.

wealth. In so doing, he addressed the neo-exclusionist agenda of Anne's reign so closely that Locke is made to appear, possibly for the last time, as a radical exclusionist. At one level, Hume's response to this agenda was that of a theorist of manners of Anne's reign who differed from Defoe, Addison and Steele only in approaching the subject as a religious sceptic. He was anxious to strip neo-Ciceronianism of its dependence on natural theology and to extend the discussion of conversation and discourse to questions about the origins of the citizen's ideas of justice, politics, morals, religion and taste. He showed that there were good reasons for believing that all our cognitive powers could be attributed to linguistic experience, gained, as he was fond of saying, in the course of common life. Thus, all human knowledge could be regarded as convention-based, gaining its authority from custom and habit. As such, he appeared as a self-confessed 'sceptical Whig' who showed that the Revolution, the Hanoverian Succession and the grubby machine politics of the Robinocracy could only be defended on *de facto* grounds as necessary for the maintenance of the political order on which justice and the progress of commerce depended.

There can be no doubt that Hume would have been content to have introduced the gist of this somewhat rudimentary line of thought into the existing language of politeness; his earliest essays suggest that he hoped for a popular Spectatorial audience. However, his engagement with contemporary discourse was more intricate and equivocal than this outline suggests. He understood the power of Mandeville's critique of politeness and he recognized the importance of pride and interest in shaping our understanding of justice, politics and morality and, explosively, religion. At the same time, he was a powerful critic of Mandeville, who had learned from Hutcheson to be wary of the language of self-love and to take note of the constraints of language in encouraging us to relate our own interests to those of the 'public' without continually indulging in prudential calculations. Hume was enabled to formulate a new, powerful and paradoxical theory of resistance which drew on two radical extremes, that of the Commonwealthman and the Jacobite. Since political conventions rested on considerations of interest, Hume was forced to conclude that the right of resistance was by its nature, universal and unlimited: 'Since 'tis impossible, even in the most despotic governments to deprive [the people] of it'. On the other hand, since the only reason we submit to government is to preserve the rules of justice on which life and property depend, the root of political obligation must lie in a 'natural' disposition to submit to establish authority.[83] All that

[83] D. Hume, *Treatise of Human Nature*, ed. L. W. Selby-Bigge, 2nd ed. ed. P. H. Nidditch. (Oxford, 1978), pp. 563–64 and 545.

could possibly limit the exercise of that 'right' was, therefore, consider-ations of prudence. In other words, the test of what constituted legitimate resistance was enshrined in manners, language and culture.

This distinctive preoccupation with prudence made Hume an acute analyst of contemporary political culture and of party in particular. It also focused his attention on parties of 'principle', which were founded on mutually exclusive beliefs about the nature of the constitution and the rights and duties which were enshrined in it. At one level, as his *History of England* showed, it made him a devastating analyst and critic of the priestcraft which so often lay at the heart of 'principles'. It also made him a radical critic of Bolingbroke's spurious attempts to abolish party distinctions altogether; these were too deeply embedded in the political system to be eradicated without running the risk of political disorder. He recognized the historical necessity of party although with considerably less enthusiasm than Cato. Like Cato, he hoped for an *éclaircissement* to close the gap between interest and principle. It would ensure that party differences were contained by a recognition that the future of liberty depended on preserving a constitution which might not be the best system of liberty in the modern world but was certainly the most complete. As the measured Tacitean disdain of 'A Character of Sir Robert Walpole' suggests, any minister who was required to manage the affairs of an imperfect polity which was plagued with party and corruption was to be regarded with sceptical detachment rather than outright distrust.[84] This, rather than Spectatorial moderation or Catonic anger, was the hallmark of Hume's celebrated sceptical whiggery.

All of Hume's understanding of the sort of prudence that was needed to preserve a far from matchless constitution stemmed from his under-standing of property. For Hume, the universal desire to secure and enjoy our temporal possessions, rather than the prospect of the rewards of the life hereafter, provided a much more plausible explanation of our willingness to enter those conventions in which we recognized the need for justice and political authority and acquired the ability to conceive of a public interest. All ideas of modern prudence flowed from remember-ing these truths, and all ideas of liberty and happiness stemmed from the sense of security we enjoyed when political authority was secure. Like Defoe and Addison, but with more acuity than either, Hume saw that security in the terrene world would naturally generate curiosity, improvement and material and moral progress, restoring trust in government and furthering the course of virtue. In this analysis, the

---

[84] *Essays Moral, Political and Literary*, pp. 574–6.

natural disposition of human beings to *forget* how they acquired their ideas of interest, their proneness to fantasy, their extraordinary vulnerability to priestcraft, constituted both the greatest strength and weakness of human nature. This was the great theme of the *History of England*. Hume's analysis of the disastrous history of the seventeenth century drew on Harrington and Clarendon to show how opinion and priestcraft had combined to obscure contemporaries' understanding of the historic changes which were taking place in the distribution of power and property as a result of the decline of feudal tenures. It was a demonstration of the depths of folly into which superstition and enthusiasm could plunge apparently prudent men. Only Humean prudence had the power to close the gap between the neo-exclusionist politics of party and a neo-Harringtonian perception of the changing patterns of power and property which were characteristic of the modern age. It was a sceptical language of manners, of great power and complexity, which would be developed with epochal consequences during the reign of George III by the great historical jurists of the Scottish Enlightenment, and it would be used by Burke to analyze the causes of the French Revolution, the catastrophe which brought about the destruction of the early modern state.

IV

The development of a language of manners marks a break in the continuities of early modern political thought in Britain. It was evident to Defoe and Hume, as it has been ever since, that the foundations of modern British political thought had been laid during the seismatic upheavals of the seventeenth century. As they saw, it was a century which had seen the birth of the politics of 'principle', in which questions about natural and divine rights, resistance and passive obedience, had penetrated and fractured the political and ecclesiastical fabric of the British kingdoms. But it was also the century of Grotius, Pufendorf and Harrington, which had given birth to new and less radical theories of rights and obligations, and a new means of comprehending the shifts in the balance of power and property which had taken place in the modern era. Above all, perhaps, it was the century which had witnessed a massive examination of the history of the common law which linked the ancient and modern constitution of Britain. Clarendon, Rapin and Hume's 'impartial' histories provided worrying and controversial accounts of the circumstances in which the politics of 'principle' had been created. But the remarkable and understudied scepticism and Hobbism of the period had provided valuable polemical resources with which to assail the epistemological authority of the claims about rights and duties on which those principles had been founded. This scepticism had threatened to reduce political knowledge to opinion, and opinion to the vagaries of the imagination and passions. It had demonstrated the power of priestcraft and the press to generate superstition and enthusiasm and to create the distrust of political authority which theorists of manners now feared would undermine revolution principles themselves.

We have already glanced briefly at the pressures to which defenders of the Revolution and the Hanoverian Succession responded in attempting to defend resistance in terms of conventional as well as natural rights, shifting the focus of political argument from ancient to modern sources of authority, invoking the changing interests of modern Britain rather than the increasingly tarnished example of Saxon antiquity. Indeed, we might have noticed the attempts of such High Church historians as Thomas Carte and, in the reign of George III, of that inspired fraud 'Ossian' MacPherson, to strengthen Tory claims to the ideological custody of an ancient patriarchal world regulated by the principles of pre-Saxon and Celtic feudalism. For it was not until the 'historical age' of George III, that Whigs from Catharine Macaulay to Fox and Millar would address the problem of recovering the Saxon past for Whiggery, in this way preparing the ground for the great Macaulay. The purpose of this essay has been to take a step towards advancing the claim that it was the language of manners, drawing eclectically on the resources of natural jurisprudence and Harrington, on natural theology and Shaftesburian aesthetics, that formed the cultural bridge which links the pre-Revolutionary party culture of an Exclusionist world to the post-Revolutionary world of war, empire and commerce. It was a development which reintroduced Cicero into the vocabulary of British politics as the author of a language of counsel designed for the city rather than the court and for a population whose opinions were now seen as not less important for the preservation of liberty than the advice of ministers.

This language of manners offered a *de facto* defence of an increasingly well-established political order, in which the balance of power and property was changing and the relationship between Crown, Parliament and people must change also. Hume had been able to show that, properly employed, it was a *de facto* language which sanctioned all evolutionary change, that is to say, all change which was underpinned by those patterns of consent and trust which had their roots in convention and culture. It was a language which aroused the hope that the rage of party would give way to a regular party system, that the politics of rights would give way to the politics of virtue, and that virtue would be construed as a matter of preserving liberties which were enshrined in constitutional principles, and a common law whose roots were ancient but whose fabric had been refined by the progress of society and the spread of civility and culture.

8   Political thought in the English-speaking Atlantic, 1760–1790
Part 1: The imperial crisis

J. G. A. Pocock

The sixteenth and seventeenth centuries are conveniently divisible at critical events near the end of the sixth decade of each: the accession of Elizabeth I in 1558, the restoration of Charles II in 1660. To divide the eighteenth century at 1760, the date of George III's accession, risks seeming to perpetuate ancient myths about a new departure in politics occasioned by that king's policies and personality. These myths are long exploded. Nevertheless, Britain was still a personal monarchy – it can be argued that George III was the last great personal monarch in its history – and in the history of its discourse it is in fact possible to find some new departures, taking their rise from actions the new king took, or was said to have taken, soon after his accession. The myth of George III is a fact of this kind of history, even if it presents as facts events and intentions which must be dismissed as myths from history of another kind, and this proposition has implications for the writing of history in general. There is therefore a case for commencing a chapter from the year 1760; but it is necessary to go further back in search of events and processes in political history and the history of political literature which gave what began to happen soon after that year its character.

The failure of Prince Charles Edward's attempt on the throne in 1745–46 can be seen in hindsight as the end of the Jacobite threat which since 1689 had done much to destabilize British politics by keeping alive the knowledge that there existed a dynastic alternative.[1] But the military defeat of the exiled Stuarts did not immediately eliminate everything which had kept the Hanoverian dynasty imperfectly legitimized, and it is argued that the disappearance of the Jacobite alternative,

---

[1] The literature on this, which has much affected our understanding of Hanoverian Britain, includes: Eveline Cruickshanks (ed.), *Ideology and Conspiracy: Aspects of Jacobitism, 1689–1715* (Edinburgh, 1982); Linda Colley, *In Defiance of Oligarchy: The Tory party, 1714–1760* (Cambridge, 1982); Daniel Szechi, *Jacobitism and Tory Politics, 1710–14* (Edinburgh, 1984); F. J. McLynn, *The Jacobites* (London, 1985); Bruce Lenman, *The Jacobite Risings in Britain, 1689–1714* (London, 1980); Paul Kléber Monod, *Jacobitism and the English People, 1688–1788* (Cambridge, 1989).

as and when it was perceived, did something toward a further destabilization of parliamentary politics, by obliging the contestants to confront one another on new grounds.[2] A problem for interpreters of the reign of George III is to explain how a regime, newly stabilized by its liberation from assaults in the name of dynastic legitimacy, came rapidly to find itself destabilized by assaults using the language of commonwealth patriotism and the 'good old cause'.

A combination of causes had brought it about that Charles Edward's invasion had become little more than an incursion by some Highland clans; this had been defeated, and the Highlands of Scotland had been subjected to military occupation and to policies aimed at changing their social structure and eliminating its military threat.[3] Great Britain was perhaps the only major kingdom of western Europe which believed itself open on a barbarian frontier. Yet there was little cause for satisfaction. The Highland charge was tactically obsolete, and the clans were looked on as a rabble of naked savages; but they had occupied the whole of Lowland Scotland against little opposition, and penetrated deep into the English midlands for the first if also the last time since the Roman withdrawal. The Hanoverian regime, powerful in Europe and beyond, was revealed as politically and militarily weak in both its British kingdoms (though Ireland was significantly quiescent). We proceed to consider the consequences of this revelation in Scottish and English political discourse.

In Scotland, where there was no central scene of political activity, discourse was literary and philosophical, belonging to and seeking to reinforce the polite culture of the clubs. Richard B. Sher's important study of the Edinburgh Moderates[4] recounts how a group of young clerics, dismayed by the absence of resistance to Charles Edward's men, came together to advocate a renewal of civic virtue in Scottish culture. This virtue should, as the Latin *virtus* implied, be that of warriors at need; but William Robertson and his associates were Whigs and Unionists, committed to the creation of an urbane modern culture and therefore deeply involved in the problem of how a professional army could replace feudal or kindred loyalties without furthering the corrup-

---

[2] J. C. D. Clark, *The Dynamics of Change: The Crisis of the 1750s and English Party* (Cambridge, 1982).

[3] A. J. Youngson, *After the Forty-Five: The Economic Impact on the Scottish Highlands* (Edinburgh, 1973).

[4] Richard B.Sher, *Church and University in the Scottish Enlightenment: The Moderate Literati of Edinburgh* (Princeton, 1985); and 'Adam Ferguson, Adam Smith and the problem of national defence', in Gordon J. Schochet (ed.), *Empire and Revolutions: Papers Presented at The Folger Institute Seminar 'Political Thought in the English-Speaking Atlantic'* (Washington DC, 1993), pp. 16–44.

tion to which modern societies were peculiarly exposed. Andrew Fletcher of Saltoun had, half a century before, defined this as a problem in the understanding of history,[5] and an immediate response of Scottish thinkers to the humiliation of 1745 was a renewed assessment of the history of feudal tenures and feudal arms. Henry Home, later Lord Kames, averred that it was under the Jacobite occupation of Edinburgh that he had begun writing his *Essays on Several Subjects Concerning British Antiquities* (1747), and a decade later the theme was being carried on by John Dalrymple in his *History of Feudal Property in Great Britain*, written by a student of Montesquieu and in its third edition by 1758, and in another way by Robertson[6] in his *History of Scotland*, published in 1759 and treating the reign of Mary Stuart as an effect of the persistence of Scottish baronial power. Colin Kidd has set these works in the context of a post-Union abandonment of George Buchanan's essentially baronial history of Scotland and a consequent turn from national to theoretical historiography;[7] but this does not mean that the Edinburgh or Glasgow literati were without deep national concerns. It is significant to compare Home's or Dalrymple's writings with the intense interest in the British or Gaelic origins of military tenure displayed in the *History of England* which the English Jacobite Thomas Carte began to publish in 1747. Robertson was at pains to orchestrate his *History of Scotland* with the Tudor volume of the *History of Great Britain* – now renamed a *History of England* – of which David Hume had published the Stuart volumes in 1754 and 1756. Nicholas Phillipson does not consider Hume's *History* as especially a product of the contemporary Scottish context,[8] and in 1754 it explicitly depicted Stuart England as a post-feudal society with the problems peculiar to that condition. Nevertheless, it was read attentively in Scotland, where feudal and kindred power was a more recent memory, and reinforced the historiographical initiatives being undertaken there, as they were not by contemporary Englishmen.

In correspondence with Adam Smith, since 1751 Professor of Moral Philosophy at the University of Glasgow, Hume defended his decision

---

[5]   There is a recent, but not a full, edition of Fletcher's *Political Writings and Speeches* by David Daiches (Edinburgh, 1979). The best current study is that of John Robertson, *The Scottish Enlightenment and the Militia Issue* (Edinburgh, 1985). Robertson's forthcoming edited volume, *A Union For Empire: the Union of 1707 in the History of British Political Thought* (Cambridge) will carry matters further.

[6]   An intellectual biography of William Robertson is being prepared by Jeffrey B. Smitten (University of Utah).

[7]   Colin Kidd, 'Scottish Whig Historiography and the Creation of an Anglo-British Identity, 1689–c. 1800', D Phil thesis, Oxford University, 1992.

[8]   Nicholas Phillipson, *Hume* (London, 1989) and his chapter in this volume.

to begin writing as from 1603, rather than 1485,[9] since Bacon and Harrington the conventional date from which to pursue post-feudal history in Britain. The incident is a reminder of the richness and complexity of what it has become customary to term 'the Scottish Enlightenment'. Sher's invaluable work is a study of the Moderate party in Edinburgh, in the politics of the clubs, the University and the General Assembly of the Kirk of Scotland; the history of 'Enlightenment' in Adam Smith's Glasgow and Thomas Reid's Aberdeen needs to be pursued independently. Smith's professorship of moral philosophy is a reminder of the intellectual context in which the mighty subdisciplines of philosophical history and political economy were soon to be taking shape. As Scotland belatedly but powerfully joined in the movement away from Calvinist orthodoxy which shaped Enlightenment in much of Protestant Europe, the teaching of a systematic morality based on Pufendorfian jurisprudence became an increasingly important responsibility of the professors and regents in the Scottish universities.[10] It has been shown how Pufendorf's historization of the state of nature contributed to the growth of philosophical history,[11] but this is only one aspect – however great – of the concern with natural morality and religion that engaged Smith, to give one instance, in writing his *Theory of Moral Sentiments* (1759). The concern with morality was 'modern' and 'enlightened' in the sense that it relegated predestination and the decrees of grace to the past of history, and this too was among the functions of the Moderate programme of advocating a polite and civilized society. They can be seen – this too we owe to Sher – as the intellectual arm of the lay patrons in the politics of the Kirk, intent on using landed property as a means of keeping religion civil, sociable and unfanatical; but there was the risk that the Christian faith would slip from Calvinism into some kind of Stoicism or even Epicureanism, become a mere pious moralism and be exposed to the corrosive effects of philosophical scepticism. The Moderates were recurrently embarrassed by their personal affection for the amiable but devastating David Hume,[12] and the beginnings of Common Sense philosophy at Aberdeen were shaped

---

[9] Hume to Smith, 24 September 1752, in J. Y. T. Greig (ed.), *The Letters of David Hume* (Oxford, 1932), I, pp. 167–8. Hume afterwards regretted his decision and thought he should have begun in 1485.

[10] James Moore, 'The Two Systems of Francis Hutcheson: On the Origins of the Scottish Enlightenment', in M. A. Stewart (ed.), *Studies in the Philosophy of the Scottish Enlightenment* (Oxford, 1990), pp.37–59.

[11] Istvan Hont, 'The Language of Sociability and Commerce: Samuel Pufendorf and the Theoretical Foundations of the "Four-Stages Theory" ', in Anthony Pagden (ed.), *The Languages of Political Theory in Early Modern Europe* (Cambridge, 1987), pp. 233–76.

[12] Sher, *Church and University*, pp. 60–1, 67, 72, 80–1.

by a series of friendly debates with him *in absentia*.[13] But fiercer debate went on with the hard-core Calvinists of the 'Popular' party among the clergy, and what political subversiveness there was in post-Jacobite Scotland arose as their positions became evangelized and radicalized. John Witherspoon left Edinburgh for New Jersey in 1768, leaving behind him a series of satiric blasts, written over the previous fifteen years, at the Moderates and their infidel associates, and headed unwittingly for a new life as an American revolutionary and the founding father of Common Sense in the universities of the New World.[14]

In England the military impact of 1745 had consequences in practice and in ideology, rather than in theory or literature. Writing some forty-five years later, Edward Gibbon recalled a process which had shaped his own experience:

Two disgraceful events, the progress in the year forty-five of some naked highlanders, the invitation of the Hessians and Hanoverians in fifty-six, had betrayed and insulted the weakness of an unarmed people. The country gentlemen of England unanimously demanded the establishment of a militia: a patriot was expected . . . and the merit of the plan or at least of the execution was assumed by Mr. Pitt who was then in the full splendour of his popularity and power. In the new model [!] the choice of officers was founded on the most constitutional principle, since they were all obliged . . . to prove a certain qualification, to give a landed security to the country, which entrusted them for her defence with the use of arms . . . But the King was invested with the power of calling the militia into actual service on the event or the danger of rebellion or invasion; and in the year 1759 the British islands were seriously threatened by the armaments of France. At this crisis the national spirit most gloriously disproved the charge of effeminacy which in a popular Estimate[15] had been imputed to the times; a martial enthusiasm seemed to have pervaded the land, and a constitutional army was formed under the command of the nobility and gentry of England . . . With the skill they soon imbibed the spirit of mercenaries; the character of a militia was lost; and, under that specious name, the crown had acquired a second army more costly and less useful than the first. The most beneficial effect of this institution was to eradicate among the country gentlemen the relics of Tory or rather of Jacobite prejudice. The accession of a British King reconciled them to the government and even to the court; but they have been

13 Peter J. Diamond, 'The Ideology of Improvement: Thomas Reid and the Political Philosophy of the Scottish Enlightenment', unpublished PhD dissertation, The Johns Hopkins University, 1986.

14 No biography or full-length study of Witherspoon is currently available. There are several essays on him in Richard B. Sher and Jeffrey B. Smitten (eds.), *Scotland and America in the Age of the Enlightenment* (Princeton, 1990).

15 John Brown, *An Estimate of the Manners and Principles of the Times* (1759). Brown's moral philosophy, formed as a critique of Shaftesbury, has been studied by James E. Crimmins, 'John Brown and the Theological Tradition of Utilitarian Ethics', *History of Political Thought*, 4, 3 (1983), pp. 523–50.

since accused of transferring their passive loyalty from the Stuarts to the family of Brunswick; and I have heard Mr. Burke exclaim in the House of Commons: 'They have changed the idol, but they have preserved the idolatry!'[16]

Gibbon's historical judgement is entitled to respect, and he here summarizes a process of importance to the themes of this chapter. The Hanoverian dynasty remedied the military weakness which had disgraced their domestic rule by converting the militia into a national institution, thus depriving it of the potentially republican or Jacobite character which it had borne as a symbolic expression of country opposition to court and regime. They were, in effect, co-opting patriotism, in that era a term – as Bolingbroke's choice of titles reminds us – commonly subversive in its connotations; and they were more able to do this when William Pitt became their minister while retaining the aura of a patriot leader.[17] The Seven Years War had begun with disasters and disgraces which called down the jeremiads of such as John Brown; but the formation of the national milita – no weekend army, but one with which Gibbon spent two years intermittently in camp – coincided with great victories at sea, in Canada, in India and in Europe, which seemed to liberate Britain from dependence on the interests of Hanover and brought the dynasty success in the blue-water strategies for which Tory and other critics of the regime had long been calling. Service in the militia between 1759 and 1763, in Gibbon's opinion, cured families like his own of the Jacobite sentiments in which his father had been active in 1745, and their reconciliation with the dynasty was ensured by the accession of George III, born in England, educated in the Church of England, son of the prince to whom Tory and patriot eyes had been turned, and 'glorying in the name of Britain' (and even Briton). The militia helped in a diversity of ways to make his realm the formidable defensive and oceanic power it was to be in the second half of his reign,[18] though an enduring mistrust of Jacobites and Presbyterians alike prevented its extension to Scotland until the Revolutionary wars with France.

But all of this was bought at a price. During Pitt's ministry the costs of war contributed to doubling the national debt, which since Anne's reign

[16] Georges A. Bonnard (ed.), *Edward Gibbon: Memoirs of My Life* (New York, 1966), pp. 109–11 (slightly emended).
[17] Marie C. Peters, *Pitt and Popularity: The Patriot Minister and London Opinion during the Seven Years War* (Oxford, 1980).
[18] For this, see in greater depth Eliga H. Gould, 'To Strengthen the King's Hand: Dynastic Legitimacy, Militia Reform and Ideas of National Unity in England, 1745–60', *Historical Journal*, 34, 2, (1991), 329–48; and his doctoral dissertation, 'War, Empire and the Language of State Formation: British Imperial Culture in the Age of the American Revolution', The Johns Hopkins University, 1992.

had been feared by Tories and commonwealthmen alike as the most potent source of national corruption and was soon to be stigmatized as a main cause of the crisis over American taxation. David Hume, neither Tory nor commonwealthman, developed in his essay 'Of Public Credit' (first published in 1752) a new and alarming account of the capacity of national debt to subvert and render meaningless an entire social structure.[19] Perceiving if not this then allied dangers, the new king withdrew his support from Pitt and Newcastle, and thus withdrew Britain from a war which to some promised and to others threatened the acquisition of a universal empire of the seas and the Americas. By his breach with Pitt, George III threw over the support of London 'patriotism', a vocal street and journalistic force which under aldermanic leadership had appeared in a Tory role during his grandfather's reign; while his breach with Newcastle was presented as part of his strategy of detaching the crown from association with the court Whig connections who saw themselves as guardians of Revolution principles. The king had lost the Patriots without gaining the Whigs; and the *ralliement* of Tory and former Jacobite gentry groups to the dynasty, of which Gibbon speaks, encouraged many to express, and many to experience, the fear that the Hanoverian monarchy was in some way falling into Stuart courses and betraying the Revolution principles which had brought it to the throne in 1714. It was always when the crown was perceived as becoming false to its own nature that the politics of early modern England became dangerously unstable.

The dynasty was relegitimized; but in an England as much divided as stabilized by its historical memories, a great deal of the reinforcement it now received was regarded as dubiously legitimate by the dynasty's traditional supporters. Because the sometime Jacobite Bolingbroke had tried to mobilize Country support in a Patriot programme addressed to Frederick Prince of Wales, it was believed that his son had been educated to make himself independent of the Whig aristocrats in parliament, that this threatened a reversion to Stuart use of the prerogative, and that the dynasty itself was endangered by these sinister promptings. A summary of the juvenile essays written by George when Lord Bute was his tutor[20] shows that there is a little, though a very little, in the notion of a Patriot atmosphere surrounding him; but Bute was a Scottish Unionist and therefore in the last analysis a Whig, who

---

[19] Istvan Hont, 'The Rhapsody of Public Debt: David Hume and Voluntary State Bankruptcy', in Nicholas Phillipson and Quentin Skinner (eds.), *Political Discourse in Early Modern Britain* (Cambridge, 1993).
[20] John Brooke, *George III* (London, 1972), pp. 107–23.

could promote Patriot thinking only in the hope that it might bring the two nations closer together. If he was a patron of Bolingbrokean or Old Whig writers in London, he was a supporter of the Moderates in Edinburgh.[21] In England, however, he and his pupil encountered a rhetorical and imagistic firestorm of an extraordinary kind, which tells us a great deal about a deeply monarchist society in which the monarchy was still insecurely legitimized.

The 'myth of George III' arose from the contradictions of this situation. His early political initiatives gave rise to the myth that he was surrounded by evil counsellors who wanted him to act as Bolingbroke's patriot king, but this pales into insignificance beside the accompanying myth of the Scottish evil counsellors who were supposed to be undermining his monarchy by teaching him Jacobite doctrine, in precisely the manner of the imagined Arminians and Jesuits of old. From Vincent Carretta's *George III and the Satirists from Hogarth to Byron*[22] – the most remarkable monograph so far produced by a member of the 1987 Folger seminar – comes the image of 'Sawney', the demonic punchinello wrapped in plaid and whispering flattery in the king's gullible ear, who persisted in caricature for thirty years, so long as Bute, Mansfield, Wedderburn or Dundas was available to play the part, and who must have done much to drive the Scottish Enlightenment into fruitful intellectual isolation. A king who 'gloried in the name of Britain' by way of indicating that he was not a devotee of Hanoverian interests was accused of being a Scottish puppet for his pains, and a venomous anti-Scotticism hard to differentiate from anti-Semitism arose with Wilkes and Churchill to infect Adams and Jefferson, William Cobbett and Thomas Love Peacock. Meanwhile, this politically radical English chauvinism merged with Whiggish fears of Highland Jacobitism and Tory dislike of Lowland Presbyterianism to ensure that Pitt's national militia was not extended to include Scotland. The Edinburgh Moderates thus found the restoration of military virtue an option denied them.

But evil counsellors are part of the fantasy of personal monarchy. Bute was the last statesman in British history to be singled out by a king as his 'Friend', by his enemies as his 'Favourite', and to be publicly accused of the seduction of the monarch's mother; but the necessary counterpart of the evil counsellor is the good king, who would rule well if he were not deceived. Behind the apparent republicanism of Old Whigs who cherished the memory of Charles I's execution, the apparent nostalgia of High Churchmen for a Stuart dynasty rendered sacred by its martyr

---

[21] Sher, *Church and University*, pp. 117, 147.   [22] Athens, GA, 1990.

king, we perceive a political culture which valued its monarch enough to maintain violently contradictory images of him in his positive and negative roles. Carretta's history of George III's appearances in caricature, ballad, satire and poetry both high and low throughout his reign is a study of the strange intensity with which the English comic genius treated a figure with whom it became obsessed as it had been obsessed only with Sir Robert Walpole before him. The relations between extreme disrespect and affectionate loyalty are hard to work out, and the phenomena presented raise the problem of distinguishing between subversion and carnival. 'The myth of George III' is both instant and permanent; from a very early point in this reign, print culture and popular culture present the king as either the victim or the agent of a conspiracy of malignant figures to subvert and corrupt English and American liberties, and many of the major works of political literature to appear between 1760 and 1790 – Wilkes and Churchill's *North Briton*, Edmund Burke's *Thoughts on the Present Discontents*, *The Letters of Junius*, Thomas Paine's *Common Sense*, *The Declaration of Independence*, William Blake's *America* – were in their several ways concerned with maintaining this image of conspiracy. The attempt to establish a politics of politeness, studied by Nicholas Phillipson in the preceding chapter, seems on this face of things to have given way before a politics of paranoia. Perhaps this was why David Hume at the end of his days feared the triumph of a new kind of fanaticism – that of principle. On the other hand, the alternative of carnival and mockery remained open, at least to the English.

During the 1760s, parliamentary and popular politics in England became much concerned with the affairs of John Wilkes, a jovial adventurer who did not pretend that his derisive defiance of the ruling order was intended to do much more than win him a place within it. The slogan 'Wilkes and Liberty' may have meant little more than that, and the widespread proliferation of Wilkite banquets, petitions and clubs may possibly be regarded as a nation-wide explosion of rough music; an attempt by carnivalesque means to recall the ruling order to a proper sense of itself. On the other hand, there were proposals abroad for more frequent parliaments, fewer borough and more county members, and other recurrent expressions of the occasional early-modern demands for parliamentary reform;[23] and in a memorable work over fifteen years ago, John Brewer mobilised the evidence for the existence of sizeable urban groups discontented by the prevailing parliamentary and even social structure, and looking for new ways to associate outside the grip of noble

---

[23] John Cannon, *Parliamentary Reform, 1640–1832* (Cambridge, 1972).

and gentry patronage on both.[24] It is the problem of 'the people',
recurrent or apparently so for the next seventy years; who and what were
they, and what did they betoken? An important literary product of this
period is Edmund Burke's *Thoughts on the Cause of the Present Dis-*
contents (1770);[25] important horizontally for those in search of the
'discontents' and their 'cause', important vertically for those studying
the growth of an extraordinary political mind. Acting on behalf of the
Whig families excluded from the king's councils, Burke painted a vivid if
fictional picture of evil counsellors manoeuvring 'behind the curtain' –
exceeded in vehemence only by the almost Swiftian savagery of the
anonymous Junius – and developed a defence of noble advisors to the
king, who might form parties and conduct political campaigns to bring
themselves back to his favour. Burke invited the 'people' to associate
themselves with these natural leaders, and drew down a rebuke from
Catharine Macaulay,[26] who saw Burke's aims clearly enough and
thought that the 'people' should act of themselves and speak with their
own voices. But though by birth a Sawbridge, of a London aldermanic
family with a long history of agitation both Tory and popular behind it,
she was not looking for the rise of newly emancipated classes. In the
History of England from the Accession of James I to that of the Brunswick
Line, in the first five volumes of which (1763–71) she upheld against
Hume, with formidable eloquence and research exceeding his, the
history of the 'good old cause', her eye was always on a pantheon of
virtuous republicans – Pym and Hampden, Milton and Vane, Russell
and Sidney – who might if not betrayed by baser actors have lifted the
people out of their habitual deference and debauchery and made them
worthy of a commonwealth.[27] She was a Roman republican; her
democracy demanded heroes. We need to look elsewhere if we are to find
harbingers of a middle-class future.

The rhetoric of parliamentary corruption entailed a rhetoric of
parliamentary reform, which might go so far as aiming at the creation of

[24] John Brewer, *Party Ideology and Popular Politics at the Accession of George III*
(Cambridge, 1976). See also his article, 'English Radicalism in the Age of George III',
in J. G. A. Pocock (ed.), *Three British Revolutions: 1641, 1688, 1776* (Folger Institute
Essays (Princeton, 1980).

[25] F. P. Lock, ' "The Organ of a Discontented Faction": Burke's *Thoughts on the Cause of*
the Present Discontents', in Schochet (ed.), *Empire and Revolutions*, pp. 121–40.

[26] *Observations on a Pamphlet entitled: Thoughts on the Cause of the Present Discontents*
(1770).

[27] Rolando Minuti, 'Il problema storico della libertà inglese nella cultura radicale dell' età
di Giorgio III. Catharine Macaulay e la rivoluzione puritana', *Rivista Storica Italiana*,
98, 111 (1986), 793–860. This is the closest study of her historical thought currently
available. See now Bridget Hill, *The Republican Virago: the Life and Times of Catharine*
Macaulay, Historian (Oxford, 1992).

a virtuous electorate, independent enough to resist corruption of either
their representatives or themselves; whether this end were best pursued
by enlarging the electorate or defining it more rigorously was a question
susceptible of more than one answer. It is certain that the rhetoric of
virtue and corruption had for some time introduced into British political
discourse the notion that the corrupt state of the representation of the
'people' or 'kingdom' – for which it was as easy to blame 'the influence of
the Crown' as that of the aristocracy – was at the forefront of the
problems of political society. It was an achievement of the Wilkes
agitation to re-inject this issue into pamphlet literature and popular
meetings; Whig connections dissatisfied by their apparent ejection from
the king's confidence might adopt what attitudes toward it as they saw
fit, as the caution behind Burke's bold statements makes clear. This is
perhaps the simplest answer that can be given to the question whether
political 'radicalism' existed in Georgian England;[28] in Scotland it
seems to have been less of an issue. It has now to be noted that the
rhetoric of parliamentary corruption was available to American colonists, and came to exercise a considerable power over their minds, as they
grew accustomed to challenging the authority of parliament to tax or
legislate for them; but the American issue was to raise problems greater
and more complex than the representation of the British people in its
parliament, and to end by challenging the whole concept of parliamentary government.

The reign of George III witnessed the transformation of English
political thought, already enlarged into British by the union with
Scotland, into something larger still: a debate over the political structure
of the English-speaking Atlantic which was to end in its disruption, and
the creation of the United States as a derived but profoundly different
political culture, operating a discourse distinctively its own. This
disruption involved civil war, but was fought over and within the
'empire' rather than the 'realm' – imperfectly distinguished as these
terms were – and was therefore capable of being styled in Roman terms a
bellum sociale rather than a *bellum civile*. The Social War in Roman
history was not fought between Roman citizens, but between Romans
and their confederates or *socii* who were subject to Roman *imperium* but
enjoyed less *jus* than was accorded Roman citizens. In Georgian history,
the War of the American Revolution involved no fighting among the
English and Scots of the metropolitan island, but was waged with

[28] J. C. D. Clark has pointed out that no phenomenon was yet reified under that name, but
currents of argument known as 'commonwealth' or 'republican' are traceable and the
adjective 'radical' may on occasion be applied to them. See Martha K. Zebrowski, 'The
Corruption of Politics and the Dignity of Human Nature: The Critical and Constructive Radicalism of James Burgh', in Schochet (ed.), *Empire and Revolutions*, pp. 67–94.

colonists who began by considering themselves Englishmen, then claimed the status of dominions confederated with the crown, and were compelled finally to declare themselves independent Americans no longer British. It seems better to style this process a revolution than a rebellion,[29] since the Declaration of Independence successfully proclaimed that it was a rebellion no longer; and to study its revolutionary character in a volume such as this is to study the advent in British political discourse of a series of problems which arose from its history, but with which it was by its history ill equipped to deal.[30]

These may be summarized as a single terminological problem, that of 'empire'.[31] Since the Act in Restraint of Appeals in 1533, the primary meaning in English of 'empire' or *imperium* had been 'national sovereignty': the 'empire' of England over itself, of the crown over England in church as well as state, the independence of the English church-state from all other modes of sovereignty. The exercise of this sovereignty had involved England in a series of tensions and contradictions, between the crown and the crown-in-parliament, between the crown-in-parliament and the government of the national church, which had given rise to a series of civil wars, dissolutions of government, conspiracies, revolutions, foreign wars, and a period of dynastic and therefore ecclesiastical uncertainty which as late as 1760 was only recently terminated. If there was one thing which civil war and dissolution of government had etched in letters of fire and blood on the English historical memory, it was that the unity of king and parliament must at all costs be maintained, and that this necessitated the maintenance of a national church under royal and parliamentary authority. Parliamentary indulgence to Dissenters was not more than an incident of this edifice; the Toleration Act was a partner to the Test and Corporation Acts rather than a competitor with them. All this had recently been re-explained, with great authority, by William Blackstone, in reviving the common-law tradition of legal reason as a pillar of parliamentary monarchy.[32]

---

[29] Cf. J. C. D. Clark, *Revolution and Rebellion: State and Society in England in the Seventeenth and Eighteenth Centuries* (Cambridge, 1987).

[30] For a full exploration of this theme, important to the present chapter, see Jack P. Greene, *Peripheries and Center: Constitutional Development in the Extended Polities of the British Empire and the United States, 1607–1788* (Athens, GA, 1986; New York, 1990).

[31] Richard Koebner, *Empire* (Cambridge, 1961), and New York, 1965), though posthumous and incomplete, has not been surpassed, and deals with the problem of British American empire for most of its length.

[32] David Lieberman, *The Province of Legislation Determined: Legal Theory in Eighteenth-Century Britain* (Cambridge, 1989), ch. 2, 'Blackstone's Science of Legislation'. Robert S. Willman, 'Blackstone and the "Theoretical Perfection" of English Law in the Reign of Charles II', *Historical Journal*, 36, 1 (1983), 39–70; John W. Cairns, 'Blackstone, the Ancient Constitution and the Feudal Law', *Historical Journal*, 28, 4 (1985), 711–17.

The unity of crown, parliament and church, so far as it could be maintained, both formed and necessitated a unified sovereignty that could not be compromised without threatening – especially in times of dynastic instability – a resumption of the processes which had led to civil war and dissolution in the remembered past. This, it may be proposed, was enough to have ensured that the union of England and Scotland to form the kingdom of Great Britain in 1707 must be an 'incorporating' and not (as had been suggested) a 'federating' union.[33] The English crown and parliament could not relate themselves to a crown of wider *imperium* without giving up the unity which was England's only shield against civil war (as the Scottish threat in 1704 to repudiate the Act of Settlement had reminded their neighbours). Therefore the kingdoms and their parliaments had been united to form a single sovereignty which was in essence that of the crown-in-parliament as shaped by English history; only the need to maintain a Scottish-Presbyterian church-state at the side of the English had retained for the Union something of the character of a confederation subject to a treaty, as Blackstone did not fail to point out.[34] He wrote as an English Tory, anxious to maintain that any modification of the Church of England's ascendancy would amount to a breach of the Treaty of Union;[35] we have to think of the Union enduring through a half-century of Jacobite persistence and Tory uncertainty. It was not English hegemonic solidarity, but underlying English instability, which accounts for the uncompromising insistence on the undivided sovereignty of the crown-in-parliament. The language of mixed government, descending from the *Answer to the Nineteen Propositions*, was as has been sufficiently shown a language of conjoint sovereignty.[36] When Bolingbroke imagined a 'patriot king' leading his people against his parliament, the author's Jacobite past sprang to his readers' minds; when George III was depicted by angry Whig aristocrats and their publicists as playing the same role, Wilkes and Churchill portrayed him in the clutches of crypto-Jacobite evil counsellors. But the rhetoric of the 'commonwealthmen', separating the powers of mixed government to a point which approached republicanism, could no less

---

[33] John Robertson (ed.), *A Union for Empire: The Union of 1707 in the History of British Political Thought* (Cambridge, forthcoming); see in particular the editor's own contributions.

[34] Blackstone, *Commentaries on the Laws of England* (Oxford, 1765; facsimile, Chicago, 1979), I, pp. 97–8.

[35] Blackstone's Tory origins are emphasized by Clark, *English Society, 1688–1832* (Cambridge, 1986), pp. 59, 189. See also Robert Willman, 'The Politics of Blackstone's *Commentaries*: Whig or Tory?', in Schochet, (ed.), *Empire and Revolutions*, pp. 279–308.

[36] C. C. Weston and Janelle R. Greenberg, *Subjects and Sovereigns: The Grand Debate over Legal Sovereignty in Stuart England* (Cambridge, 1981).

easily be denounced as playing into Tory and neo-Jacobite hands; it is perhaps the lurid spectres haunting English historic memory, together with the ease with which subversive and sinister intentions could be attributed to political actors, which accounts for the paranoia and conspiracy mania of which the age after 1760 is full. The colonists of America were about to venture on this crowded and dangerous scene, and prove themselves no exception to its insecurities and fantasies.[37]

The imposition of Stamp Act duties on the colonies was a decision to provide revenue for the consolidated military empire that had emerged from the peace of 1763 in the North Atlantic and on the American continent (its critics thought it a misguided attempt at 'universal empire' and a dangerous expansion of the national debt). The Act may be thought a product of the growing imperial bureaucracy occasioned by the militarization of the British state,[38] but legislatively rather than administratively considered, it was an attempt by Parliament to make law for the 'empire' as a whole. What followed was to reveal the deep ambivalences of the term just placed in quotation marks, and to oblige both metropolitan and colonial British political thought in an attempt to resolve these ambivalences, in which they were neither willing nor well equipped to engage. Concepts of 'empire' and 'confederation' were about to force themselves on a debating public which lacked language capable of controlling them. To the English, history dictated that 'empire' should connote the sovereignty of the realm over itself; but just as the *imperium* of the Roman people had been extended over the widening zone of subject provinces, so the sovereignty of the English (latterly the British) crown had come to be exercised over a diversity of colonies, established (as the name 'colonies' connoted) by settlement rather than by conquest. Only Ireland was held to be a kingdom established by conquest, the subjection of its parliament to that at Westminster being assured; it was merely beginning to be debated whether the Protestant settlers were subject to the conquering power or shared in its exercise.

The terms 'the empire', 'the British empire' (it may institutionalize the entity too much to use the capital 'E') therefore denoted both the sovereignty of the British realm over itself and the extension of its sovereign's authority over a diversity of subject dominions in the Atlantic archipelago, the Caribbean and the north American continent.

---

[37] Richard Hofstadter, *The Paranoid Style in American Politics* (New York, 1965); Gordon S. Wood, 'Conspiracy and the Paranoid Style: Causality and Deceit in the Eighteenth Century', *William and Mary Quarterly*, 3rd Series, 39, 3 (1982), 401–41.

[38] John Brewer, *The Sinews of Power: War, Money and the English State, 1688–1783* (New York, 1988).

'Realm' and 'empire' were therefore non-identical without being distinct, and the over-riding necessity of maintaining the unity of crown and parliament dictated that the primary meaning of 'empire' should be this institution's sovereignty over its 'realm'. Since all subjects within the realm were held to be represented by the parliament in which the crown exercised empire, it was an easy step to assuming that all subjects within the 'empire' were under the authority which represented the realm, and it was to prove hard to assert otherwise without compromising the unity and sovereignty of the realm itself. These assumptions were rendered even more persuasive and pervasive by the circumstance that the majority of the European inhabitants of the Caribbean and American colonies were English – and strongly Whiggish Englishmen to boot – who held themselves to enjoy by birthright the protection of the law over which the crown-in-parliament exercised sovereignty.

It was to appear an evident flaw in this conceptual structure that the colonies were not represented in parliament; but the point of this is less that the colonists resented their exclusion than that its existence underlined the fundamental ambiguity of their status. Were they within the realm or without it? If their charters conferred on them the status of corporations, were they trading corporations akin to the East India Company – a view which contemporary 'mercantilist' theory might recommend – or civil corporations like those of Bristol or Norwich; and if the latter, why were they not represented in parliament? The learned in law and history could find no better answer than that they resembled counties palatine like those of Chester and Durham, to which the crown had deputed certain regalian powers that rendered unnecessary their representation in the parliament where the crown exercised its sovereignty; but the earl of Chester and the bishop of Durham, in any case somewhat archaic figures, were not royal governors holding the crown's commission to govern with the advice of local legislative assemblies, whereas the existence of colonial legislatures was to be of crucial importance in the crisis impending. It might be more simply asserted that the legal status of colonies had never been determined, and that the identification of 'empire' and 'realm' – of 'empire' meaning 'sovereign monarchy' with 'empire' meaning 'extensive or enormous monarchy'[39] – meant that the British empire altogether lacked the *jus publicum*, regulating the relations between its components under sovereignty, which would have constituted it am 'empire' in the sense understood by civilian jurists. It could alternatively be asserted that there existed an

[39] The use of these eighteenth-century terms is a reminder that the twentieth-century connotations of 'imperialism' are not directly relevant here.

informal code of usages and understandings which regulated the government of the colonies, and that this 'informal empire' constituted an 'unwritten law' or 'constitution' possessing the authority of immemorial custom and an 'ancient constitution'. Some American scholars uphold while others question this very English reading of the situation before the Stamp Act.[40]

The colonial reaction to the Stamp Act duties revealed that colonists did not consider themselves members of chartered corporations, but of civil societies capable of generating their own governments and ruling themselves in their own way. The origins of this self-perception were in some cases religious; in others they lay in the circumstance that the colony was an agrarian society, in which settlers had become proprietors and exercised the rights of property, which entitled them always to freedom under law and in some patterns of belief to constitute 'peoples' in whom resided the original of government. The former claim did not necessarily entail a collision with the authority of parliament, though the rooted belief that as Englishmen they were not to be taxed without the consent of their own representatives carried it in the direction of the second, which did. This latter claim, juristic and very often Lockean in character, carried the seeds of the belief that the 'peoples' of the colonies were distinguishable from the English or British 'people', were not and perhaps could not be represented in the British parliament, and were consequently not included in the obligation to obey its laws. It can be seen for the first time adumbrated in the writings of Richard Bland of Virginia and James Otis of Massachusetts,[41] who averred correctly enough that the mainland colonies had not been established by conquest, and were settled by English subjects in the full enjoyment of their natural civil rights and inherited English liberties. These, they began saying, included the right not to be taxed but by consent of their representatives, and this consent was given in the colonial legislatures meeting by authority of the Crown as itself exercised by the royal governor. It was the unstated implication, that since the colonists were not represented in parliament their consent to taxation was given in a locus outside parliament, that was in the end to destroy the Atlantic structure. Later, Bland and other writers made use of Locke's assertion

---

[40] See n. 88 and Robert C. Tucker and David Hendrickson, *The Fall of the First British Empire: Origins of the War of American Independence* (Baltimore, 1982).
[41] Richard Bland, *The Colonel Dismounted, or the Rector Vindicated. In a letter ... containing a Dissertation upon the Constitution of the Colony* (Williamsburg, 1764); *An Inquiry into the Rights of the British Colonies* (Williamsburg, 1766). James Otis, *The Rights of the British Colonies Asserted and Proved* (Boston, 1764). The first and second are in Bailyn (ed.), *Pamphlets of the American Revolution, 1750–1765* (Cambridge, MA, 1965).

of the right of the subject to emigrate from the realm, leaving behind his property and his obligation to obey, and developed the thesis that the settlers in America had entered a wilderness and a state of nature, acquiring the right to make what terms or contracts they would with the king they had left behind them.[42] This argument was not easily reconciled with the contention that colonists had remained Englishmen and brought the rights of Englishmen with them, unless it were contended that they had exercised a natural right to assume English rights insofar as these coincided with the former. To say this would be to infuriate any English reader, who would see in it a colonial claim to be English when it suited them and not when it did not, and was a little further than Bland or Otis had desired to go. There was a middle path, that of asserting that the colonists had set forth under the king of England's protection and remained in allegiance to him under his laws, but were not subject to him 'in' the Westminster Parliament; only 'in' the several colonial legislatures. This argument rather rapidly became that put forward by a wide concurrence of colonial resolutions and public and private writings, amounting to a claim that the 'empire' must be seen as constituting an enlarged confederacy of many legislatures, each separately connected with the crown;[43] though there was widespread willingness to concede that the crown and parliament of Great Britain formed a preponderating partner and exercised an imperial jurisdiction over the relations between the empire's components, not, however, extending so far as to tax the subject's property without the consent of the legislature in which he was represented.

It is not easy to assess the conceptual sources of this doctrine. Though much of its scaffolding is Lockean, Locke had not concerned himself with federal theory or with the relations between a number of peoples each of whom was the origin of its own government. Colonial theorists were already turning toward reliance on the writings of Grotius, Pufendorf and Vattel; toward the great exponents of *jus gentium*, each of whom had been a citizen in a confederacy of states; Dutch, German, and in Vattel's case Swiss. But George III was a king, not an emperor; he

---

[42] Yuhtaro Ohmori, ' "The Artillery of Mr. Locke": The Use of Locke's *Second Treatise* in Pre-Revolutionary America, 1764–76', unpublished PhD dissertation, The Johns Hopkins University, 1988. A recent study of pre-Revolutionary American historiography (Thomas P. Cole, 'History and Historical Consciousness in Colonial British America: A Study in the Construction of Provincial Cultures', unpublished PhD dissertation, The Johns Hopkins University, 1992) finds this reading altogether lacking. Instead, the history of each colony is typically seen as moving from early and deficient charters to imperial sovereignty and civil society.

[43] The most recent study of this debate is that of Jack P. Greene, *Peripheries and Center*. Koebner, *Empire*, remains highly informative.

gloried in the name of Britain, and would not look favourably on an argument which would make him the sole link preventing his several dominions from being related to one another in a state of nature. The doctrine which colonial indignation was beginning to put together must collide directly with the instinctive belief of the English – to which the Scots were now parties – that by 'empire' was meant the sovereignty of the realm, the unity of the king who was its representative in one way with the parliament that represented it in another. The colonial argument posed a radical threat to this unity (the historic shield against absolutism, civil war and anarchy); it proposed to separate the king from each of his legislatures in order to make him the sole connection between them all, and it conveyed an alarming message that law, the rights of Englishmen beyond seas and their titles to their lands in America, emanated from the king's sole person and not from his person in his parliament. In the doctrine of empire as confederacy some in England thought they recognized Bolingbroke's Patriot King writ large on an imperial canvas; and a situation arose in which metropolitan and colonial advocates could accuse one another of being Tories, in different senses of that protean term.

British (meaning Anglo-Scottish) political discourse contained no theoretical language of confederation, and there was probably no way in which the one could have been made to accommodate the latter – which of course renders all the more remarkable the speed and conviction with which the essentially English colonists adopted it. The implicit claim that the American colonies were civil societies, or 'states', capable of entering into treaty relations with the crown, may appear in retrospect the decisive step toward independence, war and revolution. But long before that happened, metropolitan spokesmen found themselves faced with a task which had not confronted English or British discourse before: that of redefining the 'realm' in its relation to the term 'empire'. Writers with personal experience or detailed theoretical knowledge of the colonies saw, in the words of a leader among them, Thomas Pownall, the necessity

that Great Britain may be no more considered *as the kingdom of this Isle only, with many appendages of provinces, colonies, settlements, and other extraneous parts*, but as A GRAND MARINE DOMINION CONSISTING OF OUR POSSESSIONS IN THE ATLANTIC AND IN AMERICA UNITED INTO A ONE EMPIRE, IN A ONE CENTER, WHERE THE SEAT OF GOVERNMENT IS.[44]

---

[44] Thomas Pownall, *The Administration of the Colonies, wherein their Rights and Constitution are Discussed and Stated*, 4th edn (1768; reprinted New York, 1971), pp. 9–10. There are extensive discussions of Pownall in both Greene and Koebner, though the latter is displeased by his style. In later editions Pownall changed 'a one' to 'a single'.

This was not so much a vision of universal empire as a consequence of the English perception that sovereignty must be the unity of the realm, so that empire must by definition be drawn into a single realm, one and indivisible. It was the Tudor imperative; local power must not compromise the empire over church and state. There were formidable obstacles: Ireland for one, and for another Benjamin Franklin's widely-accepted demographic predictions,[45] foretelling a day when the population of America would so far exceed that of Britain and Ireland that the centre of empire must move across the Atlantic. Pownall was one aware of this prophecy, and there was another – Josiah Tucker, the brilliant if unmanageable dean of Gloucester[46] – coming to the conclusion that Britain must become independent of its colonies before this happened, since otherwise the empire would be ruled by dissenters (and slave-holders). But Pownall and others were aware of a more immediate problem: what were the colonies in relation to the realm and how might they be united more closely with it? Politically, the immediate problem was that of inducing them to obey parliamentary sovereignty; constitutionally, the question must sooner or later arise whether they ought not to be represented in parliament at Westminster. This was not a matter of all men having an equal right to representation, but a far more ancient recognition that to make subjects part of the sovereign body was the best way to make them accept its sovereignty over themselves; since taxes had been given by assent of the realm in parliament, they had been collected far more efficiently than before.

Colonies, Pownall held, were originally palatinates; when the government of England had been that of a feudal monarchy, the king had been able to extend his suzerainty over dominions other than the realm he chose to incorporate with his person, and had done so in such cases as Chester, Durham, Jersey and the other islands.[47] Of the case of Ireland Pownall had little to say; perhaps deliberately, out of a wish to avoid the thorny subject of conquest. This state of affairs had lasted through the reign of Charles I, when Virginia and Massachusetts had been considered outside the realm and the competence of parliament. But with the Restoration of 1660, it had been established that sovereignty did not reside in the king alone, but conjointly in King, Lords and Commons;

---

[45] *Observation concerning the Increase of Mankind* (1751); *The Interest of Great Britain with Regard to her Colonies* (1760).
[46] George Shelton, *Dean Tucker and Eighteenth-Century Economic and Political Thought* (New York, 1981); J. G. A. Pocock, 'Josiah Tucker on Burke, Locke and Price; A Study in the Varieties of Eighteenth-Century Conservatism', *Virtue, Commerce and History* (Cambridge, 1987). Despite these two publications, a full-length examination of Tucker remains desirable.
[47] Pownall, *Administration*, pp. 59–63.

the empire of the realm was in the realm itself. It was no coincidence that at that time the former palatinate of Durham had followed the principality of Wales, 130 years before, into full incorporation within the realm and representation in its parliament; and that parliament had at the same time assumed competence to legislate for the colonies. For the change in the locus and structure of English sovereignty meant that dominions beyond sea were now subject not to the crown alone, but to the crown and realm incorporated; that is to the king and people of what later became Great Britain.[48] It must follow, of course, that any colonial claim to be subject to the crown but not to parliament was an implicit regression to feudal monarchy. Pownall does not say this, but there were colonial spokesmen who recognized and accepted the implication; and Josiah Tucker was in a few years to notice the interesting affinity between the Lockean arguments colonists were by that time putting forward and a pre-modern or even feudal view of the relations which must arise between men in the state of nature. There was no middle way between asserting the king's purely personal authority over the colonies and casting off that authority altogether; indeed, the former argument by then looked like a way-station on the road to the latter.

Pownall's argument, however, was that the logic of political history required that as a people became part of the empire exercised over a realm, outlying parts of that people must be incorporated and represented within the realm, since it was a solecism that one part of a people should be subject to the authority of another. He therefore held in principle that all palatinates, including colonies, should sooner or later be given representation in parliament; but his attitude to the question of American representation is, in detail, a mixture of the cautious and the visionary. On the one hand, he remarks that if the time is not ripe for incorporation of the colonies in parliament, the colonial legislatures must be left – as, by custom so long established as to be almost constitutional, they are at present – to find means of raising the revenue parliament may require of them.[49] On the other, he accepts Franklin's demographic projections so far as to remark that it is a mere matter of political science that the centre of empire should move westward with the redistribution of population.[50] Here we may very well feel that he was underestimating the historical toughness of the English if not the British political structure; the former's resistance, already displayed in 1707, to incorporation within any larger and alien system. Certainly he touches only glancingly on what might have proved a most recalcitrant

---

[48] *Ibid.*, pp. 125–33, 139–42.   [49] *Ibid.*, pp. 149–52.   [50] *Ibid.*, pp. 37–38.

problem: the question whether incorporation in the 'empire' would mean incorporation in the ecclesiastical structure which 'empire' had been proclaimed to maintain. The Union of Great Britain looked most like a federation at the point where it was a union between two church-states; but the colonists in America were deemed to be English rather than Scots, had no national church of their own, and could not be said with any conviction to be members of the church as by law established. American political culture was already, as it has remained, deeply sectarian and congregationalist; it was the perceived threat of incorporation within a royal and episcopal church that drove colonists to political reactions as violent as any provoked by the stamp duties. A case can and has been made for presenting the American Revolution as one more of the British wars of religion.[51]

It is a commonplace that proposals for giving the colonies representation in the British (or 'imperial') parliament were not much supported on either side of the Atlantic. The Stamp Act Congress in 1765 gave out that it did not consider this step practicable or desirable;[52] as Adam Smith would have understood, men who were magnates in colonial politics were not much interested in finding themselves back-benchers 3,000 miles away. At Westminster itself, it happened that both Pownall and William Knox, another leading writer on American questions,[53] were adherents of George Grenville, and were therefore attacked, in parliament and in print, by Edmund Burke, writing in the interest of the Rockingham faction which had no desire to see Grenville return to power.[54] Burke derided all proposals for colonial representation in parliament, and affected to believe that all that was necessary was a return to the system of informal empire which had benignly ruled by a series of customary understandings. In his later speeches, he went so far as to advocate recognizing the colonies in their status as palatinates, and leaving them undisturbed in it. One may ask whether this presents Burke at his most farsighted, though the insistence on informality and pragmatic avoidance of doctrine may foreshadow the growth of his political philosophy. In the Grenvillean writers, at all events, he was confronted by men who thought the imperial crisis struck at the roots of the self-conceptualization of the British realm and empire, and could be dealt with only by a drastic if essentially conservative re-conceptualization of its structure and history. Beyond the Atlantic, those who had

---

[51] J. C. D. Clark, 'Heterodoxy, Sectarianism and the American Revolution', a paper presented to the American Historical Association meeting in Chicago, December 1991.
[52] Koebner, *Empire*, p. 182.
[53] Greene, *Peripheries and Center*, pp. 107–8; Koebner, *Empire*, pp. 148, 178–81, 339.
[54] Koebner, *Empire*, pp. 185–92.

begun to put forward doctrines of confederation which the parliament of the realm could not be expected to accept, but felt they were receiving no response from it which might indicate ways of moving forward, were being forced by the logic of the situation into a re-conceptualization of themselves with ultimate revolutionary consequences. Pownall, Knox and other British writers were attempting to find conceptual alternatives and were thinking seriously about realm, empire and history. In the context provided by such a volume as this, it is a comment on the traditions of British historical understanding that American (and in Koebner's case Israeli) historians appear to have given them more attention than they have received in the British literature. The doctrine of informal empire has struck deep roots, and even American historians frequently subscribe or defer to it, while British appear anxious to maintain Seeley's 'absence of mind'. Their reluctance to look outside the political structure of England is a greater handicap than even the American tendency to treat the political autochthony of colonial society as among those truths held to be self-evident, and therefore in no need of explanation.

The colonial literature of the 1760s extended beyond Bland, Otis and Franklin. John Dickinson, with his usual caution, declared in his *Letters of a Pennsylvania Farmer* (1767) that the colonies were 'as much dependent on Great Britain as one perfectly free people can be on another', though in the next year it was Franklin's opinion that 'no middle ground' could be maintained.[55] In a long-term perspective, perhaps, greater significance may be attached to John Adams' *Dissertation on the Canon and Feudal Laws* (1765), since here may be found the earliest formulation of the thesis of American exceptionalism. Neither of these ancient and repressive codes, Adams proclaimed, had taken root in British America, and it would not have been impossible for him to add that American culture was founded in principles like those of Locke. In 1769 William Robertson published in Edinburgh his *View of the Progress of Society in Europe*, arguing that both laws had been important in the progress of post-classical civilization, and in 1774 Protestant opinion everywhere was to be convulsed by the Quebec Act, which seemed to establish both under guarantee of the British crown.[56] Adams had his own agenda, which he did not trouble to hide. By 'feudal law' he meant to repudiate the notion that colonists in America held their lands under obligation to the king; he thus exposed the strategy behind their claim to be subject to him in his own person but not in his parliament.

[55] Greene, *Peripheries and Centre*, pp. 110–112.
[56] Philip Lawson, *Imperial Challenge: Quebec and Britain in the Age of the American Revolution* (Kingston and Montreal, 1989).

By 'canon law' he meant any suggestion that the authority of an episcopal or an established church was entailed by that of the Crown in its American dominions; he was implicitly identifying the prelatical with the popish in the manner of Milton or Prynne. And it should be noted that he placed 'canon' first and 'feudal' second; the ecclesiological component in American thinking was awake and roaring. There were established congregational churches in the New England colonies, and in Virginia an episcopal church with no resident bishops, so that the gentlemen of the parish vestries conducted its affairs. But the overall complexion of colonial religious life was pluralist to the point of being sectarian, and the deepest fears could always be awakened by the threat, real or fancied, of an American episcopate established by royal authority.[57] Enlightened Protestantism had reached the point where the sectarian and the secular were hard to tell apart, and the anti-clericalism latent in the puritan could be reinforced by that overt in the *philosophe*. The campaign against royal authority in an established church was now to be joined by a very similar movement mounted in England itself.

We are here in a position to advance a strong argument in favour of J. C. D. Clark's theses[58] that the American revolution had much of the character of a war of religion, and that what has been called political radicalism in Britain was less proto-democratic than a movement of anti-trinitarian dissent. In 1772, the Feathers Tavern Petition sought relief for Anglican clergy from subscribing to the more Athanasian of the Thirty-Nine Articles. Those whom it sought to relieve were those within the Church of England and its ordained priesthood whose opinions might be termed 'Socinian' in the sense that they had reservations or specific difficulties about the Nicene theology of Christ's divine and human nature and the holy and undivided Trinity, which must be upheld by any church which desired to maintain that it was of the body of Christ present on earth since the Ascension.[59] John Locke, a layman, had been of their number,[60] and their difficulties can be traced back at least to William Chillingworth in the 1630s. Yet some of their persuasion – or lack of persuasion – had always remained communicants within the Church of England, discussing their problems with their brethren and not congregating or communicating on a basis of shared belief in a way which would have incurred the penalties of the Act of Uniformity, from which the Toleration Act had exempted only those dissenters who

---

57 Carl Bridenbaugh, *Mitre and Crown* (New York, 1962).

58 *English Society, 1688–1832*, passim, and n. 52 above.

59 The classical study is that of H. J. MacLachlan, *Socianism in Seventeenth-Century England* (Oxford, 1951).

60 John Marshall, 'John Locke and Socinianism', in M. A. Stewart (ed.), *Seventeenth Century Philosophy in Historical Context* (Oxford, 1991).

were trinitarians. At the Feathers Tavern a number of these – mainly from Cambridge, where a 'Socinian' connection had been maintained at Peterhouse by Edmund Law[61] – emerged from the closet and publicly sought relief from subscribing those Articles they could not accept. Failing to secure this aim, some of them left the Church and found themselves in association with unitarians whose lineage could be traced back to a controversy over the Trinity which had divided English Presbyterianism early in the century, as well as with independent groups persisting since the Commonwealth. Under the collective name of Rational Dissent,[62] this anti-trinitarian alliance now began calling not only for relief from the Thirty-Nine articles, but for repeal of the Test and Corporation Acts which were pillars of the Anglican church-state. To the logical, outspoken and chiliastic mind of Joseph Priestley, the time had come for the fall of all religious establishments and the recognition of Christ in his true nature, that of a human being divine in mission only. By the time he published his *History of the Corruptions of Christianity* in 1782, he had come to see that the unitarian programme of the separation of church and state was in England and Scotland a demand to be realised only through 'the fall of the civil powers';[63] and only the American Revolution was to prove capable of achieving it. In what were by then the United States, it was a goal pursued by many if not most churches, and certainly not by unitarians alone; but the correspondence of the aged Adams and Jefferson almost half a century later[64] shows how far they had come to see it as pre-eminently the goal of that rational persuasion, which Jefferson thought would become the universally accepted American creed.

In the United Kingdom and especially its southern realm, Rational Dissent was recognized as a serious challenge, not least because it had arisen within as well as without the established church and enjoyed a measure of support from members of the political aristocracy. It claimed a calm and sober rationality, far removed from fanaticism and enthusiasm; it appealed to the aristocratic virtue of liberality, generosity and

---

[61] Clark, *English Society*, pp. 311–15; John Gascoigne, *Cambridge in the Age of the Enlightenment* (Cambridge, 1990).

[62] A full history of the rise of this term, and the political as well as religious movements with which it is associated, seemed a desiderandum at the moment of preparing this volume for publication.

[63] Joseph Priestley, *History of the Corruptions of Christianity* (Birmingham, 1782), II, p. 484. Cf. Gibbon, *History of the Decline and Fall of the Roman Empire*, ch. 54, n. 49 (in J. B. Bury's edition). See further R. K. Webb, 'A Christian Necessity: The Context and Consequences of Joseph Priestley', in Schochet (ed.), *Empire and Revolutions*, pp. 45–66.

[64] Lester J. Cappon (ed.), *The Adams-Jefferson Letters: The Complete Correspondence between Thomas Jefferson and Abigail and John Adams* (Chapel Hill, NC, 1959, 1988), e.g. pp. 368, 373–4, 378–86.

condescension toward those of differing opinions, and it was in this sense that the movement against the Articles and the Acts helped to re-introduce the adjective 'liberal' into the English political lexicon.[65] In its incessant suggestion that religious beliefs were matters of opinion only, Rational Dissent voiced the adiaphorism long established within the Church of England itself, with which that church had been glad to go along in its erastian polemics against nonconformity, until the point was reached at which it saw that a church based only on the sharing of opinions was not a church in communion with Christ.[66] The demand that the church should no longer be the national communion would have been enough to bring matters to that point, had it not been made – as it was – by those who could not fully accept the Nicene and Catholic definitions of Christ's divinity. The hidden demand behind the 1689 Act of Toleration – that anti-trinitarians in both the established and the nonconforming churches should observe silence and maintain privacy – was being exposed and challenged. Furthermore, rational dissenters might be genuine in their opposition to fanaticism and enthusiasm; but their doctrine of a single God who governed the universe according to the laws of reason might in a very few steps become the identification of God with the principle of reason itself, immanent in the laws governing the universe and the workings of the human mind. Once that happened, God and universe, mind and matter, would be reduced to a single principle and the intellect would be of the same substance with that which it comprehended and worshipped. A long way back in both Christian and philosophic thinking lay the diagnosis of 'enthusiasm', by which was meant any belief in personal inspiration and any heterodoxy smacking of pantheism or materialism, as the error of the mind taking its own conception of God for the presence of God himself and thus unconsciously falling into self-worship. David Hume, in both his essays and his history,[67] had given a sceptical and unbelieving form to a diagnosis ancient among orthodox believers, and his scepticism had been uneasy in the presence of the philosophic atheists of Paris, in whose insistence that mind was matter understanding the universe and itself he recognized an 'enthusiasm' which Diderot did not deny.[68]

---

[65] The point is explored by J. E. Cookson in *The Friends of Peace: Anti-war Liberalism in England, 1793–1815* (Cambridge, 1982).

[66] J. G. A. Pocock, 'Religious Freedom and the Desacralisation of Politics: from the English Civil Wars to the Virginia Statute', in Merrill D. Peterson and Robert C. Vaughan (eds.), *The Virginia Statute for Religious Freedom: Its Evolution and Consequences in American History* (Cambridge, 1988).

[67] Hume, *Essays*, 'Of Superstition and Enthusiasm', 'The Natural History of Religion', vols. V–VI of completed *History of England*.

[68] Wilda Anderson, *Diderot's Dream* (Baltimore, 1990).

There were few Diderots among the English rational dissenters – Priestley's Christian materialism is a horse of another colour – but the encounter between reason and rationalist enthusiasm was as old as the encounter between Locke and Toland.[69] Dissenters petitioning for relief and repeal used a language strongly Lockean enough to restore that philosopher to a controversial role in English discourse. Those who studied him closely knew him for a forefather of the Socinianism which had till now remained silent within the Church of England, so that the orthodox had been able to use him as a Newtonian advocate of reasonable religion; but the skeleton was now out of the cupboard. If there was to be no national church and political society no longer an ecclesiastical community, it must be founded only on the common rights of men under civil government; and conversely, Locke had stated that doctrine in language drastic enough, anti-Filmerian enough and sufficiently anti-clerical to make his *Treatises of Government* an armoury of weapons in the hands of those opposed to religious establishments. There began to appear a radically dissenting Locke, who to the extent that the attack on the established church entailed attack on the aristocratic and royal regime which upheld it could become a radically democratic Locke as well; and a view of society as existing exclusively for the maintenance of civil rights and their free enjoyment laid the foundations of that incessant criticism of institutions which has become the *raison d'être* of the liberal intellectual. The rational dissenters were the forefathers of the British Left.

The first phase of the unitarian campaigns belongs to the 1770s, a time in English political history when Whig displeasure with the policies of George III, radical discontent (both Commonwealth and Tory in its provenance) with royal and aristocratic management of parliament, colonial assaults on the legislative omnicompetence of parliament itself, and rational dissenting attempts to erode the Anglican church-state, seemed to converge in a general destabilization of institutions. In North Britain – as the former kingdom of Scotland liked to term itself – the scene was different. There was no threat to the Presbyterian establishment other than the steadily decreasing Calvinism of its Moderate managing elite, and perhaps this is a reason why there are few signs of discontent with Scotland's parliamentary status under the Union. Scotsmen had little incentive to align themselves with the chauvinistically English malcontents of the south and the only significant stress revealed by the Scottish political literature of the 1770s is the gathering pessimism of Hume, who – with his eye fixed on the politics of the

---

[69] Margaret C. Jacob, *The Radical Enlightenment: Pantheists, Freemasons and Republicans* (London, 1981).

capital – spent the years up to his death in 1776 predicting that the
growth of public debt and religious and political fanaticism would lead
'those insolent rascals in London and Middlesex'[70] to force a choice
between anarchy and absolutism fatal to the balance of the constitution.
These dark foretellings were the product of Hume's understanding of
British and general history,[71] but the years in which he put them
forward were those in which his friends among the Edinburgh and
Glasgow Moderates produced that series of great historical syntheses
which we see as the achievement of 'the Scottish Enlightenment'; Adam
Smith's long-unpublished *Lectures on Jurisprudence* (1761 and 1766),
Adam Ferguson's *Essay on the History of Civil Society* (1767), William
Robertson's *View of the Progress of Society in Europe from the Subversion
of the Roman Empire to the Accession of Charles V* (1769), John Millar's
Observations Concerning the Distinction of Ranks in Society (1771) and
finally – a work which both belongs in this series and transcends it –
Adam Smith's *Inquiry into the Nature and Causes of the Wealth of
Nations*, published in 1776, shortly before Hume's death. All these
authors were deeply affected by Hume, yet wrote out of concerns
theoretically broader than his; they drew from him the encomium 'this is
the historical age and this the historical nation'.[72] He meant Scotland;
England produced nothing comparable before 1776. Catharine Macaulay's *History of England from the Accession of James I to that of the
Brunswick Line*, published serially between 1763 and 1771 – after which
there was a ten-year hiatus – is the work of a formidable scholar whose
knowledge of the sources outdistanced Hume's, but it voices the outlook
of London patriot circles with memories of the Good Old Cause, whom
he must have thought the 'insolent rascals' threatening the death of the
constitution, and who had none of the philosophic originality of the
Scottish Moderates. England, in Hume's view, was too far gone in
faction and fanaticism to produce great history, and he was mystified
and delighted, in his last months of life, to receive the first volume of
Edward Gibbon's *History of the Decline and Fall of the Roman Empire*, as
work by an Englishman which stood among and equalled any of the
giant works of the Scottish Enlightenment.

These works arose from a variety of concerns, with history and
especially modern history, and with Scotland's, Britain's and Europe's
place in it. Robertson's *View of the Progress of Society* was a prelude to

[70] Greig, *Letters*, XI, p. 303.
[71] J. G. A. Pocock, 'Hume and the American Revolution: The Dying Thoughts of a North
    Briton', in *Virtue, Commerce and History*. Hont, 'Rhapsody of Public Debt', pp.
    125–42.
[72] Greig, *Letters*, II, p.230.

his larger history of Charles V's attempt to maintain European and American empire, the first on that scale since the Roman; he aimed – as after him did Gibbon – to study the sources of a modern plurality, almost a confederacy, of trading states in a condition of society where conquest and empire had given way to commerce, liberty and sovereignty. The Enlightened programme of replacing supernatural with social morality, and (in Protestant cultures) the decrees of grace with the practice of polite reason, necessitated an ethics of natural law, which since Pufendorf's time had become more and more a historical inquiry into the formation and progress of society.[73] The obstinate persistence of a belief in civic virtue, which required in the citizen an ability to appear in arms for the defence of his country, obliged the Scottish Moderates, following Daniel Defoe's replies to such as Andrew Fletcher, to trace the history by which this had ceased to be necessary, and the denizen of polite and commercial society had grown able to let himself be defended by semi-skilled professionals. In this part of their enterprise they were burdened by the English refusal to extend the national militia to Scotland, and the poems ascribed to Ossian, which James Macpherson began publishing in 1760, kept alive the myth of heroic armed virtue in the national (if Gaelic) past.[74] The Europe-wide cult of Ossian, rivalled only by the personality cult of Jean-Jacques Rousseau, revealed, however, the historical fragility on which the philosophy of polite and commercial society was built. Was not the enlightened and sociable modern threatened with specialization and distraction, effeminacy and corruption? Was not the heroic and virtuous ancient a regression to feudalism and a slave economy, barbarism and savagery? Where in the historic process might unity of personality be found? For Scotsmen, who both hoped and feared that Ossian and Fingal might still be alive in the mountains not far to the north, this was a poignant question.

Polite and commercial Europe, in the somewhat dubious representative of post-Petrine Russia, was extending its frontiers against both Ottoman despotism and the remnants of Central Asian and Mongol nomadism, whose history, with that of Confucian civilization, was being revealed by the Jesuit discovery of China; and in the American and African continents, European commerce and agriculture were expropriating societies based on hunter-gatherer and pre-arable tillage economies. From these historical experiences the ancient type-figures of the savage and the shepherd acquired the peculiar importance which they

[73] Istvan Hont, 'Language of Sociability and Commerce'.
[74] Sher, *Church and University*, ch. 6; Robertson, *Scottish Enlightenment*, pp. 104, 122.

held in Scottish and other Enlightened schemes of stadial history.[75] Both the inner tensions of Western society and its need to justify its hegemony over ancient empires and indigenous cultures – the two imperatives are not identical – necessitated the construction of an ideology of plough and market, according to which only the appropriation of land through cultivation, the mixture of labour with the soil, and the consequent growth of free tenures and exchange relations, laid the foundations of law, literacy, money, sociability and the progressive humanization of personality.[76] Nearly all the Scottish writers, and Gibbon with them, leaned toward the thesis that the hunter and the herdsman were more heroic but less human than the ploughman or the modern. Robertson pressed the analysis of North American savagery close to the point where it became a thesis of racial inferiority;[77] Adam Smith took the bold step of identifying the 'age of shepherds' as marking the beginnings of appropriation and civility; but it was the Englishman and former colonial governor, Thomas Pownall, who insisted that forest tribes like the Algonkian Indians were perfectly capable of regulating their hunting grounds by laws, treaties and just wars.[78] He was in a minority (at least among philosophers) when he extended the *jus gentium* to the Five Nations.

With Pownall, the imperial problem is audible once again. During the early and middle 1770s, relations between the king-in-parliament and the continental colonies moved toward open violence. Massachusetts was proclaimed in rebellion and its charter withdrawn; the Continental Congress issued a *Declaration of the Causes of Taking up Arms* and launched a preventive strike against Canada; the passage by parliament of the Quebec Act, guaranteeing the position of the French Catholic clergy, aroused the ancient spectres of the Popish Plots and the monarchy's complicity. These violent events, however, continued to be discussed in terms of the location of sovereignty within the empire. Either parliament, and the British people as represented in it, enjoyed a final and absolute sovereignty over what the latter were obliged to think of as 'our' empire; or the colonies were in the last analysis self-representing and self-governing 'states' – this term was beginning to be used – in each of which the crown exercised sovereignty only by authority and consent of the regional legislature. And if a 'people' existed only as represented and embodied in its own sovereign govern-

---

[75] R. L. Meek, *Social Science and the Ignoble Savage* (Cambridge, 1976).

[76] J. G. A. Pocock, 'Gibbon's *Decline and Fall* and the World-View of the Late Enlightenment', in *Virtue, Commerce and History*; '*Tangata whenua* and Enlightenment Anthropology', *New Zealand Historical Journal*, 26, 1, (1992), 28–53.

[77] In his *History of America* (1778).

[78] Pownall, *Administration*, pp. 259–60 and note.

ment, there must be as many 'peoples' as there were 'states'. The colonists, insisting that they were English (or British) and inherited all the rights of Englishmen, were in fact engaged in the fragmentation of the British people – an enterprise in which only Andrew Fletcher had theoretically engaged at the time when that 'people' was in process of formation.

Englishmen could see that the American programme entailed the separation of crown from parliament, threatening the unity of 'empire' which was the only guarantee against civil war and dissolution of government, those deep and still bleeding wounds in their historical memory. To some this appeared a Tory proposal; others, seeing well enough that a crown enjoying legislative authority in twenty or more parliaments at once would possess it in none, took it with greater perspicacity to be a republican. It made little different which you called it, observed that 'constitutional Whig' Josiah Tucker; since the Glorious Revolution, Jacobites and republicans had played interchangeable roles.[79] Scots committed to the Union adopted the same imperial positions; among the most vigorous defenders of the sovereignty of parliament we find Allan Ramsay, portraitist son of the author of *The Gentle Shepherd*,[80] James Macpherson the editor of Ossian,[81] and a few years later Adam Ferguson himself.[82] Only Adam Smith, walking in the footsteps of Hume, attempted an independent analysis and did not share his friend's political pessimism. The Protestants of Ireland, horrified by the Quebec Act and concerned for the autonomy of their own parliament, were a good deal less solid in their support of imperial authority. The most incisive analysts – those especially who took seriously Benjamin Franklin's predictions that, for demographic reasons, the centre of power in a unified empire must someday migrate across the Atlantic – could see that if the sovereign unity of the crown-in-parliament were the issue, it could as well be secured by ceasing to govern the colonies at all as by either reducing them to subjection or accepting their proposals for an imperial confederacy. Josiah Tucker was the strongest proponent of this view; he is rather the antithesis than the mirror-image of the commonwealthman and militia officer John Cartwright,[83] author of *American Independence the Interest and Glory of Great Britain*. Like

[79] References in Pocock, *Virtue, Commerce and History*, p. 176, n. 83.
[80] Greene, *Peripheries and Center*, pp. 107, 109; Ramsay, *Thoughts on the Origin and Nature of Government* (1768).
[81] Greene, *Peripheries and Centre*, p. 130; Macpherson, *The Rights of Great Britain Asserted against the Claims of America* (1776).
[82] Sher, *Church and University*, pp. 264–7, 273–4; Ferguson, *Remarks on a Pamphlet Lately Published by Dr. Price* (1776).
[83] John W. Osborne, *John Cartwright* (Cambridge, 1972).

Thomas Hollis, the Old Whig of Lincoln's Inn,[84] and the vociferously seditious London aldermen and liverymen – the 'disaffected patriots'[85] or 'insolent rascals of London and Middlesex' – Cartwright raises the question of just why English radicals who wanted to democratize parliament gave their support to Americans who wanted to reject its authority. Did they see it as a closed and oligarchic corporation, and hope by weakening it to appeal to the authority of the people? Had Cartwright – who wanted to rediscover Anglo-Saxon liberties in the assembly of arms-bearing freemen in the county militia – a Fletcherian vision of the empire as a confederacy of primitive democracies? In the one authentically radical Scottish voice of these years – that of John Witherspoon in New Jersey, soon to be a signatory of the Declaration of Independence – we hear the very words of the laird of Saltoun; he held that an extensive empire must be a federative not an incorporating union, and that a loosely linked confederacy might be copied elsewhere in the world as a means of general peace.[86]

There was another and more conservative response open to those in British politics who still sought reconciliation with the colonies. These terrible issues had not been raised before the Stamp Act, and it was possible to look back to an age of innocence before anyone had been foolish enough to stir them up; an attitude attractive to those disposed to blame everything on the policies of George III after 1763. Given that the competition for sovereignty among legislatures was incapable of any resolution by agreement, it was possible to argue that it should never have been allowed to break out. Here, inherited patterns of English thought offered their aid; it could be held that the government of empire had been a mixed government which it was dangerous to analyze too closely, an ancient constitution resting on custom and usage which required only to be left alone or – if it were not too late – restored. The former part of the argument spoke with the voice of Pym in 1628, the *Answer to the Nineteen Propositions* in 1642, or indeed Philip Hunton a year later; it was dangerous to define the shared powers of a mixed government with precision, and once war broke out within one it contained no authority that could settle the conflict. But the voice was no less that of Harrington and Hume, the great analysts of civil war; the ancient constitution was at bottom incoherent, and once changing social conditions, or changes in the minds of men, revealed this there was no way back. It was possible for colonial spokesmen in the eighteenth

[84] W. H. Bond, *Thomas Hollis of Lincoln's Inn: A Whig and his Books* (Cambridge, 1990).
[85] John Sainsbury, *Disaffected Patriots: London Supporters of Revolutionary America, 1769–1782* (Kingston and Montreal, 1987).
[86] Greene, *Peripheries and Center*, pp. 155, 172.

century, as for American historians in the twentieth,[87] to argue the existence of an unwritten and unspoken ancient constitution, which guaranteed to colonial assemblies the conventional understanding that they would be allowed to work out pragmatically their relations with the crown, and which only parliament's grasping at sovereignty had disturbed. The difficulty, however, was (and is) that this argument entailed the existence of two ancient constitutions,[88] one for the realm which entailed the sovereignty of king-in-parliament and one for the empire which did not; and the peoples of the realm were unaware of the existence of the latter. Thomas Pownall, moreover, had dismissed it by means of a historical analysis; it had been possible to govern overseas dominions as counties palatine while the crown was still personal, but not after 1660 when it was incorporated in parliament; and on this hypothesis it was anachronistic for Burke, in the *Speech on Conciliation with the Colonies* which he delivered in 1775, to propose recognizing the colonies in their ancient status as palatinates. Burke's eloquence against the unpractical insistence on abstract principles forms part of the emergence of his characteristic political philosophy; but on this occasion it was directed not only against those on the ministry benches and in the colonies who had posed an intractable problem, but against those writers formerly in the Grenville interest who were trying to find solutions for it.

What is noteworthy about Burke's speech for the historian of discourse is its attempt to mobilize the philosophical history of society in demonstrating that the Americans were already a distinctive people who could be governed only in ways suited to their distinctive character. He want so far as to envisage the settlers on the trans-Appalachian grasslands regressing to the nomad stage and becoming 'a race of English Tartars', who would destroy the frontier defences of a government which sought to command them.[89] His imagination in fact revealed the difficulty of applying Scottish four-stage theory to North America,

---

[87] *Ibid.*, pp. 144–50.

[88] John Phillip Reid, *In Defiance of the Law: The Standing Army Controversy, the Two Constitutions, and the Coming of the American Revolution* (Chapel Hill, NC, 1981). This problem is perhaps one source of the long-standing American interest in Coke's observations on Bonham's Case and in the possibility that ancient constitutionalism contains a doctrine of judicial review limiting the powers of Parliament. Reid's 'two constitutions', however, refer less to a metropolitan versus an imperial constitution than to a seventeenth-century view of an immemorial law that might limit even parliamentary supremacy (Bonham's Case again), versus an eighteenth-century 'ancient constitution' which was what parliament said it was. Historians who question this antithesis may still learn much from Reid's emphasis on the power of the standing army issue to delegitimize governmental measures in metropolitan eyes as well as colonial.

[89] *Works of the Rt. Hon. Edmund Burke* (Rivington edition, London, 1826), III, pp. 63–4.

where the natives had become neither mounted herdsmen nor grain-growing ploughmen, and was mercilessly derided by his most pertinacious critic Josiah Tucker.[90] Burke came closer to the historical uniqueness of English-speaking America when he described its religious culture as 'the dissidence of dissent, the protestantism of the protestant religion', less the holding of particular dogmas than the constant search after new assurances, 'agreeing in very little but the principles of liberty'.[91] Freedom of religion was coming to be equated with religion itself, as New England in particular embarked on the journey from congregationalism toward unitarianism; but Tucker seized on this too as a demonstration that Americans were becoming ungovernable on English principles and were better outside the empire than within it. He saw Burke as the pawn of a conspiracy by dissenting and anti-trinitarian enthusiasts to keep the colonies within the empire until the demographic changes predicted by Franklin enabled the forces of dissent to rule old and new England alike;[92] he seriously desired a British proclamation of independence from, rather than for, the American settlements. His proposals were too extreme even for Samuel Johnson; but they make it clear that the heart of the American problem for Britain was less the maintenance of imperial control than the preservation of essentially English institutions which the claims of empire were calling in question. What has been called 'the fall of the first British empire'[93] was the structural opposite of 'the decline and fall of the Roman empire', with which it could so easily be compared; for Rome had suffered the loss of the institutions of the res publica in the attempt to control provinces, and Britain was about to lose her American provinces rather than modify her political and ecclesiastical institutions to accommodate them. The historian of the Roman empire recalled that as a member of parliament in the North majority he had 'supported with many a sincere and silent vote the rights, though not perhaps the interest, of the mother country'.[94]

During 1774–5 the leading American spokesmen – John Adams in Massachusetts, James Wilson in Pennsylvania, Thomas Jefferson in

---

[90] Tucker, *A Letter to Edmund Burke, Esq., Member of Parliament for the City of Bristol . . . in Answer to his Printed Speech . . .* (Gloucester, 1775). Replies to Burke's speech were also written by John Cartwright and the former Jacobite John Shebbeare.

[91] *Works*, III, pp. 53–5.

[92] *The Respective Pleas and Arguments of the Mother Country and the Colonies* (Gloucester, 1775); *A Series of Answers to Certain Popular Objections against Separating from the Rebellious Colonies* (Gloucester, 1776).

[93] E.g., by Tucker and Hendrickson, *Fall of the First British Empire*.

[94] Gibbon, *Memoirs of My Life*, p. 156. There is a discussion of the circumstances in which empire in America might menace Britain with the fate of Rome in Pownall, *Administration*, pp. 92–98, 162–3, 176–7.

Virginia[95] – reiterated their theme that the colonies had been settled in the state of nature (whether this meant the wilderness in which they had acquired lands from the savages by purchase or conquest, or simply the space jointly occupied by sovereigns in the *jus gentium*) and had therefore admitted the crown to only a share of that sovereignty which they exercised over themselves. This was to claim the status of perfect states, and the crown's role as linking its dominions in a confederacy began to look less than minimal. When Jefferson proposed that the king should veto acts of the British parliament which encroached on the powers of colonial legislatures, it is hard to believe that his intentions were other than ironic; he meant to unmask the crown's absolute refusal to accept the role he was offering it. The sword was out of the scabbard by now, but – as had happened in no previous British civil war – the king was entrenched in his parliament, and lines were being drawn from which there could be no retreat. But the *Declaration of Independence* was preceded, in order of both time and events, by Thomas Paine's *Common Sense*, a text as anomalous as it was powerful, and correspondingly difficult to locate in an explicatory context.[96] Paine was an Englishman, and so described himself on the title-page of his anonymous Philadelphia pamphlet; recently arrived in Pennsylvania from London, where Benjamin Franklin had introduced him to a Club of Honest Whigs that met in Fleet Street. Yet his rhetoric is not precisely that of the Old/True/Independent/Honest Whigs of the Commonwealth tradition, and was later to diverge even further from it on the all-important question of national debt. Commonwealth rhetoric often dwelt upon an idealised national past from which it was possible to inherit an endangered but real legacy, the rights of true-born Englishmen; Paine carried a bitter anti-Normanism so far as to assert that Englishmen inherited no rights at all, enjoyed no constitution, and would never have either until they constructed a written constitution of their own. He departed from the rhetoric of ancient virtue and its modern corruption, and might seem at first sight to substitute one more revolutionary in a post-classical sense; to remedy corruption there must be a total dissolution, followed by a reconstruction on first principles. Yet *Common Sense*

[95] John Adams, *The Letters of Novanglus* (Boston, 1775); James Wilson, *Considerations on the Nature and Extent of the Legislative Authority of the British Parliament* (Philadelphia, 1774); Thomas Jefferson, *A Summary View of the Rights of British America* (Williamsburg, 1774). See further John Dickinson, *An Essay on the Constitutional Power of Great Britain over the Colonies in America* (Philadelphia, 1774); Alexander Hamilton, *The Farmer Refuted* (New York, 1775); Greene, *Peripheries and Center*, 134–5, 249.

[96] Jack Fruchtman, 'The Rhetoric of *Common Sense*', in Schochet (ed.), *Empire and Revolutions*, pp. 95–120.

is not a call for an English revolution, but for an American separation: 'it is time to part', it is ridiculous to suppose that an island may govern a continent, Americans owe no loyalty to Great Britian. This 'Englishman' – and there are senses in which it was long before Paine ceased to be one – expressed the most savage alienation from English institutions, and launched bitter attacks on the personal conduct of its monarch ('the royal brute of Great Britain'), with no further effect than to demystify English government in Pennsylvanian eyes and so prepare the way for a total separation. Paine was a journalist of genius,[97] who repeatedly discovered and created publics which had not previously known that they existed or that they wanted to hear what he proceeded to tell them; but though his English formation luridly indicates the lengths to which delegitimization of George III's monarchy had in some cases gone, the public created by *Common Sense* was an American and not a British revolutionary public. Paine was repudiating Britain altogether, whether or not his subsequent career bears out the faith on which he acted in 1776.[98]

The American Revolution was therefore an American secession and not a British revolution.[99] When the *Declaration of Independence* was received in London, the *Annual Register* previously edited by Burke – who had withdrawn from attending in parliament and can only with difficulty be said to have adopted any attitude toward the American Revolution, properly so called – correctly perceived that its intention was to convert a rebellion and civil war into a war between states.[100] George Washington, who had hitherto in his dispatches referred to Gage's troops as 'the ministerial army' – thus placing himself in a long line of noble commanders reluctantly in arms against evil counsellors – could now change his language and call them 'the British army'. The effect of the *Declaration* was to affirm and enact that Americans were not British any longer. It did so by employing the language of English argument to perform two affirmative actions.[101] One, undertaken at the

[97] Eric W. Foner, *Tom Paine and Revolutionary America* (New York, 1970).

[98] Gregory Claeys, *Thomas Paine: Social and Political Thought* (Boston, 1989).

[99] I would like to this extent to modify the opening words (intended to be paradoxical) of '1776: the Revolution Against Parliament', originally published in *Three British Revolutions: 1641, 1688* and *1776* (Princeton, 1980) and subsequently in *Virtue, Commerce and History*.

[100] It is worth adding that the *Annual Register* regularly dealt with American events in the section headed 'History of Europe'.

[101] The reading of the *Declaration* that follows is elaborated in J. G. A. Pocock, 'Republics, States and Empires: The American Founding in Early Modern Perspective', in Terence Ball and J. G. A. Pocock (eds.), *Conceptual Change and the Constitution* (Lawrence, 1988), and *The Politics of Extent and the Problems of Freedom* (Colorado College Studies 25) (Colorado Springs, 1988).

outset of the *Declaration*, was the separation of one 'people', the American, from another 'people', the British. The second, achieved in the *Declaration's* closing words, was the erection of thirteen colonies into free and independent 'states', 'united' with one another in a sense less immediately important to define than was their separation from a fourteenth 'state', that of Great Britain, with which their relations were henceforth to be those of peace or war, as was normal between independent sovereignties. The *Declaration of Independence* was soon – perhaps immediately – to be considered the charter of a new American civil society; but an examination of its language shows it to have been initially a document performed in the discourse of *jus gentium* rather than *jus civile*. The rhetoric which declares all men to have been created free and equal decrees the right of Americans to be a people and to found states; it leads to the declaration that the British people, to whom the American was previously familially bonded, are now 'enemies in war, in peace friends', occupying the role of a state to which the American states are now related by the laws which obtain between nations. The American revolution is a process in the creation of states; that some of these states are democratically constituted is a consequence, but not at this stage a necessary or immediate one.

It also follows that the *Declaration* does not contain, but rather repudiates, any suggestion that revolutionary processes are going on, or should be, within the government of Great Britain. The British people are indeed reproached for their continuing support of the King and his ministers, and this is made a further reason why the American people should separate themselves from them; in the last analysis, it is the British people on whom the American people are now declaring war. But war is one thing and revolution is another; there is not much suggestion in *Common Sense*, and none whatever in the *Declaration of Independence*, that George III's government over the peoples of Great Britain has been dissolved by malpractice, and the ties that are dissolved in the latter document are those binding one people to another – the ties hitherto constituting a confederation between peoples. Nor does it immediately appear that 'the American people', or the thirteen states constituting it, has undergone a dissolution of civil government or regressed to a Lockean state of nature. The colonies now declared states have long possessed civil governments, and in that sense are states already; what they are doing is less equipping themselves with governments than asserting or repossessing the sovereignty by which they act as states, in a 'state of nature' which is less that preceding the establishment of civil government in a theory of political society than that obtaining between sovereigns in a theory of the law of nations. Hence the importance of

Grotius, Pufendorf and Vattel, alongside Sidney, Locke and Hoadly, in the triadic incantations of Founders' rhetoric.

The *Declaration of Independence* is very importantly a Lockean document, but it cannot yet be seen as a Lockean politics of the relations of government to society, a Lockean political ecclesiology of religious liberty, or a Lockean political economy of individual property and rights. All the more or less Lockean grievances which it recites against the misgovernment of George III must be taken in the context of the specialized ultra-Lockean move originally performed by Bland and Otis: the exploitation of Locke's insistence on the right of emigration to maintain that settlers going forth of the realm established natural societies only naturally related to the realm's government. The logic of that argument was to convert the crown's dominions into a confederation, but that logic had barely been perceived before it was employed by the *Declaration*'s authors in proclaiming the confederation dissolved. The nature of civil government in the newly independent states, or in the union newly proclaimed but not yet defined between them, had next to be taken up, but it was not the *Declaration*'s purpose to address it. Perhaps this is paradoxically why it became necessary to treat the *Declaration* as the foundational charter of a new civil society which textually it was not and took some time to become. And in the context of the British history from which it severed American, 1776 was not a Lockean moment of dissolution and reversion, but yet another of those occasions which have ensured that these processes have never occurred in the history in which they were invented. Not even Paine summoned the British peoples to revolution.

9 Political thought in the English-speaking Atlantic, 1760–1790 Part 2: Empire, revolution and the end of early modernity

J. G. A. Pocock

The preceding chapter began with an apologia for commencing its narrative about the time of George III's accession. This chapter, the last in the historical series constituting the volume, must conclude with an apologia for breaking off the narrative at about the midpoint of his reign, instead of carrying it on to the end of his successor's, on the grounds that historical events – including events in the history of political discourse – occurring about the outbreak of war with revolutionary France, increasingly belong to a history shaped by forces other than those which have been invoked in holding this volume together. The themes to be treated are: the recovery of imperial monarchy from the shock of the American crisis, accompanied by the final exit of the United States from the history of British discourse into a discourse and a history of their[1] own; the British response to the revolution in France and the circumstances attending the twenty years of war which followed; and the case for positing an 'end of early modernity' at the outset of this period. The organising concepts will continue to be the history of the order laid down in English church and state by the Tudors, and the implications of the Scottish accession to this order and the American departure from it; but the order will be depicted as existing in a world even more remote from that in which it was first created than was the world brought into being during William III's reign, and diminishingly governed by that world's organizing concepts.

If this volume has had a single theme, it has been one more English than British or imperial: the construction, crisis and survival of the unified sovereignty in church and state proclaimed during the reign of Henry VIII. That sovereignty fell into a crisis, nearly but incompletely

---

[1] Historians of American political speech have noted that 'the United States' was generally used as a plural noun before the Civil War, but as singular after it.

revolutionary, during the civil wars, dissolutions of government and other violent disturbances between 1637 and 1689, and the great discourses of authority and liberty, in matters civil as well as ecclesiastical, which concern historians of political thought and philosophy, are part of that crisis. But the Tudor structure was restored on two foundations: a unity of king-in-parliament, not complete until long after 1689 and often if misleadingly described in the language of mixed government first made official in 1642; and the renewed establishment of a national church whose ascendancy was (after 1689) both mitigated and reinforced by a limited toleration. The discourse of the Hanoverian regime after 1714 was the discourse of Tudor sovereignty modified but restored, though at the same time never free from insecurities of which some were older than others. This is why it is valuable to describe it as an *ancien régime*, while insisting that it did not fall with others in the general crisis of the closing years of the eighteenth century.

In the process of ensuring its survival of the deep but temporary crisis of 1688, this regime committed itself to a long series of wars in Europe, of which the Glorious Revolution itself may be considered as a detail. In pursuing that commitment – often most unwillingly – the English sovereignty was obliged to transform itself into a powerful military and financial state; to enlarge itself into Great Britain by the Union with Scotland in 1707; to take its place in the power politics of post-Ludovican Europe before and after 1713; and to pursue – by no means unwillingly and with a dynamism generated out of itself – maritime empire in the Caribbean, North America and India. A major consequence for this volume has been the rapid transformation of British political thought traceable from the decade 1688–1698, when the matter of discourse, without ceasing to be one of authority and right – a discourse of law – became in addition one of wealth, manners and historical change – a discourse of culture – in which the British *ancien régime*, like and yet unlike other regimes in Europe, debated its own suddenly-realized modernity and the changes in political, historical and religious consciousness which that entailed. We are soon to enquire whether the decade of the 1790s witnessed a similar transformation.

This chapter and its predecessor explore a series of crises arising after 1760 in the regime established in 1689 and 1714. Some arose internally, from the conditions of the Hanoverian succession itself, and were considered by contemporaries in the light of their understanding of sixteenth- and seventeenth-century history. Others arose imperially, from the expansion of the realm of England into the kingdom of Great Britain, the problems presented by the dependent kingdom of Ireland, and the momentous if transitory establishment of an English-speaking universal empire in the North Atlantic and Alleghanian America. The crisis of George III's monarchy between 1763 and 1783 was both a crisis within the realm, and interrelatedly a crisis in the relations between realm and empire. A further series of problems arose from the transformation of Britain into a European power, taking part in both the politics and the culture of the *ancien régime* which emerged from the *siècle de Louis XIV*. When that Europe entered the revolutionary crisis we term the *caduta dell'Ancien Régime*, the British *ancien régime* responded in ways distinctively its own, conditioned in due measure by its own past history. To understand that response, we must return to the American secession of 1776 and its ratification in 1783.

I

Because the American revolution was a secession from the British political system, it wounded that system but did not challenge its structure. There was no attempt to bring about a dissolution of government within the three kingdoms, and though the language of mixed government was strong enough to generate a great deal of concern about the corruption of parliamentary rule, the American condemnation of the system as irretrievably tainted, and departure to construct a mixed government along republican lines, led to a British reaffirmation of the sovereignty of the crown-in-parliament, a principle of which the mixed government declared in 1642 had never been more than a specialized formulation. This can be understood if we follow out the rhetoric of 1776, first of those who had endorsed the claims of the former colonies and then of those who differed from these sympathizers.

In the successive editions[2] of his *Observations on Civil Liberty*, first appearing in 1776, the dissenter Richard Price carried on Hume's analysis of the imperial crisis as an effect of the growth of the national debt, and quoted at length from the recently deceased philosopher; but he did so from an advanced radical point of view. At bottom, Price's concerns were those of a rational dissenter, campaigning on anti-trinitarian grounds (he was Arian in his theology) for a separation between civil rights and religious allegiance, and he may not have been far from Joseph Priestley and David Hartley in seeing the American

---

[2] *Observations on the Nature of Civil Liberty, the Principles of Government, and the Justice and Policy of the War with America*, was first published in 1776 and claimed eight editions by 1778. *Additional Observations on the Nature and Value of Civil Liberty, and the War with America* was first published in 1777 and was in a third edition by 1778, when the two were published together as *Two Tracts on Civil Liberty, the War with America, and the Debts and Finances of the Kingdom* (see Da Capo Press reprint, New York, 1972).

revolution as presaging the 'fall of the civil powers'[3] which maintained the Mammon of religious establishments. The individual for the sake of whose liberty he desired a reformation of politics was essentially concerned with rational self-determination in religious and therefore in civil life, and though he desired an enlarged and therefore more virtuous electorate he had no objection to seeing excluded from it those too shiftless and dependent to be worthy of representation.

Price was a moralist first and a democrat (to the extent that he was one) by way of consequence.[4] He infuriated those of his time who believed in the primacy of civil society and its authority, incurring the wrath of figures as diverse as Adam Ferguson, Josiah Tucker, Edmund Burke and John Adams;[5] and all these saw that he insisted on the moral autonomy and responsibility of the individual to the point where all government was necessarily imperfect except in very small self-governing republics. There were parallels with Rousseau (as Tucker saw) and would be with Kant (as soon as anyone in Britain heard of the philosopher of Königsberg), the consequence of Price's Rational Dissent which moved the locus of morality and religion to the austerity and freedom of the inner life; but it was rapidly seen that he had made the ability to satisfy the individual conscience the test of any government's legitimacy, and was not hopeful that any government could meet that test. His critics therefore accused him of enthusiasm, asked what morality there could be if government were perpetually delegitimized by

---

[3] The phrase employed by Priestley in *A History of the Corruptions of Christianity* (Birmingham, 1782), II, p. 484, and 'recommended to public animadversion' by Gibbon at the end of ch. 54 of the *Decline and Fall* (vol. V, 1788). For instances of this often millennial expectation among unitarians, see Clarke Garrett, *Respectable Folly: Millenarians and the French Revolution in France and England* (Baltimore, 1975), Jack Fruchtman, Jr., *The Apocalyptic Politics of Richard Price and Joseph Priestley: A Study in Late Eighteenth-Century English Republican Millenarianism* (Philadelphia, 1983); J. van den Berg, 'Priestley, the Jews and the Millennium', in David S. Katz and Jonathan I. Israel (eds.), *Skeptics, Millenarians and Jews* (Leiden, 1990); and R. K. Webb, 'A Christian Necessity: The Context and Consequences of Joseph Priestley', in Schochet (ed.) *Empire and Revolutions* (Folger Shakespeare Library, 1992), pp. 45–66.

[4] D. O. Thomas, *The Honest Mind: The Thought and Work of Richard Price* (Oxford, 1977) and n. 42 below.

[5] Adam Ferguson, *Remarks on a Pamphlet Lately Published by Dr. Price* (Edinburgh, 1776); Josiah Tucker, *Treatise Concerning Civil Government* (London, 1781); Edmund Burke, *Reflections on the Revolution in France and the Proceedings of Certain Societies in London Relating to that Event* (London, 1790); John Adams, *A Defence of the Constitutions of the United States* (London, 1786). Price had received the letter of Turgot to which Adams took exception. For Adam's *Defence*, see further Gordon S. Wood, *The Creation of the American Republic* (Chapel Hill, NC, 1969), pp. 565–92, and J. G. A. Pocock, ' "The Book Most Misunderstood Since the Bible': John Adams and the Confusion about Aristocracy', in Anna Maria Martellone and Elizabetta Vezzosi (eds.), *Fra Toscana e Stati Uniti: il Discorso Politico nell'Età della Costituzione Americana* (Florence, 1989), pp. 181–201.

the conscience, and enquired into the foundations of authority entailed by their more conservative ethics. Thought not a major philosopher and remembered in part for the replies he provoked, Price is a notable figure in the transformation of British nonconformity into the ethos of perpetual dissent from the practices of government which has marked the intellectual Left.

More immediately, he serves to remind the reader of this volume that the campaign against the Thirty-Nine Articles and the Test and Corporation Acts, which Rational Dissent had been conducting at intervals since the Feathers Tavern petition, was an aspect of the imperial crisis and the demands for parliamentary reform which recurred during the American War. If government was to be divorced from confessional identification, it must seek a basis in a general theory of rights and religious liberty must itself become one of those rights for which government existed. Such doctrines could be found in John Locke, who now emerged as the intellectual hero of Americans and Rational Dissenters alike, forcing the established regime to recognize the radicalism of a figure it had long sought to co-opt. At the same time, persistent Whig and Old Whig discontent with the regrouping of factions sought by George III joined with American attacks on the absolute sovereignty of the crown-in-parliament to encourage the image of a representative corrupted by the executive and in need of reform by the obligation – sought as far back as the New Model Army and the Good Old Cause – to address itself more often to the people it represented. To the ancestral demand for more frequent parliaments was now added the charge that a corrupt representative corrupted the people themselves, and that a reform of the system was needed to discover and preserve the more virtuous electorate on which it must rest.

The movements aimed at reform of the governing system during the late seventies and early eighties were multi-faceted and cannot be Whiggishly treated as mere anticipations of the reforms of the next century – though it is proper and important to ask how far they were continuations of older 'commonwealth' and 'county' discontents, and how far indications of the emergence of new social structures, based less on domestic industry and elite patronage and more upon class;[6] an answer to such questions cannot be attempted here. Richard Price, an advocate for the admission of dissenters to full civil rights in parliament and out of it, clung as long as he could to the American programme of substituting for a unified empire under parliamentary sovereignty a confederation of independent legislatures with a central council – he

[6] John Brewer, 'English Radicalism in the Age of George III', in J. G. A. Pocock (ed.), *Three British Revolutions: 1641, 1688, 1778* (Princeton, 1980).

called it a 'senate' but it would have been more like a *Reichskammer-gericht* – to resolve their differences. Here was the familiar Tory-flavoured design of separating Crown from Parliament; but it must be asked how far Price (and John Cartwright) were aiming at reducing both to a greater dependency on the 'people'. The unity of the English crown and parliament is the guiding thread of Anglo-British history in this period; it could not be adjusted to meet the demands of the American colonies and would survive losing them to independent statehood. The 'democratic' demands of the seventies and eighties were in some measure demands for the separation of crown and parliament, the better to subject them to the 'people', and had within that measure undertones both Tory and republican; the fact that they were linked to a programme for separation of church and state underlined the truth that it was the edifice of Tudor sovereignty over an 'empire' ecclesiastical as well as civil that was still so persistently at stake.

How far this empire, challenged and overthrown on the eastern seaboard of North America, was at risk in its homeland – how far, to borrow language from a great historian, the history of the kingdom of Great Britain may be included in that of a *crisi, crollo* or *caduta dell'Ancien Regime in Europa*[7] – is a problem. Herbert Butterfield raised over forty years ago the question of how far it was at risk as an effect of the imperial – and structural? – crisis. His *George III, Lord North and the People*[8] examined the events of 1780 on the hypothesis that the Yorkshire, Middlesex and London petitioning movements of that year exhibited Britain in a condition where revolution could be (as it was) envisaged as a possible outcome. The proposition that the kingdom was in a condition of potential revolution, however, too easily degenerated into an exploration of the probabilities of one occurring in actuality; and as none occurred in fact, the positivist historiography of the 1950s too readily dismissed the hypothesis as one not even worth exploring. What emerged beyond question, however, was that language was current which envisaged the uncorrupted freemen affirming their Anglo-Saxon liberties by assembling in tithings and hundreds to petition – an act initially peaceable and deferential, but potentially tumultuous and disorderly – for a better representation in parliament, whose systemic base their own assemblies might provide; and that it was

---

[7]   Franco Venturi, *Settecento Riformatore, III: la prima crisi dell'Antico Regime* (Turin, 1979; English translation by R. Burr Litchfield, *The End of the Old Regime in Europe, 1768–1776: The First Crisis*, Princeton, 1989), ch. 12; *Settecento Riformatore, IV(1): la caduta dell'Antico Regime (1776–1789). I grandi stati dell'Occidente* (Turin, 1984), chs. 1–11. Litchfield, *The End of the Old Regime in Europe, 1776–1789: I: The Great States of the West* (Princeton, 1991).

[8]   London, 1949.

possible to look beyond the grass-roots in country and town to the grand spectre of a general convention of 'the people', to whom power might revert were parliament decreed so corrupt as to be dissolved. This never happened, and we may say that it was never probable or even possible that it would happen; but history consists not only in what did happen, but of what those living in it knew or believed might happen, and it is the case that the intention of convoking or invoking such a convention figures regularly in the treason trials of the 1790s, as an indicator of revolutionary designs that must be proved or disclaimed.

None of this happened, and the year 1780 witnessed the strong disinclination of such parliamentary Whigs as Burke to have anything to do with parliamentary reform or relief for dissenters. In June occurred the calamitous Gordon Riots in London, which discredited popular action by depicting it as reverting to its atavistic and fanatic origins. Yet the scenario had been written for a revolutionary counter-history, in which power should have reverted to the 'people', assembled to affirm their native virtue even in arms – for John Cartwright's fantasies of Saxon freedom[9] entailed a militia more Andrew Fletcher's than Edward Gibbon's. Such would have been what the discourse of the age termed a 'patriot' revolution, and it is tempting to remark that the only European state flung into revolution as an immediate result of the American war was not Britain but the Republic of the Netherlands, where the failure of the House of Orange in the Fourth English War provoked *de Patriottentijd*, an unsuccessful rebellion appealing *aan het volk van Nederland* against Orangist and regent elites alike in representing the Dutch *ancien régime*.[10] But we should not allow the continental to blind us to the insular perspective. In 1782 may be dated a 'patriot' revolution in another European kingdom: that of Ireland, where a Protestant militia officered by the nobility and gentry held a grand national convention in the county Tyrone and the town of Dungannon, and successfully demanded the convocation of the Patriot Parliament, to emancipate itself from the imperial control of the British crown-in-

[9] *Take Your Choice! Representation and Respect: Imposition and Contempt: Annual Parliaments and Liberty: Long Parliaments and Slavery* (London, 1776); *The Constitutional Defence of England, Internal and External* (London, 1796); *An Appeal, Civil and Military, on the Subject of the English Constitution* (London, 1799), *The English Constitution Produced and Illustrated* (London, 1823). John W. Osborne, *John Cartwright* (Cambridge, 1972).

[10] Simon Schama, *Patriots and Liberators: Revolution in the Netherlands, 1780–1813* (New York, 1977); I. Leonard Leeb, *The Ideological Origins of the Batavian Revolution, history and politics in the Dutch Republic, 1747–1800* (The Hague, 1973); Margaret C. Jacob and W. W. Mijnhardt (eds.), *The Dutch Republic in the Eighteenth Century: Decline, Enlightenment and Revolution* (Ithaca, NY, 1992). The last grows out of a conference held at the Folger Shakespeare Library during 1987.

parliament.[11] Echoing what had been American demands for independent legislatures under a common crown, the Irish Volunteers attracted the excited interest of militia-minded English reformers and dissenters, and seemed for a moment to presage the triumph of Fletcherian alternative politics. But there was no Scottish equivalent; the Americans had abandoned their British and Irish sympathizers; the English movement had collapsed; and we see in hindsight patriot Ireland moving into the sequence of failed Catholic relief, the advent of the United Irishmen and an Irish brand of Jacobinism, the rebellion of 1798, the backlash of Orange loyalism, and the fateful Union of 1801. The *ancien régime*, if we are using that term, reconsolidated its empire and transformed itself; which is not to say that it fell.

Much of its response – including the ultimate necessity of a union with Ireland – is presaged by Josiah Tucker.[12] His significantly-titled *Treatise Concerning Civil Government* (1781) is a treatise written against Locke, the first systematic attack on his politics since the days of Charles Leslie; but Tucker's Locke was emphatically the Locke of the movement for repeal of the Test Acts and relief from the Thirty-Nine Articles. We have seen how he took up Burke's account of the American 'dissidence of dissent' as an argument for British separation from the colonies; in his *magnum opus* Tucker now argued that the identification of moral, religious and political liberty was a Lockean error on which Price, Priestley and the Americans all relied, so that Locke appeared a founding father of Socinian and enthusiastic politics incompatible with civil government. Government depended on the individual's capacity to alienate rights to the sovereign and to see himself represented by others, but to make his moral self-determination the prerequisite of each rendered him incapable of doing either. Tucker considered Locke's insistence on a civil right to religious liberty the fatal step which had made him a precursor of Rousseau – whose condemnation of representation as a moral anomaly Tucker quoted with ironic satisfaction – and had led Price to set up the moral liberty of the individual as a prerequisite to the legitimacy of any government whatever. Tucker was a bitter critic of the Burke of 1774–75, but in his 1781 attack on Price in his pro-American vein he had anticipated much of what Burke would say of him in his pro-French attitude eight years later. He had not quite come to terms with the Locke who had remained a communicant in the Church of England, but he had rediscovered (if the Church had ever forgotten) that Locke who could be exploited by anti-trinitarians within and

[11] R. B. McDowell, *Ireland in the Age of Imperialism and Revolution, 1760–1801* (Oxford, 1979); F. G. James, *Ireland in the Empire, 1688–1770* (Cambridge, MA, 1973).
[12] Above, p. 264, n. 46; detailed references in *Virtue, Commerce and History*, there cited.

outside the Anglican communion and appear an apostle of religious and civil dissent on both shores of the Atlantic Ocean.

Tucker did not consider this Locke an exponent of progress and enlightenment, but employed an extensive knowledge of Scottish philosophic history and political economy in presenting him as an essentially archaic thinker. The state of nature was historically speaking a state of savagery; therefore civil rights could be established only in the course of history, and those who sought to ground them in nature antecedent to history were incapable of developing them beyond the slaveholding and feudal stages of society. This had been the predicament of all the giants of seventeenth-century political theory; Filmer and Hobbes, Harrington and Sidney, sharing with Locke the misfortune of living before the age of Walpole, had been obliged to choose between erecting a patriarchal monarchy and making every man a patriarch.[13] Tucker laid stress on Locke's role in writing the *Fundamental Constitutions of Carolina*, as on his possible complicity in Monmouth's invasion of 1685, to present him as an advocate of both slavery and rebellion, like his American admirers at the time of writing. Samuel Johnson had asked why 'the loudest yelps for liberty' were heard from 'the drivers of negroes',[14] and Tucker thought he knew the answer. Like Adam Smith, he held that republicans were necessarily slaveholders, and added that slaveholders were generally republicans; Locke shared with the philosophers of antiquity an archaic and unhistorical, because economically undiversified, image of the natural man and his liberty; the American revolution was a rebellion of Atlantic slave plantations against the commercial and political disciplines of the modern world; and the Locke-quoting unitarians of England and Wales – Tucker noted that there were few in Scotland – joined them in holding a doctrine of religious liberty as archaically enthusiastic as their doctrine of civil liberty was archaically republican. As for the reformation of the English parliamentary franchise, most of its advocates were demagogic noblemen – Richmond, Bedford, Shelburne – looking for support from the under-employed mobs of London and Westminster; if carried out at all, it should be based on the work-disciplined wage-labour forces of the new industrial towns, who understood their role in a modern economy. (Tucker, we may observe, was writing in an age of innocence before the Poor Laws and Corn Laws.)

Only an Anglican clergyman could have written political economy with his devastating insouciance and insight, but a greater mind had

---

[13] Tucker, *Four Letters on Important National Subjects, addressed to the Right Honourable the Earl of Shelburne* (Gloucester, 1783), p. 97.
[14] Johnson, *Taxation not Tyranny*, in Donald J. Greene (ed.), *The Works of Samuel Johnson* (New Haven, CT, 1977), V, pp. 451–4.

been before him in 1776. Adam Smith's *Enquiry into the Nature and Causes of the Wealth of Nations* is a work of comprehensive genius and must therefore be presented in a number of overlapping contexts.[15] First, it was part of a programme in jurisprudence,[16] to understand which it is helpful to emphasize the component 'justice' in the compound title of Smith's 'lectures on justice, police, revenue and arms'; an attempt to show how the moral and material goods of society were distributed and regulated by the laws of the human mind. In the course of this attempt, Smith was led to inquire into juristic and ethical problems:[17] the relations between rich and poor countries, the rights of the poor and the justice of their causes in times of scarcity, such as were disastrously overtaking parts of Europe during the 1760s. He explored the proposition that though the relations between rich and poor were not finally just, nevertheless a highly productive economy was to be preferred to one which required moral regulation precisely because it could not produce enough for all. Smith borrowed the term 'police', little used in English, from the French; among its possible meanings he singled out the circulation of the produce of the countryside into the towns, a task at which the French economy seemed to be failing in the 1770s like the Soviet economy in the 1980s. A 'nation' from this point of view seemed to be a territory politically unified to form a large trading area.

In the second place, the *Wealth of Nations* is part of a programme in moral philosophy,[18] in which Smith had been engaged since he began teaching rhetoric and *belles-lettres* to Glasgow students in the 1750s. Human morality was necessarily sociable, and could not exist without a systematic exchange of goods, ideas and beneficent actions; commerce was therefore a prerequisite of manners and morals alike. It was necessary to conduct a detailed investigation into the processes of production and circulation in a society, and of the formation of the human individual through engagement in these processes; specific

---

[15] The recent literature on Smith is large and various. Donald Winch, *Adam Smith's Politics: An Essay in Historiographic Revision* (Cambridge, 1978); A. S. Skinner, *A System of Social Science: Papers Relating to Adam Smith* (Oxford, 1979); Istvan Hont and Michael Ignatieff (eds.), *Wealth and Virtue: The Shaping of Political Economy in the Scottish Enlightenment* (Cambridge, 1983).

[16] Knud Haakonssen, *The Science of a Legislator: The Natural Jurisprudence of David Hume and Adam Smith* (Cambridge, 1981).

[17] Istvan Hont and Michael Ignatieff, 'Needs and Justice in the *Wealth of Nations*: An Introductory Essay', and Hont, 'The Rich Country–Poor Country Debate in Scottish Classical Political Economy', in Hont and Ignatieff (eds.), *Wealth and Virtue*, pp. 1–44, 271–316.

[18] Richard F. Teichgraeber III, *Free Trade and Moral Philosophy: Rethinking the Sources of Adam Smith's Wealth of Nations* (Durham, NC, 1986); and 'Less Abused than I had Reason to Expect: The Reception of *The Wealth of Nations* in Britain, 1776–90', *Historical Journal*, 30, 2 (1987), 337–66.

problems in ethics – the question of justice mentioned above, the relations between selfishness and benevolence, conscience and approval, in the constitution of moral personality – arose and needed to be addressed in the course of this enquiry. The individual might be naturally good, or else naturally acquisitive, naturally sociable, and naturally engaged in processes of social formation in which goodness was attained so far as might be; a problem as old as Plato's *Republic*. The growth of political economy in the Scottish Enlightenment appears as the latest phase in the long history of European humanism and humanist philosophy.

But without departing from this context, it is possible to present the *Wealth of Nations* as, in the third place, part of a great eighteenth-century programme of enquiry into the history of society.[19] Since the addition of Pufendorf to Locke at the foundations of Scottish natural jurisprudence, the sociability of mankind had been perceived increasingly as a historical process, developing through a sequence of stages of appropriation, distribution and production; and the humanist dimension of the enquiry, together with the problems peculiar to Scotland and Britain in the century after 1689, had led to an incessant concern with the question of 'arms', identified by Smith as the fourth term in the summation of his Glasgow lectures. What was the role of weapons, as a means of military valour and a constituent of civil personality, in the historic movement from heroic barbarism through political virtue to modern politeness; what would be the ethical consequences if 'virtue' in this sense were to be given up? This set of concerns recur throughout the text of the *Wealth of Nations*, and there is no reason to suppose that they are finally resolved; rather, we are to see Smith and his text as poised on the historical hinge between the standing armies of post-Utrecht Europe and the democratized citizen armies of the century and a half between 1793 and 1945.[20]

Fourthly and lastly, 'the wealth of nations', if taken in isolation, would paradoxically convey the mercantilist message inherent in the growth of such proto-sciences as 'political arithmetic', *police, Statistik* and cameralism: that productivity and population, the counterflow of imports and exports, were indices to the wealth and power of states, and that governments maintained their competitive as well as their normative sovereignty by regulating such phenomena. Smith, of course – as a whole history of his debate with mercantilist and physiocratic proposi-

---

[19] See above, pp. 272–4, and Gladys Bryson, *Man and Society: The Scottish Enquiry of the Eighteenth Century* (Princeton, 1945).
[20] J. G. A. Pocock, 'The Political Limits to Pre-Modern Economics', in John Dunn (ed.), *The Economic Limits to Modern Politics* (Cambridge, 1990), pp. 121–41.

tions makes clear – aimed to maintain that the 'wealth of nations' inhered not in states, but in the involvement of individuals in complex processes which, while helping to constitute states, were not confined within their borders and were not necessarily best regulated by their governmental powers. It is this – combined with his use on one occasion of the phrase 'an invisible hand' and his attitude toward selfishness in the constitution of the moral individual as an economic being – which has earned Smith the name of a *laissez-faire* economist; but nothing can be less justified by a survey of the multi-contextual character of the *Inquiry and Causes* than the conventional belief that it established political economy as an autonomous science independent and exclusive of history, philosophy and ethics.[21] Adam Smith was a humanist, a moralist and a historian; while as for the place of the state in his economics, it is worth remembering that he made 'revenue' the third term in his tetrad of the 1760s, and that by 1790 his acquaintance and reader Edmund Burke was proclaiming that public virtue was nowhere better displayed than in the management of the public revenue.[22] The relations between ancient and modern ethics did not disappear when solutions were found to the problems which they posed.

The contention that the wealth and power of nations existed independently of their governments and political frontiers imparted great ideological significance to the appearance of the *Wealth of Nations* in 1776. Smith was a close student of the American problem, and believed that it might be solved if colonial constituencies could be represented in parliament and the ambitions of their elites satisfied by involvement in Westminster politics (though he was not sanguine that this would in fact be done). His demonstration that commerce was not dependent on empire, and that the loss of dominion over the colonies would not after all be fatal to either trade or power, did something to ensure that British self-confidence would survive both the failure to reduce them to subjection and the partial loss of a European war waged without a continental ally.

II

Smith and Tucker present the response to the American Revolution of essentially conservative Whig Enlightenment at its most intellectually adventurous; at the high point of its grasp of history. There are historical scenarios, however, in which the ascendancy of the Whig intellect must

[21] Winch, *Adam Smith's Politics*, Hont and Ignatieff (eds.), *Wealth and Virtue*.

[22] Burke, *Reflections on the Revolution in France*, vol. VIII in L. G. Mitchell and W. B. Todd (eds.), *The Writings and Speeches of Edmund Burke* (Oxford, 1989).

be seen as about to come to an end, and to comprehend them we must revert to the American disruption of the Atlantic empire. It had been built upon the imperial monarchy of the crown-in-parliament, and this it had been usual to describe in a language of mixed government ultimately derived from Charles I's *Answer to the Nineteen Propositions of Parliament*. This language had always been two-faced; it could be used to emphasise the trinity rather than the unity of King, Lords and Commons (or else of executive, legislative and judiciary), independent agencies correcting one another or corrupting the balance of the constitution if they interfered with one another's functions; or it could emphasize (as it always had) the unity of the sovereign power whose components were exercised conjointly. When the colonies had begun challenging the omnicompetence of king-in-parliament, they had been sternly told that the latter's sovereignty was absolute, irresponsible and indivisible; a reply as Tory in their ears as it was Whig in the mouths that uttered it. There were Whig and Commonwealth malcontents, however, busy accusing the king and his friends of separating themselves from parliament and corrupting it, and the colonists and their sympathizers easily assumed that when the two Houses affirmed the authority of king-in-parliament, they had been corrupted into affirming that of the king alone. Americans consequently had recourse to that language which was called republican because it insisted on the essential separateness of the three powers, loudly voiced the virtue of the citizen as the only guard against corruption, and even saw an appeal to the uncorrupt people as the remedy for corruption in their rulers and representatives.

The independent United States confronted after 1783 the double problem of how their free institutions were to be kept from corruption, and of what were to be the relations between the states proclaimed in 1776 to be at once free and independent, and in some undefined sense united. Was this union to be a pure confederacy, held together by treatise alone, or was it to be one of those, ancient and modern, which had transferred some powers at least to a central agency? By the end of the 1780s the great invention of Federalism had furnished American political culture with a discourse and agenda of its own,[23] which forever separated it from its British parent, and it is a difficult historical problem

---

[23] There is a vast and often classic historical literature on this subject. Of particular relevance to the approach taken here are: Gordon S. Wood, *The Creation of the American Republic, 1776–1787* (Chapel Hill, NC, 1969); Jack P. Greene, *Peripheries and Center in the Extended Polities of the British Empire and the United States, 1607–1788* (New York, 1990), and Peter S. Onuf, *The Origins of the Federal Republic: Jurisdictional Controversies in the United States, 1775–1787* (Philadelphia, 1983).

to determine what elements in American discourse are British-derived, what rejections of Britain, and what derived from elsewhere. There was no British discourse of confederation, except for those Scots who remembered Andrew Fletcher,[24] and the inveterate determination of the English to maintain the unity of their government – since they knew what its dissolution had cost them – rendered them incapable of listening to any such arguments; it is therefore the more remarkable that colonial spokesmen had responded so quickly in 1764 with programmes to reconstitute the empire as a confederacy. Independent and precariously united, they sent to Europe – for all the world like the Romans of old sending to Athens for laws – for books on the subject of confederacies, and by an extraordinary feat of political inventiveness came up with the doctrine of a national government twofold in character, both a civil government exercising sovereignty over individuals and a federal government exercising authority over states.

The discourse of Federalism lies outside – if only just outside – the history of political discourse which is British; it was precluded, if at the same time mysteriously invented, by everything which had shaped English history and the Anglo-British mind. We can however trace certain contributions made by the latter to the debates at Philadelphia and the authorship of the *Federalist Papers*: the belief in a common law inherited by all Americans as former Englishmen, which disposed them to accept a common legislative sovereign exercising *imperium* or empire in a civilian sense; the notion of empire in its most modern form,[25] meaning a sovereign capable of assuming and funding public debts, navies and standing armies; the protean concept of representation, which on the one hand rendered the individual a consenting agent in the actions of his sovereign,[26] on another made his choice of a representative his mode of exercising the inalienable right to be taxed only with his own consent, and with a third offered him the means of exercising by proxy in an 'extensive empire' the virtue he could exercise in person only in a small republic. By a brilliant feat of rhetoric, James Madison identified representative government with the republic, saying that politics in which the citizens ruled directly were merely democracies;[27]

---

[24] John Witherspoon was clearly one of these: Green, *Peripheries and Center*, pp. 155, 172.
[25] The second sentence of *The Federalist Papers* (no. 1 in any edition) declares that the ratification debate will determine the future of 'an empire in many respects the most interesting in the world'. Hamilton is the author here, and a study of the meanings 'empire' had for him would produce multiple and interesting results. See Gerald Stourzh, *Alexander Hamilton and the Idea of Republican Government* (Stanford, 1970).
[26] J. R. Pole, *Political Representation and the Origins of the American Republic* (London, 1966).
[27] *Federalist*, no. 10; see Jacob E. Cooke (ed.), *The Federalist* (Middletown, 1961), p. 62.

but that he needed to pull this off is evidence of the strength of the republican paradigm. No sooner had the colonies been advised that they were now kingless states than questions of aristocracy and democracy, the separation of legislative from executive, and the rest of the republican lexicon arose to dominate their discourse, and the spectres of virtue and corruption began to haunt the American mind.[28] The predominant weight of their Anglo-British inheritance thrust them towards a republic which should exercise sovereignty and empire; but there was a counter-vailing tendency in the same inheritance that thrust them towards a republic of separated powers, which should safeguard virtue by exclud-ing the executive from the legislature. *Jani Anglorum facies nova*; the double meaning of the *Answer to the Nineteen Propositions* was still at work. When Alexander Hamilton was seen to aim at a standing army, a national bank, and an executive maintaining by patronage a body of supporters in the legislature, Madison was allied with those who accused him of designing an 'English' system of government, and Jefferson detected the baleful influence of Hume's teachings behind the whole affair.[29]

As the Americans defected from Whig parliamentarism, they took a great deal of Whig intellectual property with them. It seems safe to date a steady if by no means uninterrupted decline in British respect for the language of mixed government from the need they had felt to instruct their colonies past and future that the authority of king-in-parliament was sovereign and absolute, final and unanswerable, one and indivisible, and that the legislature was in the last analysis identical with the state. The legislative power lay with the king in parliament, and there were

---

[28] At this point commences the vehement and often confused discussion by American historians of the role of opposition ideology, republicanism and the concept of virtue in American values, initiated by Bernard Bailyn's *The Ideological Origins of the American Revolution* (Cambridge, MA, 1967). There are useful bibliographies of this debate by Robert E. Shalhope, 'Towards a Republican Synthesis: The Emergence of an Under-standing of Republicanism in American Historiography', *William and Mary Quarterly*, 3rd series, 29 (1972), 49–80, and 'Republicanism and Early American Historiography', *ibid.*, 46 (1989), 341–75. The most recent contributions at the time of writing are: Bruce Ackerman, *We The People: I, Foundations* (Cambridge, MA, 1991); Joyce O. Appleby, *Liberalism and Republicanism in the Historical Imagination* (Cambridge, MA, 1992); and Shelley Burtt, *Virtue Transformed: Political Argument in England, 1688–1749* (Cam-bridge, 1992), which returns the issue to its historical as well as its historiographical starting point. What the present writer could wish might be his last word on the subject may be found in 'States, Republics and Empires: the American Founding in Early Modern Perspective', in Terence Ball and J. G. A. Pocock (eds.), *Conceptual Change and the Constitution* (Lawrence, 1988), pp. 55–77. This too grows out of a conference organised by the Conference for the Study of Political Thought at the Folger Shakespeare Library during 1987.

[29] Lance Banning, *The Jeffersonian Persuasion: Evolution of a Party Ideology* (Ithaca, NY, 1978).

still those who held that the king made laws and summoned the Commons if not the Lords simply to advise him in doing so; but one need not go so far in order to contend that king and parliament were one and not several counterbalancing forces. There were those also who denied the existence of any rights which the subject did not alienate to the sovereign; the point about natural rights was that the sovereign protected them, not that they set limits to his capacity to do so. Both clerical and philosophical voices could be heard which had always mistrusted Locke and now found an opportunity of speaking out. The road lay open to a rigorous parliamentarism which held that each subject was represented in parliament – even if this involved giving the vote to as many subjects as possible – and that parliament was therefore sovereign in legislating for him. It was a long road to any such state of things, but a step had been taken.

A small but possibly a real indicator of this change of mood may be found in the odd fact that the drafting of a government response to the *Declaration of Independence* was entrusted to a none too prominent figure named David Lind, who enlisted the aid of an even more obscure person named Jeremy Bentham.[30] He may be thought of as beginning in 1776 his road towards the later declaration that natural rights were 'nonsense on stilts', but it was in the same year that he published his *Fragment on Government*, the first burst of fire in what has been called 'a lifetime's dialectic' directed against Blackstone's *Commentaries*.[31] Bentham is a difficult figure to place in any English context from which his thinking might have taken shape,[32] and his affinities with Cesare Beccaria tempt one to characterize him as perhaps the only English representative of the Late Enlightenment, codificatory, bureaucratic and atheistic. But his background was Tory and his first works appear in a context of hardening governmental authority; to think of him as an English proto-Jacobin merely increases one's sense that England was a highly idiosyncratic society. Blackstone, as we know, had been troubled by an increasing willingness of parliament to legislate, and had laboured to place legislation in the classic frameworks of seventeenth-century legal reason and eighteenth-century mixed government.[33] Bentham saw

---

[30] Douglas Long, *Bentham on Liberty: Jeremy Bentham's Idea of Liberty in Relation to his Utilitarianism* (Toronto, 1977), pp. 51–4.

[31] Professor J. H. Burns presented to the seminar his article 'Bentham and Blackstone: A Lifetime's Dialectic', since published in *Utilitas: A Journal of Utilitarian Studies*, 1 (1989), 22–40. See also Schochet (ed.), *Empire and Revolutions*, pp. 262–78, and Robert Willman, 'The Politics of Blackstone's *Commentaries*: Whig or Tory?' *ibid.*, pp. 279–308.

[32] Professor Burns observed that it was his duty to convince the director of the seminar that Bentham was a human being; I replied that one must resist the constant temptation to regard him as a monster from inner space.

[33] For references, see above, pp. 257–8.

both as mystifications erected to fetter and obfuscate legislation, and sought to break them down and liberate the legislative capacity by furnishing it with a new science of utility. He would not within his very long and eccentric lifetime become the accredited philosopher of a pragmatic alliance of bureaucrats and parliamentarians, and it may well be misleading to make the young Bentham into a prophet of the nineteenth century; but there is a symbolic appropriateness about his first appearing in 1776.

In 1783 and 1784 George III won a series of victories, overthrowing the coalition of Fox and North on the India issue and finding the ministry of the younger Pitt confirmed by the unreformed electorate, which were to cement his control of parliament for longer than he was able to exercise it in person. It was the effective end of the destabilisation of his relations with the Whig families that can be traced as far back as 1763, and in some ways the end of the classic age of Whig constitutionalism and commonwealth opposition. David Hume's diagnosis of the possible death of the British constitution was turning out a little too simple. There was no need for 'absolute monarchy' as the alternative to a 'republic' if the Crown's authority in Parliament could be confirmed, and we may doubt if it had really been challenged. What was taking shape in response to Whig and radical discontents was the true shape of English absolutism: the undisputed sovereignty of the king-in-parliament. A drastically non-religious utilitarianism might strengthen this tendency, but at the same time established religion was reacting against the assaults of Rational Dissent and enlightened skepticism. At those levels where moral philosophy indicates ideological change, we note that in Scotland, 1785–88 were productive years for Thomas Reid,[34] whose philosophy of *Common Sense* was in due course to sweep the Scottish universities – and with John Witherspoon as an agent the American – with the assurance that the mind possessed faculties or powers in which moral judgement could be grounded.

In England, William Paley's politics were Whig of a kind, but something much less 'enlightened' in the Scottish sense came about when his *Principles of Moral and Political Philosophy* (1785) were made part of the philosophy curriculum at Cambridge. Where Oxford political theologians continued to inculcate the divine law of subordination to monarchy, Cambridge acknowledged that almost unitarian streak in Anglicanism which had led several pupils of Edmund Law of Peterhouse

---

[34] See, most recently, Knud Haakonssen's introduction to his edition of Reid's *Practical Ethics* (Princeton, 1990), and Peter J. Diamond, 'The Ideology of Improvement: Thomas Reid and the Political Philosophy of the Scottish Enlightenment', PhD dissertation, The Johns Hopkins University, 1986.

to join those petitioning for relief from the Thirty-Nine Articles.[35] Law was now Bishop of Carlisle and Paley dedicated the *Principles* to him; they combine a deep veneration for John Locke with a mistrust of his doctrines on natural rights and the original contract. It was in accord with the most conformist side of the Lockean legacy that Paley taught a natural theology in which humans appeared as sentient organic beings, created to find their way toward God by the exercise of the powers placed in them, but not equipped to know more of the theodicy of God's government of the universe than those limited powers permitted them to see. This theology leant strongly toward Socinianism in a general sense, and in Thomas Robert Malthus a few years later – he was educated as a unitarian first and an Anglican after – it was to produce an anthropology and theodicy markedly unorthodox. But though Paley was historically situated at a point where unitarian theology could produce a liberationist materialism like Joseph Priestley's, his thought turned toward utilitarianism rather than unitarianism; we see in him – as we do in the career and writings of Richard Watson, Bishop of Llandaff[36] – how the Low Church tradition could inculcate submission to the social order no less effectively than the high,[37] substituting for a willing subordination to the power of a loving God a prudential subjection to his ultimate goodness, rather to be calculated than known.[38] Radical anti-trinitarians outside the Church of England demanded speculative rights against the ecclesiastical and civil order; cautious anti-Athanasians within it preferred utility to rights and enjoined the intellect to obey that order as demonstrably the probable best, and all that could be known of the will of God. Churchmen of this typically but not exclusively Cambridge kind were to study the economy of the human world and in the next generation the geology of the natural world; there was to be a conformist clerical science.

The years after the American war were years of the renewal of both empire and imperial discourse. The circumstances of the king's victory over Fox and North remind us that India and its affairs were beginning to enter the vocabularies of British politics, and nefarious and corrupt

---

[35] See above, pp. 268–70.
[36] *A Brief State of the Principles of Church Authority* (London, 1773); *An Address to the People of Great Britain* (London, 1798); *Miscellaneous Tracts on Religious, Political and Agricultural Subjects*, 2 vols. (London, 1815).
[37] For the High Church style, see Clark, *English Society*, part I, chs. 3, 5 and 6.
[38] D. L. LeMahieu, *The Mind of William Paley: A Philosopher and His Age* (Lincoln, 1976). Clark, *English Society*, emphasizes both Paley's conformism and its Low Church character. See Mark Francis, 'Naturalism and the End of Legitimacy in William Paley's Political Theory', in Schochet (ed.), *Empire and Revolutions*, pp. 309–332, published as 'Naturalism and William Paley', *History of European Ideas*, 10, 2 (1989), 203–20.

though the intrigues of Calcutta and Madras generally were, high intellectual debates in London and India accompanied them. Over Cornwallis' land settlement in Bengal[39] and during the long-drawn-out impeachment of Warren Hastings, it was discussed whether Hindus were naturally servile, so that empire over them was necessarily despotic, or whether they possessed property and a capacity for legal individuality, so that their rulers might progress through enlightened absolutism towards constitutional liberty. Sir William Jones' researches into Sanskrit laid the foundations for Aryan and Indo-Germanic speculations in the next century, and for a long debate as to whether company rule should operate through Indian elites trained in the Indian classics, or exclusively through anglicised elites trained in European learning. In North America, Loyalist settlements in Canada proper and the maritime regions around the Gulf of St Lawrence inaugurated the age of the crown colonies, in which there was no doubt that governors, often military men, directly exercised their sovereign's authority, representing him in his personal, imperial and parliamentary character.[40] In both realm and empire, to say nothing of the church, the American crisis had underlined the essential unity of crown and parliament in the English regime and its history, so that the king had nothing more to do than renew his mastery and the parliament's confidence. Josiah Tucker might feel that American independence had done what he hoped of it.

III

All this was bought at a price, in continuing discontent both aristocratic and popular; and the indications just given of moves toward a new style of politics are rather predictive than descriptive. The great defender of the Hanoverian system in the age about to commence was, after all, one of its most restless and discontented members. Politically, the regime after 1784 was constituted by the return of powerful Whig elements to

[39] A good discussion of these issues may be found in Rolando Minuti, 'Proprieta della Terra e Despotismo Orientale: aspetti di un dibattito sull'India nella secondo meta del settecento', in *Materiali per una storia della cultura giuridica*, 7, 2 (Bologna, 1978), 29–176.

[40] S. N. Mukherjee, *William Jones: A Study in Eighteenth-Century British Attitudes to India* (Cambridge, 1968); Garland Cannon, *The Life and Times of Oriental Jones: Sir William Jones, the Father of Modern Linguistics* (Cambridge, 1991). It is worth noting that Jones, a highly radical Whig, conducted friendly correspondence with Josiah Tucker as a fellow member of the Literary Club. For the crown colonies, see Mark Francis, *Governors and Settlers: Images of Authority in the British Colonies, 1820–60* (London, 1992).

supporting the monarchy as they had helped create it; the 'Whig party' of Charles James Fox[41] was a fragment of historic Whiggism. Intellectually, the best known of the public debates touched off by arrival of the news of French revolution in England were debates within the print culture between fragments of the Whig inheritance; unitarian and democratic elements, with roots in the dissenting and commonwealth pasts, hailing the French upheaval for their own purposes and countered most famously by Edmund Burke, articulating the perplexities of aristocratic opposition and drawing massively on Whig, Scottish and Anglican ideological resources. His polemic against Richard Price and those like him was a polemic against the radical Whiggism which Fox was prepared to use but Burke increasingly unable to stomach; the English debate about the French Revolution was at once a debate about the new era the revolution had created and a continuation of an ongoing debate about the national past and its values. Because the English possessed a radical inheritance of their own, their discourse was intensely self-centred and controversial; and for this reason their response to the French Revolution was the most national, the most particularist, and in the end the most counter-revolutionary in Europe.

On the 101st anniversary of William III's landing in Torbay, and the 184th anniversary of the Gunpowder Plot, Richard Price preached a sermon, *On the Love of Our Country*,[42] to a London society formed to celebrate the Glorious Revolution and inculcate its principles as the members understood them. He seemed to regard the forced removal of Louis XVI from Versailles to Paris one month before as an affirmation of values expressed in 1688, which included in the English case the right 'to cashier kings for misconduct' and in the French the right to compel their monarch into unity with his people. Price spoke also as a rational dissenter and foe to religious establishments, and his language could be read as expressing approval of the National Assembly's actions in confiscating the lands of the French church and rendering it economically dependent on the state. It was so read by Edmund Burke, whose *Reflections on the Revolution in France and on the Proceedings of Certain Societies in London Relative to that Event* appeared the next year.[43] The *Reflections* is a work of genius, which like other political classics occupies a multiplicity of contexts and is hard to encase within any combination

---

[41] F. O'Gorman, *The Whig Party and the French Revolution* (London, 1967); Austin Mitchell, *Charles James Fox and the Disintegration of the Whig Party*.

[42] Now available in D. O. Thomas (ed.), *Richard Price: Political Writings* (Cambridge, 1992).

[43] For its formation, see F. P. Lock, *Edmund Burke's Reflections on the Revolution in France* (London, 1985).

of them, but its starting points are those of British political discourse in 1789.[44]

Burke's attention focused on two phenomena: Price's association of praise for the French Revolution with a radical reading of 1688–89, and the implications of the nationalization of the lands of the French church as security for a new public loan. He read these events together, as evidence for the interpretation already sketched by Josiah Tucker. Price and the rational dissenters were the heirs of the regicide sectarians of 1649, and like them were being encouraged by renegade aristocrats for their own ends. This opened Price and the Revolution Society to the charge of enthusiasm, but like Tucker – and in a sense like himself analyzing American religion in 1775 – Burke saw them as converting an extreme thesis of spiritual liberty into a politics which left nothing of man except his right to be free (like 'the flies of a summer'). Unlike Tucker he did not attack Locke, and indeed never mentioned him in the text of the *Reflections*; but the interpretation of 1688 which he put forward was (and always had been) the antithesis of Locke's – there had been no dissolution of government and no re-foundation of monarchy in popular choice, but the necessity of maintaining the ancient constitution had justified emergency action within its structure, designed to leave it otherwise intact. This in turn had provided Englishmen with a context of known laws, known morality, and known religion within which they acted, and which made the rationalist enthusiasm of the French permanently alien to their nature; but there was a clear implication that the rational dissenters like Price were in their turn aliens within the English nation. Burke did not apply this analysis to the Americans before or after 1776, nor were Federalists in a position to make much use of him in contesting the applicability of French principles in the United States; he was defending a British constitution which they had repudiated.

When he considered the revolution of 1789 in the setting of French history, Burke saw it as the work of two social forces: the creditors of the French crown, acting as a 'monied interest' in the sense denounced by Tories of the generation of Swift and Bolingbroke, who had seized the state itself to issue new loans designed less to repay their debts than to

---

[44] For the reading of the *Reflections* which follows, see J. G. A. Pocock: 'The Political Economy of Burke's Analysis of the French Revolution', ch. 10 of *Virtue, Commerce and History*; introduction to *Burke's Reflections on the Revolution in France* (Indianapolis, 1987); and 'Edmund Burke and the Redefinition of Enthusiasm; The Context as Counter-Revolution', in François Furet and Mona Ozouf (eds.), *The French Revolution and the Creation of Modern Political Culture*, vol. 3: *The Transformation of Political Culture, 1789–1848* (Oxford, 1989); and Iain Hampsher-Monk, 'Philosophy and Rhetoric in Burke's *Reflections on the French Revolution*', in Schochet (ed.), *Empire and Revolutions*, pp. 165–86.

extend their credit and control of affairs; and the *gens de lettres*, acting in the decay of the *académies* as an organized faction within the state, whose zeal for the destruction of the Christian church had moved them to seize its lands as security for the monied interest's extension of public credit.

Burke saw the church less as Christ's body than as an estate sacred within the structure of civil society, which must like other estates be secured by independent property of its own; he therefore employed an Anglican rhetoric older than Laud himself, which denounced Henry VIII for the brutality which had failed to endow the Church of England at the time of the dissolution of the monasteries. There was an implication that dissenters aiming as a disestablishment of the church aimed like the French at a new spoliation. Burke's argument here was a two-edged weapon which could be used against the course of English history, and he spent time demonstrating that the British national debt was secured on the growth of the economy, and not like the French on the confiscation of the property of a constituent order.

He was developing a thesis of the Revolution as the revolt of modern economy and modern history against itself. Public credit and paper money were capable of rendering property meaningless and destroying the reality of society; the resulting ideological vacuum would be filled by the energies of an atheist and intellectual enthusiasm, and Burke specifically associated the spread of state indebtedness with the prevalence of intellectual conspiracies like those of the Bavarian Illuminati and the French *gens de lettres*. It was from this foundation that he constructed in his later writings the image of Jacobinism as an international fanaticism, religious in every respect but its atheism, in which the unchained intellect revolted against property and society; an extension and modernization of Hume's earlier account of enthusiasm. Enlightenment in England and Scotland had always been directed against revolutionary sectarianism as much as ecclesiastical tradition, and if we are to attribute to Burke an image of 'the Enlightenment', we must say that in 'the Revolution' he saw 'the Enlightenment' as turning against itself, in the grip of those powers of the mind which could produce enthusiasm without religion. But there was an Enlightenment to be defended against itself, and the constitution in church and state which Burke was defending was rooted not in mere hoary antiquity, but in the movement of history from ancient to modern.

When in a famous passage he lamented the fall of the age of chivalry, implicit in the humiliation of Marie Antoinette, Burke was relying directly on the historiography of William Robertson. Chivalry in the noble class, like learning in the clerical – Burke called them 'the spirit of Christianity and the spirit of a gentleman' – had been essential features of the growth of civility, manners and politeness which had brought Europe out of barbarism and rendered commerce once more possible. Burke faulted 'our economical politicians' – presumably the Scottish political economists – only for making manners dependent on commerce, where the relation was historically the reverse. Commerce could not exist without a previous foundation in manners, and the Revolution destroying the first and second estates was destroying the only conditions under which there could be a third. Burke sometimes wrote of reveolution as the work of 'burghers' and 'middle classes', but saw it less as their triumph than their suicide; the future it created would belong to nihilistically fanaticized power elites, not to social classes at all. In his later and increasingly apocalyptic writings,[45] it is the fabric of modern manners, rooted in the history of Europe, which must be protected against the despotism of anti-social intellect; the concert of Europe and the *douceur de vivre*. He proclaimed the Revolution a phenomenon both religious and anti-religious, an offensive against Europe from within, comparable only to that of Islam from without; and declared that it had caused Europe to revert to the condition it had been during the Wars of Religion, which the civilization of enlightened manners had attempted to terminate. Burke was a deeply European thinker, his understanding of Europe rooted in English, British and perhaps Irish historical experience; and this is one reason why, though we are not to take him as the representative voice of the reaction against the Revolution, he illuminates that reaction more profoundly than any other voice of his times.

IV

Of the various responses which were now made to the *Reflections*, some appear to have been drawn from patterns of oppositional rhetoric already existing – old commonwealth in the case of Catharine Macaulay,[46] rational dissent in the case of Joseph Priestley[47] – while others appear to have spoken with newer voices. James Mackintosh's *Vindiciae Gallicae* declared that Scottish historical philosophy was better capable than Burke realized of explaining, and to that extent justifying, the phenomenon of revolution. Thomas Paine's *The Rights of Man* brought its author's journalistic genius into action in articulating

---

[45] For these see Mitchell (ed.), n. 98 to previous chapter, and R. B. McDowell (ed.), *The Writings and Speeches of Edmund Burke* (Oxford, 1991), IX. Some – but not the *Letters on a Regicide Peace* – are collected in Daniel E. Ritchie (ed.), *Edmund Burke: Further Reflections on the Revolution in France* (Indianapolis, 1992).

[46] *Observations on the Reflections of the Right Honourable Edmund Burke on the Revolution in France* (London, 1790).

[47] *Letters to the Right Honourable Edmund Burke* (Birmingham, 1791).

and disseminating positions that were to become part of working-class discontent well into the nineteenth century. If we could discriminate between old and new in these ideological structures, we would be well placed to determine how far there existed in Britain a discontent and criticism of the existing order which was not merely that to which it had been exposed for a century, but resembled the 'revolutionary' and 'jacobin' tempers to be found in France and other parts of western Europe; as well as how far there were discontents articulating the mentality induced by new social structures and patterns of behaviour.

The existence of a recorded radical past may have rendered England (perhaps Britain) unique among the cultures of Europe in 1789 – where else may the equivalents of the Levellers, the Good Old Cause, the Old Whigs and the Commonwealthmen, be found? – and there are signs of tension as well as sympathy between this tradition and the Rights of Man. Catharine Macaulay, in an adjective interestingly recalling William Walwyn, described it as a 'beggarly' thing merely to claim Anglo-Saxon liberties as the heritage of freeborn Englishmen,[48] and those charged with sedition in the 1790s sometimes obtained acquittal from juries by affirming that they claimed only such liberties and not the universally subversive 'rights of man' asserted by the French (as well as by disclaiming the intention to call a Convention). More probingly, the existence of a native radicalism obliges us to ask whether even those who wanted to push beyond the liberties of freeborn Englishmen were not moved by sympathy with the French Revolution and the desire to assimilate it to their own demands – as was visibly the case with Richard Price – rather than by a revolutionary impulse indistinguishable from it; whether, in short, those who came to be known as 'English Jacobins' were not fellow-travellers, to use a later parlance, rather than revolutionaries. Certainly, the problem soon arose of the 'double standard': whether the deeds of French revolutionaries should be judged by a relative, and those of British governments by an absolute standard of morality. On the other hand, it was easier to convince Englishmen that their liberties were thoroughly corrupt than that they had never had any; that their government was in the wrong in the wars which began in 1793 than that they should rise and overthrow it. Since French armies never landed in England, the belief that they would receive a substantial welcome was never put to the test, and we cannot test the counter-hypothesis that the rhetoric which presented the regime as widely delegitimated was not more than the rhetoric of a traditional society, as

---

[48] Quoted by Minuti, 'Proprietà della Terra e Despotismo Orientale', pp. 818–19, n. 83. Cf. Hill, *op. cit.*, p. 229. She was an energetic researcher in the British Library, where the Thomason Collection was now to be found.

the devastating caricatures of Gillray and Cruickshank could easily suggest. In Scotland there was less of such rhetoric; in Ireland there was a genuine and organized Jacobinism,[49] drawing on sources at once Catholic, Presbyterian and Deist, whose history will have to be independently studied.

Paine's *The Rights of Man* dominates conventional histories of discourse, though his views were not necessarily identical with those of the artisan members of the corresponding societies of London, Norwich and Sheffield.[50] It owes its prominence in the historiography not merely to the selective preferences of historians, but to the extraordinarily wide sales which it enjoyed; allegedly as many as two million copies. Hannah More's *Cheap Repository Tracts*, inculcating the virtues of deference to established authority, rivalled but not equalled it in sales, and there is a problem of deciding how far the regime's survival was due to repression and how far to persuasion. Popular loyalism and popular rebelliousness can both be detected; but it is less important to attempt a late-Georgian public-opinion poll than to compare simultaneous and competitive discourses. *The Rights of Man* differs sharply from older commonwealth rhetorics, less because of its insistence that England had never enjoyed a constitution than in its rejection of the long-standing abhorrence of paper money and public credit. Since his days as an auxiliary of the Philadelphia banker Robert Morris, Paine had been vigorously of the opinion that a national debt could stimulate an economy if not aristocratically mismanaged; and his recipe for revolution in England as well as France could be described as a programme for taking the national debt under democratic control. The second part of *The Rights of Man*, with its remarkable proposals for social insurance, seems to fit into this pattern, and there is a real case for considering Paine the first anglophone theorist of democratic revolution in a capitalist society.[51] He never returned to Britain to lead one, but ended his days in France and America writing prophecies of the imminent collapse of the British system of war finance, which were not to be fulfilled. Perhaps the achievement of *The Rights of Man* was to employ its author's genius for invective, derision and the creation of a mass public in the foundation of a sub-culture of disrespect, just as that of its successor *The Age of Reason* was the creation of an overlapping culture of working-class infidelity, in which may be read the rejection of a God and after-life that had become

---

[49] Marianne Elliott, *Partners in Revolution: The United Irishmen and France* (New Haven, 1982).
[50] Albert Goodwin, *The Friends of Liberty: The English Democratic Movement in the Age of the French Revolution* (Cambridge, MA, 1979).
[51] Gregory Claeys, *Thomas Paine: Social and Political Thought* (Boston, 1989).

the spiritual police of established society. To consider Paine as an orchestrator of mass opinion is to open the question of how far and when popular politics in England ceased to be the preserve of independent radical artisans and became the politics of a society divided into antagonistic classes; a problem central to any thesis that Britain between 1789 and 1848 passed through a *Sattelzeit* and entered a new modernity.

Alongside a popular culture of disrespect, part infidel and part evangelical, and a middle-class unitarian culture of moral and political disapproval of the war effort[52] – between them the progenitors of the British Left ever since – we have to note the persistence of an Anglican culture of loyalism, deference and subordination to monarchy and established church. Hannah More and the pulpit clergy behind her had their own mass public, and the long war against France aroused popular loyalism and popular discontent in conflicting proportions; this was still a traditional culture in which turbulence was not always as subversive as it looked. In the face of the first anti-war movement in the modern sense, the right to think one's own country in the wrong, and even to hope for its defeat in an unjust cause, became something which it was important to some to assert, and to others to contest. Burke, writing of the Foxite Whigs' vote against appropriations for the French war, pronounced that this was the end of patriotism as it had been known in his time; and the age of the revolutionary wars was that in which the word 'patriotism' lost its meaning of a love of country which might lead to revolt against its institutions, and acquired that of a popular and on the whole conservative chauvinism, which it still retains.

Among the responses to Burke's *Reflections* we hear the voices of Mary Wollstonecraft and that no less complicated figure William Godwin, in both of whom it can be said that a Rousseauan *transparence* merged with the 'candour' praised by the extreme unitarians engaged in substituting the pursuit of truth for received religion and moving in some cases toward a philosophically idealist atheism. Wollstonecraft rebelled against Rousseau's *Emile* and passed from *A Vindication of the Rights of Man* to *A Vindication of the Rights of Women*;[53] Godwin went on from *Political Justice* to explore a philosophical anarchism which made him the post-Rousseauan dissenting sage of the counter-revolu-

---

[52] J. E. Cookson, *The Friends of Peace: Anti-War Liberalism in England, 1793–1815* (Cambridge, 1982).

[53] It will be noticed that this is the only mention of that memorable publication. We know at present how to write history of discourse by and about women; not yet how to write history of male-centered national political discourse as affected by the presence of discourse by and about women. Possibly, but not certainly, it was not so affected at the time of which we write. See, however, Marilyn Butler, *Romantics, Rebels and Reactionaries: English Literature and its Background, 1760–1830* (Oxford, 1981).

tionary period.[54] In their initial responses to the French Revolution, however, we hear the same note struck as in William Wordsworth's 'bliss was it in that dawn to be alive' and the earlier prose of Samuel Taylor Coleridge: the union of a post-Christian antinomianism in which God was becoming absorbed by the powers of the human mind with the revolutionary hope of a future illuminated and controlled by liberated reason. Tucker and Burke, in their harsh hostility, were respectively justified in their belief that Socinian politics and rational dissent could lead through enthusiasm to the mind's objectification of itself.

William Blake was the first English revolutionary poet since Milton, and probably more systematically so than his predecessors;[55] but where Milton could find contact with a widespread discourse of millenarian typology, Blake was constrained to invent his own myths and his own religion, and address his readers from the caverns of his secondary world. This did not debar his imagery from having roots in the past, just as in Vincent Carretta's study he appears as much an eighteenth-century satirist as a prophet of romanticism. Wordsworth lived closer to the junction of a *pays idéal* with a *pays réel*, and recorded in his verse the crisis of patriotism which arose when he discovered that he could not really wish the defeat of his own country, whose liberty-centred values he had identified with those of revolutionary France. Finding himself at a time when the Revolution was turning into a military empire, he imagined an ideal Britain to oppose it: in the first place the anti-tradition of 'the elder Sidney, Marvell, Harrington, young Vane and others who called Milton friend' – the Socinian and republican heroes of Toland's 'commonwealth canon' and Catharine Macaulay's lost opportunity – but later in a form which idealized the history of Britain as it actually had been shaped by established authority, and led Wordsworth to end his days venerating the imagery of church and king.[56] Godwin continued to idealize the history of the Puritan Commonwealth;[57] Coleridge by 1830 had reached the point of writing *On the Constitution of Church and State*

---

[54] Don Locke, *A Fantasy of Reason: The Life and Thought of William Godwin* (London, 1980); Peter H. Marshall, *William Godwin* (New Haven, CT, 1984); Mark Philp, *Godwin's Political Justice* (Ithaca, NY, 1986); Gregory Claeys, 'From True Virtue to Benevolent Politeness: Godwin and Godwinism Revisited', in Schochet (ed.), *Empire and Revolutions*, pp. 187–225.

[55] David V. Erdman, *Blake: Prophet Against Empire* (Princeton, 1977), would be considered Old Guard by J. C. D. Clark; but perhaps this is no bad way to treat Blake.

[56] James K. Chandler, *Wordsworth's Second Nature: A Study of the Poetry and Politics* (Chicago, 1984).

[57] *History of the Commonwealth of England* (London, 1824–28). See John Morrow, 'Coleridge and the English Revolution', *Political Science*, 40, 1 (1988), 128–41.

according to the Idea of Each,[58] in which he blended the visions of
Harrington and Burke to write the history of an ideal England where the
landed interest maintained the idea of conservation, the mercantile
interest that of progess, and both joined in endowing and incorporating
the literary class as a 'national church' which would maintain 'the idea of
each' without degenerating into the revolutionary *gens de lettres* whom
Burke had identified and dreaded. Coleridge's re-imagination of the
Matter of Britain had as its subversive counterpart William Cobbett's
History of the Reformation (1824), a savage denunciation of everything
which had happened in England since Henry VIII, dissolving the
monasteries, had laid the foundations of modern aristocracy and agrarian capitalism.

It is noteworthy that Coleridge believed himself to be reviving a
buried English Platonism or neo-Platonism which had been forced
underground by Baconian and Lockean philosophies from the time of
the Restoration of Charles II; a version of intellectual history not unlike
that implied in Blake's denunciation of 'the single vision and Newton's
sleep'. A Platonist revival could take diverse forms: conservative and
High Church in a way that looked back to the Cambridge Platonists, the
Laudians and deeper into the Anglican beginnings, republican and
enthusiast in the form that had led to the creation of the myth of Milton
and his friends. When Blake in one way and Shelley in another explored
the revolutionary possibilities of gnostic imagery, they were drawing on
the resources of magian antinomianism in a way that would have caused
no surprise to those who had been attacking Rosicrucianism, Platonism
and the enthusiasms of the Radical Enlightenment as far back as the
1650s. Though Shelley knew there had in fact been no universal
conspiracies of Illuminati like those imagined by Burke, Robinson and
Barruel, he rather wished there had been.[59] English revolutionary
romanticism and philosophical idealism alike had sources deep in the
English religious past, and continued to rely on them well into the age of
industrialisation, Chartism and the bogus political Gothicism of the
young Disraeli. These are among the ways in which we can look back
from the *Sattelzeit* of 1780–1830 into the history covered in the present
volume.

---

[58] John Morrow, *Coleridge's Political Thought: Property, Morality and the Limits of
Traditional Discourse* (New York, 1990); 'Coleridge and the National Church', in
Schochet (ed.), *Empire and Revolutions*, pp. 333–49.

[59] Seumas Deane, *The French Revolution and Enlightenment in England, 1789–1832*
(Harvard, 1988), a book which valuably studies how counter-revolutionary thought was
directed against Rousseau, Holbach and Condorcet, and examines the neo-Platonist
revival in England.

V

It remains to state the case for breaking off this volume at the beginning of the alleged *Sattelzeit*, and merely looking ahead to a few of the latter's characteristics, instead of attempting to survey it in full. The seminars on which these chapters have been based originally dealt in turn with a series of fifty-year periods, and another seminar (leading to another chapter) could certainly have dealt with the half-century separating the end of the American war from the parliamentary reform of 1832. The decision was however taken to terminate the enterprise at about the outbreak of the war against revolutionary France, partly on the grounds that the period following witnessed the rise of new patterns of discourse, suggesting the presence of new historical phenomena, on a scale sufficient to suggest the coming of a new age and the intervention of what is here termed a *Sattelzeit*. This term should not be used to denote a mere period of transition, in which old forces yield progressively to new ones; it is more likely to be one in which old patterns of discourse persist while new arise, both interacting vigorously to produce new discursive situations and perhaps an intensified sense of their historicity. For this reason the last few pages have leapt ahead to glance at the writings of Cobbett in 1824 and Coleridge in 1830, of which each can be explained in terms of patterns of discourse familiar to students of the eighteenth century, and each advances a complex and fairly sophisticated reading of English history. Much that was Hanoverian persisted into the reigns of George IV and William IV, and historians used to date the end of the eighteenth century at the deaths of Wellington in 1854 or of Palmerston in 1865. The history of a *Sattelzeit* should not become a mere trading of punches between the concepts of continuity and discontinuity, but a case may be made for holding that such a history could not be written without introducing concepts generically unlike those which have been used hitherto. In the present instance, this becomes a case for saying that the period 1780–1830 witnesses 'an end of early modernity' and the introduction of concepts which may usefully be termed 'modern'.

This volume began by studying the historical circumstances in which England became an 'empire', i.e. a monarchy equally sovereign in church and state, and has traced through the medium of recorded discourse the history of that sovereign structure through a series of crises, breakdowns, recoveries and expansions; it is not without poignancy to present that history in the last years of the twentieth century. The regime established to maintain parliamentary monarchy and the alliance of church and state throughout the eighteenth century did not disappear in 1783 or 1793; historians have used the concept of a 'long eighteenth century' beginning in 1660 and persisting for about 170 years, and more recently J. C. D. Clark has argued that a British *ancien régime*, monarchical, aristocratical and confessional, endured until 1829–32, when it was brought to an end by the self-inflicted triple hammer-blow of Catholic emancipation, repeal of the Tests, and reform of the old representative structure. There is much to be said for this interpretation, and the history of a discourse either justifying or challenging the regime based on the Restoration and the Revolution, the Test Act, the Act of Toleration and the Septennial Act, could clearly be carried down to 1832 and the end of our *Sattelzeit*. But a case can nevertheless be made for the view that this could not be done without entering a new world, in the presence of historical innovations even more drastic than those of 1689–1721, and that there is a real sense in which 'early modernity' is left behind in the era of the Napoleonic wars and the Corn Laws.

This chapter has sketched the beginnings of a British reaction, following the American challenge to the sovereignty of parliamentary monarchy, against the image of a mixed government, a conjoint sovereignty of king, lords and commons in equilibrium, which can be traced back to the First Civil War and was conventionally termed 'the glory of our matchless constitution'. Instead, it began to be insisted once again that there could be only one sovereign, that this sovereign was legislative, and that the legislative sovereign was in truth the state. By fits and starts and temporary stoppages, this was to lead in time to a rigorous nineteenth-century positivism, which combined an uncompromisingly sovereign view of the state's action with an uncompromisingly individualist view of its origins, and the more we enter upon this climate of thought the further we are from the Whiggism which incessantly celebrated and debated the Revolution of 1688–9.[60] The rise of this mode of discourse was furthered by the advent of utilitarianism, whether in the Christian form given it by Paley or the philosophic form given it by Bentham, encouraging both submission to the will of the legislator and the exertion of that will to bring about results perceived as beneficial, and promoting (again very slowly and intermittently) a transition from a Lockean government which existed to protect property to a bureaucratic state which existed to police the environment in which property acted. To speak of such a transition is, of course, to telescope fifty years of history into a single movement; but it is fair to find portents of change in the appearances of Bentham in 1776 and Paley in 1785.

[60] See Mark Francis and John Morrow, 'After the Ancient Constitution: Political and English Constitutional Writings, 1760–1832', in Schochet (ed.), *Empire and Revolutions*, pp. 351–3 and *History of Political Thought*, 9, 2 (1988), 283–302. The obvious and necessary counterpoint is provided by Macaulay, celebrating 1688 in the light of 1848.

The administrations of the younger Pitt – always a Whig, but never the apostate Old Whig and Patriot his father had been – witnessed the formation of a regime more closely allied with the monarchy, more bureaucratic and more repressive than its Hanoverian Whig predecessors. But this was also the regime which began and conducted twenty years of war against the French Revolution, and we have seen that the impact of that event was to produce a debate over the meaning of 1688, which looked back to 1649 and even to 1533. Burke continued the impassioned defender of Whig aristocratic politics as he understood them, and his indictment of Jacobinism as a force altogether new in the world's history was part of his deeper reflections on the macro-historical context in which the transformation of British monarchy between 1688 and 1714 must be situated in order to be understood. That was the context of conservative Christian enlightenment and commercial modernity,[61] and indicated how Britain as a counter-revolutionary power could promote the European renewal of the old struggle against universal monarchy, appearing after Burke's death in a new Napoleonic form. The Britain of those decades could join a European coalition and imprint its own ideas upon it.

Burke's fears of a subversion of the British regime from within – deeper than the situation warranted, but not unrelated to it – were fears of the revolutionary capacity of anti-trinitarian Rational Dissent, which he thought likely to carry sympathy with the French to the point of adopting their principles; this is the point at which we can see his indictment of revolution as the Anglican-enlightened indictment of enthusiasm transformed. In the careers of Wordsworth and Coleridge as ideologues we can trace rational enthusiasm running first in a strongly revolutionary direction, then flowing back on itself in the form of an increasingly conservative and indeed Anglican idealism (in Coleridge's case historicism). But at the same time we should observe in Paley, in Watson and later in Malthus how the Socinian and anti-trinitarian strains descending from latitudinarian groups within the Church of England began to develop a utilitarian submissiveness to the established order, which joined hands with the High Church doctrine of subordination on grounds far more catholic and traditional. It is in the figure of Malthus that we can perceive this very un-Tory recommendation of

---

[61] J. G. A. Pocock, 'Clergy and Commerce: The Conservative Enlightenment in England', in R. Ajello (ed.), *L'Età dei Lumi: Studi Storici sul Settecento Europeo in onore di Franco Venturi* (Naples, 1985), I, pp. 523–62, and 'Conservative Enlightenment and Democratic Revolutions: The Leonard Shapiro Memorial Lecture for 1988', *Government and Opposition*, 24, 1 (1989), 81–105.

authority encountering a new series of perceptions of the social order, which differentiate our *Sattelzeit* from the age preceding it.

Burke feared fanaticization at a level which was beginning to be called that of the 'middle class' (or classes), more expressly than he feared discontent or insurgency in the populace at large; his reference to 'a swinish multitude' was interpreted in ways he did not altogether anticipate. An adherent of the Whig aristocratic order, he was in touch with a tradition that still looked upon the vulgar as the *mobile*, the 'mob', the 'multitude of many people which make a noise like the noise of the sea'[62] when set adrift by a failure of leadership on the part of their natural superiors; as a momentary if ever threatening failure of the natural order. He focused his fears on Rational Dissent and its potential for fanaticism, on the unchained energies of the mind which could do more damage than the irrational fury of the multitude ever could; and when he wrote of the decay of the vertical social ties connecting client with patron, it was the danger of a revolutionary 'middle class', a horizontal stratum held together by the instant communication of uncontrolled ideas, that he chose to highlight. His Loyalist contemporaries and successors, however, John Reeves[63] and Hannah More, chose a simpler and apparently more obvious target: the need to dissuade the 'lower orders' from becoming disaffected by sympathy with the French Revolution; and though their language was that of a deeply traditional inculcation of deference and subordination, it may be asked whether they were not recognizing a politics of class more modern than anything Burke recognized. Hannah More's adversary was not 'the sermons of the Revolution Society' or 'the proceedings of certain societies in London', but the enormous sales of Paine's *Rights of Man* among a public assuredly dissenting but perceived also as plebeian and artisanal, even as labouring.

Voices began to be heard from those, artisans if not yet proletarians, who declared that their capacity for labour was their property and a source of the value of what it produced, so that they had a right to share in its profits; and were heard at the same time from those nearer to what would later be known as a proletariat, a class of impoverished labourers whose need to work and produce could not find employment.[64] A

---

[62] This text (Isaiah xvii, 12) was set as epigraph to vol. 2 of Clarendon's *History of the Rebellion* ((Oxford, edn of 1733), p. 289).

[63] Reeves reverted to the seventeenth-century Tory position that the king was sole legislator and called Parliament to assist and advise him; Fox sought to have him condemned by the Commons. Clark, *English Society*, pp. 263–5, and J. A. W. Gunn, *Beyond Liberty and Property: the Process of Self-Recognition in Eighteenth-Century Political Thought* (Kingston and Montreal, 1983), ch. 4, part 2.

[64] E. P. Thompson, *The Making of the English Working Class* (Harmondsworth, 1968).

problem in poverty and pauperisation began to create new perceptions of the practice and history of the poor laws and to induce changes in the vocabulary attending the phenomena,[65] while the passage of the Corn Laws raised questions of political economy capable of being framed in such a way as to present both the economics and the politics of nineteenth-century Britain as a clash not only of interests but of classes. This was the setting in which Malthus's writings on population, which began appearing in 1798, earned economics the name of a 'dismal science' increasingly indifferent to human values. His way of thinking can in several respects be traced far back into the preceding century; his ethics and theology had roots deep in the latitudinarian past, and he continued to present economics as a branch of social morality.[66] But in his harsh delineation of both the political and the divine economy and his recommendation of submission to its laws, he seemed to belong to both the past of hierarchical order and the present of conflict between classes; more, however – and however misleadingly – with those transforming economics into an objective science for use in positivist legislation than with those continuing and modifying the traditions of political economy in its Scottish sense. To recognize Malthus as a Christian thinker in the succession to Locke and Paley is to recognize the power of early modern discourse in a state and society no longer early modern; to recognize, in other words, the necessity and at the same time the difficulty of breaking off this volume at the point it has reached. The decade of the 1690s saw the beginnings of great changes, which were dealt with by the construction of a discourse still neo-classical and intimately bound up with both ancient and modern values; that of the 1790s carries one out of, though it does not leave behind, the parameters of early-modern discourse. That at least must be the thesis exposed to criticism and the construction of antitheses in other works by other authors.

The work of Istvan Hont, Gregory Claeys,[67] Gareth Stedman Jones[68] and others is exploring in depth the political, economic and social thought of the *Sattelzeit* in which the intellectual patterns of the

[65] Gertrude Himmelfarb, *The Idea of Poverty: England in the Early Industrial Age* (New York, 1984).

[66] Donald Winch, *Malthus* (Oxford, 1989); Patricia James, *Population Malthus, His Life and Times* (London, 1979); Eric Heavner, 'Food, Sex and God: The Christian Social Theory of Thomas Robert Malthus', unpublished PhD dissertation, The Johns Hopkins University, 1992.

[67] *Machinery, Money and the Millennium: From Moral Economy to Socialism, 1815–1860* (Princeton, 1987); *Thomas Paine: Social and Political Thought*; *Citizens and Saints: Politics and Anti-Politics in Early Modern Britain* (Cambridge, 1989).

[68] *Languages of Class: Studies in English Working-Class History* (Cambridge, 1985).

nineteenth century took shape in tangled interrelations with those of the eighteenth. The roots of this discourse in the past cannot be overemphasized; language of a kind basically Anglican and ecclesiological endures with it, and is reactivated rather than extinguished in the age of Newman and Gladstone, as the Church of England responds to the end of the Anglican church-state; it has been demonstrated by J. W. Burrow how concerns so arising found expression in the historiography of Freeman and Stubbs.[69] Yet these historians are classics of what we remain agreed on calling 'Whig history', and the 'Whig' discourse of the parliamentary constitution continues into the nineteenth century as a language no less dominant and rather more salient than the discourse of the church.[70] The Holland House circle, conducted by the heirs of Charles James Fox, patronized both the Edinburgh Reviewers, engaged in the revision of Smithian political economy,[71] and the historiographic revisions of Sir Francis Palgrave – soon to be enlarged in England into the Indo-Germanic mark thesis[72] – and Sir James Mackintosh, of whom were sprung Henry Hallam and Thomas Babington Macaulay. In the last-named, the shades of Fox and Burke joined hands and the Whig tradition was restored.

The most suggestive survey we have at present of the transition from eighteenth- to nineteenth-century theoretical discourse is *That Noble Science of Politics* by Collini, Winch and Burrow,[73] in which the scene is laid north of the Tweed and passes from Dugald Stewart's Edinburgh to that of Francis Jeffrey, and then by way of Holland House to a reborn scientific Whiggism at the beginning of the reign of Victoria. To some it seems[74] that a more Anglocentric story could usefully be told, passing from Paley by way of Bentham to Austin; one less philosophical and more positivist. But it is to Collini, Winch and Burrow that this volume must hand on the torch. We close, then, with that *Sattelzeit* in which political economy was transformed in the move from Smith to

---

[69] J. W. Burrow, *A Liberal Descent: Victorian Historians and the English Past* (Cambridge, 1981).

[70] J. G. A. Pocock, 'The Varieties of Whiggism from Exclusion to Reform: a History of Ideology and Discourse', in *Virtue, Commerce and History*, pp. 215–310.

[71] Biancamaria Fontana, *Rethinking the Politics of Commercial Society: The Edinburgh Review, 1802–32* (Cambridge, 1986).

[72] J. W. Burrow, *Evolution and Society: A Study in Victorian Social Theory* (Cambridge, 1966). Sir Francis Palgrave, *History of the Anglo-Saxons* (1831); *The Rise and Progress of the English Commonwealth: The Anglo-Saxon Period* (1832) in *Collected Works*, vols. V–VII (Cambridge University Press, 1921).

[73] Stefan Collini, Donald Winch and J. W. Burrow, *That Noble Science of Politics: A Study in Nineteenth-Century Intellectual History* (Cambridge, 1983).

[74] This thesis was trenchantly argued by Mark Francis and John Morrow in presenting to the seminar their paper, 'After the Ancient Constitution: Political Theory and English Constitutional Writings, 1765–1832'.

Ricardo,[75] philosophic radicalism was developed by the later Bentham and James Mill,[76] the foundations were laid of a liberalism far removed from that connoted by the word in its present usage,[77] Coleridgean historicism prepared the next phase of the humanist critique of society,[78] the Scotland of William Robertson became that of Sir Walter Scott, the ancient constitution was transformed by the mark thesis, Anglican high ecclesiology declared itself besieged as the Oxford Movement, the foundations were laid of the England known to Marx and Engels, and – last but not least – the typographic culture of the age of unlicensed printing, of the broadsheet, the pamphlet, the treatise and the folio which have been the unsung material of this book, gave way to the professionalized journalism of the Edinburgh, the Quarterly, and the Westminster Reviewers. The worlds of George Thomason, Roger L'Estrange, Jacob Tonson and John Almon were replaced by the landscape of Victorian Britain and the rise of the professional classes.[79]

---

[75] Mark Blaug, *Economic Theory in Retrospect* (4th edn, Cambridge, 1985).

[76] William Thomas, *The Philosophic Radicals: Nine Studies in Theory and Practice, 1817–41* (Oxford, 1979).

[77] J. W. Burrow, *Whigs and Liberals: Continuity and Change in English Political Thought* (Oxford, 1989). The paradox is that Victorian liberals defended the public virtue of the individual against the levelling effects of egalitarianism.

[78] John Colmer, *Coleridge: Critic of Society* (Oxford, 1959). Duncan Forbes, *The Liberal Anglican Idea of History* (Cambridge, 1955).

[79] H. J. Perkin, *The Origins of Modern English Society, 1780–1880* (Toronto, 1969).

Epilogue

10 Why should history matter? Political theory and the history of discourse

Gordon J. Schochet

Introduction

This chapter, unlike its predecessors in this volume, is concerned more with the present than with history. My points of departure are the modern state – especially in its English-speaking form – and its political theory and politics in the late twentieth century. That state, its theory, and the world they both occupy are all 'products' of the past, and I have an interest in the way they were 'produced', a process that is still under way. My concern, therefore, is not so much with the reconstruction of the past as with understanding its use by the present and how it seems to constrict modern possibilities. Although no full theory of historical change is offered or even hinted at here, pieces of a partial theory are scattered through my argument.

Like the other contributors, I approach political thought as a 'discursive' or 'linguistic' phenomenon and regard language, broadly conceived, as the primary source of historical continuity. It is the principal means by which, individually and as members of cultures who share traditions, people make sense of and participate in their worlds.

Throughout, I treat the state as something of a linguistic construct that is maintained by a continuous commentary on its tradition, a kind of political hermeneutics. I contend that the modern Western state is wedded to a participatory and even democratic ideology and that a significant part of its history – and of the internal conflicts that populate the histories of individual states – has been about the fulfillment of that commitment. In the English-speaking world, much of this contention can be cast in terms of the vocabularies of 'rights' and 'liberties' and the growth of 'constitutional' government and is conventionally known as

I am very much indebted to John Pocock for his careful and patient reading of this chapter and especially for his assistance in clarifying and sharpening the arguments. As usual, Lois Schwoerer has lent me her unfailing and ever-supportive critical eye, for which, as usual, I am most grateful.

'liberalism'.[1] But the expansion of political participation, the diffusion of political power, and the growth of a concomitant discourse have rarely been achieved as a result of the intentional pursuit of lofty principles. Rather, in all but a few cases, they have been granted by a grudging ruling establishment that had exhausted its other options.

All this means, then, that the state is inherently unstable and has been in a condition of impending crisis virtually since the post-Reformation period. Initially, that instability was manifested in persisting religious and political struggles, which were eventually overshadowed – as became evident in the eighteenth century – by the demands of commerce and empire. Now, at the end of the twentieth century, the institution-alized form of the state is facing new and severe tests: the nations of Western Europe are organizing themselves into a supra-national entity with substantial sovereign powers that threaten the integrity of its individual member states and the autonomy of their citizens; the United States is labouring to maintain a participatory civil society amidst the divisions of 'multi-cultural' pluralism; and the collapse of the commu-nist and colonial empires has left weak states that are racked by ethnic and religious conflicts over the entitlements of indigenous and identifi-able peoples to control their own destinies.

The very forces that created the modern state out of the wreckage of the Holy Roman Empire – religious diversity, national (or ethnic) territorial sovereignty, political secularism, economic competition, and industrial and technological development – now threaten to destroy their own accomplishment by making coherent, unifying public discourse impossible. I argue below that civil societies require common or shared vocabularies that contain their identities and act as centralizing and nearly sovereign forces. Such discourses invariably reflect the interests of the dominant segments of society, which both invites and throws into perspective questions about the hegemonic quality of the discourse: as

[1] See John Dunn, *Western Political Theory in the Face of the Future* (Cambridge, 1979), for a similar claim.

The growing evaluative use, redefinition, and historical extension of 'liberalism' back into the seventeenth century – by its advocates and enemies alike – have transformed it into a label and virtually destroyed whatever descriptive utility it may have had. I have, therefore, generally avoided using the term and have resorted to the more cumbersome but apparently still neutral locutions of 'juridical discourse', 'constitutional state', and 'vocabularies of rights and liberties'. No matter what the term 'liberalism' might mean, it seems to me to be a serious conceptual and historical error to equate it with participatory doctrines of 'popular sovereignty' and the invocation of rights and freedom in the twentieth century. Cf. Francis Fukuyama, *The End of History and the Last Man* (New York, 1992). While I share – on different grounds – some of Fukuyama's pessimism, I certainly dissent from his Nietzschean teleology and am unpersuaded by his general argument.

feminists and multi-cultural pluralists in the United States rightly object, exclusionary biases and narrow cultural values are unavoidable, and it is difficult for outsiders to find legitimate voices with which to enter the conversation, let alone contest their exclusion from it. The self-proclaimed virtue of pluralism, and of the political ideology that surrounds it, has long been that the openness and the very contestability of the discourse are important parts of what holds the community together – virtually a tacit agreement to disagree. But this becomes a sadly ironic commentary when, as is the case at present, the principles of membership and participation themselves are contested: the pluralism of the modern state is increasingly being undermined by this *post*-modernist dilemma.

The leitmotif of my argument is that the past and the present of a civil society must be held together if that society is to survive at a level of consciousness in which its members can participate.[2] In some elemental but hardly trivial sense, that continuity is always there, for even the conceptual breaks are part of the uninterrupted passage of time and can be accounted for and made intelligible in terms of an overall coherence. The trick is to encapsulate all this in a story that makes sense to those who hear it, for politics is not inherently or self-evidently coherent. To the extent that it itself is historically continuous, the public discourse of a society performs precisely this function. Its goal is to create, and even sanctify, a tradition that tells a people who they have been and are and allows them to ponder who they might become. At this point, discursive continuity and academic history can stand as partners in the same enterprise. One of the objectives of this book and of the larger project of which it is a part is to write the history of English-language political thought in just this way. The presumption and hope are that the continuity can be presented without uncontrollable distortion – and the discontinuities explained and incorporated – and in a way that will retain authenticity even when legitimately challenged. In these terms, this chapter is something of a free-floating commentary – an 'excursus', as the seventeenth and eighteenth centuries would have termed it – on the history presented in the rest of the volume. It is an attempt to tell an incorporating story *about* that history that addresses some of the most profound dilemmas of contemporary politics.

---

[2] Also running just beneath the surface of the principal argument is something more than a half-hearted endorsement of the post-modernist *rejection* of 'foundationalism', which, to my mind, has been a kind of brooding presence in the epistemological firmament since the publication of David Hume's *Treatise of Human Nature*. At the same time, however, I am deeply troubled by the empirical reality of the *loss* of foundations and even more disturbed by the piety of recent attempts to root our lives in a restored 'morality'.

From early-modern Britain to the twentieth century: democratic citizenship and the people

A narrative about the movement of the primary locus of authoritative discourse from the court, to Parliament, and finally to the popular press and some semblance of the 'people' can be constructed from the 300-year history of British political thought presented in this volume. The movement coincided with – and helps to account for – both the changes in the general features of public discourse and the gradual but evident expansion of participating membership in the political community.

Despite the appearance in this narrative of a large-scale trend in the direction of wider (more democratic) participation, it is important to keep in mind that the history of English-language political thought is not one of straight-line development, not the history of successive modes of expressing political relationships, each overwhelming and succeeding its predecessor.[3] Varying and often competitive conceptualizations frequently coexist and even become entangled with one another. Triumphs and defeats – if, indeed, that is what they are – can be but temporary rearrangements. And, perhaps most important, the supplanting of a discursive fashion is not always the end of its life. It may continue to find supporters long after it has fallen from favour. In fact, there is something altogether problematic about defining political societies in terms of single, dominating languages of political justification.

Despite these caveats, it is possible to discover trends or tendencies and to establish the lineages of twentieth-century political ideology – which is one of the objectives of studying the history of political thought – in early-modern Britain. My intention here is neither to make that narrative more explicit than it already is nor to discuss it as a series of linked, causal sequences. My aim, rather, is to suggest some ways in which the political thought of early-modern Britain gave rise to the political theory and ideology of the English-speaking world in the twentieth century. My conclusion will be that many of our contemporary problems inhere in that bequest.

Courtly discourse in the sixteenth and early seventeenth centuries, as we have seen, was largely a discourse 'of counsel', dominated by the Crown's advisors and favourites. Although it was predicated upon strong monarchical powers, it did not entail absolutism. It shared conceptual territory with the 'civic humanist' and republican rhetoric of Renaissance Europe – which itself could be traced back to classical

---

[3] Cf. Sheldon S. Wolin, 'Paradigms and Political Theory', in Preston King and B. C. Parekh (eds.), *Politics and Experience: Essays Presented to Professor Michael Oakeshott on the Occasion of His Retirement* (Cambridge, 1968), pp. 125–52.

antiquity – and competed for hegemony with a common law perspective that purported to comprehend a tradition long predating the Norman conquest of England. The sense of tradition and continuity embodied in the common law would eventually overwhelm what there was in England of the Roman or civil law[4] and would become, by mid seventeenth century, the primary vocabulary of parliamentary opposition to the alleged excesses of Charles I. The common law was concerned with historic English 'liberties', with land law and tenures, and with the proper possessions and entitlements of Englishmen (that is, with what came to be called their 'rights' and 'property'). It was a set of concerns peculiarly well-suited to oppose the claims of the monarchy.

This opposition was not something that occurred suddenly or univocally. The basic vocabulary had already found a welcome place in the writings of the Marian Exiles, who had adapted continental resistance theory to their peculiarly Scottish and English purposes.[5] And a growing parliamentary restlessness had been evident since the reign of James I. But the clearest and most forthright appearance of common law notions in political discourse came in the debates on the Petition of Right in the parliament of 1628. Those debates, dominated by lawyers, were rife with the vocabularies of 'liberty' and 'propriety' as fundamental entitlements of Englishmen which were enshrined in and protected by the common law and which limited sovereign power.[6] By the 1640s, Parliament had extended this argument and was claiming to be the

---

[4] Donald R. Kelley, *The Human Measure: Social Thought in the Western Legal Tradition* (Cambridge, MA, 1990), ch. 10 (see esp. pp. 168–76, and refs.); Brian P. Levack, 'Law and Ideology: The Civil Law and Theories of Absolutism in Elizabethan and Jacobean England', in Heather Dubrow and Richard Strier (eds.), *The Historical Renaissance: New Essays on Tudor and Stuart Literature and Culture* (Chicago, 1988), pp. 220–41 (also available in Gordon J. Schochet (ed.), *Law, Literature, and the Settlement of Regimes*, Proceedings of the Folger Institute Center for the History of British Political Thought (Washington, DC, 1990), II, pp. 5–28); and J. G. A. Pocock, *The Ancient Constitution and the Feudal Law*, rev. edn (Cambridge, 1987), esp. ch. 1.

Richard Hooker, although not himself an opposition writer, couched his *Ecclesiastical Polity* in the legalistic, Scholastic vocabulary of natural law, showing the extent to which this discourse was already influencing the ways in which the political and religious orders were conceived. See Charles Gray, 'Category Confusion as a Confused Category', in Schochet (ed.), *Law Literature*, pp. 221–6.

[5] Quentin Skinner, *The Foundations of Modern Political Thought*, 2 vols. (Cambridge, 1978), II, chs. 8–10; Jane Dawson, 'Revolutionary Conclusions: The Case of the Marian Exiles', *History of Political Thought*, 11 (1990), 257–72; J. H. M. Salmon, *The French Religious Wars in English Political Thought* (Oxford, 1959), chs. 5 and 6; and Donald R. Kelley, 'Ideas of Resistance before Elizabeth', in Dubrow and Strier (eds.), *The Historical Renaissance*, pp. 48–76 (also in Schochet (ed.), *Law, Literature*, pp. 29–48).

[6] My understanding of the Petition of Right debates owes much to an unpublished paper by J. G. A. Pocock, 'Propriety, Liberty and Valour: Ideology, Rhetoric and Speech in the 1628 Debates'.

surest guardian of those liberties because it represented – and, therefore, in an important legislative sense was – 'the people' from whom its legitimacy was derived.

Again, this was not a new claim. The notion that the 'people' were the source of governmental authority traced its English roots to Scholasticism and to sixteenth-century Protestant resistance theory to which it was conceptually related. In the hands of parliamentary apologists in the 1640s, it provided a response to the claim that Charles I's authority was derived from God.[7] More than that, however, this argument invited questions about the identity and political status of 'the people' (whoever they may have been), preparing the way for the full-blown populist doctrines of the nineteenth and twentieth centuries. The Levellers, using essentially the same juridical vocabulary that the parliamentarians had employed, charged that Parliament did not represent the people and demanded a more extensive distribution of liberty and a much wider participation. The demise of the Commonwealth set the stage for Harrington's republican call for a redistribution of political power based on the ownership of land rather than the intrinsic rights of the people.

By 1660, the restoration of the Stuart monarchy had mooted both Leveller calls for liberty and Harringtonian republicanism. The immediate legacy of the Interregnum was not the sovereignty of the people but religious sectarianism. Conflicts born of that religious diversity were to dominate English politics for the next century and one-half. But the locus of political discourse had shifted from the court to parliament and, increasingly, to the political press; and counsel had given place to the protection by the law of the people's rights, liberty, and propriety as the central concerns of that discourse.

Somewhere beneath the surface of public debate, Philip Hunton's dissolution theory[8] remained alive. And the failure of parliament in the Exclusion Controversy to become, as Shaftesbury had hoped it would,

---

[7] John Sanderson, *'But the People's Creatures': The Philosophic Basis of the English Civil War* (Manchester, 1989), is a conceptually exaggerated but none the less insightful examination of the rival ideologies of the 1640s from the perspective of what Walter Ullmann denoted as the 'ascending' and 'descending' theories of political authority.

As Edmund S. Morgan has observed:
The fiction that replaced the divine right of kings is our fiction, and it accordingly seem less fictional to us . . . In England and America at least, it [the myth of the sovereignty of the people] has worked for three centuries, providing the few with justification for their government of the many and reconciling the many to that government. It has furnished the stability that die-hard adherents of divine right had declared impossible, yet it has also provided the leverage for political and social changes that have brought our institutions into closer proximity to its propositions. (*Inventing the People: The Rise of Popular Sovereignty in England and America*, paperback reprint (New York, 1989), p. 38)

[8] See above, pp. 153–4.

the font of opposition politics – partially through the unwillingness of some of its members to vote for Exclusion and partially because of the crown's constitutional power to prorogue and adjourn that body – summoned Locke's restatement of dissolution theory in the *Two Treatises*. His formulation was truly radical, for it appreciated and built upon the limitations inherent in constitutional politics and, unlike Hunton's account, actively embraced and urged revolution as the appropriate remedy for political impasse. Locke's 'any single man' was not to be taken altogether literally – and certainly did not include Colonel Thomas Rainborough's 'the poorest he that is in England'[9] – but his defence of the right of revolution came to rest in the 'people', whose socio-economic status Locke left somewhat ill-defined.[10] They were the custodians of their own interests and therefore the source of sovereign authority, which was conveyed as a conditional *trust* to the government. This was a far cry from the 'inferior magistrates' of sixteenth-century resistance theory, but it was still not a thorough-going doctrine of popular sovereignty.

Apart from its firm justification of resistance, Locke's *Two Treatises* was couched in a constitutional framework that, for all its moderation, shared much with the opposition ideology of the 1640s. As Hobbes, Locke and the Levellers all appreciated, rights-based theories are potentially double-edged: on the one side, they validate constitutional regimes that are designed to protect the legitimate entitlements of their members; on the other, these same theories justify resistance when the government exceeds its authority and threatens rather than protects the people (whoever they may be). Thus, while Locke's writings played no

---

[9] *Puritanism and Liberty: Being the Army Debates* (1647–9), ed. A. S. P. Woodhouse (London, 1938), p. 53.

[10] Richard Ashcraft, *Revolutionary Politics and Locke's 'Two Treatises of Government'* (Princeton, 1986), is the fullest – if somewhat overstated – account to date of Locke's radicalism. For 'the people', see especially ch. 6. Cf. Gordon J. Schochet, 'Radical Politics and Ashcraft's Treatise on Locke', *Journal of the History of Ideas*, 50 (1989), 491–510.

The question of who comprised the relevant political population for Locke has been much discussed in recent years. For economically-based considerations, see C. B. Macpherson, *The Political Theory of Possessive Individualism: Hobbes to Locke* (Oxford, 1962), ch. 5; and Neal Wood, *The Politics of Locke's Philosophy: A Social Study of 'An Essay concerning Human Understanding'* (Berkeley, 1983), chs. 2 and 6. For feminist appraisals, see Lorenne M. G. Clark, 'Women and John Locke: Or, Who owns the Apples in the Garden of Eden?' *Canadian Journal of Philosophy*, 7 (1978), 699–724; Melissa A. Butler, 'Early Liberal Roots of Feminism: Locke and the Attack on Patriarchy', *American Political Science Review*, 72 (1978), 135–50, reprinted in Mary Lyndon Shanley and Carole Pateman (eds.), *Feminist Interpretations and Political Theory* (University Park, PA, 1991); Teresa Brennan and Carole Pateman, ' "Mere Auxiliaries to the Commonwealth": Women and the Origins of Liberalism', *Political Studies*, 27 (1979), 183–200; and Pateman, *The Sexual Contract* (Stanford, 1988).

direct role in the expulsion of James II in 1688–9, and Locke himself seems to have desired a more radical outcome,[11] the Glorious Revolution, by and large, was conducted and defended in a legitimist (if somewhat extra-constitutional) manner that shared the conceptual vocabulary of the 'Second Treatise'.

Republicanism – if temporarily muted by the events of the late 1680s – was still very much alive and was to play a central role in radical political and religious thinking in Britain and America over the course of the next century.[12] Algernon Sidney's voluminous *Discourses concerning Government*, finally published in 1698, fifteen years after its author's execution for his alleged role in the Rye House Plot, enjoyed far more popularity than did Locke's *Two Treatises*,[13] and the moral and political *philosophy* of the eighteenth century was as much – if not more – concerned with virtue as it was with rights.

The discourse of virtue, which was part of republican theory, stood alongside a legalistic discourse of individual rights and liberties which itself was hardly an invention of the mid-Stuart period. Drawn from Scholastic conceptions of the *jus naturale* – which themselves could be traced back to the Roman law[14] – and from the common law,[15] it represented a legalistic, voluntarist, and conventional conception of the political world. And it was fully compatible with the spiritual and religious individualism of Luther's 'priesthood of all believers' and the epistemological individualism of the new science, of Hobbes' *Leviathan*, and of Locke's *Essay concerning Human Understanding*. This conceptualization increasingly served as the linguistic vehicle for oppo-

---

[11] Ashcraft, *Revolutionary Politics*, pp. 590–601; cf. Lois G. Schwoerer, 'Locke, Lockean ideas, and the Glorious Revolution', *Journal of the History of Ideas*, 51 (1990), 531–48.

[12] The literature on political republicanism continues to grow, but J. G. A. Pocock, *The Machiavellian Moment: Florentine Political Thought and the Atlantic Republican Tradition* (Princeton, 1975), remains the standard work on the subject. For the role of republican thought in Restoration and early eighteenth-century English religion and theology, see J. A. I. Champion, *The Pillars of Priestcraft Shaken: The Church of England and Its Enemies, 1660–1730* (Cambridge, 1992).

[13] Alan C. Houston, *Algernon Sidney and the Republican Heritage in England and America* (Princeton, 1991), is a full and careful study. Suggesting that Sidney conflated arguments about virtue with conceptions of rights, Houston is not altogether willing to regard him as a republican. This mingling of the two vocabularies also demonstrates the 'impurity' of discursive modes.

[14] The most concise discussion of this complex lineage and development remains A. P. d'Entrèves, *Natural Law: An Introduction to Legal Philosophy* (1951), 2nd edn (London, 1971), esp. chs. 1–4 (in both editions). In greater detail, see Richard Tuck, *Natural Rights Theories: Their Origin and Development* (Cambridge, 1979), and Kelley, *The Human Measure*, chs. 3–10.

[15] Richard Tuck, 'The "Modern" Theory of Natural Law', in Anthony Pagden (ed.), *The Languages of Political Theory in Early-Modern Europe* (Cambridge, 1987), ch. 5.

sition politics.[16] In many respects, the growing hegemony of juridically based politics provides a discursive means of accounting for what Henry Sumner Maine in his well-known aphorism, called the 'movement from Status to Contract'.[17] At one time – when it was still in the hands, and defined an important part of the domain, of lawyers – the components of this legal language comprised a relatively stable and clear vocabulary. But as it became politicized, it became less precise and more contestable. Emerging from the strict confines of the law, this terminology began to complement and then compete with humanist rhetoric as the common law and its lawyers assumed increasingly important roles in civil affairs.

There are obvious signs of the competition between them in Hobbes' attack on the courtly discourse of counsel in *Leviathan*, which was self-consciously written in a legalistic manner and chapter 25 of which was devoted to the shortcomings and dangers of counsel. The initial problem was the confusion of counsel and command, both of which employed the 'Imperative manner of speaking'. In the former case it was exhortative rather than directive, and the intent of counsellors was, generally, to advance their own interests rather than those of the sovereign to whom their advice was given. Moreover, counsellors often lacked the experience and perspective that were necessary if one was to advise about the 'Administration of a great Common-wealth'.[18] Hobbes then deftly turned his general argument against counsel into what his contemporary readers would have recognized as attacks on the notion of king-in-parliament, on all forms of mixed monarchy, and on the pretensions of Stuart parliaments:

who is there that so far approves the taking of Counsell from a great Assembly of Counsellours, that wisheth for, or would accept of their pains, where there is a question of marrying his Children, disposing of his Lands, governing his Household, or managing his private Estate, especially if there be amongst them such as wish not his prosperity? . . . And though it be true, that many ey[e]s see more than one; yet it is not to be understood of many Counsellours; but then only, when the finall Resolution is in one man. Otherwise, because many eyes see the same thing in divers lines, and are apt to look asquint towards their private benefit; they that desire not to misse their marke, though they look about with two eyes, yet they never ayme but with one.[19]

[16] See chs. 3 and 5 above.
[17] Henry Sumner Maine, *Ancient Law* (1861), introd. J. H. Morgan, reprinted, Everyman's Library (London, 1917), p. 100.
[18] Thomas Hobbes, *Leviathan: Or The Matter, Forme, and Power of Commonwealth Ecclesiastical and Civil* (1651), ed. Richard Tuck (Cambridge Texts in the History of Political Thought; Cambridge, 1991), ch. 25 (pp. 176 and 180).
[19] Hobbes, *Leviathan*, ch. 25 (p. 182). For further and more general discussions of Hobbes' sensitivity to language and his uses of rhetoric, see Gigliola Rossini, 'The Criticism of Rhetorical Historiography and the Ideal of Scientific Method: History, Nature, and Science in the Political Language of Thomas Hobbes', in Pagden (ed.), *Languages of*

Hobbes' attack certainly did not signal the end of humanist rhetoric, which persisted in a revived and somewhat altered form in civic humanist (or 'Harringtonian' republican) theory. Eighteenth-century discussions of 'politeness', manners, and 'virtue' were not so much revivals of this discourse – for it never really disappeared or went underground[20] – as they were responses to the world created by 'commerce' and 'business', which generated relationships based on interest and prudence. The claim, in large part, was that politeness would civilize. The private relationship of 'friendship' was derived from virtue and needed to be insulated from that business world by privacy and leisure, which produced a strange rhetorical union of Christian with moral (Ciceronian) virtue. Humanist politeness supplemented and to some degree altered the juridical and interest-based discourse of natural law and natural rights that had been inherited from the seventeenth century.[21] Part of Adam Smith's genius in *The Wealth of Nations* was the suggestion that the successful pursuit of commercial interests and economic independence could help a nation achieve virtue, thus uniting what otherwise appeared to be sharply divergent political perspectives.[22]

The eighteenth-century versions of virtue and of the related notions of 'civility' and 'politeness' did not signal a return to Renaissance humanism. Rather, they manifested a desire to co-opt the emerging commercial ethos and to transform it into the foundation of a modern state while minimizing the harsher, alienating aspects of the business world.[23] This reappearance of what were basically Ciceronian and

Political Theory, ch. 13; David Johnston, *The Rhetoric of Leviathan: Thomas Hobbes and the Politics of Cultural Transformation* (Princeton, 1986); Quentin Skinner, 'Thomas Hobbes: Rhetoric and the Construction of Morality,' *Proceedings of the British Academy*, 76 (1990), 1–61, and '"*Scientia civilis*" in classical rhetoric and in the early Hobbes', in Nichollas Phillipson and Quentin Skinner (eds.), *Political Discourse in Early Modern Britain* (Cambridge, 1993), pp. 67–93.

20 M. M. Goldsmith, 'Liberty, Luxury, and the Pursuit of Happiness', in Pagden (ed.), *Languages of Political Theory*, ch. 10, esp. pp. 225–9, and, more generally, Shelley Burtt, *Virtue Transformed: Political Argument in England, 1688–1740* (Cambridge, 1992), esp. chs. 1 and 2.

21 Istvan Hont, 'The Language of Sociability and Commerce: Samuel Pufendorf and the Theoretical Foundations of the "Four-Stages Theory" ', in Pagden (ed.), *Languages of Political Theory*, ch. 11.

22 Nicholas Phillipson, 'Adam Smith as Civic Moralist', in Istvan Hont and Michael Ignatieff (eds.), *Wealth and Virtue: The Shaping of Political Economy in the Scottish Enlightenment* (Cambridge, 1983), ch. 7. Alexander Hamilton, generally regarded as the champion of interest and commerce, has similarly been read as one concerned with economic independence as a precondition of national virtue; see Gerald Stourzh, *Alexander Hamilton and the Idea of Republican Government* (Stanford, 1970).

23 See Maurice M. Goldsmith, *Private Vices, Public Benefits: Bernard Mandeville's Social and Political Thought* (Cambridge,1985); and Nicholas Phillipson, 'Politics, Politenes, and the Anglicisation of Early Eighteenth-Century Scottish Culture', in Roger A. Mason (ed.), *Scotland and England, 1286–1815* (Edinburgh, 1987), ch. 11, 'Politics and

courtly values was a reaction to an impersonal, remote, and growing political bureaucracy. It is significant both that this resurgence of humanist discourse emanated from Scotland and that it is initially evident at the time of the political and legal union of the two kingdoms. Scotland had remained a civil law society and had thereby retained much of its humanist heritage throughout the seventeenth century, a fact that has been obscured until very recently by the indifference of historians of Britain to pre-eighteenth-century Scottish affairs.[24] The union provoked questions about the relationships between the two legal systems that brought humanist considerations back to the front of political discourse.

Echoes of the older, republican or civic humanist notions of 'virtue' and 'corruption', 'community', 'duty', and 'responsibility' survived for a while in the United States.[25] On the European continent, partially as negative responses to the French Revolution and partially in the more congenial context of philosophical idealism, they continued to exert a strong hold on conceptualizations of the political world. In that attenuated and sometimes unrecognizable form, reverberations of humanist republicanism would appear in Anglo-American political thought throughout the nineteenth and twentieth centuries in criticism of the discourse of rights and liberties.

But for the most part, after the French and American revolutions, the vocabularies of virtue and corruption and of civility and politeness were to play diminished roles in politics. Coleridge was certainly concerned with political virtue,[26] and there is a line of idealist political theory that connects him to John Stuart Mill[27] (who was much influenced by von Humbold as well), to Mill's critics,[28] and runs to T. H. Green and his followers.[29] But until the latter part of the twentieth century, idealism

Politeness in the Philosophy of David Hume', in *Politics, Politeness, and Patriotism*, Proceedings of the Folger Institute Center for the History of British Political Thought, ed. Gordon J. Schochet, V (Washington, D.C.: Folger Shakespeare Library, 1993), pp. 305–318, and above, pp. 240–3.

[24] The work of Maurice Lee, Jenny Wormald, Brian Levack, Roger Mason, and John Robertson constitutes a series of striking exceptions to this generalization that actually underscores the point.

[25] The issue of 'republicanism' in the United States has spawned a vast literature. See, most recently, Gordon S. Wood, *The Radicalism of the American Revolution* (New York, 1992), pp. 95–225.

[26] John Morrow, *Coleridge's Political Thought: Property, Morality, and the Limits of Traditional Discourse* (New York, 1990), esp. 27–31 and 94–5.

[27] J. W. Burrow, *Whigs and Liberals: Continuity and Change in English Political Thought* (Oxford, 1988), pp. 15–18 and chs. 5 and 6.

[28] See Benjamin Evans Lippincott, *Victorian Critics of Democracy: Carlyle, Ruskin, Arnold, Stephen, Maine, Lecky* (Minneapolis, 1938).

[29] On philosophic idealism in nineteenth-century British political thought, see A. J. Milne, *The Social Philosophy of English Idealism* (London, 1962), and Peter P. Nicholson, *The Political Philosophy of the British Idealists* (Cambridge, 1990).

and virtue-politics were outside the mainstream of English-language political discourse. A series of anxieties about the presumed 'bankruptcy' or 'demise' of the 'liberal' state has recently sent political theorists and social critics scurrying about in search of alternatives, and many of them delight in what they take to be their 'rediscovery' of humanism. But that is a story for another place.

The story of the 'people', however, takes a novel twist at the start of the eighteenth century. Nicholas Phillipson has reminded us of the rise of 'Grub Street' and the emergence of a popular press,[30] a phenomenon that was abetted by the lapse of the Licensing Act in 1695.[31] This did not mean that the press was now free and unfettered any more than passage of the Act of Toleration had meant that dissenters were to have genuine religious liberty.[32] What it did eventually mean, however, was the emergence of a relatively new vehicle for discourse that could be directly aimed at an increasingly large 'public' that existed at the middling and lower ranges of society. It is impossible to know how much genuine 'public opinion' there was in eighteenth-century Britain, and even more difficult to determine the extent to which the press was responsible for creating and informing that public. It does, however, seem reasonable to presume that the working-class consciousness that trade unionism, utopian socialism, and Marxism were to tap and augment would not have been possible without that popular press.

By the nineteenth century, then – by that time that what we call the early-modern period of British history was drawing to a close – the 'people', whose existence had been so vaguely referred to in the previous 300 years, was about to acquire an identity. And by the twentieth century, most of the white males in that group would be eligible to claim the same rights, liberties, property, and *political* and legal equality their predecessors had been slowly and painfully extracting from a grudging state and church for many, many years.

This infusion of the masses into participatory politics in Britain and the United States occurred just as religion was declining as a unifying social force, leaving the new secular state without the means of bonding its members together. It was a prospect that would have terrified Thomas Hobbes and Samuel Parker alike, for it was their worst political nightmare violently come to life.

---

[30] Above, p. 216.
[31] See Lois G. Schwoerer, 'Liberty of the Press and Public Opinion: 1660–1695', in J. R. Jones (ed.), *Liberty Secured? Britain Before and After 1688* (Stanford, 1992), ch. 6.
[32] I owe this comparison to G. C. Gibbs, 'Press and Public Opinion: Prospective', in Jones (ed.), *Liberty Secured?*, p. 237.

Inclusion, exclusion, and access

For the most part, the principal terms of twentieth-century English-language politics were in place by 1800. The meanings of these terms have shifted somewhat over the intervening 200 years as they have been applied to different circumstances, but the words themselves have displayed a remarkable – if deceptive – persistence and adaptability. This vocabulary came from the newer and increasingly hegemonic juridical discourse and comprised the more-or-less coherent body of doctrine that would come to be known as 'liberalism'. The so-called 'triumph' of that liberal ideology was facilitated by the dominance in British philosophy after Hume of 'empiricism', an outlook that is sympathetic to a skeptical individualism in morals and politics. The legal construct 'state' eventually replaced the more humanistic 'commonwealth', and its members were 'citizens' in a modern sense whose 'rights', 'interest', 'properties', and 'liberties' were the reasons for political action as well as limitations on public 'authority'.[33] The point of politics was to protect and enhance rights and liberties – which were now conceived as *entitlements* that preceded organized politics and government rather than as *privileges* which were their creations – and not to pursue civic virtue. Central to all this were a *procedural* (rather than a *substance*-based) understanding of politics and the growing importance of the political *individual* who voluntarily became subject to legal and political rules, both of which reflected the needs of a society that was becoming increasingly diverse and pluralistic.

The substitution of interest for personal virtue as the ultimate end of *politics* was accompanied by a transformation in the meaning of *justice*. Ever since Aristotle, the term had possessed a moral as well as an economic (or legal) meaning, both having to do in the final analysis with 'desert' and giving people their 'due'. The former and more prevalent notion conceived of justice as a distinctly human attribute – something like what twentieth-century philosophers might call a disposition to be equitable – and one of the ends of life. It is familiar in the challenge thrown down to Socrates in Plato's *Republic*: 'Do not merely show us by argument that justice is superior to injustice, but make clear to us what each in and of itself does to its possessor, whereby the one is evil and the other is good'.[34] The economic or 'distributive' conception of justice generally attaches to institutions and practices rather than persons and is

---

[33] 'Liberty' and 'authority' were *words* the two discourses shared, but they sharply differed about their conceptual meanings.
[34] Plato, *Republic*, II. 367b, trans. Paul Shorey, in *The Collected Dialogues*, ed. Edith Hamilton and Huntington Cairns, Bollingen Series (New York, 1961), p. 613.

closer to 'fairness' than it is to goodness. This *modern* notion of political justice, like the politics of which it is an integral part, is essentially procedural, and is epitomized in John Rawl's famous dictum, 'Justice is the first virtue of social institutions'.[35] It is all that remained to the state once personal justice was consigned to the realm of 'private' morality.

The vocabulary that the modern Anglo-American state inherited from early-modern Britain is an evaluative and characterizing vocabulary, on the one hand, and a vocabulary about the distribution of goods and services provided by the political order, on the other. Other than by relying on such term as 'fairness' and 'equity' that are external to that discourse, however, this vocabulary says nothing about the objects or extent of distribution. Those *to whom* goods are to be distributed are pre-defined as 'citizens' and/or members who are presumed to be entitled to equal shares.

From the late twentieth-century perspective, categories of people who, historically, have been excluded – legally or *de facto* – from the larger class of persons who receive equitable shares of the goods and benefits the state distributes are conspicuously absent. In particular, this vocabulary in its original form did not mention race, class, and gender, to say nothing of people with disabilities. These are all relatively recent conceptual innovations: the introduction of the first and second can be traced to the late eighteenth and mid nineteenth centuries; gender and disability are late twentieth-century political concepts. In the first instance, these categories represent demands for a widening of citizenship to include persons who are excluded from its benefits in violation of the standards of justice and of such practices as rights and liberty.[36] More than that, however, their use in contemporary political discourse suggests that mere extension of the franchise and other political entitlements to previously excluded groups is insufficient to eliminate discriminatory practices that exist in the society itself below the level of self-conscious politics. There is something problematic and – to say the least – at variance with the dominant ideology in the way that citizenship and overt political participation decline in significance as their ranges are increased.

These complaints have their roots in the notion of 'equality', in an insistence that some disadvantaged members of society are entitled to

---

[35] John Rawls, *A Theory of Justice* (Cambridge, MA, 1971), p. 3.
[36] I have taken the notion of practice from Michael Oakeshott and Richard Flathman. See, generally, Oakeshott, *On Human Conduct* (Oxford, 1975), pp. 55–60, and, more specifically, Flathman, *The Practice of Rights* (Cambridge, 1976), esp. pp. 11–29. Flathman's entire book is directly related to my argument here, as is his *The Philosophy and Politics of Freedom* (Chicago, 1987).

the same benefits as others. As Stanley Benn and Richard Peters observed some time ago:

The demand for equality has never been intended in practice as a general plea that all men [sic] be treated alike. Egalitarians have always been concerned to deny the legitimacy of certain sorts of discrimination resting on some given differences, i.e., they have challenged established criteria as unreasonable, and irrelevant to the purposes for which they were employed. Claims to equality are thus, in a sense, always negative, denying that propriety of certain existing inequalities.[37]

In these terms, appeals to equality are attempts to eliminate what are known as 'relative deprivations'.[38] Equality itself has always had a problematic if not uncomfortable relationship with the legalistic, procedural politics of the Anglo-American world, and especially with the 'liberty' that is central to that politics.[39] Hobbes and Locke, for instance, both started with the natural equality of the state of nature, but both soon moved – in profoundly different ways – to civil societies that contained substantial inequalities; the 'equality' of the American Declaration of Independence was compromised from the start by the existence of slavery and the restriction of the franchise to males; and the simple if impractical egalitarianism of Bentham's 'felicific calculus' gave way to John Stuart Mill's search for qualitative distinctions among pleasures in *Utilitarianism* and his endorsement of unequal freedom in *On Liberty*. Even John Rawls' defence of equality in *A Theory of Justice* is presented in terms of 'the priority of liberty'.[40]

There is a much more radical conception of equality that comes out of the French Revolution. This is the implicit doctrine of Richard Price's

[37] S. I. Benn and R. S. Peters, *The Principles of Political Thought : Social Foundations of the Democratic State* (New York, 1965), pp. 131–2 (originally published as *Social Principle and the Democratic State* (London, 1959)).

[38] Relative deprivation is the subject of W. G. Runciman, *Relative Deprivation and Social Justice: A Study of Attitudes to Social Inequality in Twentieth-Century England* (Berkeley, 1966), esp. chs. 12–14, an analysis of the concept that has not been equalled in the subsequent theoretical literature.

[39] This issue is often seen as a conflict between liberty and equality, between a Locke–Mill tradition, on the one hand, and a Rousseau–Marx tradition on the other. Isaiah Berlin's classic defence of 'liberalism' against Rousseau in *Two Concepts of Liberty* (Oxford, 1958; reprinted in his *Four Essays on Liberty* (Oxford, 1969)), remains the place at which discussion of these issues must begin. George H. Sabine, 'The Two Democratic Traditions', *Philosophical Review*, 61 (1952), 451–74, is an excellent but undervalued account, apparently eclipsed by Berlin; C. B. Macpherson, *The Real World of Democracy* (Oxford, 1967), is a substantively related statement of these divergences in terms of 'liberal' and 'non-liberal' conceptions of democracy. Richard Norman, *Free and Equal: A Philosophical Examination of Political Values* (Oxford, 1987), is a recent, useful updating.

[40] Rawls, *Theory of Justice*, pp. 243–51. And see Pat Shaw, 'Rawls, the Lexical Difference Principle and Equality', *Philosophical Quarterly*, 42 (1992), 71–7.

1789 sermon, *Discourse on the Love of Our Country*, that so terrified Edmund Burke;[41] it is the doctrine that Thomas Paine in his *Rights of Man* (1792)[42] and, to a somewhat lesser extent, Mary Wollstonecraft in her *Vindication of the Rights of Men* (1790) used to answer Burke's *Reflections*. While that version has never been fully assimilated into English-language political discourse, it has provided important critical perspectives. Moreover, something approaching radical egalitarianism – rather than the incrementalism of Benn and Peters – is what critics of the discourse of the modern state have in mind when they call for redistributions of social and economic advantages as well as increased political entitlements. In some cases, they go even further and insist that the achievement of justice and equality are impossible within the current rights-based 'individualist' framework, for that way of conceiving the social and political worlds is inseparable from the interests of the white, male power-structure and, accordingly, must be replaced.[43]

The other side of this radical, redistributive egalitarianism consists in the distinctively modern notions of 'welfare' and 'need', the contents of which we increasingly think of as 'social justice'. These too are missing from the political vocabulary that was the bequest of early-modern Britain, but they are very much present in modern politics. They suggest bases for special redistributive entitlements as consequences of unwarranted and disabling relative deprivations and run counter to the deeply ingrained reliance of Anglo-American political beliefs and practices on 'merit'[44] and the separation of the public and private realms of life. Thus, the claim that these notions suggest aspects of a virtue-oriented politics should occasion no conceptual surprise. The demand for public and political redistribution, while hardly a call for a return to

[41] See Jack Fruchtman, Jr., *The Apocalyptic Politics of Richard Price and Joseph Priestley: A Study in Late Eighteenth-Century English Republican Millennialism*, Transactions of the American Philosophical Society, CXXIII: 4 (1983), ch. 3.

[42] See Gregory Claeys, *Thomas Paine: Social and Political Thought* (London, 1989), ch. 3.

[43] See, for instance, Pateman, *Sexual Contract*; Elizabeth Fox-Genovese, *Feminism Without Illusions: A Critique of Individualism* (Chapel Hill, NC, 1991), especially chs. 8 and 9; and Mary Ann Glendon, *Rights Talk: The Impoverishment of Political Discourse* (New York, 1991), ch. 5.

[44] On the general subject of social justice, see David Miller, 'Review Article: Recent Theories of Social Justice', *British Journal of Political Science*, 21 (1991), 371–91, and his *Social Justice* (Oxford, 1976), Part I; ch. 4 contains an interesting discussion of needs, as does his 'Social Justice and the Principle of Need', in Michael Freeman and David Robertson (eds.), *The Frontiers of Political Theory: Essays in a Revitalized Discipline* (New York, 1980), ch. 6. For philosophic accounts of the concept of needs, see Garrett Thomson, *Needs*, International Library of Philosophy (London, 1987), and David Braybrooke, *Meeting Needs: Studies in Moral, Political, and Legal Philosophy* (Princeton, 1987), the latter of which is very important on needs as the ends of social policies. George Sher, *Desert* (Princeton, 1987), examines a related concept, shows its relationship to 'merit', but has little to say about politics *per se*.

'civic virtue', is based upon a presumption that 'the quality of life', however private it may finally turn out to be, cannot be detached from the political process.[45] At the same time, it must be emphasized that this blurring of the line between politics and the rest of society is not necessarily incompatible with the more generally pervasive vocabulary, but it will certainly require adjustments in that discourse over the long haul.[46] What all this illustrates, in short, is the openness and flexibility of living political discourses, the persistence of older conceptualizations even though they may have fallen from favour, and the generally precarious condition of politics in the modern state as apparently new demands are made on old forms.

Political systems develop categories of membership as well as justifications for their policies of inclusiveness and exclusion. These categories initially favour the ruling segments (or classes) of the society by whom they are devised and whose interests they reflect and further. Historically, civil membership in western Europe and the societies and cultures it spawned was restricted to white males who shared religious beliefs and socio-economic status. People who were not members of the established (or favoured) religious confession, who did not own sufficient amounts of 'property', who were not caucasian, or who were not male – to list the bars in the order in which they were removed in the Anglo-American world – were deemed unfit for full, participating citizenship.[47] At best, they were relegated to positions of tutelage and were the *objects* of public policy rather than its sources; their relationships to the civil society were through their social and political 'superiors'.

Except in the area of religion – which will be dealt with separately – these exclusions rested on a series of presumptions about the natural, hierarchical organization of the world that reflected equally natural differential capacities and 'fitness' for citizenship among humans. These views went back at least to the Aristotelian conception of humans as

---

[45] This is the burden of the argument of Judith N. Shklar, *American Citizenship: The Quest for Inclusion* (Cambridge, MA, 1991), ch. 2.

[46] Two recent attempts to deal with these problems within the larger framework of 'liberal' values are Joseph Raz, *The Morality of Freedom* (Oxford, 1986), and Will Kymlicka, *Liberalism, Community, and Culture* (Oxford, 1989). On the debate between 'liberalism' and 'communitarianism' that has been raging in Anglo-American political theory for some time now, see Alan Ryan, 'Communitarianism: The Good, the Bad, & the Muddly', *Dissent*, 36 (1989), 350–4. Also of interest but rather more libertarian in outlook is Stephen Macedo, *Liberal Virtues: Citizenship, Virtue, and Community in Liberal Constitutionalism* (Oxford, 1990). Although they all use 'historical' materials, none of these works is particularly self-conscious about history and historical change.

[47] Children, too, were – and still are – denied the rights of full, participating citizenship, but if the other criteria were satisfied, the obstacle of age was eventually removed – but by natural, not political, processes.

political beings by nature. But the gradual shift away from the naturalistic and somewhat 'communitarian' language of virtue to the more voluntarist and interest-based vocabulary of rights and liberties brought with it an implicit questioning of these presumptions. The working out of the 'logic' of rights, so to speak, moved in the direction of equality; it was the antithesis of natural hierarchies. If the natural order consisted in rights and liberties rather than in status and station, the long-run problems would be to justify what appeared to be arbitrary differentiations and exclusions and to explain impositions. Privilege has always been suspect and in need of defence, but so long as the traditional view of society was essentially intact, privilege remained relatively secure. In the long run, it was undermined by the transformation of sixteenth-century and Scholastic vocabularies of opposition into natural law and constitutional theories of the state and by demands for rational justification. The ideology of constitutionalism would eventually prove hostile to claims of natural privilege, and justifications that did not look to the sovereign entitlements of the people would become irrelevant. All this, conceptually at least, would leave what political theorists are fond of calling the 'abstract', 'autonomous' individual, cut loose from the natural ties of society. And in these terms, we can see why *political obligation* emerged as so important to the discourse of the secular state.

The modern state, tradition, and the political hermeneutics of 'pluralism'

In its participatory incarnation, the modern secular state is strikingly unlike the churches from which it has managed to separate itself over the past 300 years. By design and reputation, it has made its central concern temporal justice, not salvation, and its governors accountable to 'the people', not some transcendent authority. But that is not the whole story.

Rather more like sectarian churches, the essences of individual states are enshrined in primal, authoritative, and often arcane 'texts' that are functionally comparable to holy writ and according to which their actions are evaluated. These are not necessarily 'texts'[48] in the literal sense, but are often congeries of constitutional documents, commentaries, and interpretations, laws and judicial decisions, inspiring speeches, letters, and literary works, philosophic essays, symbols, and even

---

[48] For a general discussion of these issues, focusing specifically on the work of Charles Taylor and Richard Rorty, see Charles B. Guigin, 'Pragmatism or Hermeneutics? Epistemology after Foundationalism', in David R. Hiley *et al.* (eds.), *The Interpretive Turn: Philosophy, Science, Culture* (Ithaca, NY, 1991), esp. pp. 89–93.

abstract ideals and concepts. Together they comprise a 'text' – better known, perhaps, as a 'tradition'[49] (see below) – that requires a hermeneutic reading no less than do the foundational works of a Christian church.

Part of the issue of a textual canon in the histories of ethical and political thought has to do with the relatively recent emancipation of those subjects from theology. This entanglement is fully evident when we consider the dependence of so much pre-nineteenth-century – and not a little present – moral and political theory on assertions of divinity and the will of God. We have no trouble with the existence of canons in the religious and theological realms and with authoritative, hermeneutical interpretation of those texts; they are essential to the exhortation and justification that are inherent in religious rhetoric. One of the hallmarks of the modern temper is its skeptical turn of mind. What makes traditional, theological – or theistically based – ethics and politics troublesome from that skeptical perspective is the apparent substitution of authoritative hermeneutics for judgement and of faith for reason.

It is not surprising that non-theological ethics and politics are often derived from self-interested and/or utilitarian principles. Social philosophy has always been concerned with the subordination of human will and desire to some behavioural standards and, of equal importance, with the justification and legitimation of those standards. Its task, in short, is to make humans conform to norms of order and restraint. Theology easily and efficiently accomplishes this task by providing a comprehensive, self-contained system of rules that restrains and establishes relationships among otherwise independent wills that are motivated by the individual self-interests. The problem, once divinity is abandoned, is to find some functional analogue for God and the commandments of sacred law. As John Locke presciently puts it in his *Epistola de Tolerantia*, 'The taking away of God, even only in thought, dissolves all'.[50]

A 'natural law' that is not dependent upon a supreme being is the holy grail for some devotees of modern, secular ethics and politics.[51] But even natural law is ultimately problematic, for its supra-human transcendence reintroduces the same objections that plague divine mystery.

---

[49] Or even, to readers of T. S. Kuhn, *The Structure of Scientific Revolutions*, 2nd edn (Chicago, 1970), a 'paradigm'.

[50] John Locke, *Epistola de Tolerantia: A Letter on Toleration* (1689), ed. Raymond Klibansky, trans. J. W. Gough (Oxford, 1968), p. 135.

[51] I do not wish here to enter into the contemporary debates about 'foundationalism' and the extent to which it is a uniquely – or even distinctly – 'modern' quest other than to observe that similar ventures, such as the Roman *jus gentium* and even Aristotle's classification of 'constitutions', were *predicated* upon rather than demonstrative of the existence of a coherent natural order.

Thus, the starting point for secular morality and politics remains a world of independent wills that must somehow be connected.

Modern ethics, the focal point of which increasingly is individual 'conscience', has looked for some other-regarding principle of action to replace divinity and natural law. Political justification, which is concerned with social wholes and their continuity over time, has tended to appeal to abstract principles such as 'liberty', 'rights', and 'justice',[52] and – more recently – 'virtue' and 'community' as values by which everyone should be motivated. Beyond that there is almost always at least an *implicit* reliance on some kind of historical standard that determines continuity and is what is generally meant by 'tradition'. This sort of retrospection looks to historical practice for standards and establishes and sanctifies a canon of texts and personalities that have made or contributed to the 'tradition'.

Functionally, once a canon is established, it fills the void left by banished (or departed) holy writ. The practice of looking to a canon for validation is apparently a deeply ingrained habit that satisfies an important social need. It provides standards for judging our values and institutions that go beyond our immediate preferences. A tradition expressed in a canon ties us to our forebears and furnishes us with a living, cultural identity to pass on to our successors.[53] Possessing a canon, to which we are committed, commits us as well to the hermeneutic practice of interpretation.

This political hermeneutics is generally not the preserve of a priestly caste that is empowered to provide authoritatively definitive interpretations of a tradition (although there are certainly those who aspire to such a status). It is, rather – especially in a participatory state – a more public and contentious activity in which all citizens may well find themselves playing for very high stakes, including the definition of membership and the control of the state itself. But the aim, like that of religious interpretation, is to clarify and explicate the 'text' from which legitimacy is derived and to validate or attack certain actions as they conform to or exceed the bounds revealed by the interpretation. It can even happen that the contentious debate itself becomes the source of a

---

[52] Rawls, *Theory of Justice*, is an excellent example of this practice. His conception of 'justice as fairness' and its derivation from a hypothetical contract agreed to behind a 'veil of ignorance' is designed precisely to incorporate independent, self-interested, personal wills into a system of social justice without appealing to transcendent categories. His attempt to derive justice from individual interest and entitlement places Rawls in a tradition – if I may here be allowed that term – that runs from Hobbes, through Bentham, to H. L. A. Hart.

[53] See Conal Condren, *The Status and Appraisal of Classic Texts: An Essay on Political Theory, Its Inheritance, and the History of Ideas* (Princeton, 1985), esp. chs. 8 and 9.

new legitimation, and delves into its own legitimacy at a further level of contentiousness.

The form of religious disputation and justification in traditional apostolic or fundamentalist Christian churches is fairly well known.[54] Churches generally claim to be derived from ancient, venerated texts or bodies of doctrine and to remain true to and consistent with the principles on which they were founded. Christ, the apostles, and the early Church fathers are seen as *law-givers* whose directions must be followed. But these founding principles, the texts that contain them, and the bodies of interpretation and practice that have grown up around them are often ambiguous and – because they are essentially 'other-worldly' – mysterious. It is the existence of mystery as an integral part of religion that necessitates licensed interpreters whose task it is to make divine will and the past intelligible and meaningful to the present and to settle conflicts about the requirements of holy writ and whether certain practices are actually in conformity with them.

A church that claims apostolic succession for its ministry needs to demonstrate that its clergy has descended without interruption from the founders. Those who would depart from or challenge the legitimacy of that descent are called 'heretics', 'schismatics', or even 'sinners' and are to be excluded from full, participating membership in the church. 'Purifiers' would correct the church's erroneous departures from its foundations by eliminating improper practices and illegitimate historical accretions – including, in some cases, the necessity of apostolic succession – and returning to what they understand as the original and true doctrine.

The history of religious sectarianism, by and large, is the history of unresolved disputes along these lines. Unsuccessful reformers who are not reabsorbed into the offending church or persecuted out of existence, driven by the need to escape 'ungodliness', may separate into new religious associations that are based on rival interpretations of scripture. Christian history since the Reformation is replete with denominations – each with its own hermeneutics – that began their lives in precisely this manner. The long-term social and political response to this religious pluralism is toleration and religious liberty, and the recent, liberal Christian response has been ecumenism. Both practices owe their origins

---

[54] The discussion that follows is not meant to apply to any specific church, but the fortunes and demeanours of the Church of England in the sixteenth and seventeenth centuries have never been far from my thoughts. Peter Lake, 'The Laudians and the Argument from Authority', in Bonnelyn Kunze and Dwight D. Brautigam (eds.), *Court, Country, and Culture: Essays on Early Modern British History in Honour of Perez Zagorin* (Rochester, 1992), pp. 149–75, is an excellent examination of an aspect of the Church of England's history in terms similar to the ones I have used here.

more to pragmatism than to principle; they would be unnecessary, to say nothing of unthinkable, in a world with a single, hegemonic church.

In terms of dealing with internal divisions, the modern state would appear to be at its greatest functional distance from my model of the traditional church, which, as I have already suggested, it resembles in other respects. The state is intentionally and irreducibly pluralistic and participatory, and its devotees hope on these grounds to avert secessions and separations. To extend the comparison to religious organizations, we might describe it as 'latitudinarian' and 'Presbyterian' (but certainly not Quaker), and therein lies one of its chief ideological difficulties. Thomas Hobbes and the High Church enemies of toleration and comprehension in Stuart England equally appreciated the near impossibility of reconciling the need for a genuinely authoritative political structure with the demands of pluralism.

Over the last 300 years, states have become more inclusive and diverse in their memberships. In the English-speaking world, the fostering of divergent rights and interests has replaced the harmonious achievement of civic virtue as the end of politics. The generation and persuasively coherent interpretation of the culture's fundamental 'texts' – a genuine 'political hermeneutics' – has become all the more essential if these societies are to be held together and all the more problematic because of the wide range of needs and entitlements that must be represented.[55] It is in part for this reason that *the law* looms so large in the modern world, and the myth of legalism and legal neutrality are so close to the ideological bedrock of the modern secular state.[56] At the same time, however, it is no longer self-evident that the state ought to be held together as a political community. Indeed, numbers of people are confident that it should not survive, and therein lies a significant part of the post-modernist perplexity.

The institutions and practices that define a society are also parts of its history; they did not suddenly appear but took shape and have endured

[55] See Judith N. Shklar, 'Facing up to Intellectual Pluralism', in David Spitz (ed.), *Political Theory & Social Change* (New York, 1967), ch. 12. Irreducible pluralism is one of the central themes in the work of Isaiah Berlin; see especially 'Does Political Theory still Exist?' in Peter Laslett and W. G. Runciman (eds.), *Philosophy, Politics, and Society*, 2nd ser. (Oxford, 1962), pp. 1–33 (reprinted in his *Concepts and Categories: Philosophical Essays*, ed. Henry Hardy (New York, 1979), pp. 143–72). Equally important are Bernard Williams, 'Conflicts of Values', in Alan Ryan (ed.), *The Idea of Freedom: Essays in Honour of Isaiah Berlin* (Oxford, 1979), pp. 221–32, and, at greater length, *Ethics and the Limits of Philosophy* (Cambridge, MA, 1985). In rather a more self-consciously relativist form, pluralism underscores Richard Rorty's attack on 'foundationalism' in *Philosophy and the Mirror of Nature* (Princeton, 1979).

[56] Judith N. Shklar, *Legalism: An Essay on Law, Morals, and Politics* (Cambridge, MA, 1964).

over a period of years. (The most radical historical nominalist would not question this simple fact.) The vocabulary or discourse in which a society is described and characterized to and by its members – its political discourse – is a subset of the language that is generally available. It is no less historically rooted than any other institution. And, like those other institutions and like the larger language itself, this political discourse changes over time, as each generation makes its own additions and subtractions and as surrounding and supporting institutional arrangements decay, disappear, are replaced, and evolve into something else. Society is in a constant state of flux; even the historian does not have the luxury of unmoving targets, for part of what history is about is that process of change. The trick – which is both the end and the bugbear of the historian's quest – is somehow to determine where and how change occurs.

Attention to discourse – and to what are fashionably called 'discursive modes' – does not *solve* the problem by any means, but it does bring the target more sharply into focus. Discourse and language open up a series of fascinating issues and help to minimize the artificial disciplinary boundaries that separate political thought and political philosophy from literature, history, and rhetoric, as well as from semiotics, art, and other non-verbal forms of representation. They direct our attention – as students of the subject and as political and social beings – to unwitting, unexpressed, and sometimes intentionally suppressed assumptions and modes of arguing that are implicit in political concepts and might otherwise escape detection. They provide us with the tools and force us to look beneath and beyond immediate verbal expression for coherences as well for incongruities.

As creatures of the cultures we inhabit, we are formed by – and contribute to – the languages we speak, the beliefs (including prejudices and ideologies) we acquire, the interpretative manners and standards of 'justification' and 'proof' we are taught, and the institutions we encounter. In politics, the institutions, practices, and languages always affect and refer to the interests of others; part of what politics intends is authoritative control over those interests. Short of successful revolutionary innovation, sudden and profound changes in the conduct of political life are difficult to conceive. This is not because 'authoritarian' (as distinguished from 'authoritative') politics is in disrepute and some degree of participation is ideologically required in the political world of the late twentieth century, for it is not clear that in non-revolutionary conditions authoritarian rule would be any more successful than a popular assembly in radically altering a state's political concepts and language. The cause seems to lie more in the fact that like distributions of power, political languages in participatory states are so complex that it is difficult to effect an intentional remodelling except in a revolutionary context, and even there, the result is likely to resemble the 'newspeak' of Orwell's *1984*.

When conceived in terms of its discourse, politics seems to be limited to what Michael Oakeshott called 'the pursuit of intimations' that inhere in the 'tradition' we have acquired from the past.[57] To put it in the more familiar terminology of the sociology of knowledge, we can never escape the conceptual and linguistic 'iron cage' of our political cultures, although we can certainly bend the bars a bit. If political efficacy is the measure, normal – that is, non-revolutionary – politics may be incapable of moving beyond the exploration of possibilities that are already present, and political theorists may be similarly constrained by the discourses they inherit. (By the same token, one of the primary tasks facing a regime installed as a result of successful revolution is to stabilize itself as the bearer of a new orthodoxy.) This is not necessarily to move with Oakeshott entirely to the political conservatism that he somehow extracted from his relatively unexceptionable sociology. It does not follow that politics is always or even best conducted in ways that are consistent with past practices, for the language may reveal implications that were not intended or even known or cared about before. And it may be now possible – Burke and Oakeshott to the contrary notwithstanding – in the contemporary context of nearly instantaneous international communication, growing 'internationalization' of economic and ecological concerns, and increasing cultural dispersal – for the standards and 'intimations' of one society rapidly and successfully to 'migrate' to, influence, and become parts of the politics of another.

It is primarily through the law that the state confronts and deals with its members. As Tocqueville predicted, the law in democratic societies has become the principal means by which important social issues are resolved and the conflicts that arise almost naturally from the phenomenon of pluralism are adjudicated. It is doubtful, however, whether the law can sustain the burden of defining and preserving the pluralistic society that is now placed on it. *Lex loquens* cannot be *vox populi*, for a diverse people cannot have a single voice unless it is imposed on them. But an imposition would be the destruction of the very pluralism it is allegedly preserving. Even more to the point, the law is not the voice of a

[57] This is the argument of Oakeshott's defence of tradition against what he called 'rationalism' in his famous inaugural address, *Political Education* (1951), which was republished with an appendix specifically on 'The Pursuit of Intimations' in his *Rationalism in Politics and Other Essays* (London, 1962), itself republished with a number of additional papers in a 'new and expanded edition', ed. with a new foreword by Timothy Fuller (Indianapolis, 1991).

neutral arbiter either; rather, it reflects varying prejudices and social interests.[58] Increased participation in the law-making process has become one of the important goals in the internal conflicts of pluralistic states.

The dilemma of the post-modern state almost seems to invite the kind of creative genius that established and held together the *pax Romana* and, until its break-up in the sixteenth century, Christian Europe. There is an increasing urgency about showing the otherwise diverse members of various communities that what they have in common is more important than their differences. Something like that seems to be occurring in the creation of the European Community, which might lead to the replacement of the modern state with some unprecedented form. For the genius of Rome may have been the accidental outcome of practical necessity rather than the calculated result of political insight. The preservation of local, territorial identities may have been the only possible solution to the problem of ruling so far-flung an empire. It is easy to forget that the kind of day-to-day, hands-on mode of governing at a distance that we take for granted and which makes the Roman accomplishment seem so great has been made possible by the advent of modern technology and rapid communication. The *jus gentium* as the 'one from the many', so to speak, and the keystone of that Roman feat, may have been a reflection of a metaphysics that is no longer viable. Roman Catholic Christianity ultimately became the force preserving the Roman (later, significantly, *Holy* Roman) Empire, but it was based on other-worldly concerns and an interpretative imposition of the sort that is neither appropriate to nor acceptable in modern, secular politics. The difficulty with all this is that without some kind of ideology of metaphysical union, it is not clear either what will hold the state together or what will become of participation at anything other than a relatively low level of political organization. Pluralism is then transformed into an ideology of great convenience to those exercising power at higher and more inclusive levels.

Diversity is an especially difficult problem in the light of modern technology. Industrialization and 'division of labour' seem to create value pluralism within what were previously relatively homogeneous societies. Rapid communication has expanded the size of the relevant community without decreasing the differences within it. It is ironic that

---

[58] This is the point of departure for the critical legal studies movement, adherents of which then argue that law can also be used self-consciously for reform. See, in general, Mark Kelman, *A Guide to Critical Legal Studies* (Cambridge, MA, 1987), Martha Minow, *Making All the Difference: Inclusion, Exclusion, and American Law* (Ithaca, NY, 1990), and, for the British perspective, Peter Fitzpatrick (ed.), *Dangerous Supplements: Resistance and Renewal in Jurisprudence* (London, 1991).

the bland homogenization of cultures that was once so feared as the inevitable consequence of what Marshall McLuhan called the 'global village' has not occurred. Although Coca Cola, the products of American television, and Levis jeans have become 'cultural icons' and global commodities, they have not overcome the ethnic factors that separate various peoples.

That same technology has meant, increasingly, that the concerns and policies of one nation have important ramifications for the rest of the world. Wide-spread industrialization has created a consciousness of a world-wide ecology, just as international commerce has created a world-wide economic system. But the resolution of the resulting problems is no closer than is universal adherence to international law. 'National interests' protected by territorial sovereignty are the primary obstacle to the effective solution of all these issues. Voluntary compliance simply does not work, and coercion is impossible in a universe dedicated to autonomy. In short, sovereignty and national diversity mean that the problems of the international world are those of the single, pluralistic state writ large, which are among the very forces that eventually destroyed the Roman Empire. We have not moved very far from Hobbes' assertion that nations face each other in a state of nature.

It is difficult to be optimistic about the future of the late twentieth-century state, for it appears to be inherently incapable of solving the very problem that provides its identity, secular diversity in its many aspects. The international picture is hardly more encouraging. Increasingly, the dominant image – not unlike that of the seventeenth-century Stuart theory of political dissolution – is of the failure of politics resulting in destructive, military conflict. Far from the 'end of ideology' that was seen in the 1950s, we are today living in an age of ever-increasing ethnic and ideological struggles, the end of which, left unchecked, is almost always war in one form or another.

Political philosophy and theory alone cannot help us find the way out of this morass. There is certainly not much to be found in any academic political philosophy that is divorced from the political struggles that historians of political thought so well understand.[59] At some point, architectonic political philosophy breaks down because it can neither accommodate nor adequately account for the incoherences that are the

---

[59] See John Dunn, 'The Future of Political Philosophy in the West', in his *Rethinking Modern Political Theory: Essays, 1979–83* (Cambridge, 1985), ch. 10, esp. pp. 187–89, where he stresses that 'prudence' and the 'view from here and now' must be the starting points of political philosophy. Also relevant is his 'Political Obligations and Political Possibilities', in his *Political Obligation in Its Historical Context: Essays in Political Theory* (Cambridge, 1980), ch. 10.

stuff of political life; it is replaced by a lower order of theorizing that partakes more of incremental advocacy than it does of principled justification.[60] But long before that point is reached, a socially sensitive political theory can help to understand our goals and objectives and appreciate the inherent limits of our politics before these too collapse.

Political discourse and argument are far less open-ended than some contemporary analysts would like to believe. Growing numbers of academic critics and other 'intellectuals' who appear to be in agony over what they see as the 'bankruptcy' of modern politics are unrelenting in their calls for the wholesale rejection of prevailing 'liberal' values. Their presumption seems to be that political language can be legislated and that the meanings of concepts can be prescribed. But the germ of Oakeshott's claim – shared with sociologists of knowledge, cultural anthropologists, and proponents of the new 'social epistemology' – is the recognition that the conventions of tradition and social meaning emerge from society, not from fiat. Social and political languages and the intimations they carry cannot be so readily contained; changes in them occur gradually and as the results of societal usage, not stipulation. To argue otherwise is to overstep both the role of the political theorist and the bounds of social possibility, however praiseworthy the substantive aims may be. The confrontation of reformist politics by, at best, the ever-grinding and slow processes of social change or, no less likely, what amounts to structural intransigence, is not so much sobering as it is distressing.

What then, is the legitimate task of the political theorist if it does not extend to the imposition of conceptual forms on civil society? The answer to that question is inseparable from the issue of audience: who, aside from students, occasional colleagues, and fellow critics, actually listens to and is influenced by the claims of modern-day political theorists? And that audience carries rather little political weight. This limitation is partially a result of the academization of the activity of theorizing about politics and what amounts to the practical disengagement (if not naiveté) of its practitioners, who are often frustrated by the relatively slow pace of change and by the intrusion of prejudice and ideology on ideals and standards. Academic political philosophy is a distinctly modern phenomenon – part of the cultural legacy of the Enlightenment – for isolation from the political public was not an early-modern problem. Actual politics, unlike modern theory and philosophy,

---

[60] Cf. Fukuyama, *The End of History*, for an unconvincing, Hegelian argument to the contrary, and Karl R. Popper, *The Poverty of Historicism*, 3rd edn, reprinted (New York, 1964), esp. ch. 21, for a defence of the incrementalism that he calls 'piecemeal engineering'.

is more rhetorical and practical than coherent and reflects power and shifting interests rather than principles. Appeals to 'rightness' and justice and even claims of inconsistency may be excellent ways of expressing unwarranted deprivations and of galvanizing the victims, but they are of little use by themselves in attempting to persuade people to change their behaviour, especially if they are being urged to act contrary to their perceived interests. The great masses of people and most political actors are not moved by lofty ideals, and raising the public 'consciousness' of citizens is a long and arduous project with relatively little chance of success.

The area that remains for the political theorist to occupy begins to look rather like the domain of the historian, for it is increasingly more analytic, explanatory, and even descriptive than it is persuasively normative and rhetorical. The primary tasks are to provide accounts of the concepts and political languages in use in a culture and to elucidate their meanings and relationships and their statuses *vis-à-vis* other institutions. This certainly includes examinations of possible inconsistences, their causes, and possible ways of eliminating them. It is not unlike Oakeshott's 'pursuit of intimations', although it need not be wedded to his conservative suspicions of 'rationality'. Political theorists understand better than most analysts the implications of having one set of values and concepts rather than another. Part of their stock in trade, as it were, is an appreciation of what our discourse implicitly and explicitly commits us to, what kinds of things it renders impossible or impermissible. Anything more than that, alas, moves them outside the bounds of their professional competence. Recommendations about specific policies or about other discourses that might or should be adopted are entitled to no special standing on account of their having been made by political theorists.

The 'language' of politics, history, and the politics of diversity

A peculiarly *political* discourse is not fully – and perhaps not at all – separable from the more general modes of communication that prevail in society. Rather, politics draws on, contributes to, and helps shape that larger discourse in ways that are not altogether determinate. In other words, while we know *what* we are talking about here, we do not quite know *how* it works. All this becomes a series of *conceptual* claims and distinctions, perhaps even abstracted 'ideal types' – to repair to a vocabulary that is no longer fashionable but retains a distinct utility – and it might be the case that we can do no more than call attention to the apparent paradox or difficulty of talking about talk. The whole business is extremely complicated, and much of what is believed to be the case is rather more the product of speculative theorizing than it is of empirical investigation.

Politics itself is not reducible to discourse and language and vocabulary (although it certainly uses them); politics is about stakes, interests, and conflicts. Political theory, as something akin to ideology, is about the *justification* of political systems and recommendations. It is expressed in – i.e., uses – and is concerned with language; but as a day-to-day activity, politics is about the possession and manipulation of *power* – sometimes even power for its own sake, a Hobbesian insight that seems to have been lost to modern consciousness – and about the satisfaction of interests. It is the political theorist as commentator, who, in rather a detached manner, adds his discourse about language and concepts, imposing a degree of purposive self-consciousness that is rarely achieved in politics itself. Yet, even the lowest levels of political activity have recourse to verbal expression, which occurs in words that are intelligible to the relevant audience, that is, in some part of the existing political discourse of the community. The politician's craft, to no small degree, consists precisely in these sorts of communication, which is one of the principal ways that civil societies and our awareness of ourselves as members of them – which is sometimes termed 'civic consciousness' – persists over time.[61]

As the common lawyers understood, and Hume and Burke – to say nothing of Hegel and Marx – well appreciated, the past has become the present, carrying part of itself forward in the process. In the same way, today's present will give rise to, be incorporated into, and eventually be overwhelmed by some future. We know that the passage of time is as inevitable as calling attention to it is trivial and even trite. But beyond these commonplace assertions, it is difficult to say precisely *how* this transformation occurs.

But there is a *politics* – or at least a political component – to its conduct. Politics involves the establishment and maintenance of order, the management of change, and the intrusion of authoritative intention and control into human affairs. It is irreducibly about stakes and contests and is driven by choice. It is a conscious, human activity. However 'accidental' some of its effects may be, however deeply rooted it may be in some instinctive drives for self-preservation and power,

---

[61] See Donald Hanson, *From Kingdom to Commonwealth: The Development of Civic Consciousness in English Political Thought* (Cambridge, MA, 1970), and Stephen L. Collins, *From Divine Cosmos to Sovereign State: An Intellectual History of Consciousness and the Idea of Order in Renaissance England* (Oxford, 1989).

politics is not unwitting. The movement from the world of unreflective, primitive being in which people were at the mercy of mysterious, natural forces – if such a movement ever occurred and if such a world ever existed[62] – to a world where at least some people *intentionally* construct and manipulate institutions and practices and thereby influence life is simultaneously the pre-condition and creation of politics.

By definition, choices actually made must have reason(s) behind them; they must be the outcomes of some deliberative processes, however attenuated and distorted those processes may be. Even the failure to act when confronted with difficult options is none the less a decision and can be accounted for in the language of volition and will. Similarly, Hume's dilemma that weighed the pain of a scratched finger against the destruction of the world[63] and A. J. Ayer's reductionist, 'emotive' description of the preference for one mode of moral or religious behaviour over another[64] can be comprehended in these terms.

What is relevant here is not the place of choice and volition in everyday life but their roles in the political process. In many important senses, choices and decisions that concern the welfare or interests of other people and that purport to be legitimate or authoritative (or are made in opposition to alleged misuse or misappropriation of the mantles of legitimacy) – that is, where someone other than the decision-maker has something at stake – are political. This rather broad conception suggests some of the points at which politics and other forms of social regulation, especially morality, intersect, for it is one of the constant facts of life that people encounter authoritative structures that make decisions that directly impinge upon their interests. For present purposes, however, this notion needs to be qualified – without attempting to formulate a concise definition of politics – by restricting its range to the

---

[62] Once popular amongst political theorists and philosophers who readily employed anthropological and sociological examples to illustrate their arguments – perhaps a twentieth-century analogue to otherwise discredited state of nature theories – this sort of speculation is no longer fashionable. See, for instance, Robert M. MacIver, *The Modern State* (Oxford, 1926), esp. chs. 1 and 10, and the same author's *The Web of Government* (New York, 1947 and 1965), chs. 2 and 3 in both editions; and H. L. A. Hart, *The Concept of Law* (Oxford, 1961), ch. 4. See also E. Adamson Hoebel, *The Law of Primitive Man* (Cambridge, MA, 1954), chs. 1, 2, and 12; and, more generally, Peter Winch, 'Understanding a Primitive Society', *American Philosophical Quarterly*, 1 (1964), 307–24, and the literature it generated in response, much of which is reprinted and/or cited in Brian Wilson (ed.), *Rationality* (Oxford, 1970), and Fred R. Dallmayr and Thomas A. McCarthy (eds.), *Understanding and Social Inquiry* (Notre Dame, IN, 1977). Winch's article is reprinted in both volumes.

[63] "'Tis not contrary to reason to prefer the destruction of the whole world to the scratching of my finger'. David Hume, *A Treatise of Human Nature* (1739–40), II, iii, 3; text from the second L. A. Selby-Bigge edition, ed. P. H. Nidditch (Oxford, 1978), p. 416.

[64] A. J. Ayer, *Language, Truth, and Logic* (London, 1936, 1946), ch. 6 in both editions.

'public' realm, that is, to formally structured 'civil society' or the 'state' or one of their historical analogues.

Putting all this together, we can say that politics is concerned with the management of public affairs of a state over time, that is, with controlling how and what parts of a public life will persist, be transformed, and pass into the future.[65] The political process thus superintends for the entire society the determination of how much like the present the future should be.[66] As changing conditions need to be dealt with and accounted for within an existing structure, what standards and guidelines are to be applied and followed? Who determines and has charge of those standards? What are the criteria for deciding that a proffered policy or change satisfies the standards? And, perhaps most important, who sees to it that the standards are adhered to? On what grounds and by whom are the standards enforced?

These are among the central questions of politics, and their importance has been recognized and addressed with increasing frequency since the sixteenth century. Indeed, once the political process is perceived as placing an undue burden on people who seek redress, it is almost a certainty that these issues will be joined in one form or another. Their significance is something of a reflection of the emergence over the past four centuries of law as the primary vehicle of political control. All these questions have to do with 'sovereignty' and what in the twentieth century has been called 'constitutionalism'. The one addresses the nature and locus of the supreme power to make and enforce laws in a society and the other the formal as well as the substantive limitations on that power.[67]

So conceived, disputes about the legitimate exercise of sovereign power and the proper extent of constitutional entitlements and guarantees presuppose the existence of a relatively accessible and more-or-less intelligible vocabulary that can sustain political discourse and which contains the standards and the means of assessing their operation. The

---

[65] Obviously, the effects of the political process range far beyond the public life of a community, and one of the great debates of the late twentieth century is precisely about how great that range should be. 'Privacy', as a fence against political intrusion, is a battle-cry used by the Left and the Right alike. That issue, however, cannot be further pursued here, but I am not unmindful of its significance.

[66] This claim that politics is intimately involved in the construction of the future is something of a hyperbole that pertains to the kind of abstracting and *explaining* what politics is about in which theorists engage.

[67] Sovereignty in this Bodinian form is discussed in chapter 5 above, pp. 150–2. For constitutionalism and especially the differences between the modern and classical conceptions, see Gordon J. Schochet, 'Constitutionalism, Liberalism, and the Study of Politics', in J. Roland Pennock and John Chapman (ed.), *NOMOS XX: Constitutionalism* (New York, 1979), ch. 1.

appearance and development of such a vocabulary is an anthropological concomitant to the persistence of a civil society over time. A society's identity is asserted, maintained, and justified in large part through its political discourse, which determines the way it describes itself both to its members and to the rest of the world. This discourse enables a society to persist over time, for it is the conceptual vehicle that effects self-conscious movement among the past, the present, and the future.[68]

A society's belief systems, its myths, what A. D. Lindsay called its 'operative ideals',[69] as well as its ideological 'cultural system'[70] all go into the making of – and are inseparably intertwined in – its public language. That language and the concepts it contains and supports, accordingly, bear their society's fundamental presuppositions and prejudices, which are part of the heritage that is passed on to the next generation. Two substantial qualifications must be introduced: first, this process does not operate at the level of consciousness for all language-users (or even for some language-users all the time); second, language is not an entirely passive reflection – mere consequence and 'superstructure', as it were – of the society's *other* institutions.

Much of what we believe to be the case about the world is grounded in verbal representation of which we are simply unaware and which we therefore do not question. This is of significance not only in the realms of unreflective, vulgar discourse and propagandistic ideology. Even in so lofty an arena as the United States Supreme Court, as Martha Minow has pointedly demonstrated,[71] assumptions about status and equality

---

[68] The general theoretical position implicit in these remarks has been more fully developed in Gordon J. Schochet, *The Authoritarian Family and Political Attitudes in Seventeenth-Century England: Patriarchalism in Political Thought*, 2nd edn (New Brunswick, 1988), ch. 14; 'Patriarchalism, Naturalism, and the Rise of the "Conventional State"', in F. Fagiani and G. Valera (eds.), *Categorie del Reale e Storiografia: Aspetti di continuità e trasformazione nell'Europa Moderna* (Milan, 1986); and 'The English Revolution in the History of Political Thought', in Kunze and Brautigam (eds.), *Court, Country, and Culture.*

Much of this is commonplace to those historians of political thought who conceive of their subject as 'discourse', but there are substantial differences on the particulars. This reconceptualization has been among the driving forces behind the Folger Center, and many of its premises unite the contributors to this book, several of whom have already addressed the subject above. For further discussion, see especially Anthony Pagden, 'Introduction', and J. G. A. Pocock, 'The Concept of a Language and the *métier d'historien*: Some Considerations on Practice', both in Pagden (ed.), *Languages of Political Theory*, and Pocock, 'Texts as Events: Reflections on the History of Political Thought', in Kevin Sharpe and Steven N. Zwicker (eds.), *Politics of Discourse: The Literature and History of Seventeenth-Century England* (Berkeley, 1987).

[69] A. D. Lindsay, *The Modern Democratic State* (Oxford, 1943).

[70] The allusion is to the classic essay by Clifford Geertz, 'Ideology as a Cultural System', reprinted in his *The Interpretation of Cultures: Selected Essays* (New York, 1973), ch. 8, from *Ideology and Discontent*, ed. David Apter (Glencoe, 1964). See also in the Apter volume William Converse, 'The Function of Belief Systems in Mass Publics'.

[71] Minow, *Making All the Difference.*

and access to entitlements are deeply embedded in – and protected by – the seeming neutral language of the law. These presumptions go unquestioned because they are unrecognized and may mask (even while they claim to dispel) the perpetuation and legalization of inequities and injustices.

Only when there is – which there usually is – an apparent conflict among representations (verbal and otherwise) – when, for whatever reason, things seem out of kilter and some of our words have lost their meanings[72] or taken on objectionable connotations – do we find it necessary to question and doubt and to look for a new coherence. To the extent that we consciously *use* the available language and its inherent complexities to construct a new coherence, we are actively *creating* new meanings and representations, not merely reflecting those that exist somewhere else. An awareness of this process and of the cultural structure that supports it is a powerful political tool that can be used, as Minow does, to unpack the baggage that concepts and words invariably carry and to argue for change.

A *living* language is inherently unstable. Its *function* is to enable a community of users to *communicate* by participating in a universe of shared signs and symbols. Communication, at some point, involves explanation and justification, which, in their turn, rest upon the representational and analogical aspects of language. But linguistic representation and the transfer of meaning through verbal icons is always imprecise. The language is used and heard – which is to say interpreted – by people with differing perceptual frameworks and intentions. Meaning is thus *ascribed* by individuals and not *legislated* for the relevant community as a whole. (Even dictionary definitions – the closest thing we have to legislated meanings – are often multiple and/or ambiguous.) Despite this relative open-endedness of meaning, ascriptions are neither random nor arbitrary, for there are constraints – including, in the final analysis, dictionaries – on the range of permissible interpretations available to the community of users.

'I don't know what you mean by that', 'Those things are not at all alike', and other such objections and requests for clarification are signposts that mark the outer bounds of specific communications. They are commonplace responses that illustrate the open and rich texture of verbal exchange and signal an invitation to participate in a conversation from which the expansion or alteration of shared meaning may emerge.

---

[72] This latter phrase and the conceptual information it conveys are borrowed from James Boyd White, *When Words Lose Their Meaning: Constitutions and Reconstitutions of Language, Character, and Community* (Chicago, 1984), a work that has contributed a great deal to the general tenor of my sense of the social (and political) character of language and linguistic change.

More often than not, however, such failures to understand and mis-understandings pass unremarked upon. In many cases, they may not even be noticed. By and large, people hear and understand what they want or are prepared by their socialization to hear and understand.

None of this is particularly earth-shaking; it simply makes explicit what is generally taken for granted when we consider the ways languages and vocabularies operate. But when it is applied to politics and to the deployment of public languages, it opens up several important issues. In the first place, political talk is often intentionally ambiguous and even vague; the speaker's purpose may be to permit a wide latitude of interpretation – to let people hear and understand what they want to – not to be precise.

Second, much political vocabulary is ambiguous by its nature and derives its meaning only from its use in specific contexts. Some of that ambiguity results from the fact that many important political words – such as 'justice', 'rights', 'authority', 'liberty', etc. – have an irreducible evaluative content or function. They are used rhetorically or 'persua-sively', not descriptively; the aim is to characterize behaviour or prac-tices by showing that they are properly comprehended by the word in question, and/or to persuade an audience to adopt the speaker's attitudes to them. This is equally true of seemingly descriptive words that also carry substantial normative implications, such as 'murder', 'theft', 'property', 'riot', and 'abortion'. The normative may be at the same time deeply divisive.

Related to this ambiguity is the fact that political notions are generally less stable than many other kinds of concepts and are often 'contes-table'.[73] The concepts or words themselves can be the goals of political conflict, and significant parts of their contents or meanings can be determined by political prescription that attempts to impose itself on public usage. Contests for power and control within a state – for possession of the cloak of sovereign entitlement – are often struggles for control over the generation and use of the justifying political language, for the power of naming is part of the power to control.[74]

---

[73] I take this term from W. B. Gallie, 'Essentially Contested Concepts', as reprinted in his *Philosophy and the Historical Understanding*, 2nd edn (New York, 1968), ch. 8. See also William Connolly, *The Terms of Political Discourse*, 2nd edn (Princeton, 1983), ch. 1.

[74] As Lewis Carroll so aptly put it in the famous exchange between Humpty Dumpty and Alice:

'When *I* use the word', Humpty Dumpty said, in rather a scornful tone, 'it means just what I choose it to mean – neither more nor less'.

'The question is', said Alice, 'whether you *can* make words mean so many different things'.

'The question is', said Humpty Dumpty, 'which is to be master –that's all'.

(*Through the Looking-Glass and What Alice Found There*, ch. 6.)

The political discourse of a rigidly stratified society that is more or less closed will be the preserve of a relatively self-contained elite whose members have enough in common to minimize all but the ambiguities born of political conflict. (Certainly, ruling elite groups fight amongst themselves for power, but those battles involve the 'circulation of elites', which can be contained within the discourse, and therefore the power, they share.) But when access to the mechanism of legitimation is widespread and cuts across the major divisions in a society, the misunderstandings and ambiguities that are endemic to verbal communication are increased. The ideological and linguistic bonds that help to give a society coherence and hold it together are threatened because the commonality of values that generates and supports cultural norms has been lost. In short, participatory states whose members consist of numbers of relatively diverse (or changing) populations are difficult to govern. They are liable to split apart into numerous, distinct, relatively homogeneous groups that exist precisely because of their coherence but which are entirely too small to be politically and economically viable. Heterogeneous communities, on the other hand, are no less problematic, for they are not single cultures but actually consist of several distinct societies with divergent and potentially conflicting values and objectives.[75] Although this is everyday wisdom, its importance to the understanding of societal belief systems and political languages would be hard to exaggerate, for it is the one of the principal sources of the post-modernist dilemma.

It is at least ironic that while the material and ideological conditions of the contemporary world encourage the development of secular self-consciousness and identity – which, in general, we believe to be good – the apparently unavoidable and increasingly uncontrollable intensification of that process undermines and threatens utterly to subvert those very conditions – which is certainly bad. Identity, in these terms, is based as much on 'difference' and 'exclusion' as it is upon similarity and shared values, and its assertion is invariably part of a claim of deprivation and/or oppression at the hands of a ruling, 'hegemonic' part of the society. What begins as a series of complaints about the injustice of relative deprivations and about the denial of rights or entitlements becomes – in the face of apparent intransigence – an attack on the very principles of authority and legitimacy. In the Eastern European, Middle Eastern, and post-colonial contexts, it becomes as well a separatist

---

[75] It was precisely this problem that Rousseau had in mind when he distinguished between a 'multitude' and a 'société', an 'agrégation' and an 'association'.(*Social Contract*, I, v, para. 1.)

demand for territorial, ethnic sovereignty. These newly emerging and re-emerging states, one presumes, will have the ideological advantage of coherent 'foundations' even while they lack the material and political prerequisites for the existences they claim.

All this, in an interesting but tragic way, is something of an apparent reenactment of the quasi-legal 'invention' or 'creation' of 'the people' in the American Declaration of Independence. Although the conditions of 1776 do not obtain in the late twentieth century, some of the conceptual problems are the same: what are the limits on the entitlements of identifiable groups to declare themselves 'peoples' and to engage in the political activities *vis-à-vis* other such 'peoples' appropriate to their newly acquired status? The 'Balkanization', as it were, of groups that feel sufficiently oppressed into separate and therefore self-governing people with rights to assert and defend their existence, even by arms, is extremely difficult to deal with. We have no formulaic way of specifying the circumstances under which such actions are legitimate or, if independence and separation are not 'legitimate', of determining the political association to which separating 'peoples' are already obliged. Presumed answers to questions such as these are implicit in the Declaration of Independence and are an important point of contact between political theorists and historians of political thought. They ought, by the same token, to be at the root of contemporary discussions of political obligation but are conspicuously absent.[76] Similarly, a reformulated analysis of obligation that attends to the problems of ethnicity and cultural conflict ought to be at the centre of contemporary political theory, but it is not. In the end, there is no theory of the state other than the very imperial impositions from which these 'peoples' are fleeing that can satisfactorily contain the world they are creating.

The internal, 'multi-cultural' politics of the industrialized, 'postmodern' state raise, in the short run, a different set of problems that, in the longer run, are no more hospitable to the survival of the secular state. Sovereign legitimacy is replaced by the illegitimate 'hegemony' of the ruling interests in society, and politics based on cultural identity is to become an unending series of 'negotiations' that takes place somewhere beneath the level traditionally occupied by the now-discredited state. In the past, however, only that state was sufficiently powerful and compre-

---

[76] However, see Michael Walzer, *Obligations: Essays on Disobedience, War, and Citizenship* (Cambridge, MA, 1970), esp. ch. 3, 'The obligations of oppressed minorities', for a compelling argument that takes on even greater significance in this respect when it is situated in the context of the author's earlier historical work on seventeenth-century puritanism, *The Revolution of the Saints: A Study in the Origins of Radical Politics* (Cambridge, MA, 1965).

hensive enough to maintain that negotiation and to protect its members, who will now be exposed to the very forces the cultural pluralists necessarily abhor. Even more paradoxical than this is the fact that *only* the sovereign, territorial state can stand up to the growing internationalization of economic and political forces that threatens it and its members. Should that state fail, the successor, as the history of British political discourse suggests, is more likely to be Leviathan than anything else.

In these terms, early-modern history can be seen as the record of how the secular state was founded on the suppression of confessional conflicts. Between the American and French Revolutions and the end of World War II, that state was relatively successful in extending its principles across gender and class barriers. But in the subsequent or 'post-modern' period, the whole enterprise has been placed in jeopardy. The shared contestability of political discourse that is necessary to virtually any civil polity that we would find acceptable is now seriously threatened by a radical hermeneutics which seems to subvert both the discourse and the state that rests on it.

A history such as the one presented in this book represents the historian as capable of showing how that discourse has moved from its past to its present, of explicating the social and historic preconditions on which it rests, and of pointing out their fragile contingency. And is precisely its responses to those contingencies that have kept the discourse alive and permitted it to sustain the pluralism of the secular state while avoiding the ever-present threat of Leviathan.

Index

Abbot, George, 123, 125
absolutism
  Caroline, 102–4, 106, 149, 151
  and George III, 299
  in Hobbes, 159, 161–2, 164
  Jacobean, 83, 90, 91, 93, 100–1, 151
  legal, 182
  opposition to, 72–3
  Stuart, 73, 90, 91, 93–5, 102, 181–3,
    186, 189
accountability
  ministerial, 100–1
  royal, 148, 196–7
Act of Appeals 1533, 8, 22, 26, 35–6, 38,
    40, 257
Act of Proclamations, 28 n78
Act of Security, 237–8
Act of Settlement 1701, 212, 237, 258
Act of Supremacy, 22, 24, 25, 26, 29, 36,
    38, 40
Act of Union 1707, 4, 9, 237, 258, 284
Act of Union 1801, 4, 290
Acts of Uniformity, 29, 173, 186, 187,
    268–9
Adams, John, 253, 267, 269, 278, 286
Adamson, John, 95, 96 n65, 115
Addison, Joseph, 223, 225–7, 235, 242
adiaphora, 41–3, 173, 270
Admonition Controversy, 43, 62
Agarde, Arthur, 97
Allen, J. W., 180
Almon, John, 317
America, political thought, 4, 266, 267,
    283, 295–6, 331
American colonies
  and church, 266, 268–9
  and nature of empire, 263–6, 276–82,
    285–94, 295
  post-independence, 295
  and representation, 256, 260–6, 274–5,
    287–8, 294, 298
  and republicanism, 291, 295, 296–7

and social war, 256–7
Stamp Act crisis, 259, 261, 266
and Whig policies, 297–8
American Revolution, 256–7, 280–1
  as religious war, 266, 268–9
amici, nobility as, 18
Andrewes, Lancelot, 115, 124 n15
Anglicanism *see* Church of England
Anglocentrism, 3–4, 283, 316
Anne
  ministries, 231–2
  and neo-exclusionism, 212–15
  and political thought, 211–45
  succession, 207
anti-clericalism
  in American colonies, 268
  in Harrington, 165–6, 168–9
  and Henry VIII, 25–6, 32, 52
  in Hobbes, 165, 170, 185
  in Locke, 271
antinomianism
  and Arminianism, 125
  decline, 195
  and French Revolution, 309, 310
antiquarianism *see* constitution, ancient
Antrim Commission, 130–2
Antrim, Duchess of, 130
Apology of 1604, 90, 94–5, 105, 110
Aristotle, influence, 14, 20, 64, 107
Arminianism, 63, 106, 123–7, 143, 212,
    240
  and Calvinism, 121, 123, 125, 127, 142
  and latitudinarianism, 120
  and popery, 129
Armstrong, B. G., 123, 125
army, standing, 169, 181 n5, 215, 219,
    229, 293
Arnall, William, 233–4
Ascham, Anthony, 160
Ascherson, Neil, 145
Ashcraft, Richard, 190, 192
Atkyns, Sir Robert, 204